ip

Radical Parody

American Culture and Critical
Agency After Foucault

The Social Foundations of Aesthetic Forms Series
Jonathan Arac, Editor

The Social Foundations of Aesthetic Forms
A series of
COLUMBIA UNIVERSITY PRESS
Jonathan Arac, Editor

Critical Genealogies: Historical Situation for
Postmodern Literary Studies
Jonathan Arac

Advertising Fictions: Literature, Advertisement,
and Social Reading
Jennifer Whicke

Masks of Conquest: Literary Study and British Rule in India
Gauri Viswanathan

Left Politics and the Literary Profession
Lennard J. Davis and M. Bella Mirabella, eds.

The Vietnam War and American Culture
John Carlos Rowe and Rick Berg, eds.

Authors and Authority: English and American
Criticism, 1750-1990
Patrick Parrinder

Reaches of Empire: The English Novel from
Edgeworth to Dickens
Suvendrini Perera

The Profession of Authorship in America, 1800-1870
William Charvat

Narrating Discovery: The Romantic Explorer in American
Literature, 1790-1855
Bruce Greenfield

The Author, Art, and the Market: Rereading the
History of Aesthetics
Martha Woodmansee

Radical Parody
American Culture and Critical Agency After Foucault

by Daniel T. O'Hara

Columbia University Press
New York

Columbia University Press
New York   Chichester, West Sussex

Copyright © 1992 Columbia University Press

Library of Congress Cataloging-in-Publication Data

O'Hara, Daniel T., 1948–
    Radical parody : American culture and critical agency after
Foucault / by Daniel T. O'Hara.
        p.   cm. — (The Social foundations of aesthetic forms series)
    Includes bibliographical references (p.   ) and index.
    ISBN 0-231-07693-2 (paperback)
    1. Criticism—History—20th century.   2. Criticism—United States.
3. Foucault, Michel.   I. Title.   II. Series.
PN94.O44   1992
801'.95'09045—dc20   92-7694
                                                                                CIP

Casebound editions of Columbia University Press books
are printed on permanent and durable acid-free paper.

Book design by Teresa Bonner
Printed in the United States of America
c 10 9 8 7 6 5 4 3 2 1
p 10 9 8 7 6 5 4 3 2

Anna M. Corcoran O'Hara
1910–1990
In Memoriam

Contents

Preface   ix

Acknowledgments   xv

Introduction: Why Radical Parody Now and Other
Questionable Matters   1

I   Constructing a Mask

1. Mask Plays: Theory, Cultural Studies,
   and the Fascist Imagination   13

2. What Was Foucault?   37

3. Performing Theory as Cultural Politics: The
   "Experience" of Critical Agency in and After Foucault   60

4. Aesthetic Relations: Michel Foucault and the Fate
   of Friendship   74

5. On the Friend Self and Lawrence Kritzman's *The Rhetoric
   of Sexuality and the Literature of the French Renaissance*   96

II Opposing Orthodoxies

    6. Revisionary Madness: The Prospects of American
       Literary Theory at the Present Time   113

    7. Critical Change and the Collective Archive   130

    8. Pragmatists of the Spirit: Late Bloom and Company   150

    9. A Postmodern Poetics of Critical Reading   165

    10. Selves in Flames: Derrida, Rorty, and the New
        Orthodoxy in Theory   179

III Reconstructing a Practice

    11. Smiling Through Pain: The Practice of Self in *The Rise
        of Silas Lapham*   193

    12. John Cheever's "Folly": The Contingent Imagination   207

    13. Imaginary Politics: Emerson, Stevens, and the Resistance
        of Style   225

    Conclusion: On Becoming Oneself in Frank Lentricchia   245

Notes   271

Index   291

Preface

I first read Emerson's "History," the opening of *Essays* (First Series), with equal amounts of awe and annoyance. He said such terrible things—terribly tempting to me because, from my limited lower-class experience then, they were beautifully untrue—and he said them with such insouciance that, like Eliot on Shelley, I thought Emerson the perfect example of the perpetual adolescent, only American-style.[1] After all these years, however, I have found that one of the things he said must really be true, so far as I now can see. Americans don't possess a definite identity as separate individuals or a people, unless lack of identity counts for an identity. Most really are middle-class, fortunately for them, and so can afford to make a virtue of their necessary lack. How else can one explain and justify our society of the spectacle and our ever-changing personas?

Emerson speaks of this lack of identity as the perpetual possibility of becoming anyone or anything. I call this "revisionary madness" here. It is as if the American psyche were the preordained virginal site for the apocalyptic perfection of all the previously unfulfilled aspirations of ever-changing humankind. This is what I take Emerson to mean by "the transmigrations of Proteus" (252)—the mask plays of a "Proteus nature" (238) performing itself through Americans as the blissfully belated heirs of world history. For him, as a major tradition in American studies recognizes (see chapter 7), all history is but the provocatively riddling figures of the same Sphinx (to follow his changing mythic archetype for this phenomenon), who in each epoch learns to read herself once again, and who in Emerson's time, as "Experience" suggests, is learning to read the human self as what the human self always aspired (albeit unwittingly) to become: the reborn native of "a new yet unapproachable America" (485). In this representative light, Emerson sees "the solid angularity" of historical fact ever sublimely dissipating, as he speaks, into the soft golden haze of poetic imagination. And in reading history, he says (in "History") that we but envision with dramatically ironic distance our own grandest or meanest possibilities writ large and memorable (238). For Emerson, then, the external is the internal and the internal the external (as Hegel claims and Kierkegaard disproves), and all is made one in the mirror of nature (or history—it hardly matters) by the transcendent will of the eternal human/divine soul.

It is my argument in the following essays that many contemporary American critics, especially the "neopragmatists," despite their sometimes programmatic dismissal of such transcendentalism in theory and despite their sometimes programmatic endorsement of the ideology of difference in all its forms—textual, cultural, socioeconomic, sexual, geopolitical—too often practice criticism as sublime, professionally self-serving individual mask play in the grand Emersonian tradition. Their self-subverting paeans to the self-made individual appears, ironically enough, precisely when they are most loudly proclaiming their devoted engagements with the grander movements of social history. I also argue in what follows that this ironic situation arises primarily from the failure of American critics to situate themselves in the historical context of the postmodern condition they repeatedly theorize and find everywhere emerging—except in their own critical lives. (On this ground I account for the recent retreat by many self-styled "oppositional" critics into the pragmatics of professionalism.) Finally, in my use of the late Foucault on "the aesthetics of existence" (often in combination with Kristeva on identity formation), I offer a positive perspective on and contemporary measure for analyzing this entire situation. I propose that because this critical practice as mask play is, so to speak, the only game in town, we play it with open eyes, putting it to what I believe are the kinds of more general socialized uses that late Foucault best exemplifies for me.

Radical Parody, then, is a reflective polemic. As such, it is often strategically reductive, satirically ironic, and even intentionally (self-)parodic. By "radical parody," I mean an ironic, even satiric kind of critical performance of another critic's characteristic position and style. It is the kind of thing I have just tried to do in my opening reflections on "History," with my boldly ex cathedra yet personalizing, rapid-fire yet lapidary assertions about (and after) Emerson. Such often implicitly antithetical performances are, as it were, dramatically beside themselves: radically plural (because they reflect both consciousnesses—that of the critic and that of the critic's critic), ironically shifting (because they are at once sympathetic and critical), and intentionally ambiguous (because they solicit strongly critical and thus often self-betraying response). As such, these performances entail pastiche as their generic mode, since they stage as dramatic visionary spectacles, using many diverse forms of discourse drawn from a variety of sources, the generally implicit self-regarding desires, what I call the mask plays of other critics. Their point is in their performances, critical judgment materializing figuratively in their textures and structures as well as in explicit arguments. Whatever the final effect, their primary aim is playfully satiric: to jollify us, where possible, out of some merely barren critical perspective. But their secondary aim is seriously satiric: to shame us, where necessary, out of a destructive idée fixe. (For more on this subject of masks, see chapters 1 and 3.) How well I have succeeded in either aim only the reader can say.

The book also has a positive thrust as suggested by the topic headings to its three major sections. I have arranged the material to correspond to the career pattern of the contemporary American critic, in the belief that we can evaluate this pattern if we can see it. Part 1, "Constructing a Mask," discusses both how practicing criticism as mask play is inescapable now and why I choose to revise and develop my "late Foucault" as a critical intervention into this context. To elucidate further, with Kristeva's analytic aid, my critical development of what I call "oneself"—that is, the postmodern subject in and after late Foucault—I include at this point a brief coda in chapter 5: "On the Friend Self." ("The friend self" is what one can at best aspire to become now as "oneself.")

Part 2, "Opposing Orthodoxies," moves to the next phase of the critical career, which is to use one's chosen mask as a constructive base for launching critiques against the dominant orthodoxies of the moment—which I believe to be neopragmatism, new historicism (especially "feminist" examples of new Americanist studies), and a certain Anglo-American appropriation of Derridean deconstruction for purposes of developing postmodern analytic aesthetics. In the second essay of part 2 (chapter 5), I offer conceptions of culture and critical agency that, unlike those informing such critical modes, put literature, canonical and noncanonical alike, potentially at the service of collective insurrectionary enterprises. This is the intention informing, however selectively, my use of literary examples. To clarify my different uses of Emerson and to account better for my privileging of literary art as cultural politics, I have included after my chapters on Howells and Cheever a chapter called "Imaginary Politics: Emerson, Stevens, and the Resistance of Style." The sampling reader may wish to turn to this, chapter 13, for a discussion of my normative model of psychic development after reading the introduction and chapters 3, 4, and 5, and before reading the conclusion. (This sequence makes up the argumentative spine of the book.)

Part 3, "Reconstructing a Practice," then outlines how, with oppositional mask in place and the revisionary weapon of the collective archive in hand, the critic turns to rehabilitate particular institutional practices—in this case, the theory and interpretation of modern poetry and realistic fiction—along lines consistent with his or her general oppositional position. (I hope to follow this outline with a more detailed portrait in a forthcoming book.)[2] Each of these essays turns to what I take to be appropriate literary examples of imaginations in action instructing their societies, in order to counterbalance the neglect or dismissal of this literary function in contemporary critical culture. I hope thereby to promote the productive interplay of criticism and the collective archive, underscoring in the process what one recent critic nicely terms "the ethical force of imaginative ideals."[3] The order of these essays unfolds the normative model of psychic development and ethical self-stylization that I derive from Kristeva and later Foucault, and repeatedly contrasts that model with the practices of self in contemporary criticism, to what I hope is the increasing instruction of the latter.

In conclusion, then, I discuss Frank Lentricchia, the American critic whose work and career for me realizes most effectively in our postmodern condition the critical ideal I propose through the mask of my "Foucault." (Frank Lentricchia, of course, is also a critic writing "after Foucault" in terms of making something of his own out of the latter's historical influence.) In this last essay, the reader can find the fullest statement of my position, even as my critical practice and generic mode here (unlike in the rest of the book) are neither parodic (radical or otherwise) nor pastichelike in the postmodern (or any other) fashion. The kind of criticism I am practicing here is closest, perhaps, to what used to be called "appreciation," for I am attempting, following Lentricchia's lead, to perform theory as a particular magnanimous act of critical identity in the general service of imaginative culture. In other words, in this essay, I am not doing what I do throughout the rest of the book (and tried to do with Emerson)— which is to reflect ironically, diversely, and parodistically on the mask play of another critic. Here I am performing, in what I hope is a definitive way, my own mask play deliberately and provocatively "against the grain" of Lentricchia's critical opponents: neopragmatists, new historicists, and "essentialist" feminists in American studies.[4] Whether I prove successful in this final "trial" only the reader can ultimately say.

A few closing notes: Although the theoretical marriage of these strangest of bedfellows, Foucault and Kristeva, forms the conceptual framework of the following analyses, I have not attempted to repeat in detail, or sometimes to repeat at all, the specifics of this critical scaffolding in every chapter of the book. My aim in not doing so is to maintain, as best I can, the meditative quality of the essay form, even when I am being most polemical. In each part, however, there are essays (chapters 3, 4, 7, 11, and 13) serving as "manifestos," which, along with the introduction and conclusion, are intended to make explicit what I hope is the fully formed, constructively critical position animating the entire volume. Last, a critical caution: the "Foucault" and "Kristeva" making their appearances here do not pretend to be anything other than my own revisionary developments for purposes of "essaying" the contemporary practice of American critical theory "after Foucault." By the way, this phrase in my book's subtitle, rather than "after Foucault and Kristeva," for example, defines precisely and comprehensively for my purposes the primary angle from which I view the present critical situation at large—which is, after all is said and done, the primary object of my concern.

Acknowledgments

I want to thank, first of all, my *boundary 2* colleagues. Through their questions, I have been able to sharpen arguments. I am particularly grateful to Jonathan Arac in this regard. As editor of a series entitled "The Social Foundations of Aesthetic Forms," he has repeatedly read and challenged my work on the imaginative dimensions of cultural politics in contemporary American criticism.

Next, I want to thank my Temple University colleagues Steven Cole and Alan Wilde, who stand out for their insight and example.

Also, I am grateful to two special friends. Frank Lentricchia has been heroically generous and cooperative as I was developing my view of his work and career. Amy Zaffarano Rowland has performed in a similar manner with respect to many conversations, over the years, on Emerson, Kristeva, parody, and the plural subject. I am deeply grateful for her unfailing vision.

Finally, I am indebted to my family. My sister, Anne O'Hara Crankshaw, my father, Daniel J. O'Hara, my wife, Joanne Recchuiti O'Hara, and my daughter, Jessica Lynn O'Hara—all have remained sources of love and joy in very difficult times. The debts I owe my late mother, to whose memory this book is dedicated, are inestimable. I only hope this gesture can suggest some of what I feel for her.

Most of these chapters were previously published, in very different contexts, and sometimes with slightly different titles, as occasional essays. I am grateful to the editors and publishers of the journals and collections concerned for permission to use them here.

"Mask Plays: Theory, Cultural Studies, and the Fascist Imagination." In *boundary 2* 17, no. 2 (Summer 1990): 129–54.

"What Was Foucault?" In Jonathan Arac, ed., *After Foucault: Humanistic Knowledge, Postmodern Challenges.* New Brunswick, N.J.: Rutgers University Press, 1988, pp. 71–96.

"Aesthetic Relations: Michel Foucault and the Fate of Friendship." In *boundary 2* 18, no. 1 (Spring 1991): 83–103.

"Revisionary Madness: The Prospects of American Theory at the Present Time." In *Critical Inquiry* 9, no. 4 (June 1983): 726–42.

"Critical Change and the Collective Archive." In Michael Hays, ed., *Critical Symptoms.* Minneapolis: University of Minnesota Press, 1992.

"The Poetics of Critical Reading." In *Poetics Today* 11, no. 3 (Fall 1990): 661–72.

"Selves in Flames: Derrida, Rorty, and the New Orthodoxy in Theory." In *Contemporary Literature* 32, no. 1 (Spring 1991): 116–26.

"Smiling Through Pain: The Practice of Self in the Rise of Silas Marner." In Donald E. Pease, ed., *New Essays on the Rise of Silas Marner.* New York: Cambridge University Press, 1991, 91–105.

"John Cheever's Contingent Imagination." In *South Atlantic Quarterly* 91, no. 3 (Summer 1992).

"Imaginary Politics: Emerson, Stevens, and the Resistance of Style." In Mehta Schaum, ed., *Wallace Stevens and Women.* Tuscaloosa: University of Alabama Press, 1992.

"On Becoming Oneself in Frank Lentricchia." In Donald E. Pease, ed., "New Americanists II," *boundary 2* 19, no. 1 (Fall 1992): 285–310.

Radical Parody

American Culture and Critical
Agency After Foucault

Take care, philosophers and friends, of knowledge, and beware of martyrdom, of suffering "for the truth's sake!" Even of defending yourself. Rather go away. Flee into concealment. And have your masks and subtlety, that you may be mistaken for what you are not, or feared a little.

—Nietzsche, Beyond Good and Evil *(1886)*

It is a familiar expedient of brilliant writers, and not less of witty talkers, the device of ascribing their own sentence to an imaginary person, in order to give it weight. . . . It is a curious reflex effect of this enhancement of our thought by citing it from another, that many men can write better under a mask than for themselves. . . . It is a sort of dramatizing talent. . . . In hours of high mental activity we sometimes do the book too much honor, reading out of it better things than the author wrote,—reading, as we say, between the lines. . . . The wit was in what you heard, not in what the speakers said. Our best thought came from others. We heard in their words a deeper sense than the speakers put into them, and could express ourselves in other people's phrases to finer purpose than they knew. . . . Swedenborg threw a formidable theory into the world, that every soul existed in a society of souls, from which all its thoughts passed into it, as the blood of the mother circulates in her unborn child. . . . Only an inventor knows how to borrow, and every man is or should be an inventor. . . . Original power lies also in selection. . . . The divine gift is ever the instant life, which receives and uses and creates, and can well bury the old in the omnipotency with which Nature decomposes all her harvest for recomposition.

—Emerson, "Quotation and Originality" *(1876)*

Introduction: Why Radical Parody Now and Other Questionable Matters

On Wednesday, June 19, 1991, Stanley Fish, a designated speaker for the academic "left," appears on the "MacNeil-Lehrer News Hour." A part of each show for the week is devoted to the "political correctness" controversy. Accordingly, Fish is to comment on the charge by neoconservative critics spotlighted the previous evening that a "radical" ideology is stifling free speech and academic freedom among students and teachers on America's campuses. In his commentary, Fish strikes a magisterial pose. He appears to be generally above the fray as he offers a generational account of the controversy.

Fish claims that many aging white male professors and their few younger disciples (some of whom may even be nonwhite and nonmale) have been made "uncomfortable" by the progress won in the academy by women and people of color. This progress is now reflected in campus codes of speech and behavior meant to outlaw insensitive, as well as inflammatory, speech and action, such as racial slurs, vulgar and sexist epithets, and intimidating and harassing gestures. According to Fish, such "uncomfortable" professors have dressed up their petty resentment at being officially constrained, for the first time in their careers, from hurting "minority sensitivities" with impunity. These uncomfortable professors claim that such codes, when taken along with curricular "multiculturalism," represent a systematic attempt by academic leftists now in control of the universities and colleges to cut Western civilization down to size. In this neoconservative nightmare, the politically correct may even intend to exclude altogether the great books of the Western tradition from their new "multicultural canon." These uncomfortable ones, Fish reiterates, allege that this politically correct degradation or exclusion of the Western tradition, when coupled with campus codes of speech and behavior, has had a chilling effect on academic freedom.

But this charge, Fish assures us, is the academic equivalent of politicians wrapping themselves in the flag. These uncomfortable professors are simply dinosaurs. Once the new generation of professors, which has recently come to power, completely solidifies its dominance via the death of the old guard, this debate will pass away—until another debate provoked by the challenge of another, younger generation arises, and all is essentially repeated, as Fish has already seen.

There are considerable ironies in this scene. First of all, that Stanley Fish comes forward as, and is taken for, a representative of the academic left is almost comical. His most infamous theoretical claim is that no practical consequences necessarily follow from theory. This is a counterintuitive claim—especially to intellectuals who, following Marx and others, believe theory can be a weapon of change. Yet, thanks in large part to this controversial theoretical claim "against theory," and to similar claims (that there is no such thing as critical self-consciousness, that a text means whatever a powerful authority figure manipulating interpretive conventions can get it to mean, and so on), Fish ended up chairing Duke University's English department, which decided some years ago to recruit the most visible (because most often controversial) figures in literary studies. Consequently, it is understandable, if still ironic, that the media would have recognized Fish, who reigned (in 1991) over the many avowed leftists at Duke, also as their representative. This mistake, if he even sees it as such, Fish never tries to correct.

Since the late 1980s, however, his position on the nonconsequences of theory has been charged by younger left-oriented critics with a passive acquiescence to the status quo, now that he has all the status one could wish. Fish, in a reply to such criticism in *PMLA*, defends himself at one point by recalling for his critics the countless otherwise unremembered acts of his progressively professional behavior. [1] From this exchange one would expect Fish to be able to speak on both sides of the political correctness issue. Given his evident sense of realpolitik, however, Fish clearly wants to be seen on the winning side in the generational war. But his rather cynical and commonplace apology for professional change (it's the generation gap again) is a weakly all-seeing pose of knowing the pallid psychological form such change supposedly always takes. Although this position may provoke uncomfortable conservative dinosaurs a little more, it certainly won't give significant aid and comfort to academic leftists, either, for the latter view change in a less Oedipal light. They see it more broadly as the consequence of political conflicts between different historical material interests and their associated ideas and principles concerning the nature of the good society. I hope my own position, to anticipate a bit, is neither so self-congratulatory as this view nor so weakly psychological as Fish's.

The ultimate irony of this scene, however, entails the worst cut of all. By means of very polished anecdotes persuasively recounted on "MacNeil-Lehrer," Fish traces the improved representation of women and people of color in the profession. He thereby produces a moral impression of progressive justice that lends considerable weight to his otherwise purely formal and rather banal generational explanation. However at odds these loaded anecdotes may appear to be with his magisterial pretense of pure historical description, this contradiction scarcely detracts from the moving epic story of the previously abjected having rescued themselves from their abjection by heroic individual and collective efforts and now having decided not to suffer any more bad-mouthing by their enemies.

All in all, then, this is very effective television, however questionable it may remain as explanation. But the power of spectacle has always been his forte, and the title of "The Great Communicator" could easily pass to Stanley Fish. (His is clearly the single most effective performance "for the left" this week.) For serious critics on the left, this may be the unkindest cut of all. Admittedly, Richard Nixon as the peace candidate in 1968 or as the American "rediscoverer" of China in 1971 may yet be even worse.

Such overdetermined scenes of multiple misrecognitions are what make contemporary American cultural life particularly ripe for parody. Roles in competing stories—within and without the academy, in master or more personal narratives—get conflated with unintended self-betraying consequences for all concerned. The occurrence of this kind of thing in a literary or critical text is the object of my critique in this book, but in a distinctive way rather different from my necessarily explicit analysis in this introduction. My chosen mode throughout the other chapters in this book is what I call "radical parody." Such textual scenes of multiple misrecognitions are already unwitting (self-)parodies (as demonstrated in my playful use of Emerson in the preface), and as I will show elsewhere in the book. My strategy in these textual cases is to parody them self-consciously and indeed reductively (and so myself insofar as I enter these textual scenes by way of critical impersonation). My aim is to help bring out and clarify in these scenes the multiple misrecognitions with a maximum of instructively parodic effect. My hope is to provide a more useful basis for critical judgment in a postmodern situation in which I am also inescapably involved.

In the case of Fish and the media, the media functions as the general postmodern storehouse of stereotypical images, roles, and stories, into which Fish walks to be dressed in the first available costume and handed the first available script with his part underlined in red. (A small amount of appropriate improvisation is naturally encouraged for greater effect.) The media, in short, act like a demonic parody or a degraded commonplace version of the high cultural tradition. In the case of a literary or critical text, an often unconscious selection from the collective archive of intertexts (or tradition) that resonates complexly within the text generally casts the writer in a more ironically typical role than he or she can recognize, even as the writer would consciously don the individual mask of choice. By parodying this complex scene of critical misrecognition radically, self-consciously, reductively, my polemical intention is to make possible a better (because stronger) conscious choice of roles to play drawn from the collective archive. To appear as the unwitting avatar of Milton's Belial, one of Satan's masters of rhetoric in *Paradise Lost,* is not so bad, I assume, as functioning blindly as the academic equivalent of Richard Nixon. But a critic would prefer, I also assume, not to be the dupe of any scene of multiple misrecognitions.

Speaking of possible misrecognitions, I also must clarify here my own position, "where I am coming from," as well as three key terms (and their variations) used throughout this book. How is it that I can see and parody, so as to make possible the correction, of these critical scenes of multiple misrecognition? To address fully that question is the aim of my chapters on Foucault (2, 3, and 4), and I primarily direct the curious reader there. In what follows, however, there is also the outline of an answer to this question.

The terms I have just alluded to are *revisionism, oppositional criticism,* and *the contingent imagination.* For me, *revisionism* is the generic master term. It refers to an interpretive practice of modern intellectuals that would re-see and reevaluate the past in light of the perceived special interests of the present. Some critics, such as Harold Bloom, believe that revisionism, in the sense of necessarily misreading the past for the special individual interest of imaginative self-aggrandizement, defines the primary meaning of the term, and in fact the "real" or "strong" essential core of all interpretation. Gaining symbolic immortality in the pantheon of Western writers is, for Bloom, the nearest thing to apotheosis or divinity that secular intellectuals can envision. Other critics, such as Stanley Fish, identify revisionism even more simply and generally as the persuasive art of rhetoric itself, a position that Bloom also ultimately endorses. But Fish argues that the contemporary special interests served are always determined by a community of interpreters and its conventions, and never solely by an individual critic's whimsical fiat.

My own view, rehearsed at length in my last two books, is most like Richard Rorty's—at least at first.[2] The present situation in the humanities is such that the community of interpreters and its conventions tends to license the practice of revisionism in Bloom's sense as professionally appropriate behavior. We are all accredited avatars of Milton's Satan, striving to revise the past as much for our personal and professional self-aggrandizements as for any other stated reasons. Informing this postmodern revisionary situation of rampant "self-creation" is what Bloom, Fish, Rorty, and others claim is their rediscovery of the good old American philosophy (or "antiphilosophy") of pragmatism. Long before the recent importation of various post-structuralisms had anticipated the present sense of antifoundational and intentionally "fictional" revisionism, there was, many claim, an ironic philosophy of contingency that had its origins in an aspect of Emerson, was developed by William James, Nietzsche, and Heidegger, and now has returned to postmodern America in the foreign dress of one poststructuralist or another. (C. S. Peirce is generally absent from this story.) This influential position explains my focus on the so-called neopragmatism of late Bloom, Fish, Rorty, Poirier, and others and my sense of its representative status as the most general or pure form of professionalism available for analysis. Theirs is a least common denominator philosophy and so far is as banal and inescapable as the postmodern media's formulaic system of categorizations. They define the American tradition in and against which all of us, I believe, still have to work.

I therefore tend to see "oppositional criticism," which may have an announced political thrust, in terms of the neopragmatist "pure form" of revisionary professionalism. The type of contemporary critical activity has been defined as professionally revisionary in this neopragmatist sense. I say this deliberately for polemical purposes. I want critics with whom I sympathize, such as my *boundary 2* colleagues and other "younger" oppositional critics, to stop and think about not just the primary motives informing their work but also its actual consequences. In occasionally discussing or alluding to the work of some would-be American Raymond Williams, I am really asking the following question: What can be pragmatically achieved in the present academic situation of revisionism that significantly distinguishes such announced oppositional work from that of a Fish or a Bloom in ways that the general public can appreciate without the trivializing distortions and misrecognitions that shape the political correctness debate? One of the worse ironies is the emergence of Stanley Fish as spokesperson for the academic left. At the risk of being unfair "in principle" to particular individual oppositional critics as a result of my intentionally overgeneralizing remarks, I launch my polemically parodic critique that "in principle" associates them with neopragmatist revisionists because I believe that oppositional criticism as it has become institutionalized is in danger of being seen as Fish has characterized it—as nothing but a species of generational revisionism. As their influential media status and institutional prominence suggest, Bloom, Fish, Rorty, and company have captured the professional mask, the mental form of revisionism, for the public sphere, against which would-be oppositional critics have had to define themselves within the academy. Even oppositional critics with more public visibility, such as Edward Said and Frank Lentricchia, not only refuse to debate in detail their political differences with a Bloom or a Fish but continue strongly to see themselves in terms of the former's revisionary paradigm and as the latter's professional allies.[3] Because of such a lack of fundamental debate and such continued pervasive misrecognition, a Stanley Fish can all too readily be taken, even by critics who should know better, as a plausible representative of the academic left. If this is not the way it is, I hope my polemic will provoke oppositional critics to show me how it is not so.

This brings me to my final term for clarification—*the contingent imagination*. By this epithet I mean the revisionary practice whereby selective social determinations—historical accidents or conditions ("facts," anecdotes, "values," opinions)—are pragmatically misread, fictionalized into desirable possibilities according to the imaginary imperatives of professionally licensed narcissists, so that, despite ostensible but perfunctory claims to the contrary, the self would formally and influentially become all in all. Stanley Fish as heroic magisterial chronicler of the epic progress of women and people of color in the profession is a good case in point. And if a Fish, a Bloom, or a Rorty can play this game, why can't everyone? In fact, isn't this now the only game in town? While Rorty and others celebrate this fate as radically revisionary, I lament it as an empty game, and parodically expose it as such (see, especially, chapters 8, 9, and 10), for this revisionary game's resulting self-serving and self-congratulatory interpretations function as imaginary substitutes for missing (because wholly relativized and disputed) universal or essential values. Once God goes, one is tempted to say, only the self remains. But it is more accurate to say, once the belief in a permanent, divinely sanctioned system of real universals goes, then all value tends to collapse into the human subject's powers of creative invention and its endless project of satisfying its desires whatever they are thought to be. This is fine so far as it goes, I suppose, but self-creation must have more of an ethical end for me than the perfection of the process. If this makes me a modern intellectual nostalgic for some "higher," more-than-human ideal of perfection, so be it. Being a leading intellectual in the vanguard of politically correct thinking (neoconservative or radical brand), or being more imaginatively inventive than one's literary ancestors in this revisionary academic scene finally defines for the general public the kind of academic difference that the recent "MacNeil-Lehrer" shows demonstrate don't finally matter: Everything comes down to purely academic spectacles.

What is needed, I believe, is a broadly transhistorical (but not God-like) perspective on the practice of interpretation and the interpretive self. No one can hope to reverse the loss of essential values and universal norms. They have their own inherent dangers as we know from Foucault's work, anyway. However, by examining Foucault's practice in volumes 2 and 3 in *The History of Sexuality* and by adapting Kristeva's developmental model of the narcissistic subject's creative response to loss and grief, I propose such a transhistorical perspective that does not simply come down to self-aggrandizing revisionism or academic oppositionalism or the long-term customary practices of formal argument (i.e., traditional logic and rhetoric). In chapters 3, 7, 11, 12, and 13, and in the conclusion, I try to show the consequences of seeing the collective archive of works as more "objective" measures and standards of creative aesthetic construction against which we must define ourselves and redefine our present moment. These aesthetic "objects" that act as measures and standards, of course, are subject to interpretive revision, but usually with greater difficulty than the work of contemporary figures due to the considerable weight and continuity in the history of their reception and aesthetic evaluation. (Noncanonical works, of course, are recovered precisely so they can begin to attain this greater density and resistance to mere fashionable revisionary commodification.) In these chapters, I try to elaborate the normative but also slowly changing literary model of psychic development against which I measure my own interpretive performances and those of others. To put it briefly, to avow magnanimously in one's work the significance of that imaginative achievement in light of which one aspires to perform one's work, however critical one may sometimes also have to be of one's "ancestor," is, for me, a necessary avowal. It is one of the major assumptions of this book, as it was one of the major arguments in my last book, *Lionel*

Trilling: The Work of Liberation, that the capacity for making such an avowal is generally being lost. (This accounts especially for my appreciative chapters on Foucault, Stevens, and Lentricchia here.) I find such avowal important because it bears witness to the often painful but necessary psychic truth that the interpretive self should recognize (although it usually chooses to repress) the reality of another's imaginative achievement as the reference point and guide of one's own aspirations and desires. That is, one ought to recognize the interpretive self as a plural subject, an internalized pedagogic pair engaged in an ongoing agonistic relation that has for its dialectical end the overcoming of *ressentiment* and the conscious avowal of a tradition. Freud thought one must begin to love in order not to get sick. We must avow our imaginary ancestors, I believe, for the same reason.

I Constructing a Mask

1 Mask Plays

Theory, Cultural Studies, and the Fascist Imagination

To Paul A. Bové

The relation between theory and politics has been dominating critical discussion for some time now. Originally, calls for theory to demonstrate its utility in various struggles came from critics on the left, such as Edward Said and Frank Lentricchia.[1] More recently, critics on the right such as Allan Bloom have repeated and elaborated, fantastically, earlier claims made by such different critics as Gerald Graff and M. H. Abrams. In Bloom's apocalyptic version, theory is merely the confused ideological reflex of a leftward politics threatening Western civilization itself with total nihilism.[2] Of course, the sensational discovery of Paul deMan's collaborationist wartime writings and the unexpected renewal of interest in Heidegger's Nazi affiliations, even now still being debated, have brought home with a vengeance this question of theory's relation to politics.[3] Although there are those pragmatically minded theorists such as Rorty and Fish—who argue that theory has at most private or purely conventional disciplinary consequences, and usually no politically revolutionary consequences at all—no one who takes the practice of criticism seriously can act as if this belief were possibly true, since just by trying to persuade others, as Rorty's and Fish's considerable influence brilliantly demonstrates, we necessarily assume the possibility of important, if unspecified, public consequences—as all of us always already know, no matter what whimsical absurdity to the contrary is avidly proposed these days.[4] *Exactly* what has been, is now, or ought to be the relation between theory and politics remains up in the air.

Klaus Theweleit's *Male Fantasies,* volumes 1 and 2, provides an opportunity to examine this relation in three ways. First, a profile of the fascist mind-set can be drawn from them. Second, this psychic profile can be compared with that of the self-critical, fascist-leaning intellectual produced in Heidegger's *Introduction to Metaphysics,* a major text by one of the most formative figures in the development of modern critical theory, and a text explicitly endorsing the "true spirit" of national socialism. And third, another profile can be drawn from Theweleit's own practice as a contemporary culture critic who uses theory, especially revisionary psychoanalytic theory, to develop an oppositional form of cultural studies with a decidedly feminist edge. Three profiles should clearly emerge for comparative analysis in what follows: that of the fascist imagination, that of an influential founder of modern critical theory, and that of a postmodern practitioner of cultural studies. These mental profiles constitute the mask plays of my title to this chapter.

Before beginning my profiles, however, I need to outline my own position and to explain my critical practice. I come to these matters from literary study and from a particular orientation within literary study that can generally be identified as "ethical." Literature, for someone like me, offers a wide and ever-changing range of possible selves not so much for one to become as for one to recall as inspirational or cautionary tales when faced with the inevitable everyday choices of living a life, pursuing a career, and understanding others and, one hopes, oneself. By doing or not doing, saying or not saying, writing or not writing this or that, one produces, consciously or not, a mental profile having "worldly" effects. In other words, will I, by this action, be or not be seen as a Bradley Headstone? What profile is given and how it is remembered—these are the complex intertwined issues that literature helps one to recognize.

This means that I believe there is no predetermined "core" or "natural" self. The self is an ever-provisional, mobile effect of specific rhetorical acts—taken in the largest sense as instances of general discursive practices—a multiple, composite construction that a selected personal style or set of styles unifies—if at all—moment by moment. Yeats's name for this overdetermined rhetorical self-effect is "mask," while Fredric Jameson analyzes such aesthetic effects from the perspective of the "political unconscious." Literary study is for me an informed and endless meditation upon the practical possibilities of self-definition as a mask. As such, in T. S. Eliot's words from "Tradition and the Individual Talent," it is a struggle against the metaphysical theory of the substantial unity of the soul. And critical theory is the philosophical reflection upon the dominant masks within a culture and their grounds of legitimacy and of moral efficacy. Cultural studies, in this light, is the critical comparison of all the different discursive practices of self within and among different cultures—a form of philosophical anthropology, to revive another, older name.[5]

Ideally, the critical intellectual is in the best position to appreciate, revise, and evaluate the production of selves. In principle, within and without disciplines, with or without an elaborated ideology, critical intellectuals, individually and collectively, whatever their particular interests may be, are political forces for cultural change—even if they often do not know in advance what change their work is in fact promoting. This is because critical intellectuals see the self as a selected style of life with ideological dimensions and as ever open to change. They recognize that the self may be different, even as it may have been different at one time. The mask plays of cultural politics embody critical agents with specific agendas that do not necessarily add up to one final goal. To put it more philosophically, these mask plays disclose mask worlds that produce heterogeneous temporalities, a teeming welter of possible futures realizing variously selected pasts in the interpretive acts of the revisionary present. Naturally, in a modern liberal democratic society, the role of the critical intellectual is just one source of imaginative authority, just one available educational resource. Our empowerment in a mass culture is significant en masse as part of the educational apparatus of the modern state, but individually it is not usually very significant at all. Even considering our institutional significance, however, we must compete for the "hearts and minds" of "the people," as they say. With more popular forms of making up selves to be found in the print and electronic media, we do so to our great but not complete disadvantage.

The argument of Theweleit's two volumes can be given diagrammatically. A large open space, either lit to a blazing white or filled with an appalling darkness, suddenly disgorges a swirling, uncannily advancing, variegated mass headed by a distinctly exotic, usually Jewish, "Red" woman—aggressive, sharp-tongued, sensuously threatening, yet inviting—who is concealing a gun or a grenade beneath her skirt. Atop a rise stands a lone "soldier-male," rigidly alert, his eyes mechanically sweeping the unfolding spectacle for the best view. He is resolutely pledged to maintain order: his uniform, skin, and heavy musculature all compose his "body armor" and are not so much extensions of his ego as that ego itself in (military) formation. He is the "man of steel," the projected figure of phallic power of the "totality machine" of the Nation. Both longing to dissolve into the mass and battling against such an enticing fate, the soldier-male would erase the mass itself. He focuses his coldly penetrating gaze on its female leader, taking aim on her voluptuous red mouth, from which streams a rising tide of filthy epithets. Suddenly, at precisely the right range, the tension-filled, sublimely straining soldier-male becomes one with his uplifted rifle, suffers a blackout of his conscious mind, and feels himself explode repeatedly into the throat of the woman, turning her face and head into a bloody, pulpy mess and scattering the crowd in all directions. The crisis surmounted, the soldier-male comes slowly to himself, waking in the midst of a now empty, silent square. The emerging future has been obliterated by means of past defenses acquired in military training and the "drill" in order to preserve the blank purity of an orderly (i.e., male-dominated) present.

This primal scene and its related variations recur again and again in the more than 250 novels, memoirs, reports, and stories forming the material basis for Theweleit's analysis. With the one major exception of Ernst Jünger, a World War I veteran, celebrator of battle as inner experience, leading literary intellectual and friend to Heidegger, the authors of these texts are ex-members of the *Freikorps*. The *Freikorps* was a German military force made up of veterans of the Great War, hired by the new "democratic" government they loathed, to keep the peace on the Polish border, in the Ruhr, and during worker "rebellions" in the cities from 1918 until 1923, when a *Freikorps*-attempted coup (the "Kapp putsch") was crushed, their units officially disbanded, and their leaders arrested or permitted to go into exile. Yet many of the *Freikorps* officers became important figures in the Nazi movement and, once in power, occupied significant positions in the Nazi regime. Rudolf Höss, a *Freikorps* leader, became the head of the Auschwitz death camp.

The language of this primal scene I have been simulating (shortly, the real thing will be given) provides my analytic focus here. When I use the phrase the *fascist imagination,* I mean this discursive scene, its variants, and the life practices that support its production. Theweleit takes these fascist works at their word. Basing his work on Deleuze and Guattari's *Anti-Oedipus,* Margaret Mahler's *On Human Symbiosis and the Vicissitudes of Individuation,* Elias Canetti's *Crowds and Power,* and other revisionist, largely feminist, critiques of psychoanalytic theories of ego-formation, Theweleit examines the reality of fascist desire that such language produces. The result of this novel approach—an approach he claims to have improvised in the process of coming to terms with these disturbing texts—is a construction of the fascist imagination in these soldier-males that sheds light on the little fascist in every man, and, more important, on the destructive history of male domination of women and the earth. These soldier-males, Theweleit finds, never developed "egos" at all in the classic Freudian sense—hence the need for revisionary psychoanalytic perspectives. Their society, an extreme instance of postromantic Western culture at large, created unloved and unloving mothers and remotely ineffectual yet authoritarian and authoritarian-sounding fathers. The sons, longing for fusion with their mothers, feared their annihilating rejection and desired total revenge against both parents for their complementary inadequacies. Like Freud's "Wolf-Man," these soldier-males never arrived at the Oedipal stage of open rivalry with their fathers. If they had, they would then have come to identify with their fathers after learning, the hard way, to renounce the original aims of their desires and to substitute new, culturally approved and at least minimally satisfying aims. Instead, these soldier-males were sent off to military school to be broken and remade, without any regard for their personal satisfaction, to learn to identify their personal redemption from incipient dissolution with the most intense experiences of pain, of self-sacrifice for the good of the whole, and of the destruction of the

Other. Becoming an integral part of a larger, all-male "corps," what Theweleit calls the "totality machine" of the Nation, enables the soldier-male to experience the ecstasy of destroying the Other while maintaining as rigorous and impenetrable a defense as possible.

Nature; femininity; temporality; the free-flowing, multifarious floods of desire—all these streaming things are dangerous threats to the soldier-male's pre-Oedipal selfhood. And Jewishness and Bolshevism are seen in terms of these threats. The same language ultimately characterizes them all: that of the bloody miasma. Culture, masculinity, monumentality, the military "totality machines," the fascist hierarchical production of reality—all these things are the encompassing shells constituting the soldier-male's fragile, rigid ego. "Warfare" and "Germanness" are the aggressive defenses of the self's and the nation's integrity. All internal and external stimuli produce and stage themselves according to this fundamental opposition of flux and form. Even the soldier-male's language functions as an extension of war into cultural politics. Parasitic on the differential play of conventional figures, this language incorporates all alterity, sucking out its life by reducing this play to terms of its obsessive polarity. It fills the resulting void with mystical paeans to and sublime displays of the fascist primal scene. Primarily antisexual—rather than perversely sexual, latently homosexual, or purely asexual—the fascist imagination, an impersonal *discursive* practice, begets itself in monumental enterprises of male bonding in authoritarian hierarchies. Following Foucault (in *Discipline and Punish*), as well as Deleuze and Guattari, Theweleit points out that, while clearly extreme, this fascist practice of the male self and society is not really far from the norm. In fact, it is closer to the norm of Western culture, particularly that of the modern state, than one would like to think. Epic texts of government and culture, the idea of mastering the earth and breeding a new superrace, transforming all others through total war into the raw materials for these projects, even to the point of universal annihilation—this scenario is the "great" work that the fascist imagination would impose upon world history. From out of the mass a people must be formed by a nation of soldier-males whose leader expresses the will of the Fatherland: forge the chosen people into a race of steel and siphon off the dross—all the rest who do not fit.

Although the approach is different and the materials had been previously unmined (this has changed in the years subsequent to the

original 1977 German edition),[6] the vision of *Male Fantasies* should
not be unfamiliar, especially to readers of D.H. Lawrence. "The Prussian Officer," for one example, stages, on the eve of World War I, the
fascist imagination as it turns against itself in the form of a lackey
soldier's shocking murder of the officer master who had beaten him
apparently in lieu of more intimate modes of male bonding.[7] What's
original about *Male Fantasies,* however, is that it gives us a "rhetoric of
fascism" that enables us to see the constellation of figures in fascism's
primal scene as a destructive style of human temporality seeking at
any cost to keep all its prospects pure. Soldier-males want no future to
become present that would mean the dissolution of past defenses, for
that's all the self there is or ever was—past defenses. Body, self, and
the Nation can only become themselves, never something they have
not already been. Others are there only as materials kept in reserve or
as threatening obstacles to the efficient operation of the psychic and
social maintenance mechanisms. Any "new order" of self or society
must always be not so much the return of as the insistence upon the
same self or society. There must not be any seductive traces of un-
mastered differences. One aspect, then, of what I am calling the fascist imagination is the collective wounded narcissism of a culture destructively in action.

Here are two "reports" by soldier-males—whose identities, like
the styles of all these texts, are indistinguishable—which enact versions of the same primal scene:

> Again he hears the metallic-sounding laughter of Ruth, Esther, Sa-
> lome [coming from the "Red" woman]: a fact as lovely as those of the
> Old Testament women. And it seems as if, in that mocking laughter,
> a mask is being lifted from another face that appears behind it: the
> head of the Gorgon, Medusa.[8]

> The last body they ride past [from a crowd of dead Bolsheviks] seems
> to be that of [the leading] woman. But it's very hard to tell, since all
> that's left is a bloody mass, a lump of flesh that appears to have been
> completely lacerated with whips and is now lying within a circle of
> trampled, reddish slush. (*T1,* 189)

Unlike Adorno and Horkheimer in *The Authoritarian Personality*—
who claim that fascism arises à la Freud from a paranoid fear of castration by the Primal Father, transferred to others who must then be
destroyed as scapegoats—Theweleit argues suggestively that soldier-

males, having already frozen their own femininity within, aim to annihilate the feminine outside themselves in all its forms as well. Of course, this murderous process of self-discipline haunts them forever. They perpetually reenact it on themselves as they kill one another. It isn't that they fear castration, symbolized unconsciously by the woman's body; it is rather that they have learned to castrate the feminine by destroying all manifestations of it in themselves and others in their field of vision (*T1, 300–62*). To petrify the Medusa in themselves forever, they must destroy woman in the world and all her sinuous surrogates, such as Jews, "Reds," and the legendary "riflewomen" (a version of the myth of the woman with a penis par excellence), to what they "essentially" are: a bloody miasma. Every threat to the maintenance of the military "totality machine" of supermales—Jewishness, socialism, sexuality, and homosexuality—everything that threatens the dissolution of their defenses into free-flowing desires, must be crushed, releasing in each solider-male the sublime sensation of his own rushing blood, a sensation that the "object" of his destruction is simultaneously made to enact in "reality." As Nietzsche's *On the Genealogy of Morals* suggests in this context, the fascist imagination is one modern enactment of a radical asceticism[9] whose origins are saturated in blood—that of the guilty Other, of course, but also that of oneself insofar as one internalizes guilt. Puritanism, in its various forms, is of course another early enactment.

Here are several particularly "eloquent" passages on this subject:

> And, finally, there is ecstasy—a state of mind granted not only to the holy man, to great writers and great lovers, but also to the great in spirit. . . . Ecstasy is an intoxication beyond all intoxications, a release that bursts all bonds. It is a madness without discretion or limits, comparable only to the natural forces. A man in ecstasy becomes a violent storm, a raging sea, roaring thunder. He merges with the cosmos, racing toward death's dark gates like a bullet toward its target. And should the waves crash purple above him, he will already be long past all consciousness of movement or transition; he will be a wave gliding back into the flowing sea from whence it came. [10]

> Breath, heartbeat, engine-roar, flying grenades, and machine-gun clatter coalesced into one rhythm: Hot human—blood—flows—here—the vapors—for—all magic—dear. The rhythm [of my words] caught and wedded itself to a text from the original version of

Goethe's "Walpurgisnacht," which [I] had read years before in passing. "Hot human blood flows here, / The vapors for all magic dear."
(*T2,* 185)

[War] gives men form and maturity in a formless age. The blood
shot through their bodies like torrents tumbling together in a snow-
thaw. Their blood . . . foamed and exploded and ancient rock
melted back to molten fire. Battle melted the snow that had frozen
our feelings; they blossomed in the surging of our blood. . . . The
blood whirled through our brains and pulsated through our veins, as
if anticipating a long-awaited night of love—but this night would
be more passionate and more furious. The enthusiasm of these virile
men made their blood seethe against the walls of their veins and
bubble through their hearts like fire. Every voice ever raised in
alarm, from Suttner to Kant, fades away like a child's murmur in
this motoric rhythm of tension and deed. In the immutable laws of
the blood, all experience sinks and is lost.

We were passed by endless streams of men—men willing to sacrifice
life itself to satisfy their will to life, their will to battle and power they
represented. All values were made worthless, all concepts void by this
incessant nighttime flooding into battle; we sensed that we were witnessing the manifestation of something elemental and powerful,
something that had always been, that would outlive human lives and
human wars. (*T2,* 186)

I have quoted at length to stress that, as the fascist primal scene
suggests, soldier-males in foreign wars or domestic "police actions"
experience pleasure only in the Dionysian release of these "blood
flows"—those from the Other, which embody, by destructive magic,
those within themselves. The symbiotic relationship of sadomasochism parallels, in Theweleit's view, the primal scene of the fascist
imagination.[11]

It is not surprising, then, to find that shaping the formation of this
fascist primal scene is the construction of the body by the military
drill. This process extends in the cadet academy to "unofficial" forms
of punishment for any "lapse," no matter how minor, in discipline.
Here is a soldier-male on the ritual of initiation into the hierarchical
apparatus of cadet society:

The cadets stood around me in a semicircle. Each one held a knout in
his hand, long leather thongs attached to a wooden stick that was used

for beating the dirt out of clothes. Glasmacher stepped forward, took me by the arm, and led me over to the table. I climbed up, not without difficulty, and lay down on my stomach. Glasmacher took my head in his hands, pressed my eyes shut, and forced my skull hard against the surface of the table. I gritted my teeth and tensed my whole body. The first blow whistled. I jerked upward, but Glasmacher held me tight; the blows rained down on my back, shoulders, legs, a frenzied fit of hard, smacking blows. My hands were tightly gripped around the edge of the table. I beat out a rhythm with my knees, shins, and toes in an attempt to expel the excruciating pain. Now all the torment seemed to move through my body and implant itself in the table; again and again my hips and loins slammed against the wood and made it shudder with me; every blow recharged the bundle of muscles and skin, blood and bones and sinews, with slingshot force, till my whole body stretched under tension and threatened to burst in its lower regions. I gave my head over entirely to Glasmacher's hands, wrenched myself shut, and finally lay still and moaning. (T2, 150)

The beating—violently and rhythmically slamming the body against the table, making it shudder—simulates the action of coitus to the point at which orgasm and incontinence alike threaten "in its lower regions." Notice the simultaneous distance from and identification with this ritual scene. The writer observes now as then the memory of his own body and its sublime flows. And warfare provides the theater where this rite of passage can be performed again and again upon the Other as if it were oneself going through it once more. As Theweleit repeatedly reminds his reader, Benjamin is right to see fascism as the ultimate aestheticization of politics, only, for Theweleit, he does not carry the material analysis far enough, down to the bone, as it were.[12] The figure Theweleit uses to characterize the soldier-males, "the-not-yet-fully-born," comes from the analysis of psychotic children.[13] The phrase is appropriate if one recalls that the military drill and the educational system equip these men with all the destructive tools required to resist any experience that would disintegrate their present arrested psychic organizations and so possibly release them toward some further development. Imagine this situation, if you will, as being like that of a baby in the womb resisting birth with a copy of Faust and a field helmet.

A disturbed form of human temporality produces the fascist imagination. For human beings, despite their strongest defenses, each moment is potentially a new birth of self, a new production of desire, another mask play, another body to be. All that one *is* depends on all that one has been, as one meets the future by becoming other than oneself once more. Repeating what one had been as one's being now stifles any future self emerging. The fascist imagination of soldier-males would fix this process of change. As Foucault's *Discipline and Punish* suggests, this culture of the soldier-males is an extreme instance of Western cultural organization into the imperial nation-state. It resists all further transformation. It seeks to master the process of transformation on every level—economic, technological, social, cultural, psychical, physical—from a total or global perspective. Such a perspective, Theweleit shows, enables the enactment of any transformation imaginable only through the scapegoat simulacrum made out of the Other. The Other becomes the bad puppet one must quell. To put it another way, and in accordance with Foucault's various analyses of the disciplinary society, the fascist imagination practices a murderous hermeneutics upon the living text of the world, producing it repeatedly as a consumable "corpus." "Woman," as we know from Derrida's reading in *Spurs: Nietzsche's Styles,* is the traditionally overdetermined name for this "raw material" of male transformation. [14] And this murderous hermeneutic is one reason why Theweleit refuses to distinguish between acts of war and acts of writing committed by soldier-males. The destruction and transformation of all alterity into one's scapegoat muse or spectral "defective" double who inspires one's destructive creation constitutes equally both kinds of action. This does not mean, however, that a certain kind of "incorrect" hermeneutic is the model for acts of war, any more than it means that the latter is the model for the former. Yet, both martial and textual practices of the fascist imagination derive from the same fundamental disturbance in the Western experience of time. The endless productions of human desire must be mastered, so as not to be experienced—except totally on one's own terms, as if from above—in registering the destruction of the Other. As Heidegger argues in *What Is Called Thinking?* "man" in the Western tradition can only become "the persona, the mask of Being" in this violent play. [15]

Our first mask play is now at an end, with the emergence of this

profile of the fascist imagination. This desiring machine stages a sublime phantasmagoria in which an "ego" incapable of object relations
and a world not finally distinguishable from the frozen floods of desire
play out roles according to the destructive designs of the fascist primal
scene. The disciplined bodies and heroic acts of soldier-males realize
this phantasmagoria through the annihilation of the Other, thereby
transforming the coming future into the insistent reiteration of the
pre-Oedipal past of primary fusion and so devastating the present into
blank purity, ultimately on an apocalyptic scale. No alterity or difference, should it appear, can be permitted to remain so. Only nothingness and oneself can be, for projecting oneself into the created void,
one can replicate oneself symbolically as part of the total fascist organization of the real, producing the missing phallus of the resurrected
Fatherland—lost in the Great War—under the monumental guise of
the state as the "super totality machine" at the pinnacle of the national
hierarchy. The imaginary becomes the real via the exhaustively symbolic formation of everyday life. The perfect aesthetic specularity of
unsurpassed narcissism consumes the present. Neither regression nor
repression occurs, as the original preoedipal psychic apparatus explicitly defines the Western rule of the earth, materially and institutionally, in an imperialist expansion and totalitarian massing of the
fascist regime. In fascism, the spirit of nihilism becomes demonically
creative, increasing and multiplying so that it may saturate and transform the entire world into its own spectral image (*T2*, 269–70).

As an experiment, and before examining critically Theweleit's own
psychic profile, I want to compare the would-be invariable, totalitarian mask of the fascist imagination with the mask play occurring
in Heidegger's *Introduction to Metaphysics*. Heidegger, of course, as one
of the major influences on critical theory—both defenders and critics
acknowledge this fact as a commonplace—is a perfect example in this
context, perhaps too perfect. [16] The recent revival of interest in the
details of his Nazi affiliations and their traces in his philosophy before
and after his famous *Kehre* or "turn" in the mid-1930s, coming on the
heels of the Paul deMan debates, makes my choice of Heidegger appear all too timely. [17] The reason for my choosing him, however, and
more specifically this text of his, is that I see there the performance of
a typically Heideggerian "turn" of a different sort. This is a "turn" on
what I now understand to be the fascist production of the real that I

have also sensed operating in critical theory for some time. In earlier studies, I argued that most critical theory transforms its textual "objects" into the raw materials for its systematic speculation, taking as "nature" what it finds already inscribed and handed down as "culture," in order to overcome all masterly influences threatening the sublime images of the self's desired autonomy. Prior texts and authors read "antithetically" become the scapegoat muses of contemporary theory.[18] Although at the time I did not formulate it this way, I can now see that this means much critical theory bears a strong family resemblance to the fascist imagination. Yet in some theorists and their most "questionable predecessors," such as Nietzsche and Heidegger, I have also seen this move critically elaborated and turned against them. I have understood this revisionary turn made upon a destructive production of the Other as "irony" and have understood such "irony" to be the sign of a critical self-consciousness expressing itself in a reflective meditation upon nihilism that justifies the practice of criticism in modern culture as an open-ended and hence "postmodern" art of self-fashioning.[19] Read in the light of all the recent debates and, especially, of these volumes, I am no longer sure what exactly to make of such "irony."[20]

An example will flesh out what I mean by "the Heideggerian turn" as "irony":

> But if we put the question in the form of our original interrogative sentence: "Why are there essents rather than nothing?" this addition prevents us in our questioning from beginning directly with an unquestionably given essent and, having scarcely begun, from continuing on to another expected essent as a ground. Instead, this essent, through questioning, is held out into the possibility of non-being. Thereby the why takes on a very different power and penetration. Why is the essent torn away from the possibility of non-being? Why does it not simply keep falling back into non-being? Now the essent is no longer that which just happens to be present; it begins to waver and oscillate, regardless of whether or not we recognize the essent in all certainty, regardless of whether or not we apprehend it in its full scope. Henceforth the essent as such oscillates, insofar as we draw it into question. The swing of the pendulum extends to the extreme and sharpest contrary possibility, to non-being and nothingness. And the search for the why undergoes a parallel change. It does not aim simply

at providing an also present ground and explanation for what is present; now a ground is sought which will explain the emergence of the essent as an overcoming of nothingness. The ground that is now asked after is the ground of decision for the essent over against nothingness, or more precisely, the ground for the oscillation of the essent, which sustains and unbinds us, half being, half not being, which is also why we can belong entirely to no thing, not even to ourselves; yet being there (*Dasein*) is in every case mine.[21]

Although the antifoundational, "abysmal" formulations are largely Heidegger's own, the resonance of the figures haunting this passage—the language of decision, overcoming, resoluteness, and powerful penetration to the brink of possible annihilation—harmonizes quite well, it would appear, with the language of the primal scene of the fascist imagination.[22] A collective subject, the "we" that Heidegger's lecture invokes, like that of the soldier-males, interrogates an "essent" (an entity or "being") in a way that holds it out to "the possibility of non-being," penetrating it thoroughly with its questioning. A wavering or oscillation of the essent occurs that discloses how all being is "an overcoming of nothingness." *Dasein,* human "being," also is disclosed in this wavering or oscillation to be "an overcoming of nothingness." So far Heidegger sounds like the philosophical equivalent of Ernst Jünger in battle. But insofar as human "being" also wavers and oscillates, pendulumlike, and one decides, as Heidegger does, to push on to the point of questioning the grounds of this very questioning, one must recognize, "ironically" enough, how one is "half being, half not being." One thus suffers the recognition of one's being the very process of oscillation itself, a process that both "sustains and unbinds." "With our question," Heidegger says, "we place ourselves in the essent in such a way that it loses its self-evident character as the essent. The essent begins to waver between the broadest and most drastic extremes: 'either essents—or nothing'—and thereby the questioning itself loses all solid foundation. Our questioning being-there is suspended and in this suspense is nevertheless self-sustained" (*IM,* 24). The authentic alienation of such devastating questioning ("we can belong entirely to no thing, not even to ourselves; yet being-there [*Dasein*] is in every case mine") is not, however, "an invention of ours," Heidegger claims; rather, it is only "the strict observance of the original tradition regarding the meaning of the fundamental question" (*IM*, 20). And this questioning attitude "must clarify and secure itself in this process, it must be consolidated by training" (*IM*, 18). Authentic philosophical discipline or "drill," imposed on oneself out of respect for the "original tradition," permits us to interrogate both the realm of other beings and ourselves. Such interrogation addresses the question of the meaning of Being even to the sublime point of envisioning total negation.

A soldierly aesthetic surely pervades these passages, but it is elaborated not only consciously—Theweleit stresses the conscious nature of the soldier-male's texts—but also self-consciously to take in and turn against the very self involved in the systematically "destructive" interrogative act.[23] That is, it becomes critical and internalized:

> To question is to will to know. He who wills, he who puts his whole existence into a will, *is* resolved. Resolve does not shift about; it does not shirk, but acts from out of the moment and never stops. Resolve is no mere decision to act, but the crucial beginning of action that anticipates and reaches through all action. To will is to be resolved. (The essence of willing is here carried back to determination [*Entschlossenheit*, unclosedness]. But the essence of resolve lies in the opening, the coming-out-of-cover [*Entborgeneheit*] of human being-there into the clearing of Being, and not in storing up of energy for "action." . . . But its relation to Being is one of letting-be. The idea that all should be grounded in letting-be offends the understanding.) (*IM*, 17)

Once again the soldierly aesthetic of the fascist imagination—the language of resoluteness and not-shirking, of coming-out-of-cover, and of enduring in the clearing of Being as an uncanny suspension in the nothingness of the entire totality itself—haunts the figures embodying the philosophical conceptions, even those figures expressing later formulations, with suggestions of the primal scene of the fascist imagination. And once again this haunting explicitly turns in on the questioning self in the very act of questioning. The self-division between earlier and later Heidegger is here played out as the potentially self-cancelling, finally undecidable, juxtaposition between earlier and later formulations. Yet this "deconstructive" *ur*-moment already begins in such "turning" in on the self. In this light, Heidegger's famous "turn" in philosophical direction after the mid-1930s would appear to be an amplification and complication of this original self-division, as a "turning" in on the self.[24]

More immediately, what can we make of the "ironic" Heideggerian "turn" that pervades this text? Heidegger would seem to understand this turning on the self in terms of the textual production of his own notorious interpretation of the first chorus in Sophocles' *Antigone* (lines 332–75) about man being the strangest, most uncanny of beings, who violently introduces nothingness into the world as the measure of Being. Heidegger in this passage "destructively" introduces such irony into the history of modern philosophy. I say this because the gist of Heidegger's interpretation is given most "tellingly" in the following self-portrait:

> Not-being-there is the supreme victory over being. Being-there is unremitting affliction resulting from defeat and renewed attempts at violence against Being: at the site of its appearing, omnipotent being [literally] violates [*vergewaltigt,* to do violence to, to rape] Being-there; Being indeed is this site, surrounding and controlling [*umwaltet und durchwaltet*] being-there and so holding it in being. (*IM,* 149)

Here the essent and its violent interrogator are both overcome by "omnipotent" Being itself, which is said to rape the latter, just as Heidegger could be said to have violated the former with his penetrating questioning. At the site of Being, all essents, including *Dasein,* are ambiguously "cleared," even as they are all surrounded, controlled, and so held in existence.

Is this entire circle of violations the allegorization of the famous hermeneutic circle of Heidegger's "destructive" critical reading? Is it, in other words, fascism to the second power? Or is it, in the "turning" in on the questioning self, the sublime release of letting being be, the necessarily violent withdrawal from Being of the nihilistic projections of the fascist imagination? Is the endless wavering and oscillation of both "subject and object" between "being and nothingness" the imagined and desired final dissolution of the Western tradition of metaphysics? Or is it the "ironic" continuation of that tradition under a prototypically "deconstructive" erasure ("clearing") that preserves as a self-consciously "ironic" textual practice what was consciously performed at last on the stage of world history as fascism and "the final solution"? Is fascism, which is militarism practiced in the name of "the people" as a total way of life, when raised to the "second power," still fascism? Or is it something else as yet unnamed and unnameable?

Despite its indeterminate, "unresolved" status, this text—supplemented and revised repeatedly over the years, so that it is literally a palimpsest laid bare—does provide us with a psychic profile. In *An Introduction to Metaphysics,* Heidegger stages what in *Being and Time* he calls "the destruction" of "tradition." By this, I do not mean to imply that the text we have been reading is simply an extended example made up of some of the missing second half of *Being and Time*.[25] Nor is it merely a prototypically "deconstructive" etymology and "discursive" genealogy of the word "Being" and its "history." But before saying more precisely what I do mean I must recall Heidegger's conceptions of "tradition" and "destruction":

> When tradition . . . becomes master, it does so in such a way that what it "transmits" is made so inaccessible, proximally and for the most part, that it rather becomes concealed. Tradition takes what has come down to us and delivers it over to self-evidence: it blocks our access to those primordial "sources" from which the categories and concepts handed down to us have been in part quite genuinely drawn. Indeed it makes us forget that they have had such an origin, and makes us suppose that the necessity of going back to these sources is something which we need not even understand. [We have] had [our history] so thoroughly uprooted by tradition that it confines our interest to the multiformity of possible types, directions, and standpoints . . . in the most exotic and alien of cultures; and by this very interest [tradition] seeks to veil the fact that it has no ground of its own to stand on. Consequently, [we no longer understand] the most elementary conditions which would alone enable [us] to go back to the past in a positive manner and make it productively [our own]. . . . This hardened tradition must be loosened up, and . . . dissolved. . . . We are to destroy [the tradition] until we arrive at those primordial experiences in which we achieved our first ways of determining [our sense of things]. . . . [In this way,] we must . . . stake out the positive possibilities of that tradition, and this always means keeping it within its limits. . . . In working out [this project,] we must heed the assignment [of destroying the tradition,] so that by positively making the past our own, we may bring ourselves into full possession of the authentic possibilities of such inquiry.[26]

Clearly, Heidegger, while using only the one word, assumes two senses of "tradition." It is, first, a present-day trivializing, rigidifying, blocking agent that inflexibly reduces to mere self-evidence all the sources of one's own being-in-the-world. It does so in order better to pursue the exotic beliefs of all other cultures, of culture itself. It really can be described historically, I think, as the internationalist "convention" of post-Enlightenment intellectual life. This is what Lionel Trilling in another context dubbed the modern "liberal imagination"—which, in the name of liberation, imprisons the mind in the most reductive categories of thought,[27] and so is not really "liberal" at all. Besides this first sense, there is also a second sense to "tradition." Still the inexhaustible sources of a culture, tradition is also the original understanding we must appropriate and define for ourselves if we are to have access to the original experiences out of which all authentic understandings come. "Tradition" in this sense can be more precisely termed "organic tradition," I think, or "heritage." This is the "primordial spirit" of a particular people that first informed—and perhaps still barely informs—their "being-in-the-world." "Ironically," of course, thanks to the "authentic spirits" of the respective languages, Heidegger insists that another culture, that of the Greeks, is part and parcel of these fundamental experiences of the German people.[28] To sum up: "convention" is the currently established reductive construction put upon "tradition" by a post-Enlightenment, liberally modernizing culture in order to trivialize, curtail, and disperse its genuine, still "uncanny" possibilities. And "tradition" as "organic" or "native" culture comprehends those sublimely primordial experiences out of which arise all authentic appropriations of "tradition." One thinks here of Heidegger's famous meditation in "The Origin of the Work of Art" (1935) on Van Gogh's painting of "peasant shoes." In short, "convention" is the seductive philistine Delilah of the blinded, bound, and dispirited Samson "tradition." Or, more topically put, "convention" is the international, modern civilization of the victorious Allies, while "tradition" is essentially the defeated, romantic culture of Germany.[29]

In *An Introduction to Metaphysics*, we see what it means to practice the liberating "destruction" of "tradition." The established "conventional" meanings of philosophical concepts and terms like "being," "physis," "idea," and their histories in the world are "destroyed" by an inventive if somewhat speciously playful etymology and an equally inventive and extravagant if also playfully specious genealogy. Heidegger thereby affiliates the Greek and German languages as the "true" conveyers of the truth of Being, while all other languages, especially Latin and its "romance" derivatives, are consigned to the status of "bad" translations.[30] He is able to perform the "release" of the question of Being, to let it be more in the fullness of what it may have originally asked. "Tradition," according to the desire animating Heidegger and staged here, is liberated to become insistently itself once again. And we have a sense of what that means: Being is itself the necessary violation of all entities, including humanity, in order to hold existence open in the clearing amid nothingness. The mental portrait emerging in Heidegger's text is that of a (self-)violating, (self-)ravishing Being that, in violating and ravishing the entire realm of entities, discloses what this text and his related texts of the time celebrate: the "flame" of "spirit" consuming all.[31] As Derrida notes, this motif of "flame and spirit" is both rare and definitive in Heidegger, defining as it does Heidegger's complicated, anxious relationship to Hegel, who is hardly mentioned here, and his less complicated, openly avowed affiliation with the "true spirit" of national socialism, which, even in the 1953 authorized and revised version, is mentioned far too avidly, especially near its conclusion.[32] The mask play Heidegger performs, therefore, is the reflective simulation of a philosophical Samson bringing down the modern "House of Being" and so freeing the "fiery spirit" of philosophy to wander errantly the Black Forest byways of the mind, in quest of the meaning of Being, a meaning spectrally synonymous with (self-)ravishment.[33]

What all this may imply for critical theory, insofar as it derives from Heidegger—and from his master in such all-consuming "irony," Nietzsche—seems considerable. In this light, the self-conscious critical practice of a "deconstructive" "irony" subverting "conventional" hierarchies of representational oppositions, even its own avowedly provisional inverted ones—all performed in the name of the "free play" of intertextuality and endless allusiveness—is apparently the "postmodern" legacy of the international critical reflection on the fascist imagination.[34] Critical theory, in other words, practices simultaneously both the invariable fascist mask and the variable "ironic" mask. The institutionalization and professionalization of critical theory would thus correspond to the incorporation of all alterity into the "new" hierarchical structures of the fascist "totality machine." It would all work like this: deconstruction consumes the highly structured Other it "reads," and professionalization then incorporates this "disseminated" Other into its own institutional organization. Deconstruction, as the final instance of critical theory, would be the explosive weapon and dissolving agent of the successful discipline of critical theory.

The part missing from this story, however, is the place of temporality in Heidegger and the critical theory he has authorized.[35] The formative problematic of the fascist imagination, as we have seen, is the annihilation of the emerging future as a hated yet seductive other self. This annihilation is carried out in order to maintain as the present a past defensive organization of the preoedipal psyche in its totally elaborated imperial form. The fascist imagination needs the Other's death, since the Other is equally different from and similar to oneself, an impossible double-bind provocation to homicidal rage that we recognize from the psychosis of celebrity killers. Just imagine the Lacanian "mirror-stage" infant as in fact "the god in the machine" of modern technology.

The hermeneutic temporality in Heidegger, on the contrary, releases the flood of unrealized or "unthought" possibilities of the past as the invading future, which voids and transforms the present. this interpretive "repetition" is actually a new redescription or creative appropriation of the "tradition" that, in Heidegger's view, the "tradition" of great thinkers itself sponsors. Such a "poetics of critical reading" stands in stark opposition to the reductively trivializing and literalizing construction of mere self-evidence put upon this "tradition" by the narrow, rationalizing constraints of present-day "convention." Heidegger's several Hölderlin "elucidations" make perfect cases in point of such "inventive" revisionism.

As with all such starkly posed extremes, however, this one too begins to express, as one reflects on the matter, more of a resemblance than a simple opposition between the contrasting poles. In fact, the Heideggerian half of the polarity between the fascist imagination and critical theory's temporal hermeneutic looks increasingly more like the self-congratulatory, bad-faith smear of its other half. Yet this may be an optical illusion. In any event, there does remain a significant difference between critical theory's Heideggerian strain and the fascist imagination.

In Heidegger, unlike in fascism, temporality is explicitly thematized and put into question as the privileged site of access to the language of the problematic truth of the Being question. This problematic thematization of time, language, and Being is present in early and late Heidegger alike,[36] and present also in Derridean deconstruction at least.[37] The question of the future in Heidegger—how we encounter our past coming toward us from the future in each moment of the present—becomes in deconstruction the question of difference in all its forms: distinction, differing, deferral—the endless postponement or apocalyptic anticlimax of scriptive "différance" and dissemination.

In this light, deconstruction would appear to be less the universal "goon squad" and dissolving agency of the hierarchical profession of critical theory, less fascism's institutionalized disciplinary "spirit," than its demonically intellectual "postmodern" parody.[38] The mask of the fascist imagination and the mask of critical theory are, therefore, not ultimately the same. Nor is the latter merely the former's self-divided speculative refinement. But, like Batman, that latter-day mask of the "dark knight" of nihilistic vigilantism, and like his antic foe, the Joker, that self-masked "first homicidal artist in world history," an artist who does "art until someone dies," these masks perform the pivotal roles in one and the same story, too.[39] It is this shifting problematic relation of masks that motivates my "radical parody" here.

Cultural studies, as practiced by Theweleit and as his practice authorizes others, combines critical theories not into a new "system" but into a new context defined by both current and past ideological configurations of the discourse of the imaginary. The problematic of temporality afflicting the fascist imagination and informing Heideggerian hermeneutics and Derridean deconstruction now reappears in the analyses of the new historicism that relate present and past discursive moments via the anecdote. Earlier concerns with self reappear as the insistence upon the productive relational powers of all the body's desiring "machines" to make, unmake, and remake serial, multiple connections, via sucking, licking, rubbing, penetrating, receiving, and so on. And the exclusive focus on white male Western masters of politics and culture reappears as a new emphasis upon the necessary interrelations of such figures with all the previously ignored and repressed bearers of Otherness—women, ethnic, racial, and former colonial groups, and all their practices of everyday life—seen now from an internationalist, "left-leaning" perspective that yet also sees classic Marxist analysis as riddled with dogmatic claims. "Liberal" civilization also reappears with this essentially pragmatic, academic "leftist" critique. Neither an ideological construction in service to a political organization, nor a speculative philosophical "worldview," cultural studies as a "field" reads the genealogy of the currently dominant imaginary in all its manifestations. This accounts for Theweleit's use in *Male Fantasies* of photographs, poster art, classical paintings, editorial cartoons, avant-garde graphics, film stills—as many cultural representations as possible of the fascist imagination, representations covering the period from the beginnings of modernity in the Renaissance to the present. Although the primary critical method is the reading of texts, the manner of reading and the selection of texts explains Theweleit's rather typical cultural-studies sneer at merely "literary" analysis. Instead of reading the symbols of canonical works by great masters for their hidden meanings and articulating the significant, "objective" forms of unique, freestanding classic texts, cultural studies, as Theweleit demonstrates, reads the material surface inscriptions of all cultural constructions as the human "desiring machine's" productions of the real. Political, military, and cultural actions are equally "creative" of historical reality. Culture is neither a Kantian aesthetic playground nor an "ivory tower" translunar paradise nor the utopian design center of the emerging world. Rather, it is just another theater in the war that is modern life: this is the war for determining the dispositions of bodies in space and of collectivities through time that Foucault labels the struggle for "bio-power."[40]

In the spirit of such postmodern discursive formulations, let me put this distinctive difference of cultural studies in the form of a revisionary Freudian parable: if the fascist imagination produces the modern male's historically constructed "id," and if critical theory stages the self-critical function of the modern intellectual's "superego," playing out its internalized critique as "ironically" self-reflective "turns," then cultural studies performs a new "ego" or "rational subject" for the contemporary subject—a mobile, multiple, and sexually

indeterminate "self" open to the body's polymorphous desires for connection and relation and opposed to all those practices cursed by Freud
with the name of the "death instinct." The masks of the soldier-male
and of the resolute vagabond of being are now giving way to the more
purely passionate face. In this context, the later Derrida could be said
to practice not, as Rorty claims, deconstruction as private fantasies
but cultural studies as the perfected form of deconstruction.[41] But,
for me, it is Foucault in volumes 2 and 3 in *The History of Sexuality* that
most effectively defines the practice of self in cultural studies.

Let me conclude, however, by following Rorty's lead for once, and
reflect on *The Postcard*. As erroneously suggested by a contemporary
reproduction of a thirteenth-century picture that shows Socrates writing and Plato speaking, Derrida imagines here his own conception as
ironically resulting from Socrates' writing about himself under the assumed name of his one-time pupil, Plato. The picture mistakenly reverses the traditional order of their names. Derrida thus inscribes the
history of philosophy at its "origins" with the contingent play of the
signifier, an act that acts as the signature of his own remarkable career
of revising that history.

Similarly, I think, this is the reason why Theweleit, whose texts
predate *The Postcard,* begins with and interweaves in these volumes an
autobiographical meditation upon fascism and upon his own family
romance, a meditation suggested by a postcard his mother saved from
his childhood. This postcard depicts a train steaming across the surface of the sea, the top of the dam upon which its rails run being concealed by the furious flood tide. Theweleit's father was a "good rail-
road man" under the Nazis, and this postcard shows the train that
travels back and forth "between the island of Sylt and the terra firma
of Schleswigh-Holstein" (*T1*, xix). Later made much of, the complex
connection of resemblance and difference among fascism, the drain-
ing of the Zuider Zee in the second part of Faust, and Freud's use of
this image to figure the aim of psychoanalysis as "Where id was, there
ego shall be," is thus personalized: it is given a historically specific
and distinctively unique signature for Theweleit's generation of German intellectuals who are coming to terms with fascism's legacy in
the emerging post-Freudian cultural context of late capitalism.[42]
This personalizing gesture has become one of the most visible hall-
marks of cultural studies.[43]

The open question that cultural studies raises in a more "local," American context is that of its very appropriateness to that context. The force of Foucault's analysis of the disciplinary society, for example, is for some readers dissipated in a pluralistic and pragmatic American culture that always already, virtually from its beginnings, appears to be wildly "democratic," "postmodern," and "deconstructive." (See chapters 3 and 7.) Similarly, the worry over the presence or absence of the fascist imagination in Heidegger or, perhaps more urgently, in Paul deMan, while raising tempests in academic teapots around the country, seems to others just so much provincial angst of an American Europeanized academic left at the discovery that two of its idols have feet of clay. That is, all this had very little or nothing to do with the masses or their culture.[44] Perhaps Rorty, one of the latest "leading" intellectuals, from whom I am, in part, drawing this possibly instructive moral about America, is in fact right: perhaps American intellectuals form at best "a band of eccentrics collaborating for purposes of mutual protection rather than a band of fellow spirits united by a common goal."[45] The possibility of a fascist brotherhood—or, apparently, of any other kind—is, in America, just the haunting specter keeping this "band of eccentrics," through the years, minimally in line. Such, anyway, is my argument in part 2 of this book.

I once saw a multiple mask from a Pacific Northwest Native American tribe: a nightmarishly monstrous head opened to reveal a dusky owl's cruelly curved beak, which in turn opened on the human "face" of an "ultimate warrior." The triple mask, to ensure good fishing, was to be worn, lightly, by a lone dancer.[46]

2 What Was Foucault?

My title means to allude, of course, to Foucault's famous essay "What Is an Author?"[1] In addition, it intends a more distant echo—that murderously innocent question that in one form or another animates Nietzsche's career: "What Is Dionysian?"[2] Besides these specialized intertextual references, however, my title cannot help but invoke a less intellectual mode of placement and definition—that of the typical, even the stereotypical. I am thinking of the way one asks what was the political or sexual orientation of someone now dead, whose literary corpus we identify, in subtler if no less discriminating ways, just as we tag the actual body by name and cause of death. Against this stark mass of more commonplace resonances, my title would project a first set of darkly twining figures, in a manner that will produce, I hope, a somewhat lighter music.

Why should we read Foucault? I raise this question after a survey of recent uses to which he has been put in the humanities.[3] Three such usages outline an answer to this second question, which leads us on, or rather leads us back to Foucault himself, and especially to the question "what is an author?"[4]

Enabling constraints—these are what Foucault provides to the three critical projects under consideration. Lydia Blanchard deploys Foucault's critique of the repressive hypothesis from the first volume of *The History of Sexuality* to frame a recovery of D. H. Lawrence's *Lady Chatterley's Lover.*[5] She finds that Foucault, like several major critics, "underestimates" (18) Lawrence's work of liberation. For Foucault sees in the novelist what he sees in Freud and his scientific and theoretical followers. Like them, according to Foucault, Lawrence merely repeats the myth of sexual liberation from Victorian repression—a myth that accompanies the climactic incitement to the transformation of sex into sexuality, which defines the modern period as the end of Western culture. Foucault quotes Lawrence from *The Plumed Serpent* and "A Propos *Lady Chatterley's Lover*" in cursory illustration, the lines from the latter essay being particularly telling in Foucault's eyes: "Now our business is to realize sex. Today the full conscious realization of sex is even more important than the act itself."[6] Blanchard in turn quotes Foucault's ironic gloss on these lines:

> Perhaps one day people will wonder at [Lawrence's] concern. They will not be able to understand how a civilization so intent on developing enormous instruments of production and destruction found the time and the infinite patience to inquire so anxiously concerning the actual state of sex; people will smile perhaps when they recall that here were men—meaning ourselves—who believed that therein resided a truth every bit as precious as the one they had already demanded from the earth, the stars, and the pure forms of their thought; people will be surprised at the eagerness with which we went about pretending to rouse from its slumber a sexuality which everything—our discourses, our customs, our institutions, our regulations, our knowledge—was busy producing in the light of day and broadcasting to noisy accompaniment. And people will ask themselves why we were so bent on ending the rule of silence regarding what was the nosiest of our preoccupations. (157–58)

Thus Foucault, in the first volume of *The History of Sexuality,* analyzes and prophetically criticizes, according to the model of the confessional rite as viewed from some utopian future, this metamorphosis of the body's interior into the field of psychosexual discourse, reading this transformation as the production of "bio-power" into or as language. Foucault also claims that this discursive practice has actually defined Western culture for most of its history, especially since the Enlightenment, and that the Victorian confinement of sex took place precisely when sexuality was beginning to be subjected to the most intense and disciplined of scientific articulations, which culminated, of course, in the invention of psychoanalysis.[7]

Blanchard's point against Foucault's lumping of Lawrence in this camp, however, is not to prove the philosopher and Lawrence's critics generally wrong and therefore the novelist and his ultimate novel particularly right. She does not use Foucault to demonstrate how Lawrence anticipates, transcends, and so precludes all the positions of his commentators, critical or not. Rather, she uses Foucault to enframe the transformation of sex into discourse. This process creates the modern conception of sexuality as the guilty secret of individual identity, which has to be openly and endlessly discussed. Blanchard then finds this problematic transformation and its founding confessional imperative already operative, in a reflective and critical, even ironic, fashion, in Lawrence's final and mistakenly abused novel (the Lawrentian motif of "sex-in-the-head").

For Blanchard, Lawrence is neither the dupe of discourse nor its demon, neither genius nor devil. Instead, like the figure of Foucault that she sees, Blanchard discovers a Lawrence who practices in his novel a kind of critical reflection, a human balance, which in his case takes the form of parody of inherited fictional and social conventions and self-parody of prophetic pretentions—that is, the sex scenes and love debates in *Lady Chatterley's Lover,* surprisingly enough, are as often as not intentionally absurd, Blanchard claims. Thus Lawrence here equally embraces and holds up to ridicule both horns of his (and, according to Foucault, *our*) imaginative dilemma of sexuality and discursiveness, of sex and talk, or what Lawrence derisively called in *Women in Love,* "sex-in-the-head."

> Foucault is right, of course, that Lawrence did want to realize sex; Lawrence, after all, maintained that the point of *Lady Chatterley's Lover* was "to think sex, fully, completely, honestly, and cleanly" (*Phoenix* II, 489). But Lawrence also argued that "in man's adventure

of self-consciousness [he] must come to the limits of himself and become aware of something beyond him. A man must be self-conscious
enough to know his own limits, and to be aware of that which sur-
passes him" (*Phoenix,* 185). *Lady Chatterley's Lover* is a study of the tension between these two ideas, between the need to rescue sexuality
from secrecy, to bring it into discourse, and the simultaneous recognition that the re-creation of sexuality in language must always, at the
same time, resist language. (32–33)

Blanchard, in short, uses Foucault to rehabilitate the reputation of
the novel within the canon of major works as established in Lawrence
studies since the 1950s. She does so, as we have seen, by reading its
weak points as parody and self-parody, consciously intended; and its
strength as Lawrence's self-conscious human finitude. Foucault thus
serves to produce another reading in an essentially New Critical or
Leavisite mode. The arch-antihumanist among poststructuralists
here helps to recuperate Lawrence's humanity, in support of the self-
serving academic morality of critical humanism in Blanchard's actual
instance of reading as a woman.

My point, despite this sudden shift in tone, is not so much to lament this familiar situation of professional assimilation of innovative
work as it is to understand it. By her reading Blanchard would pull
not only Foucault's teeth but Lawrence's, too. But the form of this
reduction is more my concern than its morality is. A double reduction
of Foucault and of Lawrence occurs, and this reduction corresponds to
or mirrors both the dilemma of the immediacy of sex being mediated
by language and Blanchard's paradoxical, compensatory resolution of
this dilemma in parody: both the parody of earlier novelistic practices
and that of Lawrence's own earlier and current practices. The innovation, useful to Lawrence studies, of discovering parody and self-
parody in *Lady Chatterley's Lover* exacts its price: the humanization of
Foucault, what I am ironically calling the profession of genius but
could just as well call the professionalization of genius. For all that
appears different, provocative, or suggestively original; all that could
mark both writers as creative, innovative, or as what used to define
the designation "genius" in its original sense as the distinctive difference of an individual;[8] all this is done away with or at least severely
modified, sacrificed to the professional constraints of doing business
as usual within the code of Lawrence studies, which is still dominated

by the critical ideology of the 1950s. And yet, despite this "conservative" humanistic use of Foucault's ideas, Blanchard, by helping to open Lawrence studies enough to insert them here makes possible, perhaps, several points among the many that would be required to modernize and then postmodernize the subfield, to bring it in line or up-to-date with romantic or Renaissance studies, theoretically speaking.[9] Whether such a transformation would be more of a burden than a boon remains, of course, to be seen.

Like my first example from literary studies, the chapter on Foucault in Allan Megill's *Prophets of Extremity,* a contribution to intellectual history, professionalizes Foucault as well as its other three "subjects." (The other figures are Foucault's assigned predecessors: Nietzsche and Heidegger, and his critical alternative, Derrida.) Although suspicious of Foucault's allegedly aesthetic or hermetic self-enclosure in discourse and of his panironic crisis mentality (or his apocalyptic thinking with a vengeance), "Michel Foucault and the Activism of Discourse" finally produces a balanced portrait of a thinker caught in the dilemma of negating both a degraded present and the compensatory radical drive to envision any ideal alternative, nostalgic or prophetic, out of suspicion of this revisionary dialectic's complicity with the will to truth in Western culture from Socrates to Sartre. In the name of a self-parodic utopianism of oppositional discourse for its own sake, Foucault substitutes, according to Megill, the activity of critical reflection for the action of revolutionary political organization, in the desperate belief that his openly admitted historical fictions may provoke, absurdly enough, long-term structural changes in the networks of discursive power in the culture. Megill argues, of course, that unless these fictions in some sense contain "truth" for their professional readers—and their good professional readers already know they cannot do so, being imaginative lies in the service of what Foucault himself terms "a politics not yet in existence"—then Foucault's histories can only be taken as novel forms of literature, as texts full, at best, of creatively misleading rhetoric:

> If the "object" is created by an elusive power, rather than power the product of knowledge (as has been held since the seventeenth century), if everything is a lie designed to aid the continuing struggle against the extant order, then it simply does not matter who, objec-

tively, is struggling against whom. Foucault gives not an "analytic" but rather a "rhetoric" of power—or, perhaps better a vision of power as rhetoric. (250)

And yet Megill redeems Foucault precisely on an aesthetic or literary basis, that is, on the basis of the power of this vision of power, as being imaginatively productive of new ideas, perspectives, visions— "images that yet fresh images beget," as Yeats would say. Or, as Megill himself more temperately puts it, "Still there is much that we can learn from Foucault. By the very fact that his writings cut across accepted categories, generating a tension with analyses of a more conventional kind, they are not only intriguing but also sharply illuminating" (256). Megill demonstrates this claim in his own brilliantly inventive and highly persuasive reading of *The Archaeology of Knowledge* (see "The Parody of Method," 226–37), as a parodic and even self-parodic text that does for Descartes's *Discourse on Method* and its legacy of Cartesianism in French intellectual circles what Joyce's *Finnegans Wake* has done for literary modernism and its legacy of Mallarméism—namely, composed its ultimate satyr play.

Like Blanchard, Megill humanizes Foucault, by which I mean that both critics cut Foucault down to size, assimilate him to the structure and procedures of their respective disciplines in ways that will stimulate more scholarly production but will leave the institutional apparatus not merely intact but actually untouched. Whatever may be distinctly, even originally challenging and so recognizably Foucauldian in Foucault, has been detached. Blanchard sets up Foucault's understandably human underestimation of Lawrence, produced by the requirement of taking a comprehensive, even "panoptical" overview in the first volume of *The History of Sexuality.* Megill isolates Foucault's essentially post-Kantian theory of the world-making-and-breaking powers of discourse, which Foucault had adopted not in blind hubris, of course, but out of a tragic dilemma—that of a post-Holocaust, post-1960s prophet of pandemic suspicion without a positive vision to announce, affirm, or sacrifice himself for. Blanchard and Megill thus reduce and then consign their "subjects" (their "Foucaults") to the sphere of literature, in the purely, even banally academic sense: in normalizing Foucault and Lawrence, in other words, they professionalize their genius of defining differences.

The double danger of such professionalization of "genius," however, lies not only in the way it normalizes whatever does not fit pre-established procedures, but also, by its very reductiveness, in the way such professionalization retroactively projects the original sublimity upon the distinctive figure that is to be normalized by professional strategies of assimilation in the first place. That is, professionalization produces at least two Foucaults—one closet humanist and one romantic genius—and thereby represses and sublimates the critical differences his discourse would make. The subject of my final example, drawn from Paul Bové's *Intellectuals in Power,* is this ironic dialectic of revisionary professionalization, seen from within a space of judgment made possible by a certain reading of Foucault.

Although Bové's critique of the professionalization of genius in this double sense of repressive sublimation appears throughout his book, it can be found most abundantly isolated in the two longest and central chapters on Erich Auerbach. These are elaborately and brilliantly done, and it would be useless to attempt to redo them here. Besides, my analysis so far suggests what I want to underscore in this revisionary process: the way Foucault, as assimilated into the humanities, is split into a more human, secondary figure and an original, more sublime figure tacitly assumed and retroactively projected by the methods of assimilation themselves. This duality has already been exemplified in Megill's reading of Foucault as a pathetic aestheticist who, in *The Archaeology of Knowledge* at least, is yet a master of parody—thus the balanced dialectic of critical humanism in action.

That certain reading of Foucault to which I referred a moment ago, Bové's enabling constraint, is also concentrated in its shortest chapter, "Intellectuals at War: Michel Foucault and the Analytics of Power." Bové argues that Foucault refuses to envision, prophetically, alternatives to things as he claims they are in our present world of what I call "professionalism unbound." Foucault thus should be seen as evading rather than succumbing to the seductive cul-de-sac of aesthetic hermeticism and utopian discursiveness that Noam Chomsky (in an interview) and EdwardW. Said (in a chapter from *The World, the Text, and the Critic,* "Traveling Theory") accuse him of. For although Foucault does claim that power is dispersed amid networks of truth, he also claims that power provokes the production of positive visions as one of its superior ruses. But for Chomsky and Said—both like Megill in this one respect—Foucault's double negation of the existing repressive order (or regime of the will to truth) and of any and all possible intelligible alternatives to it necessarily leaves him affirming only a sublime power that, like God, is everywhere and nowhere at once; that is, with a stylishly ironic metaphysics (but no real analytics) of power. In short, for Chomsky and even more so for Said, Foucault's own words—from "Fantasia of the Library" (1967)—about the hero of Flaubert's *The Temptations of Saint Anthony*—now could be seen as coming back to haunt their author; for Foucault's later texts, especially, could be seen as Said tends to see them: in Foucault's own earlier words, as "the composite result of a vision that develops in successive and gradually more distant levels and a temptation that attracts the visionary to the place he has seen and that suddenly envelops him in his own vision."[10] One could see things this way.

For Bové, however, Chomsky and Said especially have somehow failed to recognize, appreciate, or take into serious account Foucault's career-long analysis of the revisionary dialectic of critical humanism, which since Kant and the Enlightenment generally condemns the present in the name of an ideal selected from the past, in order to prophesy and oversee its apocalyptic realization in some actually utopian future.

Unlike his critics, then, Foucault (for Bové at least) recognizes the pervasively intimate complicities of intellectuals and power, of academic professionals and the ideological apparatus of the modern nation-state. By arrogating to themselves the prophetic and executive power of envisioning alternatives to things as they are, Bové argues, they ensure their continuation as repressively ineffective overseers of the privileged knowledge of liberation; that is, precisely because of its status as the phantasmic property of leading intellectuals (accredited and at least tolerated by the state), such liberation is no liberation at all:

> Leading intellectuals try to deny to the people the power of self-regulation and self-imagination, either individually or in groups, and try to prevent or at least to inhibit others from coming to political clarity. Leading intellectuals traditional or oppositional tend to as-

sume responsibility for imagining alternatives and do so *within* a set of discourses and institutions burdened genealogically by multifaceted complicities with power that make them dangerous to people. As agencies of these discourses that greatly affect the present lives of people one might say leading intellectuals are a tool of oppression and most so precisely when they arrogate the right and power to judge and imagine efficacious alternatives—a process that, we might suspect, sustains leading intellectuals at the expense of others. (227)

Thus Foucault, in Bové's eyes, should be taken seriously when in "Nietzsche, Genealogy, History" (1971) he ironically proclaims, following Nietzsche's lead from *Daybreak,* that whereas "religions once demanded the sacrifice of bodies, knowledge now calls for experimentation on ourselves, calls us to the sacrifice of the subject of knowledge" in texts that enact a universal self-parody,[11] a cosmic auto-da-fé of the transcendental pretensions of Western culture. The conclusion to *Intellectuals in Power* strongly alludes to this vision of Foucault as demonic parodist of the Enlightenment mind-set via its own savagely parodic play upon the uncannily familiar imagery of birth as death and death as birth that attends the major texts in the tradition of critical humanism from Kant and Nietzsche to Foucault and his erstwhile American disciple, Said himself:

> The temptations to build a better world, to discover the truth about human life, to rely on genius, sublimity, mastery, and prophetic wisdom: even though all these must be put aside, they will recur for a long time. The emergent cannot be forced. Forceps in the hand of male medical experts—can this image have benign force any longer? Such an appropriation of truth to political work, such a releasing of it from the shapeless, indeterminate background of the power structure of humanistic discourse might seem amoral or immoral. But the morality of humanism and its professionalization has worn out its welcome; it has announced its own betrayal of its own highest ideals, not only, as Auerbach would have it, by helping produce fascism, but by being structurally and institutionally allied with other "masters" whose "morality" is indefensible and, above all, by relying always and everywhere on death for its own survival. (310)

Well, in Bové's book, we surely have a different use of Foucault from those to be found in my other two examples. In Blanchard's exercise in literary criticism, you will recall, Foucault appears as a device to transform the Lawrence of *Lady Chatterley* into a lover of parody and self-parody. In the section of Megill's volume devoted to him, Foucault himself appears as the desperate activist of a self-defeatingly parodic discourse of antiknowledge, of heuristically fictional histories of the will to truth in the service of "a politics not yet in existence" and known in advance never to be coming into existence, since as soon as any such politics should begin to come into existence it would have to be negated as complicitous with power in the worst sense of the word. Finally, however, in Bové's text we have seen Foucault, despite the critiques of Chomsky and Said, in an even more severely grand light—as the master critical parodist of all post-Enlightenment pretensions to mastery, to end all such figures of mastery. As such, Bové's Foucault would totally empty out and leave the spaces of representation in the culture formally open to the people's own acts of self-determination and self-imagination, so long as the institution of critical humanism, traditional and oppositional, in the form of leading professional intellectuals like Chomsky, Said, or William J. Bennett, does not usurp the role of envisioning for the people the proper alternatives—of the left or the right—to things as they are.

If we are to allegorize these three uses of Foucault with the help of what to my mind appears to be an appropriate literary text, we could say that Blanchard uses Foucault in such a way as to make him (and Lawrence as well) seem more like the narrator of Thomas Mann's *Doktor Faustus,* Serenus Zeitblom, Ph.D., that ordinary, normal, bourgeois humanist who is nevertheless indirectly and unwittingly complicit in the final destruction of an avant-garde genius and of a nation. Megill, to continue this play on point of view, then could be said to transform Foucault, especially the Foucault of *The Archaeology,* into Adrian Leverkühn, Mann's self-destructive Schoenberg-like composer, who, like Nietzsche, possesses a demonic gift for sublime parody.

Finally, in Bové, Foucault emerges as the critical heir of modernist and postmodernist writers, I think, conceived along the lines of someone like the implied author of *Doctor Faustus* or *Gravity's Rainbow,* that elusive parodist of parodists, who in turn is best conceived on the original demonic model of Satan himself, or, perhaps, on the model of Fish's Belial. (See chapters 8 and 12.)

If we grant that these or similarly allegorized master figures are guiding the uses of Foucault in the humanities, what can we say is being achieved through them? First of all, new readings of Lawrence, of modern critical theory, and of post-Enlightenment intellectual history. Second, a new placement of Foucault as a figure in his own right who can serve to get more interpretive work done, of whatever sort and however its effects are intended by these or other critics in and out of the humanities. That such an enabling or empowering use of Foucault also entails forms of constraint (on Foucault's work, on the critics concerned) goes without saying. The primary constraint is the ironic reinforcement of the ruling paradigm of scholarly production and distinction that has always been the hallmark of critical humanism in the modern university: *scholarship as an individual achievement or work*. Bové's book is particularly self-aware of this ironic aspect of its own or any use of Foucault in the academy today.

Even more significant, I think, each of these uses of Foucault places him either near or actually in the sphere of literature—as, for example, a midwife to parody on Lawrence's part (Blanchard); as, for another, a parodist himself (Megill); and last, as the parodist par excellence of this very strategy of literary consignment and containment of the emergent and the different via the secularizations of the religious discourses, especially those of the prophetic texts (Bové). So in answer to my earlier question, "why should we read Foucault?" we apparently can say that we should read him because he permits us to discover the effectiveness of parody for critical discourse. In adducing such an answer we also address my title question, "what was Foucault?" by identifying him as, effectively, an intellectual parodist of the first order. That is, we should read Foucault as it appears we already do, for the parody's sake, because he was a parody himself in some sense or a self-parody of the prophetic or leading intellectual—the lead in the Enlightenment satyr play now being played out everywhere in Western culture—whose textual performances can still promote our own scholarly productivity. In the rest of this essay, I would like to examine the issue of parody and of style generally, of what it may mean to say that a critical intellectual is an author in a literary sense—issues

that are occasioned by these ironic literary institutionalizations of
Foucault in the humanities, institutionalizations whose critical practices repeatedly invoke one author figure in particular: Nietzsche.

The *locus classicus* of this question regarding the author in Foucault
is, of course, "What Is an Author?" One familiar reading of the essay,
as suggested by Megill's remarks on it and related works of the time
(1969), is to see it in the context of French intellectual life, that is, as a
symbolic revolutionary destruction of the subject of knowledge projected by the discourses of the regime of the will to truth within the
so-called liberal and democratic state. That is, one could read it as a
discursive guerilla action taken as a knowing form of therapeutic
compensation for the collapse of actual revolution. In essence, then,
one could read the essay as a belated, postmodern, perhaps parodic
and even self-parodic repetition of the romantic reaction to the failure
of the French Revolution (as classically represented by M. H. Abrams
in *Natural Supernaturalism* [1971]).

Although such a reading is comforting precisely because of its fa-
miliarity and nice balance of realistic critique and reductive psychologizing, I propose another reading: "What Is an Author?" as a socialization of the natural history of authorship to be found in Nietzsche's
Ecce Homo, particularly in sections 8 through 10 of the chapter entitled "Why I Am So Clever." I read Foucault's parodic style, therefore, not as a narcissistic economy of grandiose compensation. I see it
instead as an instrument for a kind of musiclike metamorphosis, a
singular transformation of Nietzschean themes into a different key
and register, a revisionary recategorization of Nietzsche's "naturalistic" categories demarcating the conditions of possibility for authorship that has for its primary effect the potential assimilation, along
already established institutional and professional lines, of Nietzsche's
Dionysian stance.

Before proceeding any further, I want to define what I intend by
my use of the term *parody* (or *self-parody*) in this context. Parody has
traditionally taken two forms: that of the burlesquing subplot that
ridiculously parallels the heroic main plot in Shakespeare and in
classical drama, and that of critical parody, the exaggerated imitation
of a writer's characteristic style. Originally, "a song sung beside" a
serious poem, parody achieves its broadest comic effects by applying

high-flown language to trivial matters, or, more rarely and subtly, vice versa. Parody, in short, is an antithetical song placed adjacent to some conventional work of piety.

For my purposes, however, the intellectual self-parody I am isolating can be defined as the exaggerated imitation of a recognizably characteristic position or style that the parodist in question shares with others by virtue of a network of ideological and professional identifications and associations. Even more precisely and technically, intellectual parody—what I also want to call "radical parody"—is a recognizably self-contradictory conceit of defensive hyperbole that arises from the exuberance of critical productivity, as if the parodist were almost beside himself with self-opposing forms. As we shall see, however, the intended target of such parody, some common aspect or other of the intellectual parodist's own mode of scholarly production, may only be the mask for another, more fundamental, repressed object.

I want to distinguish, in other words, this mode of radical parody, which I see as potentially operative both at any time in the post-Enlightenment cultural history of the modern nation-state and its professions and bureaucracies, and in any discourse or genre or artistic medium, from the historically specific and aesthetically limited conception of parody, in its relation to pastiche, found in Fredric Jameson's "Postmodernism, or The Cultural Logic of Late Capitalism." Jameson sees a shift from modernist parody like that of Mann's *Doktor Faustus,* with its moral imperative largely intact, to postmodern pastiche as in the wholesale "imitation of dead styles . . . stored up in the imaginary museum" of the past. "The producers of culture," Jameson claims, now practice "blank parody," a kind of neutral and neutralizing pastiche on the model of pop-art collage. [12] My own conception of radical parody would incorporate this recent development in a larger aesthetic and historical framework than that provided Jameson by the transition to late capitalism.

The fact that parody, even self-parody, is operative in Foucault's "What Is an Author?" is signaled not only by the deployment of a quotation, "What matter who's speaking, someone said, what matter who's speaking," which comes from Beckett's *Stories and Texts for Nothing* and occurs at the opening and then again, in truncated form, at the close of the essay's experimental argument as an ironic refrain or frame; it is also signaled at the very beginning of the initial statement that prefaces Foucault's text. When this statement claims that its speaker, presumably Foucault, is "conscious of the need for an explanation" simply for "proposing the slightly odd question" of the title as a serious subject for discussion and then goes on to assert that the general notion of the "author" itself remains an open question "to this day" both "with respect to its general function within discourse" and in what the speaker terms "my own writings"; or when we notice that the speaker then claims that "this question permits me to return to certain aspects of my own work which now appear ill-advised and misleading"; and we also notice, perhaps, that this speaker declares that this question even grants him the right, indeed the authority, "to propose a necessary self-criticism and reevaluation" (113) with respect to certain apparently misleading statements in *The Order of Things;*[13] and finally, when we reflect that in the space of the six short sentences of this small first paragraph of his brief prefatory statement there are five uses of the first-person singular pronoun or its reflexive pronominal/adjectival variants; then we may begin to feel, I think, that what is to follow in the text of "What Is an Author?" can be read in part at least as a revisionary parodic text of self-revision.

Even if we grant that the Foucault speaker is being wittily ironic here, even parodic and self-parodic, why should we also understand all his following remarks as similarly tainted or so stressed in part? And why should we see them, as I have suggested that we should, as a socialization of a naturalistic mode of conceiving authorship, especially since this speaker explicitly sets aside a sociohistorical analysis of the author in favor of an apparently highly restrictive rhetorical focus on "the singular relationship that holds between an author and a text," precisely by virtue of "the manner in which a text apparently points to this figure who is outside and precedes it" (115)? It is at this point that the speaker, to emphasize ironically his accredited seriousness, introduces the Beckettian citation and then digresses upon writing's self-referential nature these days and its antiheroic "kinship," in Kafka and Beckett certainly, with "death" (118). And yet, I would argue, the banality of these digressive remarks, as well as the ironic twist the speaker gives to them via the Beckett line, suggest the continuation of the opening parodic move. For the self-referentiality of contemporary writing is conceived here not as constitutive of a heterocosmic interior totality, as a great sphere burning with a hard, gemlike flame; rather, it is said to constitute a new form of exteriority, a new Mallarméan stress on the impersonal, indeed anonymous materials of the linguistic medium itself, into whose surfaces the author is said to be disappearing, practically at this very moment: a sacrificial victim of the demolition by writing of the traditional epic assumption of the writer as hero whose work wins for him and his people the serene if purely symbolic immortality of posthumous fame as a classic text of culture (117). I submit that the speaker's parodic practice at the opening as throughout the essay therefore specifically enacts the irony of the contemporary writer's "death" as theoretically thematized here by the Foucault figure in terms that—with one notable exception—even for 1969 were obviously clichéd.

A complete reading of this text along the lines suggested would continue by noting how the speaker not only suggests that "the function of an author is to characterize" in various ways "the existence, circulation, and operation of certain discourses within a society" (124), particularly by a splitting and dispersion of the subject into different, even opposing discursive positions and functions, but also makes this suggestion in a way that recalls the conventional version of ironic point of view and the implied author to be found, as the editor helpfully notes, in Wayne Booth's *The Rhetoric of Fiction* (129). That is, such a reading would further develop the innovative conventionality of this text revealed here and also in its tracing of the hermeneutic practices of today's critics who deal with today's revolutionary writing back to the medieval norms of Christian hermeneutics—specifically, to Saint Jerome's four criteria for textual authenticity (127). A fully comprehensive reading of "What Is an Author?" could indeed demonstrate, ad nauseam, the evidently knowing way this text quite literally subverts or contradicts itself by invoking innovation and disclosing continuity—and vice versa.

This parodic self-contradiction and self-subversion is seen nowhere more strikingly than in the speaker's simultaneous dismissal of and dependency on what he terms, derisively, the notion of the "transcendental anonymity" of *écriture,* by which he means the unwitting recapitulation and reinscription of "the historical and transcendental tradition of the nineteenth century" (120) upon the theoretical plane of the then newest intellectual mode, deconstruction. [14] The Foucault figure, after this outburst, proceeds to assume his own position of prominence among "those who are making a great effort to liberate themselves, once and for all, from this conceptual framework" of post-Kantian philosophy (120). At the same time he also divides "authors" into those godlike few such as Homer, Aristotle, and the church fathers who occupy "a 'transdiscursive' position" as "old as our civilization itself" (131) and "a singular type of author" that, while not classically sublime in the former sense, nonetheless remains remarkably distinctive, even uniquely original, as what "the nineteenth century in Europe produced" and left to us, namely such inescapable "initiators of discursive practices" (131) as Marx and Freud. Significantly, Nietzsche is omitted from this roster, indeed almost entirely from the essay as a whole, with the exception of one explicitly comic aside concerning the question of how one knows what to include in an author's corpus. [15] Once again, "What Is an Author?" parodies its own gestures of innovation as they are being made.

Let's take a closer look at this distinction between kinds of authorship for what it may betray about the workings of this text. A transdiscursive author, according to the Foucault speaker, authors "much more than a book . . . [authors] a theory, for instance, . . . a tradition or a discipline within which new books and authors can proliferate" (131). Such authors, like the founder of a science, produce, in Thomas Kuhn's conception of scientific revolution, an organization or paradigm for doing certain things in a discourse or cutting across several discourses that subsequent workers in the field can follow, apply, refine upon, or normalize. [16] Both Saint Jerome and Newton could function as a transdiscursive author in this sense, as could Saint Augustine and Darwin. On the other hand, initiators of discursive practices in the nineteenth-century tradition, a tradition that clearly still continues into our time, such figures as Marx and Freud, as the Foucault persona claims, produce new discursive constellations that, by their original omissions, logical aporias, and rhetorical fissures, cannot be totally assimilated into normalized discourse, even that inspired by these very original omissions.

Consequently, I would argue, such initiators of discursive practices must provoke the further production of textual innovations and repositionings by this production of memorable images of sublime disjunctiveness. These further innovations can stand in opposition, even as they must ever return to their founding ellipses in the works of the "initiators of discursive practices" from which these later texts have sprung. Instead of ascribing the innovations of such writers as Marx and Freud, therefore, to their mysterious irreducible originality that functions as a demonic or natural force of inspiration, the Foucauldian voice attributes them to the unique and founding "interstices of the text, its gaps and absences. . . . those empty spaces that have been marked by omission or concealed in a false and misleading plenitude." That is, this speaker attributes their innovations to "an essential lack" (135). Such fundamental holes in these innovative texts, in other words, provoke an equally innovative, indeed transgressive progeny simultaneously marked by its own generic blanks, which in Foucault's case takes the form of a radical, Dionysian self-parody. And in this instance of the distinction between transcursive writer and discursive initiator, Foucault's text openly self-destructs. For it reinscribes the transcendental anonymity of *écriture* just banished for recalling the Kantian problematic; more generally, it revises, under the sign of negative inversion, of the original "essential lack," the romantic or demonic conception of individual genius that, like the texts for nothing of Beckett or Kafka, "What Is an Author?" disperses—here, of course, into the four author-functions that the rest of the essay analyzes. "Foucault" limits himself, he says, to the four characteristics of the "author-function" that seem "most obvious and important":

> The "author-function" is tied to the legal and institutional systems that circumscribe, determine, and articulate the realm of discourses; it does not operate in a uniform manner in all discourses, at all times, and in any given culture; it is not defined by the spontaneous attribution of a text to its creator, but through a series of precise and complex procedures; it does not refer, purely and simply, to an actual individual insofar as it simultaneously gives rise to a variety of egos and to a series of subjective positions that individuals of any class may come to occupy. (130–31)

In any text, this Foucault is saying, we can trace the lineaments of the legal and institutional codes that permit and constrain, that determine and articulate the production, circulation, and preservation— in the largest sense, the economy—of texts and their authors. In addition, by comparing texts produced in different times and cultures, we can trace the ways our attribution of authorship is *placed* in our present culture by these legal and institutional codes. (This is one thing that doing a "history of the present" means.) Consequently, we can also learn how the attribution of authorship is an elaborate yet exact discursive practice of construction and positioning (and not one of interpretive discovery and re-creation). These procedures for constructing an author depend far more on the extant intellectual and cultural conditions than on the original intention of the individual writer. In fact, as this Foucault figure concludes, the text a writer produces in accordance with our discursive, institutional, legal, and intellectual or cultural conditions and conventions disperses the individualized subject into a series of egos or author-functions and textual positions that a reader from any class can be educated to occupy, and that the writer, as reader, can occupy as well. One thinks in this regard of Kierkegaard's or Beckett's Chinese box–like nests of narration, of their innumerable author figures and narrators, which infinitize the ironic play of point of view in their literary discourse.

In summary, these four characteristics of the "author-function" are 1) the author's determination by particularized institutional codes; 2) the author's temporally and spatially specific placement vis-à-vis other times and societies; 3) the author's culturally irregular or heterogenous construction and dissemination; and 4) the author's, indeed the subject's, serial dispersal as these author-functions into ego positions and freely accessible personas for occupation by individual readers. These four characteristics of the author-function thus constitute the primary conditions of possibility, in a discursive and textual sense, for the emergence and institution of the author in Western culture, especially since the inauguration of modernity with the rise and triumph of the bourgeoisie and their universal assumption of texts as the private property of a uniquely original individual. In such a context, all subsequent developments have been seen as precedent-setting fragmentation of authors such as Homer, whose original genius survives as a spectral ideal.

In the articulation of the discursive conditions of possibility for authorship, therefore, "What Is an Author?" clearly lies, ironically enough, well within the field of a nineteenth-century transcendental tradition of critical philosophy founded by Kant. The distinction between two kinds of authors—transdiscursive and initiating-replicates, for instance, a transcendental move: the division of an object's mode of existence into noumenal and phenomenal modes.

This text, in other words, once again proves radically self-contradictory in a way that suggests self-parody, since it apparently intends to contribute to the current effort to break free, once and for all, from this very tradition, even as it demonstrates the impossibility of such a project as anything other than a purely rhetorical gesture.

Restrictions of space prohibit a demonstration of this text within the field of the Kantian problematic. Suffice it to say that the various ways this text subverts itself—conceptually, structurally, and rhetorically—testify equally to the limits of instrumental reason (what Kant calls "the understanding") as to the imaginative power of the failure of rational representation ironically to resist the provocatively shattering effects of what Kant in *The Critique of Judgement* calls "the sublime." Although the identifiable causes differ in Kant and Foucault (nature and discourse, respectively), the textual production of the sublime effect, as such, is consanguineous.

Foucault's own recently published essay "What Is Enlightenment?" reflects on this general intellectual situation of Kant's pervasiveness (see *The Foucault Reader*). Besides, there is another, more immediate predecessor text of discursive innovation within the field of the Kantian problematic, Nietzsche's *Ecce Homo,* which relates more directly to the question "what is an author?" An examination of one portion of *Ecce Homo* not only will demonstrate how the Foucauldian text transforms Nietzsche's naturalistic and late-romantic characterizations of the conditions of possibility for authorship, but also will explain, I think, why "What Is an Author?" repeats, parodically and self-parodically (that is, transgressively) in its institutional, discursive, professsionalizing, and impersonalizing modes of socialization, the more generally romantic and demonic conception of individual genius that it would ironically disperse. That is, in deconstructing, as it were, this cultural myth theme of genius, "What Is an Author?" also reiterates, in a transformed register or key, a Dionysian problematic drawn from Nietzsche's text. As Nietzsche's *Ecce Homo* generally does, so "Why I Am So Clever" reduces and disperses, in a climactic fashion, the subject of writing that its announced author has so far impersonated in his life career. Nietzsche's self, that is, is reduced and dispersed along the discursive networks of rules for the construction of the conditions of possibility for authorship that are wholly defined according to the biological and psychological imperatives of natural history as understood from the perspective created by the canon of Nietzsche's works that their author is reviewing: in short, their natural history of the will to power.[17]

For Nietzsche, the "selection"—whether conscious or not—of "nutriment, of place and climate, of recreation" (63) constitutes the author-organism's "whole casuistry of selfishness" (66)—its defensive system of mimicry and self-mimicry, of chameleonlike effects that is claimed to have made possible the realization of this career's ruling principle or genius: self-overcoming through a form of writing that produces, almost as a side effect, a revaluation of all values hitherto operative in the history of values and value judgments on the earth. These "naturalistic" or naturalizing categories of nutriment, place and climate, recreation, these conditions of possibility for "the whole casuistry of selfishness," which in turn enables and constrains authorship in Nietzsche, enact a Dionysian destruction of the religious and moral idealism, the mystique of the great spirit and beautiful soul associated with the romantic conception of genius.

Moreover, Foucault's four "obvious and most important characteristics of the author-function" act as the revisionary reading of these Nietzschean categorizations that de-idealize their *über*-biologism, according to the largely professional economy of texts in present-day society, even as these Foucauldian revisions maintain the original critical configuration of Nietzsche's categories.

Being "tied to the legal and institutional systems" that "circumscribe, determine, and articulate the realm of discourse," for instance, rereads the first Nietzschean category of "nutriment," even as the "whole casuistry of selfishness" becomes in Foucault's hands the serial dispersal of "a variety of egos" and "subjective positions that individuals of any class may come to occupy" (131). The revisionary relationship between the Nietzschean "place and climate" and "recreation," on the one hand; and the Foucauldian cultural heterogeneity and construction of the author-function, on the other, appears too obvious to belabor at this point. The revisionary relation between these two texts can be summarized as follows: where Nietzsche's text allegorizes the author-function according to a natural history schema or code, Foucault's text allegorizes the conditions of possibility for authorship according to a textual and discursive, institutional or professionally social schema or code. The structures of these allegorizations of the author, as readings, remain, however, homologous, almost musically so, as if each were the variation of the other's theme and both were variations of a theme left unread and so unsounded.

This last point is best exemplified, I think, in a section of "Why I Am So Clever," which reinscribes the dispersed ideology of genius under the sign of creative repression, in much the same self-contradictory and self-parodic way that "What Is an Author?" reinscribes it via the speculative conception of "initiators of discursive practices," which functions as a form of critical negation. After deconstructing the author into this fiction's "naturally" defensive components of nutriment, place and climate, and so on, the Nietzschean narrator announces that he is now ready to answer at last the question implicit in the subtitle of *Ecce Homo: How One Becomes What One Is.*

According to this narrator, by means of such reductions and dispersals found in this text, as well as by such "lies" as are found in all sorts of idealisms, one can practice, knowingly or not, "the art of selfishness," of "higher" self-protection and self-defense, until one's "genius" or "organizing 'idea,'" the intention of one's life as career, has become powerful enough to leap forth "suddenly ripe," in its "final perfection"—for to be a great author, this Nietzschean narrator claims,

> The entire surface of consciousness—consciousness *is* a surface—has to be kept clear of any of the great imperatives. Even the grand words, the grand attitudes must be guarded against! All of them represent a danger that the instinct will "understand itself" too early—. In the meantime the organizing "idea" destined to rule grows and grows in the depths—it begins to command, it slowly leads *back* from side-paths and wrong turnings, it prepares *individual* qualities and abilities which will one day prove themselves indispensable as means to achieving the whole—it constructs the *ancillary* capacities one after the other before it gives any hint of the domineering task, of the "goal," "objective," "meaning."—Regarded from this side my life is simply wonderful. For the task of a *revaluation of values* more capacities perhaps were required than have dwelt together in one individual, above all antithetical capacities which however are not allowed to dis-

turb or destroy one another. Order of rank among capacities; distance; the art of dividing without making inimical; mixing up nothing, "reconciling" nothing; a tremendous multiplicity which is nonetheless the opposite of chaos—this has been the precondition, the protracted secret labour and artistic working of my instinct. (65)

The romantic ideology of individual genius, of the demon that is the great author's destiny, hereby returns from its previous diaspora in the Nietzschean text by means of the psychology of repression and unconscious creativity—a conception of the unconscious as a source of individual and individualizing ruling instincts, as capacities for domination of the entire psyche, as wills to power that function like artists, authors of one's fate. [18] Such is the Nietzschean understanding of the conditions of possibility for authorship.

As we can now see, "What Is an Author?" follows the Nietzschean precedent in more than the structure of its critical categories; it also reiterates the founding self-contradiction of the earlier text, the essential lack of that text, in its own self-contradiction between the subject's discursive dispersal into various author-functions and positions for utterance and the author's partial recuperation of the status of genius as an inspirational source of discursive initiation due to an original omission to which later writers ever must return. But whereas Nietzsche's text recuperates the ideology of genius under the sign of creative repression, Foucault's text does its recuperative work under the sign of the critical negation of a text or an entire corpus. That is, while Nietzsche envisions his organizing idea of the revaluation of all values as a natural development suddenly fully ripe and perfect in the prophet's mouth, as it were; Foucault improvises his transient speculative conception of initiators of discursive practices as an original omission, as a founding gap or provocative hole—as an essential lack often subsequently thematized in various ways and informing the corpus of later writers. This essential lack incites further scholarly innovations in the form of transgressive returns to the texts of these initiators of discursive practices—abysses that yet fresh abysses beget.

Although one can easily read the desires of Nietzsche and Foucault into these different portrayals of authorship (full mouth versus inviting slit?), I am more interested here in summarizing what we can learn from reflecting on the general question of style that their interaction helps to define, especially in comparison to the recent critical appropriations of Foucault in the humanities already discussed.

What such a comparison teaches us, I think, is that some younger scholars of the modern and postmodern in the humanities appear to be replacing irony with parody as one of the first principles of their critical judgments,[19] and to be applying this literary principle of judgment to other than conventionally defined literary works, with the result that the style of intellectual work in the texts so treated is being read as contributing to, and even at points contradicting, the explicit arguments or intentions of such works.[20] In the words of the title of Hayden White's recent book on the difficulties of doing history, it is increasingly "the content of the form" that matters in the critical conversation.[21]

As my reading of the relations between Nietzschean and Foucauldian texts suggests, such an orientation toward the symptomatology of style enables us to read the previously more esoteric, revisionary transformations of texts by other texts that have produced intellectual history, and at the same time, of course, constrains us to *humanize* that productive history via the assumption of an inevitable comic pathos that necessarily attends the fate of the critical intellectual at this time. In short, we tend to see the work of others and even our own work as chronically self-contradictory to the point of intentional self-parody. We see ourselves, in other words, as self-conscious avatars of that hero of the Nestor chapter of Joyce's *Ulysses*—that is, as figures of sublime parody—as, at best, *holy fools* of the various discourses that distort us: "On his wise shoulders through the checkerwork of leaves the sun flung spangles, dancing coins."[22] Such appears to be the culture of parody in our postmodern age.

But perhaps I had better let Foucault himself have the last word on this matter. So I will conclude with a quotation from his early book on Raymond Roussel that seems apropos: "In relation to this secret all of Roussel would be just so much rhetorical skill, revealing, to whoever knows how to read what [his texts] say, the simple, extraordinarily generous fact that they don't say it."[23] This ironic secret that Foucault refers to in relation to Roussel is naturally that of his style.

3 Performing Theory as Cultural Politics
The "Experience" of Critical Agency in and After Foucault

Foucault spends the better part of seven years re-thinking and revising the major research project of his later career, *The History of Sexuality,* between the appearance of the first introductory volume in 1978, *The Will to Knowledge,* and that of the second volume in 1984, *The Use of Pleasure.* Why? Professionally speaking, especially in American intellectual circles of the period, this is not a smart thing to do. Foucault during the mid- and late 1970s is at the height of his popularity. For in *Discipline and Punish* (1975) and related pieces of the time, he gives liberal American intellectuals a persuasive historical confirmation of their own ironic position. He simultaneously documents all-pervasive power operations in the modern state, as he so memorably puts it, down to the formation of the modern soul, and suggests that they are as much empowering as repressive, especially for what he calls specific intellectuals. Specific intellectuals are those who renounce the totalizing ambitions of a Marx or Sartre to comprehend all life in a single synoptic system— for to further liberationist ends, according to one version of the theory of power/knowledge, they instead need only work, practically yet resistantly, at the particular positions in the educational apparatus of the modern state they already happen to occupy. Rather than speak theoretically, as would-be universal intellectuals, in the name of all history's repressed people, such specific intellectuals need only speak, immediately and pragmatically, in the name of themselves and the group with which they professionally identify. While thus "radically" avoiding the coerciveness of sublime presumption, they also "conservatively" preserve intact their social role as traditional intellectuals. They can thus be "political" and comfortably placed at the same time, and with a good conscience to boot. For better or worse, much of the new historicism, the new pragmatism, and the new Americanist project derives from this moment in American theory.

So why, then, when on this roll, does Foucault break the momentum? Perhaps it is this use of his work that gives him pause? I think so. This may also account for all the self-defining interviews done in this period. However all this may be, the interregnum in his significant publications gives adversaries and former disciples alike time to put aside their awe at his brilliant displays of historical scope and interpretive penetration so as to focus their sights on the theoretical gaps and methodological problems sure to be found now in their more considered experience of his work. Besides, once Foucault has given us the excuse we need to practice the game of academic criticism as usual, why keep him around as an annoying reminder of our bad faith? (I am thinking of followers of Said and Lentricchia who accept their critiques of Foucault without question.) This is not to say that Foucault is free of problems, only that their discovery is motivated as much by purely self-serving interests of professional advancement as they are by any aspiration toward theoretical perfection. If Foucault is now "out" because of his critical provocation, I'd better not rock the boat?

What, then, are these alleged problems? Apparently, given the strong version of his theory of power (especially in *The Will to Knowledge,* vol. 1 of *The History of Sexuality*), power saturates thoroughly all the discursive fields of knowledge and practice in the modern state. Consequently, there cannot be any locatable sites of possible resistance that are not always already produced and programmed by the system of power to be opposed. In short, Foucault's theory of power is really a dystopic metaphysics leading to cynical pessimism, and not a radical politics leading to significant action.[1] Similarly, given his constructivist position on truth as nothing more than the history of the different regimes or practices of truth, Foucault cannot account for the status of his own statements as valid truth claims. Where does this leave his explanations for the great confinement of the mad, the modern formation of productive disciplines in the seventeenth and eighteenth centuries, the technological development of medical treatment, or the perfection (in the guise of reform) of the penal system?[2] Apparently, it leaves them in the limbo created by his own late admission that his texts are really critical fictions.[3] Finally, Foucault, in his many stylish critical performances, violates philosophical decorum. In itself, this is not so bad. It does strongly suggest, however, that he may be courting a Dionysian irrationalism, espousing the absurd spectacle of the gratuitous act, and embracing the thrilling mythic power of savage rituals. Just think: Foucault does all these questionable things in an influential fashion, too. One shudders to behold it, for such things surely mark him as a dangerously reactionary force, particularly when seen in the progressive light of the highest Enlightenment ideals of instrumental reason, transparent communication, and critical emancipation.[4] In sum, then, Foucault's critics find ideological, logical, and rhetorical grounds for problematizing his positions: for he leaves them, they all claim, with neither a reliable method nor a coherent theory.[5] And in the Anglo-American tradition of theoretical debate, as in a certain Enlightenment continental tradition, an unreliable method and an incoherent theory amount to a kiss of death.

In the first section of his introduction to *The Use of Pleasure,* Foucault, apparently having thought long and hard about just such problems, indicates what I think is their entirely ironic "resolution" in his understanding of "experience."[6] As in the exemplary instance of sexuality, "experience" is far from unmediated. It is rather a historically specific formation in which diverse fields of knowledge, complex sets of rules and norms with support in religious, judicial, pedagogical, medical, and literary institutions, all converge to shape the changes in the way individuals are led "to assign meaning and value to their conduct, their duties, their pleasures, their feelings and sensations, their dreams" (4). Such a formative and formidable discursive convergence as in this light "experience" becomes simply does not accede to programmatic ideological direction, cannot be theorized systematically, and is equally rational and irrational, especially given the historical inadequacies of any self-styled abstract Enlightenment brand of binary critique. "Experience" can be studied, researched, interpreted, analyzed, and reflected upon afterward, but it cannot be successfully made predictable, logical, or tasteful in advance. Whatever value oppositional intellectuals may have is by way of their interventionary historical meditations. This is why Foucault describes his work ironically as a critical history of the present, since in each of his studies he is attempting to gain the comparative distance on the present modes of "experience" that only historical research can hope to provide. And such flexible critical distance must be the primary prerequisite for any intelligent act of critical intervention. In these ways, then, experience is very like Foucault's earlier notion of "event": "the hazardous play of dominations."[7] If there are "dominations," there is also "play" among and between them, however hazardous it may be— hence the theoretical, rhetorical, and political problems Foucault's work ironically presents to those looking precisely for the very things it never pretends to give.[8] Is Foucault's unaccommodating "experience" absolutely so, and, therefore, one of the latest postmodern versions of what in literary studies we call "the sublime"? Perhaps so.[9] In any event, his critical response to "experience" is to embrace the ironic distance historical research and critical reflection permit. Foucault describes his sort of "experience" as an intellectual "curiosity" and a "passion for knowledge" to discover the ways of getting "free of oneself," of "the knower's straying afield of himself," and so of "knowing if one can think differently than one thinks, and perceive differently than one sees" (8). His "experience" is, Foucault concludes, "a philosophical exercise," and its object is "to learn to what extent the effort to think one's own history can free thought from what it silently thinks, and so enable it to think differently" (9).[10] Foucault's point is, I surmise, that in rethinking and revising *The History of Sexuality,* he has had to rethink and revise his understanding of this kind of "experience" and its history. I take him to mean by this self-revision not only the specific history of his overall intellectual project but the general historical "regularities" that, as conditions of possibility, have formed him and his "experience," as well. If I am right in this latter surmise, then what we have in the second and third volumes of *The History of Sexuality* are the broadly based and long-term historical grounds, the intellectual inventory or collective cultural archive, for the particularly representative formation of "experience" that we identify as and with Michel Foucault's life and work, his career, his oppositional style of life, and all the critical changes he suffers and would promote. The self-designated "masked philosopher" here, discreetly, let his mask slip a bit. [11]

In brief, Foucault reveals in these later volumes in *The History of Sexuality* that the self he and we largely are is a mobile, plural, and agonistic structure of interdictory moral codes and resistant ethical practices of self-stylization. We are produced by our culture to be, to a greater or lesser extent, self-fashioning individuals. The games of truth and error, knowledge and power, all coincide in the open strategic games of our "aesthetics of existence." The detailed accounts of Greek, Roman, and early Christian practices of self with respect to sexuality are the major elements in the critical construction of our genealogy as instances of "desiring man." (One notes Foucault's recognition of the limits of this tradition via the patriarchal epithet.) "Experience" for postmodern Western intellectuals, as for all those who come under the imperial sway of this culture, is a historically mediated formation enjoining the discipline of self-making based on the now-internalized ancient classical model of the pedagogic couple of mentor and student. Each of us, in short, is the "Lui" and "Moi" (the Rameau's nephew and Diderot personas, or the revisionary virtuoso without a fixed identity and the master of one style of thinking who would remain the same) all rolled into oneself, and so our "experience" is a repeated scene of instruction in which the play of culture and critical identity determines the imaginative forms critical agency may take. To explain what I mean more fully, I will elucidate the later Foucault by way of Kristeva's recent revisionary work on abjection, melancholy, and love—what more generally I refer to as her poetics of mourning and identity formation. But first, I must confront the greatest obstacle to Foucault's late work, the critique of agency mounted by his most influential precursor.

Nietzsche's *On the Genealogy of Morale* performs memorably the deconstruction of subjective agency when he shows how "the 'doer' is merely a fiction added to the deed" by the "seductions of language." [12]

Given the subject-predicate structure of Western languages, Nietz-sche argues, we cannot help but envision a subject as the underlying substantial ground of any action. It is thus language that "conceives and misconceives all effects as conditioned by something that causes effects, by a 'subject'" (481). Until Foucault's late work, his project appears to be to show, via his archeology of knowledge and genealogy of power, how impersonal and anonymous discursive practices and power-relations actually regulate and normalize everyday life so that instead of seeing such faceless forces as causes of action, we mistakenly see individual subjects as substantially "free agents" accountable for their deviations from the established norm. As we know, with the second and third volumes in *The History of Sexuality,* however, Foucault seems to believe that such "free agents," capable of performing their own "aesthetics of existence," of stylizing ethically their own sexualities, that relatively "free agents" exist among the Greeks and Romans. Thus, Foucault uses Nietzsche's own understanding of "noble" morality against his deconstructive linguistic analysis of the subject. The reason Foucault gives for his conviction is the difference he sees, thanks also to Nietzsche, between Judeo-Christian or modern secular societies that rule via an imposed, supposed "universal" norm or code, and a culture such as that of the ancient Greeks and the Romans (of the Republic), which, for some time, permits and even encourages pockets of people to develop, profess, and put into distinctive practice their own individualizing self-fashionings to serve as a rich and various collective archive of imaginative exempla for posterity to study and emulate. (The difference between this "noble" mode of emulation and the "imitatio Christi" or the statistical average ideal of our mass culture—both instances of a centralizing imperial normalization—should be clear.) Despite this historically particular difference, however, critics of Foucault still wonder how his late work on the self can be accommodated to his earlier projects often seen as disseminating the self into discursive anonymity, and thereby constituting "the death of the subject."

One way is to focus on the fact that from the beginning of his career with his study of madness, through his studies of modern disciplines of knowledge, medical technology and treatment, and penal institutions, to these last studies of sexuality, the subject in question—the madman, the modern representative intellectual, the medical practitioner and his patient, the prisoner, the self-helping stylizer of sexuality—all these figures of subjectivity are instances of a radically divided, plural agency, never a singular solitary individual. Foucault's subject, in other words, is never the Emersonian infinitely repellent orb of purely self-originating individuality, the individuality that in the clichés of neoconservative celebrations and of left-wing critiques embodies the American and bourgeois dream of a self without real precedents, possible posterity, or quotidian relations of any meaningful kind. (Clichés are at times also true.) Foucault, in contrast, always presents the subject as a fundamental conditional set of phenomena, a nominalist mass of conflicting behavioral possibilities, imposed upon by some normalizing and reifying discourse, with the alienating result that the subject is most like a colonized territory: radically split, subversively resistant and complicitously collaborative by turns, and most ready for rebellion when not regularly placated by carnivalesque spectacles of programmed saturnalias, such as the recent "War in the Gulf," a festival for television's slaves that our would-be masters performed all too perfectly.

The Hegelian master-slave analysis of subjective agency from *The Phenomenology of Spirit* informs Foucault's Nietzschean ventures, and does so transparently now in his elaboration of the mentor-student dialectic of self in *The Use of Pleasure* and *The Care of the Self*. Agency throughout Foucault is a matter of plurality, mobility, and conflict—the agon in the relation to óneself between imposing masterful discourses and exempla and recalcitrant anarchic behaviors. The model for this conflict is ever the struggle of the pedagogic pair repeatedly being reinscribed in Foucault's work like his signature until it reaches perfect clarity in these late volumes. The practices of self in Greece and Rome are, in this context, special cases, relatively open strategic games of truth and error, love and power, in what is otherwise largely a history of dominating coercive norms and the closed games of one or another imperially centralizing regime of truth. For such regimes, error embodied is ever error to be confined, excluded, treated, and disciplined. In Foucault, then, these open strategic games of love that the Greeks and Romans share between groups and pass on to posterity constitute the historically particular (or "contingent") oppositional imagination of collective agency and aesthetic relations whereby the rest of Western culture may be brought to judgment. It is not that the classical practices of self are perfectly ideal, only that they are comparatively better (because relatively "freer"), for the agents in question, than what exists in cultures of punitive commandments or demographic sanctions. Foucault repeatedly reminds us to purge ourselves of any nostalgia for their practices by recalling that they were largely made possible by slavery. Nevertheless, they may yet serve Foucault strategically as a collective archive of positive exempla for a postmodern criticism opposed to all single normalizing codes: "One law for the lion and the ox," as William Blake says, "is tyranny."

Foucault thus gives me a detailed historical model for the primarily pedagogic relation between a culture of ethical ideals and an aesthetic practice of self-fashioning, a model that has been internalized as the relation to oneself each of us is ever becoming. I rely on Kristeva, principally from *Black Sun,* to provide me with an analysis of the dynamic psychic states of intellectual identity. [13] As the critical intellectual identifies with a canonical or noncanonical example of appealing imaginative achievement, his or her psyche splits into two specularly related halves on the model of the pedagogic pair of mentor and student. A spectral scene of instruction now ensues. Its sympathetic moment recapitulates the primary mode of identification with its radically empathetic fusion experience, which in our culture the mother-child bond typically depicts. As the process of identification would become a complete (and so an impossible) incorporation of the other, however, the previously submerged ambivalence that is caused by the necessary wound to one's illusory narcissistic self-sufficiency breaks out. It does not erupt in outright projective expulsion from the psyche. Rather, this radical ambivalence results in a complex process of internalization by which the imposing other is made to the take the form of, to impersonate if you will, the self in mourning its loss of narcissistic self-sufficiency, even as the mourning self has already been impersonating, so far as it is possible, the ideal Other. The sense of loss—what Kristeva calls, after Lacan's revision of Heidegger, "the lost Thing"—also involves the loss of the loving moment of what feels like virtually total identification with the power of the Other and the replacement of this moment by the new phase of (admittedly) primitive critique. The entire process is what I mean by "mask play," and it is what Kristeva glosses in Freud's *The Ego and the Id* and *Group Psychology and the Analysis of the Ego* as the emergence of "the [imaginary] father of individual pre-history." (The imaginary father, after the abjection of the phallic mother, incorporates in fantasy form all the gender-specific characteristics of both sexes, thereby preserving dialectically the previous stage in psychic development before the oedipal complex fully emerges.)[14] The imaginary father is both the ghost of the abjected mother and the first instance or prototype of the symbolic order—that is, a mental form with personal and cultural resonance, and not a literal fact.

For the critic immersed in many examples of imposing imaginative agency, the imaginary father can never be simply a single figure. It is always a familiar compound ghost. Or, rather, it is the entire story or mask play of figures as it unfolds at the time in the critic's text. The polysemous relations in Emerson between Over-soul and Scholar, which become in Nietzsche the overdetermined relations of sublime "overman" and resentful underdog, perform such mask plays of their imaginary fathers.[15] In Kristeva, who follows in this both Lacan and Freud—who, in turn, ultimately follow Hegel—the figure of the imaginary father represents the prototype of critical (self-)consciousness, the (self-)critical faculty Freud christens "superego."[16] The more inclusive the collective archive of mask plays becomes, and so the more opportunities for complex imaginative identification and critique there are, then the more complex, various, and liberating—because less rigidifying, severe, or deadly—the critical response may be: "How can I approach the place [of the lost Thing] I have referred to? Sublimation is an attempt to do so: through melody, rhythm, semantic polyvalency, the so-called poetic form, which decomposes and recomposes signs, is the sole 'container' seeming able to secure an uncertain but adequate hold over the Thing" (14).

Culture and critical identity stage imaginative agency after Foucault as historical mask plays in this admittedly "poetic" or "literary" sense that, thanks to Kristeva, I can also analyze psychologically. From this perspective, Foucault's history of ethical stylizations of sexuality materializes the "homoerotic" fathers of the classical tradition still ironically shaping Western culture. He thereby historicizes critically his imaginary father. Writing "after Foucault" means that American critics could now engage in similar acts of historical materialization by pointedly recovering their socially, racially, and sexually different yet nurturing "imaginary fathers" in order to establish institutionally a collective archive making for critical change that is as richly diverse and provocatively inspiring as possible. Each of us, as Foucault himself admits in the end, does indeed write critical fictions.

In a recent essay, "The Adolescent Novel," Kristeva isolates a particular identity formation, resembling that of adolescence, which persists well into adulthood. Neither sheer perversity and psychosis nor pure borderline narcissistic disorder, this perpetually "adolescent" structure of personality, as an ideal psychosocial type, maintains "a renewable identity" only through "interaction with another," as the two together open themselves to "the repressed" and at the same time this opening up "initiates a psychic reorganization," "a tremendous loosening of the superego," by recalling, revising, and magnanimously avowing the imaginary father(s) of individual prehistory (8–9). Kristeva speculates that, for this perpetually adolescent personality type, sexual and identity differences, reality and fantasy distinctions, act and discourse oppositions are all fluidly traversed all the time. Such a personality, Kristeva believes, is definitive of the modern novel since Rousseau and pandemic in our culture due to "the [radical] inconsistency [in identity formation] in a mass media society" (9). I think Kristeva is basically right in her speculation, although I would also say that this adolescent personality structure predates our novel and mass media culture, since, as we know, Foucault analyzes it as the dialectical situation of classical pedagogy, and Freud theorizes it in the analytic transference.

As Foucault shows, "the aesthetics of existence" put into practice by the Greeks and Romans is later assimilated to the erotics of the married couple after Stoic and Christian scapegoating of homoeroticism. This ensures both the internalization of the pedagogic structure via the family romance and the permanent institution of the mentor-student model of education, in which, ideally, the relations are intellectually open to anything, even as the two practice an ascetic self-discipline with respect to explicit erotic pleasures. With the rise of novel and mass media cultures, this agonistic, self-overcoming structure of self, reinforced by the educational ideal, defines the identity formation of the Western intellectual. Foucault claims (in *The Care of the Self*) that "a kind of lawless universality" (37) reigns for the pedagogic pair. I take this to mean something like what Kristeva says when she claims that for the adolescent personality, while open to the spectacle of perversity, "there [are not] necessarily . . . any precise perversions" (9) in fact performed.

In Emerson's "The Over-Soul," we see the transcendental expression of this internalized pedagogic relation of the self to the self, so different from Foucault's rhetoric but, as we shall see, a prototype of Harold Bloom's influential rhetoric:

> The soul gives itself, alone, original, and pure, to the Lonely, Original, and Pure, who, on that condition, gladly inhabits, leads, and speaks through it. Then it is glad, young, and nimble. It is not wise, but it sees through all things. It is not called religious, but it is innocent. Behold . . . I am born into the great, the universal mind. I, the imperfect, adore my own Perfect. I am somehow receptive of the great soul, and thereby do I overlook the sun and the stars, feel them to be the fair accidents and effects which change and pass. More and more the surges of everlasting nature enter into me, and I become public and human in my regards and actions (400).

The imperfect "I" of human history finally realizes its perfection in the fabulous universal third person, the singularly Divine One. Despite the lip service given here to public life, the main thrust of Emerson's position clearly moves in the direction of an idealized specular identity of the individual self's given and constructed components. Fitzgerald's Jay Gatsby, composing a media personality out of his own Platonic conception of himself, is virtually peeking around the corner.

The "experience" of imaginative agency in and after Foucault, however, clearly involves all the critic's relations—philosophical, psychological, professional, political, and ethical—with the collective archive of mask plays (canonical and noncanonical alike) through which the critic comes to "experience" fully the intentional constructive power of the imaginative Other. Such "experience" possesses and is possessed by the critic, thanks to the general cultural model of the pedagogic pair and the specific psychological processes that are, respectively, the subjects of late Foucault and recent Kristeva. Ideally, the critic would form and reform an identity in his practice, an identity that is simultaneously cultural and social in its contingent or historical origins, and imaginative and individual in its immediate textual and discursive consequences. This critical identity would be a mobile plural subject whose textual practice and genre must be, respectively, radical parody and reflective pastiche. I say this because only parody and pastiche as practical style and generic mode can accommodate the postmodern critic's radically shifting, multiple, and so perhaps ultimately indeterminate identity of reflexive critical acts. [17] How successful any one critic, including myself, may be in achieving this aesthetic/ethical ideal is a matter for detailed specific judgment.

In response to the assembled and circulating mask plays of the collective archive, the critic is thus like nothing so much as the speaker in the following Wallace Stevens poem, "A Dish of Peaches in Russia." [18]

With my whole body I taste these peaches.
I touch them and smell them. Who speaks?

I absorb them as the Angevine
Absorbs Anjou. I see them as a lover sees,

As a young lover sees the first buds of spring
And as the black Spaniard plays his guitar.

Who speaks? But it must be that I,
That animal, that Russian, that exile, for whom

The bells of the chapel pullulate sounds at
Heart. The peaches are large and round,

Ah! and red; and they have peach fuzz, ah!
They are full of juice and the skin is soft.

They are full of the colors of my village
And of fair weather, summer, dew, peace.

The room is quiet where they are.
The windows are open. The sunlight fills

The curtains. Even the drifting of the curtains,
Slight as it is, disturbs me. I did not know

That such ferocities could tear
One self from another, as these peaches do. (224)

The poem takes off from a Cezanne held captive at the Hermitage in the Kremlin, a picture of which appears in a contemporary maga-

zine. It quickly becomes a meditation—sensuous, reflective, and
poignant by turns—on identity formation, the plural subject, and
the role of the collective archive in provoking a self-fashioning response. The poetic reflections move from being fantastically speculative and pastoral, to being romantically passionate and lyrical, to
being pathetically sentimental and Hallmark card–like, to being,
suddenly, starkly real and novelistic. This ironically various and dis-
tanced pastiche of generic modes composes a radical parody—an antithetical song sung beside the pictured painting, as it were—that is
nevertheless a deadly serious meditation on and critical portrait of the
then-emerging postmodern subject of late consumer capitalism. This
is the imperial subject that would immediately consume all alterity as
commodities fetched from around the world.[19] The reflective critic,
like Stevens in this regard, creates his or her similarly parodic pas-
tiches as dramatic acts of opposition, in a highly ironic style of resistance to such would-be apocalyptic consumption. By such sharp-
edged estrangement, the critic (like the poet) would thus disrupt the
efficient operations of intellectual consumerism, that repeated staging of real differences as images of difference, until there is no difference left that can make any difference (hence the poem's various tear-
ings of one self from another, virtually line by line). The critic's aim
(like the poet's) is to force the reader to pause and take thought rather
than immediately process the critical (or poetic) text by automatically
swallowing it up, in the most reductive readiest-to-hand fashion, by
using some reifying category or other.[20] (This is, of course, a pervasive danger nowadays regardless of the critic's intention.) The critic,
like Stevens, would thus attempt to recover all the hard and lasting
savor of his "lost Thing." Such "experience" of real material differences, equally pleasurable and painful, produces too much disso-
nance, cognitive and aesthetic, for our culture to countenance without significantly reductive critique and accommodation.

The critic, in other words, produces, by such improvisation, an
oppositional plural agency—not the voracious vacuity of the late
capitalist subject, but the "oneself" formed in "experience" (in the
late Foucauldian sense) and analyzed psychologically by Kristeva.
This critical agency is mobile, plural, and ever provisionally determinate. It is a revisionary "oneself" of cultural memory like the "Foucault" in the second and third volumes of *The History of Sexuality,* a

composite figure that reforms critical identity in a heroic act of historical recovery that magnanimously gives life to the poignant story of
the ancient classical culture and its erotic practices forming him and
indeed all of us in (so-called) Western civilization. Foucault's incredible combination of and remarkably coherent and cogent commentary
on the many different discourses therein excerpted—medical, ethical, philosophical, historical, literary, religious, and so on—attest to
the "classic" postmodern pastiche he has so subtly produced, even as,
in making "homoerotic" culture and its repression the central founding moment in the story of Western civilization's formation of "desiring man," Foucault brilliantly practices radical parody, a quietly but
devastatingly subversive antithetical song, with a perversely exemplary vengeance. The severely self-disciplined style in these volumes
reflects ironically, I think, on such prior sublime flourishes (and their
critics) as the Dionysian "death of man" passage climaxing *Les Mots et
Les Choses,* even as it materializes memorably his last mask play: "The
object was to learn to what extent the effort to think one's own history
can free thought from what it silently thinks, and so enable it to think
differently."

My aim in writing this book is to further such projects both by
critically reflecting (or radically parodying) those recent developments in American criticism that tend to impede such works of liberation, and by offering, especially in my discussions of Foucault,
Lentricchia, and literary works, what are here modest attempts to
participate in these contemporary struggles to redefine and revise
the collective archive of culture, so as to incorporate into it significantly diverse examples of imaginations in action.

4 Aesthetic Relations
Michel Foucault and the Fate of Friendship

O my friends, there is no friend.   —*Aristotle*
Take care that a falling statue does not strike you dead!
                             —*Zarathustra*

In Memoriam
Richard C. Newton

In responding to Jacques Derrida's critique of *Madness and Civilization* for its apparent privileging of madness as a transcendent experience beyond the language of reason, Michel Foucault makes an initial distinction between the genres of philosophical writing that proves important for the critical understanding of his entire career. I begin with this response not because I am interested in either Derrida's accusation or Foucault's defense. Rather, I am interested in Foucault's characterization of these genres and the generic subjects appropriate to them. Quite simply, Foucault here provides his readers with a guide to his own self-understanding, which is for me the point of departure for any comprehensive analysis of his work.

Foucault begins by distinguishing between the genre of "pure demonstration" and that of "meditation." Pure demonstration is a genre in which the "utterances can be read as a series of events linked one to another according to a certain number of formal rules."[1] I take Foucault to mean here the kind of formal rules of logical analysis and deduction to be found in scientific and philosophical demonstrations, treatises, and arguments. Foucault continues by identifying "the subject of the discourse" as one "not implicated in the demonstration." Instead, this subject of pure demonstration "remains, in relation to it, fixed, invariable as if neutralized" (*F*, 35). I take the subject of this genre of writing to be the subject of knowledge privileged by the disciplines of modern rationality.

The genre of "meditation," on the other hand, "produces, as so many discursive events, new utterances which carry with them a series of modifications of the enunciating subject" (*F*, 35). Through "what is said in meditation," Foucault continues, "the subject passes from darkness to light, from impurity to purity, from the constraint of passions to detachment, from uncertainty and disordered movements to the serenity of wisdom, and so on" (*F*, 35). Concerning this subject of meditation, Foucault concludes that it "is ceaselessly altered" by its own movement; its "discourse provokes effects within which [it] is caught" (*F*, 35). The discourse of meditation "exposes" this subject to "risks," making it "pass through trials or temptations," producing "states" in the subject, and conferring on the subject "a status of qualification" that the subject "did not hold at the initial moment" (*F*, 35). If, in short, the genre of pure demonstration implicates a fixed, invariable, neutralized subject, then "meditation implies a mobile subject modifiable through the effect of the discursive events which take place" (*F*, 35). Because this subject of meditation is mobile and unstable it must be contained and stabilized. So it is produced within the discipline of literature by the subject of knowledge. I take this mobile subject of meditation to be the subject of power in this sense. It is to be supervised and disciplined by the institutions and discursive practices of the invariable subject of knowledge.

For convenience's sake, and with modern rationalism in mind, I will call the subject of knowledge the philosophical subject. I will call the subject of power the modern literary subject. While the former designation is, I think, fairly self-justifying, the latter requires a few words in explanation. The mobile subject as characterized by Foucault sounds exactly like the subject to be found in Montaigne or Shakespeare. That is, the mobile subject of meditation, whatever its ancestry in the classical and Christian traditions, is the subject performed and dramatized by the rhetoric of the discourse being articulated. Interest in this subject arises from the spectacle of its transformations accomplished by its own reflections upon the very utterances it makes. As we shall see, the central generic feature of this mobile subject of meditation—its subversive revisionary instability—has been taken to be what constitutes the essence of the literary when redefined as the purely rhetorical. If the invariable subject of pure demonstration is the subject of argument, then the variable subject of meditation is the aesthetic subject, or the subject of style.

Harold Bloom in *Ruin the Sacred Truths,* for one recent example, credits Shakespearean representation with the definitive invention of modern subjectivity, by which he means (as so many other critics before him have meant) literary subjectivity. Bloom claims that Shakespeare's characters—Hamlet, Iago, Lear, Falstaff, and so on—father themselves into being by changing themselves in response to their own words: "What they say to others, and to themselves, partly reflects what they already are, but also partly begets what they yet will be."[2] Unlike Bloom, who simply reverses priorities by immediately privileging the mobile literary subject over the fixed philosophical subject, I will follow Foucault, who dialectically evades simple reversals. In the conclusion to his remarks on the genres and subjects of demonstration and meditation, Foucault clearly proposes yet another subject and another kind of writing. In fact, to anticipate my argument a bit, it would not be wrong to say that in his later work Foucault not only demonstrates how the subject of knowledge and the subject of power ironically work together to produce the modern regime of truth but also meditates upon the possibility of a different kind of working relationship between these two subjects, one that would represent a new form of relationship, a new mode of subjectivity, and so constitute a new regime of truth—a form, mode, and regime that would be new in the sense that together they would put an end to modernity as we know it—modernity, in short, against itself.

Foucault concludes this section of his response to Derrida's critique by positing a third genre of writing: "demonstrative meditation."[3] This genre would consist in "a set of discursive events" in which the "groups of utterances" were "linked one to another by formal rules of deduction" and "a series of modifications of the enunciating subject which follow continuously one from another" (*F,* 35). Foucault continues, expansively, as follows:

More precisely, in a demonstrative meditation the utterances, which are formally linked, modify the subject as they develop, liberating him from his convictions or on the contrary inducing (qui induisent) systematic doubts, provoking illuminations or resolutions, freeing him from his attachments or immediate certainties, inducing new states: but inversely the decisions, fluctuations, displacements, primarily or acquired qualifications of the subject make sets of new utterances possible, which are in their turn deduced regularly one from another. (*F*, 35–36)

Demonstrative meditation, which is what Foucault calls Descartes's *Meditations*, thus requires a "double reading." This double reading would produce, first of all, "a set of propositions forming a system, which each reader must follow if he wishes to feel their truth." Second, it would also produce "a set of modifications forming an exercise, which each reader must effect, by which each reader must be affected, if in turn he wants to be the subject enunciating this truth on his own behalf" (*F*, 36). System and exercise would thus combine the two subjects of knowledge and power in a demonstrative meditation. "Chiasma," as Foucault says, would necessarily be its definitive generic figure and convention, for the "systematic stringing together of propositions—moments of pure deduction" and the continuous exercise or rhetorical modification of the enunciating subject—for these "two forms of discourse" would have to "intersect" (*F*, 36). The result would be that "the exercise modifying the subject" would order "the succession of propositions" (*F*, 36), and the system of propositions would transform the enunciating subject. Whether Foucault is correct in his claim that Descartes's *Meditations* exemplifies this third genre and third form of subjectivity, and whether this line of response is a sound basis for beginning to answer the Derridean critique of Foucault's reading of Descartes, I find these remarks useful for understanding Foucault's writing and career, because they establish the framework within which Foucault unfolds his project.

The disciplines of modern society have privileged one form of subjectivity as universal, natural, rational, and normal: that of the invariable subject of scientific rationality. Moreover, these disciplines have produced and seek to replicate this modern mode of reason, not only by repressing other past or emerging modes but by structuring the circuits of power to reward, by selective empowerment and the ordering of discourse, those professionals who can successfully replicate the privileged mode, and to pacify, by the literary pleasures of self-decipherment and self-confession, those who cannot. And those even more "dangerous individuals" (the mad, the sexually marginal, the "creative" writer, and the prisoner; who, unlike accredited professionals, do not pursue selective empowerment or the aesthetics of compensatory reflection) are subjected to the most explicitly coercive forms of institutionalization as object lessons and raw materials for further disciplinary experimentation and revisionary improvements in supervisory techniques. Foucault's archaeology and genealogy expose how the subject of knowledge and the subject of power together compose the regime of truth in modern society along these lines. This is why it is incorrect to read Foucault as celebrating the mobile "postmodern" subject. It is, for him, the necessary, subordinated counterpart of the modern subject of knowledge.

Implicit in Foucault's analyses, however, is the assumption that there are other possible—past or future—modes of subjectivity, as we would expect given his previous remarks. This is important to remember. Being, for Foucault, becomes possible as an experience only in the specific contexts of a particular society's historically contingent practices for producing and managing these possibilities of human subjectivity. Experiences that do not fit the currently established codes and criteria are, when recognized at all, supervised and disciplined by being defined as necessarily deviant when measured against the privileged norm of the moment. Foucault produces this historical contingency by staging the styles of unreason permeating modern rationality via his various archaeological analyses and by tracing back in his genealogical exercises "the hazardous play of dominations,"[4] those moments of transition from one dominant norm to another that occur in the modern disciplinary career of this supposedly timeless, universal reason.

Because the discourse of knowledge and the disciplines of power do not saturate the spaces of representation in a culture, and because their regime of truth is hegemonic but not totally perfected, fissures of indetermination open up at various sites in the culture: in texts, in discourse, in the archive. Indeed, such fissures appear in the practices of institutions and in the play of reflection. Into these fissured spaces of nonrelation (gaps in levels of analysis, aporias, and unrecognized contradictions), everything that does not fit in the culture tends to slip and disappear, until such time as, for one set of historical circumstances or another, the dominating powers (discourses, norms, disciplines, practices) must attempt to organize, administer, and institutionalize these problematical spaces of indetermination, these original "lapses" or "outsider" enclaves in the text of being that, as "What Is an Author?" suggests, have been fabricated by the culture in order to limit, contain, and appropriate as its own the anonymous, proliferating power of discursive practices, especially that of fiction writing.

Foucault's fight from the beginning—an entirely ethical fight—has been to expose these spaces of indetermination, to analyze the discursive and disciplinary practices that have organized and represented them, in order to permit their reclamation by those subjected individuals—including himself—otherwise not permitted to represent themselves as other than standard deviations of the norm and so self-consigned to occupy as prisoners these increasingly supervised cultural spaces. In short, the subject of knowledge and the subject of power, that is, the subject of pure demonstration and the subject of meditation, have produced in modern culture an unrecognized parody of the openly dialectical subject of demonstrative meditation that Foucault envisions in his response to Derrida. Foucault's career-long task, as "Nietzsche, Genealogy, History" especially makes clear, is therefore self-consciously to parody this unconscious parody, to make it recognizable as a contingently constructed (unintentionally self-parodying) mask of reason that Hegel and Nietzsche have already theorized, respectively, as "the unhappy consciousness" and "the spirit of *ressentiment.*" Reading Foucault's performance of this metaparodic exercise permits us to recognize, via our own double reading of his reflexive practice, the complex subject of style shadowing the critical subject of his systematic, always at least implicitly, self-parodic "fictions" of modern culture. This theoretical subject of Foucault's highly ironic style is by definition composite, indeed multiple. It incorporates the conventional subjects of pure demonstration and meditation in a spectral demonstrative meditation, a shadow-play of philosophical and literary subjects, a self-conscious specular drama of the imaginary working against currently hegemonic ideologies. This drama can be realized only in the reader's fully responsive appropriation of Foucault's text. Implicit from the beginning, in the performances of Foucault's work through all its transformations, this plural subject of style becomes the explicit theme in Foucault's later work, particularly, of course, in the second and third volumes of *The History of Sexuality*. There it is fully conceptualized, via a historically cast allegory, as an aesthetics of existence, an open game of being, which Foucault and his reader can perform and revise as a textual practice of self-fashioning in a variety of ways.

What I am arguing, then, is that Foucault's career is one comprehensive critical meditation upon the subject of knowledge and the subject of power as the dialectically related masks of modern reason. The aim of this critical meditation is to work upon the limits of ourselves by means of a philosophical thinking that is also an aesthetic reshaping of modernity. This emerging, improvised, and open-ended project of subjectivity would entail a dispossession of ourselves by ourselves, practiced not in the name of a universal norm enforced by a seductive punitive code, but in that of collective self-stylizations of existence, without any prescribed end in view, that would relate the subjects of knowledge and of power as a multiple yet broadly rational subject, the "oneself" of demonstrative meditation. In this light, Foucault's career would be critical theory practiced as an art of life that cares for the self, as the tradition of critical humanism would enjoin, but in distinctively different, nonessentialist, impersonally relativistic ways. Before turning to a necessarily selective reading of *The Use of Pleasure* and *The Care of the Self,* however, there is one major problem that I must confront: that of rational agency, of the critical foundations for Foucault's own theoretical and historical analyses.

Foucault's theory of the statement in *The Archaeology of Knowledge* is actually a theory of the subject as impersonal plural agency. The statement is a construction of discourse that, despite the repetition of the same words, always entails a collective reconstruction, which takes place by means of discursive conventions that presume the possibility of one or another set of subject positions open for occupation by individuals:

> So the subject of the statement should not be regarded as identical with the author of the formulation—either in substance, or in function. He is not in fact the cause, origin, or starting-point of the phe-

nomenon of the written or spoken articulation of a sentence; nor is it that meaningful intention which, silently anticipating words, orders them like the visible body of its intuition; it is not the constant, motionless, unchanging focus of a series of operations that are manifested, in turn, on the surface of discourse through the statement. It is a particular, vacant place that may in fact be filled by different individuals; but, instead of being defined once and for all, and maintaining itself as such throughout a text, a book, or an oeuvre, this place varies—or rather it is variable enough to be able either to persevere, unchanging, through several sentences, or to alter with each one. It is a dimension that characterizes a whole formulation qua statement. It is one of the characteristics proper to the enunciative function and enables one to describe it. If a proposition, a sentence, a group of signs can be called "statement," it is not therefore because, one day, someone happened to speak them or put them into some concrete form of writing; it is because the position of the subject can be assigned. To describe a formulation qua statement does not consist in analysing the relations between the author and what he says (or wanted to say, or said without wanting to); but in determining what position can and must be occupied by any individual if he is to be the subject of it.[5]

The statement's subject, in other words, is always potentially variable or invariable, depending on the play of generic conventions and the positions open to "any individual if he is to be the subject" of the statement. The theory of the statement is also the theory of the subject of demonstrative meditation, the genre, we recall, that comprises the dialectic, chiasmic construction of pure demonstration (with its invariable subject) and meditation (with its variable subject).

These positions, these discursive sites for individuals to occupy as subjects of statements according to the conventions of the discourses in which the statements appear, these masks of words, as it were, incorporate the Other as interiorized double. This process thus produces "oneself" as the doubling of the Other, the doubling of a double. Or as Gilles Deleuze intriguingly puts it, concerning the theme that haunts the author of the memorable chapter in *The Order of Things* entitled "Man and His Doubles":

> The inside is an operation of the outside: in all his work Foucault seems haunted by this theme of an inside which is merely the fold of the outside. . . . Or, rather, the theme which has always haunted

> Foucault is that of the double. But the double is never a project of the interior; on the contrary, it is an interiorization of the outside. It is not a doubling of the One, but a redoubling of the Other. It is not a reproduction of the Same, but a repetition of the Different. It is not the emanation of an "I," but something that places in immanence an always other or a Non-self. It is never the other who is a double in the doubling process, it is a self that lives me as the double of the other: I do not encounter myself on the outside, I find the other in me. . . . It resembles exactly the invagination of a tissue in embryology, or the act of doubling in sewing: twist, fold, stop, and so on.[6]

And since this process of interiorizing the Other as a doubling in oneself involves the interiorizing and doubling of an already doubled Other (the subjects of demonstration and meditation), the result is the production of oneself as a plural agency, the conflicts and contradictions among its masks in turn productive of a dynamic discursive rationality that mediates among the masks according to the conventions of the medium in which it is working. In this respect, and as "What Is Enlightenment?" suggests, Foucault's emphasis on a dynamic, self-revising rationality separates him from other theorists of the so-called postmodern subject. As I have shown in chapter 2, the medium in which the Foucauldian "oneself" appears is one of "radical parody," whose conventions I distinguished by their "exaggerated imitation of a recognizably characteristic position or style that the parodist in question shares with others by virtue of a network of ideological and professional identifications and associations."[7] To reiterate this crucial point I want to stress the vagaries of the postmodern subject of parody and pastiche as Fredric Jameson theorizes the topic. Foucault's "oneself" already reflects critically upon, that is, already parodies in advance the subject Jameson analyses.

The subject in Foucault, then, is never an already given thing, never an original and final nature that one receives or simply is; rather, Foucault's subject is a discursive construction, an artificial, composite, variable, and rational mask. In our time, the literary subject is generally designed and produced, reactively, by scientifically defined, universally enforced, normalizing codes of thought and behavior—a situation that can only be parodied. In *The Use of Pleasure* and *The Care of the Self,* Foucault traces both the lineaments of another society's modes of subject formation (the ancient aesthetics of existence) and the beginnings of our own mode of disciplinary practice (the hermeneutics of self-suspicion). In the process, he perfects the genre of "demonstrative meditation," staging and surmounting the complicitous conflicts of the philosophical and literary subjects by stylizing these conflicts into the fateful history of male friendship. Foucault thereby re-creates these subjects of knowledge and power as the pedagogical pair that author and reader impersonate in the act of reading, an act that reproduces at the site of the text a "oneself" whose original culture's demise this text traces.

This is not the occasion for a full-scale reading of the three volumes of *The History of Sexuality* that are currently available to us. I will attempt to summarize, all too briefly and schematically, the relationship between the first volume, *The Will to Knowledge,* and the other two volumes, before selectively examining Foucault's critical practice of subject formation.

The Will to Knowledge argues that the modern idea of sexual liberation from Victorian repression disguises the fact that ever since the eighteenth century, and with special gusto in the late nineteenth century, modern society has induced individuals to talk endlessly about their sexuality as the defining mark of their individuality. The modern sciences of the human subject—medical pathology, psychiatry, psychoanalysis—have provoked individuals to confess their sexuality in order to define, analyze, categorize, and supervise the normal and the abnormal. This process actually produces the normal and the abnormal, implanting in individuals a standard by which they can decipher, scrutinize, and police themselves—on the model of the religious and moral prescriptions of Christianity.

As he pursues his history of sexuality, Foucault finds that his project's temporal horizon keeps regressing and that the relationship of sexuality to other aspects of human life becomes more complex and problematic. To keep to the seeming demands of his project requires abandoning not only his historical focus but also, and even more important, his habitual modes of thinking on the subject of power and human sexuality. Foucault makes a major discovery in this process of self-revision: there is a difference between societies in which invariable, universalizing moral codes based on religious or scientific knowledge define and discipline human sexuality, and societies in which a play of ethical stylizations, practices of the self (in relation to sex), are not only permitted but also encouraged as an aesthetics of existence founded in the problematic of friendship to the Other in oneself. In discovering this difference, Foucault does not abandon his earlier views on power and discipline or on the social foundation of subject formation; he has not suddenly embraced the ethics of liberal individualism. The subject of ancient societies is no less the incorporation of the Other, no less a discursive construction, no less the production of impersonal practices. The difference resides in the practices of the different societies, so far as the techniques of ethical subject formation are concerned.

As we have seen, the process of subject formation in modern society is a closed, but infinite, coercive game of knowledge and power played according to the strict and invariable rules of a regime of truth productive of scientific rationality and literary unreason. As Foucault puts it, the process of subject formation in ancient society best realizes—for males—the possibility of playing a different kind of game, like love, that is, more of "an open strategic game where things [can] be reversed."[8] In short, in ancient societies, there is more built-in play in the process of subject formation than either Christian or modern societies can permit.

This discovery of difference, however, does not imply automatically the privileging of ancient over modern society—for Foucault takes great pains to remind his readers that ancient society, whatever its attractions, is a slave society in which minors, women, and servants are not fully empowered (if empowered at all), even as their relationships to dominant males are nevertheless ethically problematized. The ethics of sexual stylization that Foucault discusses in the second and third volumes of *The History of Sexuality* is essentially a male ethics of self-governance and male friendship. The critical importance of this fact is clear: the desire for a return to the Greco-Roman ideal is a regressive delusion. At the same time, however, we should not overlook the resources of ancient society. The modes of "self" stylization that Foucault analyzes can be of use to our culture, in which all universalizing moral codes have been put radically into question and in which how we live our lives as sexual beings has literally become a life and death issue. Although how ancient society problematizes sexuality (and so forms the self) is bound to be very different from our own sexual problematics of the self, still we can perhaps dispossess ourselves of our habitual modes of thinking on this subject by critical historical reflection and so begin to see, experimentally, what (if any) aesthetics of existence we can now practice. This is especially promising given the problematic of friendship (to others, to oneself, to the other in oneself) that defines ancient practices of the self.

The central problematic of friendship in Greek and (still to a considerable degree) Roman culture concerns the love of boys. Especially in the Greek context, this proves extremely problematic because, according to the Greek sense of things, the sexual object is passive in the sexual act. The lover, or sexual subject, is the active agent. Whoever penetrates is the active subject (the authentic man); whoever is penetrated is the passive subject (like women or slaves). To make love to a boy who is going to become a citizen of the city-state is thus to put the future man in a highly compromising position from which he may never recover. If the boy is indiscreet, promiscuous, or opportunistic, he can never leave to posterity the memory of a beautiful life. Consequently, the aim of Greek sexual ethics is to problematize and stylize this relationship, so as to transform the different and incompatible claims of honor and love. Ideally, the lover and beloved would practice a wisely chosen moderation and so transfigure the contradictory dimensions of the relationship into a lifelong friendship, a friendship as much with the Other in oneself as with the Other outside oneself. The boy's love must therefore come not on the lover's demand, but as a rare and surprising gift, one in excess of the established terms of the relationship: it must come as if it were the affective and sexual product of an imaginative art—an art of life.

In many respects, then, the story Foucault traces in *The Use of Pleasure* and in *The Care of the Self* tells the fate of friendship; for beginning with Plato and then later even more so with Plutarch, there emerges a unitary theory of love as the quest of the subjective (increasingly heterosexual) couple for the ideal love object: the philosophical and moral truth of their relationship. Necessarily this new erotics entails the systematic scapegoating of the male homosexual. Male friendship, whether actively homosexual or not, is the highest ethical ideal of the ancient world, and the story Foucault writes is simultaneously one of its historical demise as a theme for serious philosophical speculation and its current discursive replication in aesthetic form via the practice of self that is the text of this story. As I read these two volumes, therefore, the play of subjects—philosophical and literary—that Foucault stages also formally reenacts as "an open strategic game" of aesthetic relations the reader's fate of friendship with the author. That is to say, the story Foucault tells is inescapably double: it is the true lie of the disappearance of the author into the act of reading. These volumes are also performing (and perfecting), as a historically cast specular drama of Foucault's own construction, that dialectical interplay of the subjects of knowledge and power earlier portrayed in terms of the subjects of pure demonstration and meditation. In short, *The Use of Pleasure* and *The Care of the Self* are the finest examples of Foucault's own critical mode of "demonstrative meditation."

My readings focus on two sections. The first, from opening passages in *The Use of Pleasure,* critically reflects upon the "heautocratic" or agonistic structure of the self. The second, from closing passages in *The Care of the Self,* reads the Pseudo-Lucian's *Affairs of the Heart.* My point is to demonstrate how the performance of the argument in the first section and the argument in the performance of the second section construct the subject of demonstrative meditation as the interpretive practice of the ancient aesthetics of existence.

Foucault applies to the ethical stylization of the Greeks a fourfold frame of analysis. There is, first of all, the ethical substance—that is, the material singled out for ethical stylization precisely because it is problematic in some way. Next, there is the mode of subjection, the process by which the ethical material is defined, organized, and disciplined. And then, there is the mode of transformation, the process of refinement that transfigures the originally problematic ethical material. Finally, there is the ethical telos, the goal toward which the ethical stylization works. (The ghosts of Aristotle's four causes peak through Foucault's critical framework here.)

For the Greeks, the ethical substance is the aphrodisia, the behaviors and pleasures of sex as they relate to the entire regimen of diet and household economy and, especially, as they involve the love of boys. This is because the boy, as the future citizen of the polis, is both put in the passive position as the sexual object penetrated by the active sexual subject and unable to remain in this compromising position yet still attain his full status as a man. For a society of male power, in which minors, women, and slaves are passive sexual objects, the problematic of love and honor ensues. The mode of subjection for the Greeks consists of the pragmatic strategies of use, which depend upon a continuing moral reflection on one's life. The mode of transformation, the topic of the first section I will read, is self-mastery. And the ethical aim of the Greeks is moderation: to use pleasure wisely in all matters, via a philosophical discipline of philia. The aim, finally, is to ensure the proper realization of an aesthetics of existence, which would leave to posterity the beautiful memory of lives in which the lover and beloved practice their mutual forms of ascetic self-denial, in the interest of a lifelong friendship of pupil and tutor, lies in the fact that the positions of master and ephebe, in principle, can be exchanged.

Foucault begins his remarks on self-mastery by first reflecting on the way that the Greek subject interiorizes the adversarial relation with others in an agonistic structure of the self. In the process, he makes a dubious claim about the nonontological nature of the division of the self into warring parts:

> This combative relationship with adversaries was also an agonistic relationship with oneself. The battle to be fought, the victory to be won, the defeat that one risked suffering—these were processes and events that took place between oneself and oneself. The adversaries the individual had to combat were not just within him or close by; they were part of him. To be sure, we would need to account for the various theoretical formulations that were proposed concerning this differentiation between the part of oneself that was supposed to fight and the part that was supposed to be defeated. Parts of the soul that ought to maintain a certain hierarchical relationship among themselves? Body and soul understood as two realities with different origins? Forces straining toward different goals and working against one another like the two horses of a team? But in any case, the thing to remember in trying to define the general style of this ascetics is that the adversary that was to be fought, however far removed it might be by nature from any conception of the soul, reason, or virtue, did not represent a different, ontologically alien power.[9]

In reading this one immediately asks oneself: What about Plato? But as soon as one has asked this, one also realizes that Foucault himself, in his capsule, rhetorical-question review of the various theoretical formulations of the soul's self-division, has already referred to the most famous Platonic topos for this self-division, that of "the two horses of a team." Foucault has thus anticipated the source of one's objection to his unconventional claim. He has stressed this Platonic topos of "forces straining toward different goals and working against one another." He had ironically highlighted the material thrust of the Platonic theory of the soul's self-division. Moreover, even as the reader recognizes this maneuver and seeks to evaluate it, Foucault contrasts this apparently Greek view of the matter with the most extreme version of the Christian conception of the soul's self-division into warring parts, spirit and flesh, the latter being the nest of that Eternal Enemy within, Satan. Mind quietly spinning, one now learns that in "the ethics of the *aphrodisia,* the inevitability and difficulty of the combat derived" not from fighting "the presence of the Other" in oneself, "with all its ruses and its power of illusion," as if one were involved in a metaphysical or cosmological battle; rather, this inevitable difficulty derives from "the fact that it unfolded as a solo contest," for "to struggle against 'the desires and the pleasures' was to cross swords with oneself" (*UP,* 68). Indeed, a solo contest is being enacted here. As each of one's objections is anticipated, objected to in turn, or deflected, one is almost tempted to say in response, *touché, touché*—only Foucault has already said it: "to cross swords with oneself."

Still somewhat dubious, the reader at last encounters the expected discussion of Plato. Two of the standard texts—*The Republic* and *The Laws*—are adduced, but none of the usual passages are discussed, and the *Phaedo* is not even mentioned. It is as if Foucault gives and takes simultaneously, meeting and evading the reader's presumptions. This is like a bout of shadowboxing in which feints and counterfeints prevail. Consider how the paragraph opens with a comment about the "strange," "somewhat ludicrous," and "outmoded" expression of being "stronger or weaker than oneself." These adjectives for characterizing this paradox appear initially to reflect back upon the equally old-fashioned paradoxical expression of crossing swords with oneself that ironically concludes the previous paragraph.

Foucault's argument now moves on to discuss Socrates' analysis of the paradox of being stronger or weaker than oneself in terms of the assumptions underlying ordinary language usage, as if in anticipation of the typical moves of Anglo-American analytic philosophy. As one observes Foucault citing Plato from *The Republic* on the prior division in the soul that informs this paradox, one begins to suspect that the elitist model of civic governance is implicitly shaping the Socratic assumption of an ethics of self-governance. At this point, as if in response to the reader's thought, Foucault cites a passage from the *The Laws* that confirms one's suspicions even as it also confirms that the agonistic structure of the self is being realized in the reading process:

> And it is made clear at the beginning of the *Laws* that this antagonism of oneself toward oneself is meant to structure the ethical attitude of the individual vis-à-vis desires and pleasures: the reason that is given for the need of a ruling authority and a legislative authority in every state is that even in peacetime all states are at war with one another; in the same way one must assume that is "all are enemies of all in public," then in private "each is an enemy of himself"; and of all the victories it is possible to win, "the first and best" is the victory "of oneself over oneself," whereas "being defeated by oneself is the most shameful and at the same time the worst of all defeats." *UP*, 68–69)

As one discovers the performative dimension of the argument, the question of who is in the driver's seat naturally arises. Not only does Foucault anticipate one's moves but his anticipation also evades one's objections, thereby spurring on one's suspicions. Mastery and skepticism together possess the subject of reading in this way. Necessarily, then, one interiorizes this adversarial relationship as an agonistic self structure, since Foucault and his reader position and reposition each other in this open strategic game.

As if in confirmation of this reading game, the next paragraph opens with the invocation of just "such a 'polemical' attitude with respect to oneself" (*UP*, 69), in terms of analogies drawn from wrestling and running contests. The ancient Greek stylization of existence as a virile, athletic aesthetics realizes itself here as an interpretive agon. Yet, fearing the reluctance to credit this transformation, Foucault presents the worst that can be said—seriously and comically—about this virile ascesis, for he reminds us, first, that this ascetic style sometimes celebrates the Pyrrhic victory of the extirpation of all desires. He then reminds us that, as Bion the Borysthemite wryly notes, if Socrates in his famous test slept all night beside Alcibiades and felt desire for him, then Socrates was foolish to abstain; and if Socrates did not feel desire and just slept, then his was a hollow victory indeed. After thus confirming and defending from possible critique the game of reading, the paragraph then concludes appropriately enough with a brief account of Aristotle's analysis of *enkrateia,* defined as "mastery and victory."

This analysis describes the excess, privation, and triumphant golden mean of self-mastery—the latter being, it is stressed, neither self-abandonment nor insensitivity to the other. This conclusion sounds as much like a comment upon the aim of the Foucauldian reading contest as it does a masterfully succinct account of Aristotelian virtue. The self-disciplining act of reading presented in Foucault's later works, then, produces at the site of the text an overdetermined, composite self that, imaginatively conceived, is the consequence of neither self-abandonment nor insensitive estrangement.

As we have just seen, the adversarial relation to others becomes an agonistic relation to oneself for the ancient Greeks. Similarly, the adversarial game of reading becomes the agonistic structure of the subject of reading. As a result, the firm distinctions between argument and performance, text and commentary, author and reader break down, even as the subject of reading is agonistically built up. A "oneself" or, if you will, an "Over-self," is here emerging that incorporates all these distinctions as continuous phases in a complex act of (self-)reading.

The last paragraph in this section discussing the mode of subjection in the Greeks' ethical stylization of sexuality recapitulates the positions of Foucault's major authorities on the "heautocratic" structure of the Greek ethical subject. It also underscores in this way the mask play of the "oneself" here performed via all these very figures:

> In the domain of pleasures, virtue was not conceived as a state of integrity, but as a relationship of domination, a relation of mastery. This is shown by the terms that are used—whether in Plato, Xenophon, Diogenes, Antiphon, or Aristotle—to define moderation: "rule the desires and the pleasures," "exercise power over them," "govern them" (*kratein, archein*). There is an aphorism that captures this general conception of pleasure; interestingly, it is attributed to Aristippus, who had a rather different theory of pleasure from that of Socrates: "It is not abstinence from pleasure that is best, but mastery

over them without ever being worsted" (*to kratein kai mē hēttasthai hē-donōn ariston, ou to mē chrēsthai*). In other words, to form oneself as a virtuous and moderate subject in the use he makes of pleasures, the individual has to construct a relationship with the self that is of the "domination-submission," command-obedience," "mastery-docility" type (and not, as will be the case in Christian spirituality, a relationship of the "elucidation-renunciation," "decipherment-purification" type). This is what could be called the "heautocratic" structure of the subject in the ethical practice of the pleasures. (*UP*, 70)

The irony of Foucault's mask play, in which he even gets Aristippus, the opponent of the Socratic conception of pleasure, to do his part, is apparent. The final two sentences allude to Foucault's major precursors in the modern philosophical tradition. Hegel, Kant, and Nietzsche are contrasted, via their famous topoi for the self, with the strangely Heideggerian sounding hermeneutics of self-suspicion to be found in the Christian parenthesis in Western cultural history. Made doubtful and inspired by Foucault's breathtaking performance, one is happily lost in this interpretive labyrinth of lucid masks. In this fashion, Foucault brilliantly uses the pleasure modernity takes in the self-suspicion that founds modernity by initially playing off it in his textual elaboration of the ancient aesthetics of existence. This is, in short, using modernity ironically against itself.

The subject in Foucault is thus simultaneously self-conscious and self-forgetting: it is an aesthetic construction, agonistic in its specular structure. Yet such a subject nonetheless stands in opposition to the conventional ideological work of critical humanism, with its endorsement of an imaginary individual nature. By contrast, this Foucauldian subject openly performs itself spectrally at the site of the text as an ever-renewing birth of the self. This self, in Foucault's later work, is a discursive phenomenon of style, playfully produced, shaped, and reshaped intertextually among authors, readers, and their masks. It is in this sense that the subject of Foucault's discourse is a "oneself," a kind of "Over-self," made up of these component subject positions.

The second section that I will read, from the close of *The Care of the Self*, is itself a reading of Pseudo-Lucian's *Affairs of the Heart*. This text is presented, Foucault notes, "in the quite customary form of interlocking dialogues."[10] Theomnestus, a lover of boys and women alike, asks Lycinus, the Stoic ascetic, to serve as "an impartial judge and tell him which is the better choice" (*CS,* 211). To this end, Lycinus tells the story of a debate between Charicles, the lover of women, and Callicratidas, the lover of boys. Although the latter bests his opponent in their debate, the dialogue that ensues between Lycinus and Theomnestus results in the young man's cynical privileging of physical desire that yet does little to relieve his comically painful irresolution. The truth represented by the final figures of Lycinus, the impartial anchorite, and Theomnestus, the long-suffering cynic, is thus a twin one. The presiding genius of Pseudo-Lucian's text is ironically complete and self-canceling.

Foucault begins his reading by strongly reminding us that the seriousness of Charicles and Callicratidas, the participants in the reported debate of love, is not to be taken "at face value":

> Pseudo-Lucian is being ironic when he writes the emphatic and weighty demonstrations he attributes to them. There is an element of pastiche in these pieces of bravura. Taken together, they constitute the typical discourse of the Advocate of Women and the Devotee of Boys. Traditional arguments, obligatory quotations, references to great philosophical ideas, rhetorical flourishes—the author smiles in reporting the speeches of these imperturbable disputants. And, from this point of view, it should be noted that the pederastic discourse is much more ponderous, pretentious, and "baroque" that the one spoken in favor of women, which is plainer, more Stoicizing. The final irony—Theomnestus will observe that what it all comes down to is just a matter of kisses, caresses, and hands that wander beneath tunics—will be mainly at the expense of the eulogy of the love of boys. But this very irony indicates the seriousness of the problem that is raised. And whatever enjoyment Pseudo-Lucian may have had in sketching the "theoretical-discursive" portrait of these two devotees—their rhetorical profile, in rather heavy strokes—one can see in it a contemporary example, displaying the most prominent features, of that "contest of loves" which had such a long career in Hellenic culture. (*CS,* 212)

With all this blunt talk of seriousness that is not serious but then becomes so, of enjoyment that is not quite enjoyable, of irony, of the author smiling—it is easy, perhaps all too easy, to read the description of Pseudo-Lucian and his text as an ironic portrayal of Foucault and his own text, as if Foucault while he wrote were uttering into textual existence his own autobiographical mask. Yet such obvious, broad-stroked self-irony, such fashionable *mise en abîme*–ing, if true, could only be the bitterly compensatory accompaniment of the history of sexuality Foucault has traced to this point, for this history witnesses in Plato and even more so in Plutarch the emergence of a unitary and reciprocal conception of love at the cost of systematically scapegoating the pedophile-pedagogue. In fact, "the great integrative chain of love" (*CS*, 210) now excludes, as if it were a logical necessity, the prospect of serious male bonding, actively homosexual or not, since the married heterosexual couple of equal subjects in love increasingly defines the exclusive norm of this new, largely Stoic stylistics of love. Such irony as we find here with Foucault might be a rhetorical victory that marks a historical defeat. Hereafter, for example, the love of boys is no longer a subject for serious philosophical reflection. But the operative phrase, really and ambiguously, is the optative mood of the verb in the next to Foucault's last sentence: "one can see in [Pseudo-Lucian's portrait] a contemporary example."

Such ambiguity, after all, defines the initial anecdote that serves as the pretext for the debate between Charicles and Callicratidas and that haunts the entire *Affairs of the Heart:*

> It is physical pleasure that will have the last word and dismiss the prudish speeches with a peal of laughter. And it is physical pleasure that serves as the pretext for the debate between Charicles and Callicratidas—in the form of a meaningful anecdote: a young man, enamoured of the marble by Praxiteles, had let himself be locked in the temple at night, and he sullied the statue, but as if it had been a boy. The telling of this story—a very traditional one—occasions the debate. Since the sacrilegious act was addressed to Aphrodite, was it an homage to the goddess who presides over female pleasures? But given the form in which it was carried out, was it not a testimonial against that particular Aphrodite? An ambiguous act. Should this impious homage, this profanatory reverence, be accounted to the love of women, or of boys? (*CS*, 213)

Talk about the ancients problematizing sex! But the exuberant transgressive style of this problematization is as much Foucault's own in the telling of the anecdote. Such telling, in terms of the game of reading I have been playing with Foucault, is itself telling in another sense: it ironically reflects the problematic nature of any aesthetics of existence practiced publicly as an art of interpretation and necessarily entails moments of monumentalizing appreciation of the author' mastery and of his reader's devastatingly critical deconstruction of the pretense to such mastery—and vice versa. The dangers of monumentalizing the author or reader functions, in short, are comically highlighted by this report of aesthetic relations with a statue—certainly an ironic comment upon the plight of Theomnestus. However, whether or not it is really physical pleasure that has the last word in Foucault's own text, some kind of peal of laughter, sublimely ambivalent no doubt, surely does echo in one's mind.

Pseudo-Lucian's text concludes with a victory of the love of boys, a victory that Theomnestus "immediately waxes ironic about" (*CS,* 227). This is because it is an entirely traditional victory in which the philosophical pederast evades physical pleasure in his celebration of ideal love, even as the universality of marriage is left wholly intact. This victory, then, does nothing for Theomnestus, who had originally wanted to know which love to choose, since he had found pleasure in both loves. His disappointment thus inspires his irony, as now ventriloquized, self-parodically, by Foucault himself:

> Seriously, he says, they can't make us believe that the whole pleasure of this relationship is in looking into each other's eyes and in being enchanted by friendly conversation. Looking is agreeable, certainly, but it is only the first stage. After that comes touching, which thrills the whole body. Then kissing, which is timid at first but soon becomes eager. The hand does not remain idle during this time; it glides down under the clothing, squeezes the breasts for a moment, descends the length of the firm belly, reaches the "flower of puberty," and finally "strikes the target." (*CS,* 227)

In this fashion, for one of the only times in either *The Use of Pleasure* or *The Care of the Self* Foucault impersonates here the voice of his source. We can see him now becoming at the site of the text a "oneself." This agonistically structured self incorporates as richly ambiguous interpretive acts the various positions represented by all the characters in the dialogue being read. In this dramatic style, we see staged an ironic performance of the truth of the mask play we enact in our reading of Foucault's text as we together also become a "oneself" or "Over-self."

These two sections from *The Use of Pleasure* and *The Care of the Self* show how Foucault solicits the reader to play an open strategic game of reading in which the systematic philosophical analysis of the history of sexuality in terms of forms of ethical stylization also functions as a meditative exercise of the literary subject, an interpretive practice of the self. Thus, the ancient aesthetics of existence is performed as a perpetual mask play. The supersubject of "oneself," or what I am calling the "Over-self" of "demonstrative meditation," is here repeatedly being born. The fate of friendship, as read from Foucault's *History of Sexuality,* is openly to become again and again a culture of purely impure aesthetic relations—just like making love to a statue of oneself, perhaps? But, perhaps not. O my friends, there is a friend—in this text.

5 On the Friend Self and Lawrence Kritzman's *The Rhetoric of Sexuality and the Literature of the French Renaissance*

The ancient Menander declared that man happy who had been lucky to meet even the shadow of a friend.
——*Montaigne, "Of Friendship"*

I, the imperfect, adore my own Perfect.
——*Emerson, "The Over-Soul"*

Lionel Trilling remarks in his journals that of all major American writers, only Emerson could relate to himself as a friend. [1] The relation to oneself is both a historical matter and, as an internalized reflexive (or specular) structure, a psychological phenomenon. Foucault in volumes 2 and 3 in *The History of Sexuality* details the ways in which the relation to oneself functions as an active social practice for the classical Greeks and Romans entailing the problematic erotics of a pedagogic pair. Mentor and pupil would love. But how best to realize this love without compromising either the former's authority or the latter's honor? The solution is for each of them to transform the dynamics of their interpersonal relationship into the intrapsychic agonistic relation to oneself. Each could play the specular role of friend to the other as a freely elected ascetic renunciation of physical excesses for the spectral beloved's own good. The gift of self to other would appear, paradoxically, as the refusal to give oneself in any fashion other than this self-chosen discipline of true love.[2] Unlike Hegel's master-slave dialectic, however, the origin and end of the pedagogic relation and of its internalized offspring, the agonistic relation to oneself, does not depend on the external threat of death that is then internalized, but on the psychological reality of love that is being expressed. The aristocratic class can always afford the luxury of such noble love.

Since the Renaissance, this luxury has become increasingly available, and the pedagogic dimension of the relation to oneself has become a matter of the intertextual relation of the reader and writer functions of the self because the intellectual's memory is primarily a precipitation of sublime touchstones. America, of course, has traditionally provided the most opportunity for the expression of this relation to oneself through its official embrace of the policy of universal literacy as necessary for democracy's survival. The psychic structure of reading and writing is the relation to oneself in a textual configuration I call the "friend self."

Julia Kristeva in her recent trilogy on narcissism (*Powers of Horror, Tales of Love, and Black Sun: Depression and Melancholia*) offers the best general theoretical guide to what I am calling the friend self.[3] Kristeva, especially in her clinical observations, isolates a once new but now familiar social type that has generally been characterized by Heinz Kohut and others as the narcissistic personality.[4] This new social type is, I believe, the general form the intellectual takes in a postmodern media culture. Or, more precisely, it is a democratized form of intellectuality in a postmodern media culture made possible by modern higher education.

The narcissist, postmodern style, is a radically split subject composed of a wounded ego and a grandiose ego ideal. The former is the ghost of the abjected mother, even as the latter is the specter of the imaginary father. The narcissist endlessly repeats the dynamics of the family romance by acting it out as a life. The aim is not, however, to realize in symptomatic fantasy an Oedipal triumph unavailable in everyday reality; instead, it is ever to regress from the demands of the grandiose ego ideal into the waiting arms of the wounded ego. One may want to think here of Nixon's farewell address to his staff as one memorable case of the narcissistic personality type in action. I choose

Nixon because, like Tom Wicker in his recent biography, *One of Us,* I think Nixon is more one of us than we intellectuals want to acknowledge.

The professional narcissist plays out this chronically adolescent syndrome in the text as a refusal to avow the imaginary father, the great original of the grandiose ego ideal. This refusal takes the form of a resentful (because insatiable) attack on all established authority figures in the name of marginalized Others, each of which finds its great original in the figure of the abjected mother. This critical mask play, however, cannot be an effective social critique, since it is not historically modulated and realistic enough for that. As such, it is an obstacle to the development of a well-balanced tradition of significant social critique. But there is no way around this syndrome—only the way through it.

In *Black Sun,* Kristeva theorizes an imaginative strategy for overcoming critical narcissism as the dominant mode of the relation to oneself in our postmodern culture of the simulacrum.[5] The wounded ego of the narcissist must come to recognize and avow the imaginary father underlying the grandiose ego ideal. The ego thereby recovers the exploratory relation to reality first mediated by the mother. The ego only suffers this relation to reality now as what Kristeva terms the loss of the Thing if this recognition and avowal are not forthcoming. The narcissistic form of melancholy and depression expresses itself as the nameless and unfathomable sense of powerlessness. Such unconscious mourning for the abjected mother defines the relation to the imaginary father (and his avatar, the grandiose ego ideal) as one of depression. One may learn to identify with the transitional object of the therapist in the analytic situation, or of the mask of one's chosen author. Either therapist or author can symbolically play both parental roles in the analytic or critical transference. The wounded ego can thereby release sexually ambivalent imaginative energies from repression for the creation of texts that stage the overdetermined desires of the self for autogenesis as a perpetual crisscrossing of the gender characteristics of abjected mother and imaginary father. Wounded ego and grandiose ego ideal, and their great originals, abjected mother and imaginary father, compose the major topoi of reading/writing constituting what more generally I call the friend self: "oneself."

This oneself (or friend self) is both an impersonalizing textual practice, with accessible conventions and norms of judgment, and a deeply embedded complex of personal identity themes. To become oneself, to become—like Emerson—a friend to oneself, thus means to identify with a transitional authority figure sufficiently well enough to compose and stage the public recognition and avowal of one's imaginary father. In the course of a career, however, this figure is constellated by the total play of figures in one's texts, and freely and repeatedly incorporates all the major characteristics of the immediately preceding figure in psychic development, the abjected mother. Our culture needs to abject the mother as the only way to move from the imaginary realm of semiotic wordthings to the symbolic patriarchal register of the linguistic law of object formation. Until our culture no longer needs to do so—and the revolution does not seem to be just around the corner, to say the least—the drama of becoming oneself may be the best strategy we can perform in the direction of imaginative health. Such a critical move relies upon the collective archive of texts, canonical and noncanonical alike, as a resource of authoritative masks or personas to function like therapeutic transitional objects in these plays of becoming oneself, in which self-destructive resentments at repression are overcome through learning to exercise the magnanimous power of (self-)critical love.

Consider, for example, the following excerpt from Emerson's *Journals*.[6]

October 30, 1835
How hard it is to impute your own best sense to a dead author! The very highest praise we think of any writer, or painter, or sculptor, or builder is that he actually possessed the thought or feeling with which he has inspired us. We hesitate at doing Spenser so great an honor as to think that he meant by his allegory the sense which we affix to it. (145)

This meditation anticipates Emerson's famous remark from the opening of "Self-Reliance" (1841) that "in every work of genius we recognize our own rejected thoughts: they come back to us with a certain alienated majesty" (259). But who is really speaking in this journal entry? And to whom? We say in answer to both questions, "Emerson," but what can we possibly mean? Who is being addressed as hardly imputing "your own best sense to a dead author"? Who then becomes the "we"? Why a particular dead author in this passage, who this time turns out to be "Spenser"? We so readily accept the convention of journal writing in which the author is addressing himself that we rarely think about what this practice can imply for the theory of the subject. The voice that admonishes and the "you" or "we" admonished are, first of all, the internalized pedagogic couple of mentor and student that Foucault historically meditates. Second, as Kristeva teaches us, the journal text of Emerson's "Spenser" serves as an authoritative transitional object of transference love and ambivalence that therapeutically releases both the recognition of "our" resentful hesitancy and the already emerging magnanimous gift of sublime attribution. The abjected state of resentful depression over another's sublime achievement of "thought or feeling" stems from an extravagant narcissistic sense of creative usurpation. It is as if "Spenser," one aspect of the imaginary father (that "alienated majesty"), would take possession of our poetic power, thereby abjecting us like the mother, should we fully recognize and publicly avow him as a source of inspiration. Being generously able to do so, however, frees one to become oneself, which is what Emerson is here recognizing, thereby incorporating both what he repeatedly sees as the "erect" stance of "male" creative power and the more languid posture of "female" receptivity to another's influence. This radical play of essentialized gender roles is the best we can do, it seems. How consistently Emerson "becomes oneself" in this complex sense is another question. The imaginative persona here speaking, in any event, expresses the relation to oneself in Emerson as playing the friend.

The most Emerson can say about "playing the friend" in "Friendship" (1841) is considerable.[7] The friend is the figure before whom one can be entirely naked and so sincerely truthful: "I may drop even those undermost garments of dissimulation, courtesy, and second thoughts, which men never put off, and may deal with [the friend] with the simplicity and wholeness with which one chemical atom meets another" (347). As Emerson asks, and I dare say, D.H. Lawrence in *Women in Love* also recalls, "To stand in true relations with men in a false age is worth a fit of insanity, is it not?" (347). Citing Montaigne's famous essay "On Friendship," which is devoted to the memory of his dead friend, La Boétie, Emerson remarks that with the friend one can thus afford to offer, beyond truthfulness, "tenderness"

(348). This is because, "in the last analysis," such "love is only the reflection of a man's own worthiness from other men" (352). Unfortunately, Emerson, like Montaigne, does not believe women are capable of friendship with men.

Given this admittedly patriarchal reflexive specularity, which repairs somewhat our chronically wounded narcissism, Emerson concludes that we can now understand why "men have sometimes exchanged names with their friends, as if they would signify that in their friend each loved his own soul" (352). And even when, to do our own work, we must temporarily put aside the joy of friendship, we still can recognize in what emanates from their influence upon us the "lustres" of our collective imaginative power (354). This collective imaginative power informing and transforming friends is so great that it may even magnanimously overcome a friend's relative lack of capacity, as Emerson suggests (and as does Nietzsche in his remarks on the friend in *Zarathustra*), via the metaphysically loaded trope of the sun:

> Why should I cumber myself with regrets that the receiver is not capacious? It never troubles the sun that some of his rays fall wide and vain in to ungrateful space, and only a small part on the reflecting planet. Let your greatness educate. . . . Thou art enlarged by thy own shining. . . . True love transcends the unworthy object . . . and when the poor interposed mask crumbles, it is not sad. . . . The essence of friendship is entireness, a total magnanimity and trust. . . . It treats its object as a god, that it may deify both. (354)

Visionary apotheosis of the friend self and its savage demonization occupy the extreme poles of possible self-interpretation. Learning to balance these extremes by occupying the middle ground between is the practice of criticism as radical parody.

Radical parody is the mode of critical interpretation through which the critic positions his or her text as an antithetical version of the imaginative source for one's criticism. Emerson on Spenser in the previously cited journal entry positions his text for a meditative moment beside and in experimental opposition to his source text via his wonderment at his own reading of Spenser's "allegory." Such an exploratory critical gesture is the beginning of radical parody, which continues in the form of a conceptual challenge to the source text ironically mediated by an exaggerated rhetorical imitation of its characteristic manner. The aim of this radical parody is not simply the "dark conceit" of one's own "allegory" in the forms of disguised homage or circumlocutious critique; rather, it is the staged recognition and public avowal of the gift of inspiration as, finally, a repaying of the debt to "oneself." "In Shakspear [*sic*]," as Emerson remarks in another journal entry, "I actually shade my eyes as I read the splendor of the thoughts" (145). Note well that Emerson says "the" thoughts. Emerson assumes they are not Shakespeare's sole possession but are democratically available to all. In sum, then, such tender truthfulness toward himself is what Lionel Trilling means by saying Emerson can play the friend to himself.

The friend self is thus a split or plural subject impersonating intrapsychically both the admonishing instruction of the collective archive and the contingent prodigality of the individual self. The force of education invents the plural subject and, based on the pedagogic ideal of the mentor-pupil relation, proposes that the psyche internally reform itself on this model by learning, via creative reading, to reflexively don the spectral mask of both partners to this agon. Necessarily, the self experiences this entire process as if it were the work of mourning and melancholia Freud and others suggest is definitive for self-development:

> [After the loss of the love object,] the free libido was withdrawn into the ego and not directed to another object. It did not find application there, however, in any one of several possible ways, but served simply to establish an identification of the ego with the abandoned object. Thus the shadow of the object fell upon the ego, so that the latter could henceforth be criticized by a special mental faculty like an object, like the forsaken object. In this way the loss of the object became transformed into a loss in the ego, and the conflict between the ego and the loved person transformed into a cleavage between the criticizing faculty of the ego and the ego as altered by the identification.[8]

The internalization of the pedagogic ideal as the relation to oneself necessarily loses and then reinvents in this fashion the individual teachers, actual and imaginary, we have had. Emerson in his journal entry on Spenser exemplifies the imaginative and ethical results of such a mournful process of educative discipline.

What I have been doing so far is developing my theory of the friend self by elaborating a historical-psychoanalytic-rhetorical framework as my radical parody of Lawrence D. Kritzman's parallel efforts vis-à-vis the source texts in his new book, *The Rhetoric of Sexuality and the Literature of the French Renaissance.*[9] With respect to the latter, my essay "On the Friend Self" intends to serve vicariously as conceptual challenge and exaggerated rhetorical homage, and so comparatively ironic albeit kindly critique. In this postmodern fashion of specular doubling, I would repay the debt to myself for his provocative inspiration, thereby exemplifying, I hope, my theory. *The Rhetoric of Sexuality* examines from a psychoanalytical perspective canonical and noncanonical texts of French Renaissance literature by Pernette du Guillet, Marguerite de Navarre, Sceve, Marot, Montaigne, and Rabelais. These diverse authors and texts provide Kritzman with the heterogenous materials for his critical impersonation of their themes and patterns in and as his text. He makes it clear by the sixth chapter, "Architecture of the utopian body: the blasons of Marot and Ronsard" (this lack of capitalization simulates the look of a French text), that all his chapters are to function as if they, too, were blasons whose formal arrangements articulate even as they phantasmagorically disfigure an ambivalently idealized female body. Kritzman's book, within its three-part circular structure tracing the movement of "Rhetorics of Gender" through "Figures of the Body" to "Allegories of Repression," also means to resemble, as it anatomizes, the Renaissance anatomy form. As critical analysis, finally, Kritzman's reflexive intertextuality also displays for his (and our) judgment this postmodern simulacrum of the Renaissance texts he discusses. In this fashion, Kritzman practices radical parody self-critically via intellectual pastiche.

The story that the book as a whole tells goes something like this. Female sexuality is for Kritzman a radical phenomenon disruptive of the patriarchal hierarchy. Rather than simply suppress it, the male writer can imaginatively appropriate it for his own purpose, which is basically twofold. He can learn to use female sexuality in its various conventional and unconventional modes to symbolize his own complex relation of receptivity vis-à-vis the patriarchal tradition. And he can learn to incorporate female sexuality by rhetorically assimilating its potential for disruption to his aesthetic project of simulating heroic "male" power and redefining it as critically oppositional. In this twofold self-pedagogy, the critic would become a transsexual textual entity, an imaginary specular structure of crisscrossing gender characteristics, what I call "oneself" or the "friend self." This birth of self by the self and for the self aesthetically preserves as style the male writer's sense of creative power. It rescues it from the loss of love attendent upon death or anxious fantasies of castration at the hands of the patriarchal father or the dangerously seductive woman.

Refreshingly, Kritzman uses all the resources made available by the importation of French critical theory into America to tell this story as an object lesson from which he honestly refuses to exempt himself. Of particular service to his critical project are the feminist revisions in Freudian and Lacanian analysis of Cixous, Shoshana Felman, Irigaray, Melanie Klein, and Kristeva. Although he is the editor of some of Foucault's most important fugitive pieces, Kritzman does not highlight that debt here, which appears primarily in the focus, already justified by the texts he selects to read, on the pedagogic relation to oneself, which is especially intense and on display in Montaigne's essays. [10]

The three chapters on Montaigne constitute the heart of the text: "Pedagogical graffiti and the rhetoric of conceit," "Montaigne's family romance" (a path-breaking essay), and "My body, my text: Montaigne and the rhetoric of self-portraiture." The first of these chapters reads Montaigne's "De l'institution des enfans." The second reads "De l'affection des Peres aux enfans." And the last of these three chapters reads "Sur des vers de Virgile."

Montaigne, in "De l'institution des enfans," plays off the Ovidian tradition of the Tristia, "where the author is father of a poem which ostensibly becomes his child" (59). In proposing a new pedagogic ideal, where creatively remembering cultural artifacts displaces their rote memorization, Montaigne also enfigures the relation to oneself as a prodigal son striving for mastery but refusing the conventional position of the father. Unable to control his own "conceptions," Montaigne, vis-à-vis those he would instruct, is both male authority figure bearing the imprint of the father in his quest for manly diction, and the inverse of this traditional image, a source of maternal nurturance and affection: "In activating this metamorphosis, the text transcribes the sexual indecision of Montaigne's pedagogical imperative" (69). The key to such "confusion of gender" (69) is the desire, encrypted in the stray figures of Montaigne's essay, that suggests his aim in educating others in what he does not consciously know is to ingest the cultural fathers by drinking their powerful influence down via the projected simulacrum of his pedagogical audience, so as to pass this influence on, in revised form, like a maternal figure, to stimulate the new birth of learning he envisions, which is a lucid fluency of textual being. Imaginary perversions envisioned here compose an open secret. Kritzman uses Freud's "Mourning and Melancholia" (1917) to elucidate this point with respect to Montaigne's notorious style of "relentless self-depreciation that characterizes the rhetoric of [his] self-portrait" (66). The loss of an authoritative ideal, like that of a love object, causes a grief that works to install the image of the lost ideal love within the psyche by transforming a portion of the psyche into its mask. In this way, the lost love or ideal remains alive, spectrally, even as it becomes an object for working through ambivalence via (self-)accusations and (self-)hatred. The introjection or ingestion of the patriarchal "imago" of verbal power releases Montaigne to preserve and denigrate this beloved ideal in the compromise formation of his "relentless self-depreciation."

As Kritzman reads "De l'affection des Peres aux enfans" in "Montaigne's family romance," we discover the primary biographical source for the great essayist's mournful revisionary quest for endless sexual metamorphosis: "The melancholic retreat into narcissism permits Montaigne to transfer the bond between himself and La Boétie into a bond between writer and text and thereby encrypt the deceased into the 'monumen des muses'" (77). Playing male pedagogue to an imagined male pupil, or prodigal son to imposing patriarchal tradition, or nurturing mother to the projected mask of himself as his own offspring—all these revisionary meditative positions that the critical essayist takes in his figurative romance would perform this bond between writer and text as his beloved friend's ironic monument: "To present oneself to oneself reveals a self-nurturing textuality created from an initial dual unity and which expresses, in its course, the problematics of giving and receiving as implied in the succession of generations" (78–79). Montaigne's "self" is what I call "oneself" or the "friend self," a plural subject constituted in the bond with La Boétie and repeatedly reconstituted in sexually revisionary fashion as the textual and intertextual substance of the essays, which are ever trial runs for a consummation never to come but always to envision. The self composed in the bond between writer and text rehearses the bond between Montaigne and La Boétie in terms of an exhaustive playing out of all the possibilities of the family romance, even as it also prefigures the giving birth to oneself in the essays as an immortal child of the mind. Kritzman wittily terms this narcissistic desire to give birth to oneself via one's essayistic "conceptions" "the rhetoric of conceit," which via Montaigne's sublime example defines the conventions of the essay genre as we still know it.

In "My body, my text: Montaigne and the rhetoric of self-portraiture," Kritzman, in reading "Sur des vers de Virgile," both crystallizes his position on the origins of Montaigne's essays and elaborates the substitute gratification motif as their final formal motive.

> The essays are composed in an interval of waiting, in the gap between the disappearance of the other (perhaps La Boétie) and the goal of consubstantiality, the narcissistic identification with the self-portrait. . . . The expenditure of desire [focuses] on the enterprise of displaying the writer before the mirror of his own writing. Indeed the fetishistic object of desire reflects back on the desiring subject. (137, 139)

The unspoken but strongly implied figure shaping these remarks is the period of gestation resulting, once the waiting is finally over, in the beaming appearance of the proud papa.

Montaigne, in writing on Virgil, also displays his acute awareness of the unnatural practice of his new art when compared to Virgil's poetry and its greater harmony with nature. (It's a good thing Montaigne doesn't compare his work to Homer's, which has always seemed like nature when compared to Virgil's artifice.) This self-consciousness, Kritzman believes, derives from Montaigne's sense of "how sexuality and rhetoric are interchangeable" for him, especially as he ages with only this one pleasure of writing against nature left to him (145). Yet the "natural" repression of sexuality that aging enforces ironically supplements the repression that the discipline of culture produces. Repression thus ends up functioning as a new incentive to pleasure, since the greater the repression the greater the intensities and complexities of fantasy life. "The fluidity and movement associated with the release of tension emanating from the explosive force of desire is enacted through the topoi concerning both sexuality and writing" (146).

Not only does Kritzman come gracefully (rather than mechanically) full circle in the final chapter of the book by returning to Rabelais, who was left hanging back in chapter 2, but he also provides, proleptically, for a possible critique of his postmodern simulacrum of this transgressive sexual project of French Renaissance literature. He does so in "Sexuality and the political unconscious in Rabelais' *Quart Livre*" by reading the prologue, the Chiquanous, and the Papimanes episodes in a manner that implicitly judges his own practice of radical parody as intellectual pastiche. I quote him at some length to give him his proper due. We must only remember that whatever he says about "Rabelais," whether or not new historicist in tendency, also in principle applies (like Emerson's take on "Spenser") to the critical fiction being essayed:

> Rabelais' *Quart Livre* therefore demonstrates how writing functions as an integral part of the social process of incorporation and rule; it serves power by subjugating individuals to a supra-personal discipline or authority. Chapter fifty-two of the Papimanes episode demonstrates how the misuse of the sacred [laws]—the perverse violation of the text—is a paradigm of negativity, a prescription for punishment and failure; it regenerates the paradise myth by inversion so as to produce an archeology of sadistic fantasies. [This last comment ironically reflects on Kritzman's own practice of critical blasons.] The libidinal pleasures associated with the correct use of . . . law turns against itself here through the destructive instinct for transgression or the individual's will to power against an intemperate law. (211)

Self-judgment subtly ventriloquized through the sublime mask of the other could not be better done. The differences between Kritzman's Rabelais and Montaigne define the dimensions of his imaginary father. Kritzman in *The Rhetoric of Sexuality and the Literature of the French Renaissance* thereby exemplifies what I mean by playing the friend to (and as) oneself. As Emerson in his journal entry on Spenser admonishes himself, so here Kritzman on Rabelais does the same thing. Moreover, in openly exploring the transgressive sexual transformations of intellectual identity via the rhetorical figures that he cathects meditatively, Kritzman suggests our continued derivation from or continuity with the Renaissance and dramatizes his own critical romance with respect to that derivation. This book is Kritzman's exemplary *Anatomy of Melancholy* for our time. The wounded ego and grandiose ego ideal, their great originals of the abjected mother and imaginary father, can be seen playing themselves out as the relation to oneself in the rhetoric of sexuality, self-conception, and self-delivery that Kritzman discovers at work in his source texts and especially in Montaigne's representative essays. In Kritzman's work, this pedagogic relation to oneself takes on all the sexual trappings of a truly American desire to give birth to oneself as a defense against what Emerson in "Compensation" sees all the shocking losses of our lives as finally composing: "the natural history of calamity" (301).

> The changes which break up at short intervals the prosperity of men are advertisements of a nature whose law is growth. Every soul is by this intrinsic necessity quitting its whole system of things, its friends, and home, and laws, and faith, as the shell-fish crawls out of its beautiful but stony case, because it no longer admits of its growth, and slowly forms a new house. In proportion to the vigor of the individual, these revolutions are frequent, until in some happier mind they are incessant, and all worldly relations hang very loosely about him, becoming, as it were, a transparent fluid member through which the living form is seen, and not, as in most men, an indurated heterogeneous fabric of many dates, and of no settled character, in which the man is imprisoned. Then there can be enlargement, and the man of to-day scarcely recognizes the many of yesterday. And such should be the outward biography of man in time, a putting off of dead circumstances day by day, as he renews his raiment day by day. But to us, in our lapsed estate, resting, not advancing, resisting, not cooperating with the divine expansion, this growth comes by shocks. (301–2)

While Emerson's transcendental rhetoric about the new American man ever about to be born allows equally for a sexual, economic, or political reading of these "shocks" to our "whole system of things," Kritzman's rhetoric, until his final chapter, is predominantly, even exclusively, sexual in its frisson. It is here that I would briefly mount my concluding genial critique.

The emergence of the new social type of the narcissistic personality in our postmodern age permits Kritzman to juxtapose his rhetoric of sexuality and French Renaissance literature. But he does not fully reflect in a critical fashion on its emergence in the profession of criticism or on what this may mean, positively and negatively, for literary studies. It is not that I expect him to play the Christopher Lasch of the profession; only that I would have greatly appreciated, besides the embedded self-critique in his final chapter, some additional critical discussion, by this brilliantly sensitive reader, of our institutional narcissism, since, as he knows, it has transformed our practice into fictive romances of oneself.[11] *The Rhetoric of Sexuality and the Literature of the French Renaissance* is clearly the finest American example of French critical theory in action since Geoffrey Hartman's now-classic essays.[12] Perhaps this is enough, and I am a touch ungrateful to ask for even more.

II Opposing Orthodoxies

6 Revisionary Madness
The Prospects of American Literary Theory at the Present Time

For if I triumph I must make men mad.
—*W. B. Yeats, "The Tower"*

Now must be the time to turn our backs on literary theory. Signs are everywhere that such a move would be advisable. Such distinctive American theorists as Harold Bloom, Stanley Fish, and Edward Said, each for his own reasons, have repeatedly warned the critical community about the dangers of doing theory in a post-structuralist mode. Everyone now knows or should know what M. H. Abrams and Gerald Graff—to identify just two of the more prominent and persistent opponents of theory—have been saying for years. The elusive, purely theoretical quest for the hidden rules governing *the system* of production, dissemination, and interpretation of texts, a quest generally informed by an essential concern to revise the academic study of literature, can lead only to the foolish positing of some single, all-determining principle of critical practice (Language, Power, Influence, etc.)—that is, to a speculative trap of self-indulgent rarefaction, in short, to an intellectual dead end—for the notion of there being a "system" reducible to a single magical formula is at best a hypothetical construct and at worst each theorist's fetching chimera, the fantastic image of his possible sublimity, his will to power over other theorists writ large and alone in the intense inane. In this light, doing theory now, in however self-conscious and ironic a fashion, would represent a radical and wasteful break with the often nostalgically invoked American tradition of pragmatically oriented, intellectually skeptical, and socially aware (if politically uncommitted) scholar-critics. [1]

This strange turnabout, in which the leading literary theorists and their disciples join hands with representatives of the loyal, neohumanist oppositions, is a paradox. It even smacks of the willfully perverse. [2] As I observe this spectacle of a new antitheoretical consensus forming right before my eyes, the question that strikes me is this: Why should American literary theorists—marginal figures with respect to the larger culture—appear to be so determined to wipe themselves out of the picture entirely, so to speak, just as they are witnessing the first fruits of their labors to institutionalize theory as a subdiscipline within the critical profession?

For one of the most immediately accessible examples of this revisionary exercise of turning against theory—one that, for me, suggests a plausible answer to my question—consider the following conclusion on the dangerous delusions of theory made recently in "Against Theory" by Steven Knapp and Walter Benn Michaels, two of theory's most perceptive students: Theory "is the name for all the ways people have tried to stand outside practice in order to govern practice from without. Our thesis had been that no one can reach a position outside practice, that theorists should stop trying, and that the theoretical enterprise should therefore come to an end" (742). [3] What is one to make of this provocative and deeply problematic conclusion?

The point that Knapp and Michaels make is an important one, especially in these revisionary days of neoconservative ascendency and other such ills. They reach their conclusion after arguing that in order to get the theoretical project off the ground and then keep it aloft, the theorist, no matter what the stripe, whether he or she is an intentionalist like E. D. Hirsch and P. D. Juhl or a deconstructive ironist like Paul deMan and Fish, must assume that some "ultimate" vantage point beyond the discursive field under scrutiny can in principle be envisioned and separated out from the realm of practice and what they call "true belief." [4] Only if the theorist assumes that such a synoptic view and such an apocalyptic separation are possible (even if that view is of the abyss and that separation is really a self-incarceration) can the theorist pretend to knowledge and so to a command of the underlying rules governing the field. Whatever such "knowledge" may portend—human freedom or some depersonalizing fate at the hands of Power, Language, or Precursor—makes little practical difference to the success of the theoretical project. The only thing that matters is the theorist's belief in his prospects of attaining that all-determining higher ground, however "fictional" that position is programmatically said to be by any particular theorist. Clearly, Knapp and Michaels do not believe that such a vantage point is possible or, for that matter, that belief in such a possibility is anything more than an act of bad faith, whether made in the good taste of ironic self-consciousness or not. Consequently, for them, questions such as whether the human subject masters language or language masters the human subject are meaningless, akin to the theosophists' disputes about the possibility of the dead experiencing sensual pleasure in the afterlife. In this respect, Knapp and Michaels follow Fish. For their master Fish, all objectivist, idealist, or transcendental tendencies to posit a position beyond the strident intricacies of critical practice and its wars of true belief are merely projections of the theorist's desire for such an ideal vantage point. This is the case, for Fish, no matter how hedged about such tendencies may be by ironic qualifications, opaque terminologies, and deconstructive posturings. Such tendencies, then, produce a wish-fulfilling bit of phantasmagoria, a dream of escape from the arid conflicts involved in the actual world of strenuous critical argument. One needs relief, so one simply spells it "o-a-s-i-s," or "i-s-l-a-n-d," or "t-o-w-e-r."[5]

But Knapp and Michaels do not stop with their repetition of Fish. They go on to claim that he who originally made possible their critical insight into the mechanisms of theory production has recently suffered an acute lapse from his formerly rigorous position.[6] By trying to establish his view of the reader's share in the constitution of the text as the best theory of interpretation, Fish has attempted to set up his hermeneutics (and so himself as well) as the governing principle of mediation operating among the different conflicting interpretive communities. Knapp and Michaels contend, therefore, that Fish, who had once assumed he could eradicate the crime of critical theory—with the help of his ironic theory of the reader's imaginative response to the self-consuming text—has instead perpetuated that crime. After using Fish to deconstruct Juhl and deMan and, in turn, using Fish's own arguments to deconstruct Fish himself, Knapp and Michaels, true to their principle of repressing "the theoretical impulse," refuse to offer a theory—or even an antitheory—of their own to account adequately for either the interpretive practices they have partially discussed or those they have implicitly employed. Instead, their conclusion shows, they end up calling for the death of theory. Or it might be more appropriate to say that they retreat from the sublime abyss (or is it the revisionary void?) and offer to the poor pathetic figure of the literary theorist a good old hefty Anglo-Saxon broadsword upon which to fall: "Despite his explicit disclaimers, [Fish] thinks a true account of belief must be a *theory* about belief, whereas we think a true account of belief can only be a *belief* about belief" (740).

This ironic spectacle of the "self-dispatching genius," quite explicit here, is now being staged repeatedly throughout the profession, with more or less subtlety, for other theorists by their former students and allies.[7] I point to this development not to blame or to praise anyone; nor am I interested in the phenomenon as a clue to new trends in intellectual fashions. Rather, I find this recent opposition to theory representative of the manner in which I still see the revisionary imagination operating generally in our "postmodern" culture. That is, it exhausts, virtually as it opens up, those all-too-briefly viable alternatives of intellectual production outside the normal range of conventional procedures. In light of this ironic style of the revisionary imagination, I want to propose a deliberately dramatic analogy between revisionism and madness, a self-mocking "theory" of their mutually penetrating interplay. I do so less to explain Knapp and Michaels or others away than to offer provocation in return. What follows, then, is meant to be taken as a caricature of the revisionary imagination of American literary theorists.

Schopenhauer in *The World as Will and Representation* characterizes madness as a traumatic derangement of the memory. In so doing, he provides us with a useful analogy for the more extreme forms of the revisionary imagination as they appear throughout modern culture. The madman, according to the great pessimist, remembers the past only in a highly selective, discontinuous manner, while the future appears to him as a looming blank. Ironically enough, the present appears to him more or less exactly as it does to the rest of us. As a result of his memory lapses, the madman must invent an illusory continuity for himself and an illusory context for everyone else, a textual identity and a textual world, essentially metaphorical and associative in nature and wholly rhetorical in effect. As he fills up the gaps in his memory with consoling or terrifying fictions and presses them into service, the madman begins to take these unsuccessful transfigurations of certain unbearable aspects of an irrational reality for "truthful" (i.e., "pragmatically" useful) representations of what is to him an ultimately comprehensible world. Such mad inventions quickly fall into one of two basic pathological categories: that of the melancholic's ruling obsession or fixed idea; or that of the maniac's or fool's purely random improvisations. "The madman," Schopenhauer remarks, "always carries about in his faculty of reason a past in the abstract, but it is a false past that exists for him alone, and that either all the time or merely for the moment. The influence of this false past then prevents the use of the correctly known present."[8] Like Freud after him, Schopenhauer traces in psychological terms a mode of interpretive activity that informs the shape and significance of critical practices.

One could argue, then, that each would-be revisionist structures his reading of a particular precursor or entire tradition of precursors in such a way as to suggest that at a certain point in the precursor's writing career or in the development of a tradition, he or the tradition went wrong and started to resemble Schopenhauer's madman.[9] That is, the precursor or tradition begins to become, for the revisionist, a dangerously destructive, even self-destructive, influence that can be neither contained nor rehabilitated without resorting to exorbitant, even violent, interpretive measures.

Thus the more systematic and theoretical the revisionist, the more he appears to be like the chronically anxious melancholic trotting out his master obsession at every opportunity so as to provoke and then ward off another saving attack of his self-defining anxiety. The more practically oriented "pluralistic" interpreter, who makes the most of all critical means, would accordingly become the pure fool or jolly maniac. And, of course, one can imagine some really "disturbed" critic, with little or no identity of his own—a monster of deconstructive irony, moving "playfully" between these dialectical extremes. In any event, no matter how one construes the underlying conditions for this process—whether in figures drawn from individual psychology, communal ideology, economic theory and practice, or the various histories of institutions, disciplines, and cultures—the textual consequences and the rhetorical effects appear to be the same: in case after case, the critical reader witnesses in the revisionist's text the past being condemned in the name of an enlightened ideal of "liberation" or "sanity" that is to be fully realized in some future time; this ideal, humanistic, even utopian in its dimensions, is derived by the revisionist from what are, ironically enough, essentially literary images lifted out of an even earlier fabulous or mythic past.[10] In other, more metaphorical words, the dialectic of modern revisionism runs the gamut from Don Quixote inflation to Sancho Panza reduction and back again, without any apparent end in sight. In Nietzsche's prophetic words from *Zarathustra,* words that as sublime parody illustrate perfectly both the pattern I have described and the appropriate attitude toward it, "Not only the reason of millennia, but their madness, too, breaks out in us."[11] This situation, I find, is inescapable now.

I don't think that the point has to be belabored. In "Against Theory" Knapp and Michaels, no matter what their intentions, act rhetorically like so many others these days, in a manner that suggests Schopenhauer's understanding of madness as a systematic derangement of the memory. Knapp and Michaels selectively recall portions of texts by Juhl, deMan, and Fish and fill in the gaps between them with their own cleverly argued inventions, drawn from various incompatible and generally unnamed sources (Gadamer, Foucault, Bloom, etc.), all so that they can point out exactly where the critical theorist repeatedly goes wrong. In this way they can make a "valid" call for him to close up shop. What they have done, in order to triumph over their tradition, is to revise it into oblivion.[12] But their triumph is a hollow one, since in place of it they offer only the same old spectacle of critical practice we have known for years. It is as if in fulfilling the dialectical pattern of revisionary interpretation, by playing in their essay the Panzaic critics to the entire tradition of Quixotic theorists, Knapp and Michaels have destroyed the world of their fathers, only to return us to that of our grandfathers, the world of the new critics and the gentleman-scholars of literary history (that is, the world of true belief par excellence, before the advent of Northrop Frye). The irony of such a fulfillment is, of course, that Knapp and Michaels would not fit into such a world. [13]

The effect of their polemic is that it leaves the field open to the long-established and well-heeled native American fly-by-the-seat-of-one's-pants critical pragmatists and know-nothings, who have been waiting in the wings ever since the late sixties for such boring annoyances as critical theory, feminism, affirmative action programs, and so forth to disappear; we then can go back to doing business as usual, waging our polite and sensible battles over the sources and significances of some line in Pound's *Pisan Cantos* or Joyce's manuscript drafts of *Finnegans Wake*. [14] I am not saying that Knapp and Michaels consciously intend, as Richard Rorty apparently does, to take us back to John Dewey, Williams James, and "Ol' Virginie," only that the effect of their argument, especially on students, is likely to make unavailable, or at least less attractive and ever so much more difficult, a career option that has only recently been introduced in the profession and that has been so strenuously fought for—doing critical theory. [15] It is almost as if the attitude informing their essay were "Well, we are making places for ourselves, so to hell with all those coming after us." But perhaps this is too harsh a characterization, and their attitude would be better characterized as that of a latter-day Samson in the temple of his enemies, blind, self-destructively powerful, and full of the Lord's righteous anger at all the degradation he senses around (and within) him. I suppose, however, that whether the antitheoretical impulse underlying the essay is cynical or moral makes little practical difference, for the rhetorical effect is essentially nihilistic, and so even in the best possible light the essay aids and comforts the champions of the status quo.

Yet even this conclusion would not be so bad. After all, we have been living so long with one apocalyptic nihilism after another appearing in our culture that one more hardly seems to matter. The problem with Knapp's and Michael's argument lies in its antidemocratic, genius-will-out assumption that one can just do criticism. What they fail to realize is that by clearing the air of theory they have also taken away from students the means necessary to do criticism at all. They fail to realize, in other words, that the primary function of critical theory is not to make the theorist king of the hill but to submit to others for evaluation models for doing criticism. The questions of intention and meaning, of knowledge and belief, do not center around the possibility of apocalyptically envisioning an absolute vantage point separated from critical practice. The critical theorist need not aspire to become the pope, nor need he be seen as the Antichrist. Theorists' models are always experimental, "proved," if that is the right word, by the fact that they aid in getting certain kinds of intellectual work done. (And only some form of "truth" or effective knowledge can ever provide such aid.)[16] While we may want to quarrel with a particular model, so long as we are engaged in teaching students how to read and understand texts, then we must provide them with models of critical activity that they can assimilate and learn to execute successfully, with the ultimate sign of success being, of course, the student's production of his or her own more workable model. At the very least, we must provide students with a style of intellectual production that they can admire and find morally satisfying.

The question, however, is not primarily one of educational self-interest—that to stay in the big business of higher education we need to do certain things to maximize our position vis-à-vis the sciences; rather, the question is more broadly educational. Given that we have a certain number of students who are still committed to the study of literature and its relations to the entire range of cultural production, how do we meet our responsibilities to serve their needs and to reinforce that commitment? Do we attempt, in short, to preserve, develop, and enlarge their access to all the means whereby they can express and establish themselves as critical thinkers in their chosen vocation? Or do we allow the nihilistic implications of theory to combine with the economic fiats coming from Washington, the various state capitals, and college administration offices to destroy the profession by reducing the study of literature to an adjunct of the teaching of composition? Shouldn't we try to defend the profession or, if not, propose viable alternatives to it? It is all too easy today to succumb to cynicism and despair or, worst of all, to become reconciled to the silly spectacle of professional opportunists, old and young alike, anxious for their careers, perpetually jockeying for position, just like a bunch of drones buzzing around their one and only queen.

What, then, should the critic do? What is the critic's role? What ought it to be? What can it be? To begin to answer such questions, I want to examine now the interpretive practices of two of our most influential critics, Emerson and Frye. By focusing on these figures respectively from the distant and the more recent past, I hope to abstract from the rhetorical strategies in two of their central works those underlying principles of critical activity that may provide us with the basis for a viable model of doing criticism that we can learn to practice for our own collective benefit. My project, then, would be an example of "monumental history" in Nietzsche's sense of the term in "Of the Advantage and Disadvantage of History of Life." I turn to the past not to find some all-determining overview but rather to recover from other bad times inspiring possibilities of imaginative survival that may be applicable in this time of revisionary nightmares.

The two works by Emerson and Frye are "The Divinity School Address" (1838) and "The Imaginative and the Imaginary" (1962). Both are lectures, given from generally unconventional points of view to potentially hostile audiences composed almost entirely of experts on the topics. Emerson and Frye both attempt to distinguish the principle of authentic creativity in religion and literature from the degraded conventional forms available in their cultures. And both attempt to convert their audiences to their points of view. To this end, they argue synoptically, ranging widely over the entire sweep of religious and cultural history for their examples, and conclude their performances on an emotional, even prophetic note, as they defend the freely creating mind against the enormous pressures of society, in a valiant attempt to make possible a more enlightened, free, and humane future. In other words, they embrace the dialectic of revisionism, refuse to remain stuck in its reductive phase, and attempt to turn it to their own visionary purposes, against the background of darkening hopes in the times that saw, respectively, the movement to the Mexican War and the debacle in Vietnam.

The differences between the pieces are of no less interest. Emerson, of course, eschews all mediating structures standing between the individual soul and its visionary prospects as he separates the true religion of moral sentiment from its fallen embodiments in historical creeds, including that of Christianity. In trying to convert his audience of newly ordained Unitarian ministers to his "doctrine of the soul," Emerson condemns as preposterous impositions all the dogmas, rites, and traditional practices to which these young ministers plan to devote their lives. For Emerson, such degraded and degrading forms encourage a self-defeating imitation of outworn practices. For this reason he admonishes his audience, in a more radical fashion than even his heirs Knapp and Michaels do, "to go alone; to refuse the good models. . . . Imitation cannot go above its model. The imitator dooms himself to hopeless mediocrity. The inventor did it because it was natural to him, and so in him it has a charm. In the imitator something else is natural, and he bereaves himself of his own beauty, to come short of another man's."[17] Following from this radical advice ("dare to love God," he also enjoins us, "without mediator or veil"), Emerson concludes that not even a new religion can be efficacious, since one cult makes little difference (81). All cults are gratuitous obstacles to the freely creating soul, that genius of the race that acts through the genius of individual men. Only the new Teacher of the venerable but always fresh doctrine of the soul can make a real difference. For only such a Teacher will be able to unite in his visionary oracles the various fragments of the religious and scientific cultures of Emerson's time:

> The question returns, What shall we do?
> I look for the hour when that supreme Beauty which ravished the soul of those Eastern men, and chiefly of those Hebrews, and through their lips spoke oracles to all time, shall speak in the West also. . . .
> I look for the new Teacher that shall follow so far those shining laws that he shall see them come full circle; shall see their rounding complete grace; shall see the world to be the mirror of the soul; shall see the identity of the law of gravitation with purity of heart; and shall show that the Ought, that Duty, is one thing with Science, with Beauty, and with Joy. (82, 84)

Emerson would thus complete and make whole the fragmentary oracles of past beauty by replacing the educational apparatuses of American institutions with this immediate vision of spiritual reality, a vision that the inspiring presence of the prophetic Teacher, who glows with truth, will represent in the minds of his auditors.

Frye, on the other hand, not only concedes to his psychiatric audience an important mediating role (they help the suffering individual adjust to the harsh realities of social life), but he assumes that all institutional operatives should ideally stand in a similar position. Unlike Emerson, who proposes his antinomian, radically revisionary

doctrine of the freely creating soul, Frye barely sketches in but nonetheless heavily relies on the solid "doctrinal" basis of his theoretical
system as adumbrated in the *Anatomy of Criticism* (1957).

In fact, as he traces the development of Renaissance literary notions
of melancholy and mania to the psychoanalytic complexes of anxiety
neurosis and mass hysteria, one observes how his own essay repeats in
miniature the major visionary theme and form of the larger, genially
satiric work. Finally, Frye turns not to the idea of a prophetic educator
who will radiate a new vision of health and spiritual freedom but to
the implicitly moral visions embedded in two canonical texts, *Don
Quixote* and *The Prelude*—visions so subtle and refined that only the
discerning if self-effacing literary critic can make them manifest to
others, thanks to his powerful historical memory. The critic is able to
discern and then teach others to discern "the solid core of moral reality
in the middle of [Don Quixote's] fantasy that holds the loyalty not
only of Sancho but of the teachers of his adventures."[18] Thus, the critic enables us to recover "the child's vision" of "a golden age," "something that makes Quixotes of us all, and gives our minds, too, whatever dignity they may possess" (165). Similarly, it is the critic in
Wordsworth who can read in his dream of the "semi-Quixote," who
flees from "some unimaginable catastrophe" while carrying a stone
and a shell that are also books representative of words and numbers, a
parable of the plight facing any imaginative person living in apocalyptic times. Wordsworth's semi-Quixote bears the emblems of "the
two great instruments that man has invented for transforming reality" (166). That is, the critic, like the fictional visionary, must seek to
preserve human culture, no matter what the odds.

Frye concludes his lecture by endorsing and updating Wordsworth's remarkable vision of the semi-Quixote in order to win over his
audience of presumably tough-minded psychiatrists. First, Frye
quotes Wordsworth as the latter testifies to having realized how much
akin to this Don Quixote figure he actually is, how fully he identifies
with "a Being thus employ'd." Wordsworth goes on to say that given
a similar intimation of apocalypse he could go upon "a like errand,"
leaving all else behind and come to share completely in "that maniac's
anxiousness." Second, Frye rounds out his elucidating commentary
on the apparently apocalyptic vagaries of the visionary imagination by
revising Wordsworth and Cervantes and making them appropriate for

our time: "Perhaps in the age of the useless bomb-shelter it may be easier for us than it was even for Wordsworth to understand that if the human race is to have any future at all, it can only obtain it through a concern for preserving its powers of creation which it will be difficult, if not impossible, to distinguish clearly from a 'Maniac's anxiousness'" (165–66). Subtly, carefully, Frye insinuates into the mind of his audience this possible distinction between the authentically creative visions of the truly imaginative creator and the anxiety-ridden phantasmagoria of the neurotic, only to end up suggesting that, given such an age as ours, so literally apocalyptic, this distinction, so important to preserve, may turn out to be moot, as the visions of the creator and the nightmares of the madman come to seem, to neither's benefit, in the glittering shadow of the mushroom cloud, identically eerie.[19]

The differences between Emerson and Frye could not be any more striking than in their conclusions. Emerson stands proudly at the beginning of the historical processes that formed the institution of literary study, and he freely projects his prophetic image of the Teacher to come, the Messiah figure to whom he sees himself as precursor.[20] This quite open self-portrayal accounts for the self-conscious circular structure of his talk. For what at the end of the lecture he predicts for the Teacher, he himself has already partially fulfilled in his rhapsodic, biblical-sounding opening:

> In this refulgent summer, it has been a luxury to draw the breath of life. The grass grows, the buds burst, the meadow is spotted with fire and gold in the tint of flowers. The air is full of birds, and sweet with the breath of the pine, the balm-of-Gilead, and the new hay. Night brings no gloom to the heart with its welcome shade. Through the transparent darkness the stars pour their almost spiritual rays. Man under them seems a young child, and his huge globe a toy. . . . One is constrained to respect the perfection of this world in which our senses converse. How wide; how rich; what invitation from every property it gives to every faculty of man! . . . it is well worth the pith and heart of great men to subdue and enjoy it. The planters, the mechanics, the inventors, the astronomers, the builders of cities, and the captains, history delights to honor. (67)

Clearly, Emerson is doing here what he calls for at the end of his talk and creating a vision, apparently like that of the Hebrew prophets, which, in uniting the laws of the spirit with those of matter, goes much further than any biblical precedent. In short, Emerson structures his performance as a self-fulfilling prophecy by playing Christ to his own John the Baptist.[21]

Everything crucial about Emerson's lecture is in the Protestant. Romantic, visionary tradition; and everything crucial about Frye's lecture fits the Anglo-Catholic, commonsensical, modernist tradition of criticism.[22] Whereas Emerson sounds like a prophet and projects himself as thee precursor of the new, strangely sensual, and materialistic Messiah to come, Frye not only sounds like a professional academic but projects himself as the Sancho Panza–like appreciator (rather than denigrator) of all the semi-Quixotes in our Western literary tradition:

> In Part Two of the book, Quixote and Sancho come into the dominions of a duke who has read Part One, and who, to amuse himself, makes Sancho the governor of an island. We are perhaps less surprised than he to learn that Sancho rules his island so honestly and efficiently that he has to be pulled out of office in a hurry before he starts to disintegrate the Spanish aristocracy. We are even less surprised to find that Quixote's advice to him is full of gentle and shrewd good sense. The world is still looking for that lost island, and it still asks for nothing better than to have Sancho Panza for its ruler and Don Quixote for his honoured counsellor. (165–66)

If Frye in his more genial manner would play, as do Knapp and Michaels in their reductive fashion, Sancho Panza to all our quixotic visionaries, he must know that he appears to his audience of plain honest men like the "honoured counsellor" in his reading of *Don Quixote*. Frye's sense of his possible self-images and of his audience's possible self-recognitions is every bit as powerful and acute as Emerson's, only in a different register—that of critical irony rather than of the critical sublime. Such self-conscious art unites Emerson and Frye, despite the differences previously underlined.

In fact these works now begin to resemble each other again. When Emerson adopts the prophetic mode and strikes the heroic stance as he points to the early version of the central man trope, he stresses how this new Teacher is to be incarnated in his own texts by means of the self-fulfilling circular structure of his talk. Similarly Frye, although he adopts the plain-speaking mode and strikes an ironic posture, also points to a great facilitator of the moral vision now implicit in literary texts—that reflexive critic who is cut, subliminally at least, in the minds of his auditors as they attempt to follow his authoritative citations and interpretations of texts not immediately available to everyone's memory. My point is not, however, that Emerson and Frye are the same and that both of them are touched in the head because, à la Knapp and Michaels, they set themselves up as hermeneutic gods; nor is it that Frye fulfills Emerson's prophecy of the new Teacher and Knapp and Michaels fulfill Frye's worst fears concerning a "Maniac's anxiousness"; rather, what I hope to suggest by comparing Emerson and Frye is that some experimental, yes, even "theoretical," generalizations about their practices can be made, generalizations that could suggest the outlines of a model of doing criticism that one could characterize—good heavens!—as rational and affirmative.

But can one really abstract common critical principles from these related but also very different works? Naturally, I believe that one can. So far as I can see, there are six such principles of critical activity.[23] I term the first one the "principle of opposition." Whatever the religious, political, or aesthetic ideology of the critic, he or she should strive to maintain an oppositional stance vis-à-vis the dominant conventions in the discipline and, more generally, in society. This principle should not be implemented blindly, of course, nor in a reflexlike manner. The critic's opposition must arise from the particular situation of the profession. Consider, for example, how Emerson confronts directly the bankruptcy of the clerisy with his doctrine of the freely creating soul, a prophetic provocation, as it were. Or take Frye. He patiently and wittily traces the origins of psychoanalysis back to its roots in the literary imagination and so disarms in advance the audience's potential critique of literature. In both cases the critic opposes the specter of historical or psychological determinism on behalf of the human imagination. Such a stance must continue to be adopted given the various determinisms of the right and the left, of the old guard and the deconstructive cutting edge.

My second principle is that of "accommodation." It follows naturally from the first. It requires the critic, in turning to the past or the future for inspiration, to address directly and honestly, without the coy evasions of self-conscious irony, the intellectual needs of the interpretive community. Frye, for instance, gives his lecture in 1962 amid the bomb-shelter craze, a time that saw not only the beginnings of American escalation in Vietnam but the Cuban missile crisis as well. This background explains, in part, Frye's manner of updating the moral vision embedded in the texts of Wordsworth and Cervantes.[24] Frye accommodates the vision of these texts and the situation of his time to one other. Similarly, Emerson enunciates his "doctrine of the soul"—that there are immutable spiritual laws arising out of man's moral nature that can make prophets of us all—in order to rouse himself and his audience from its dogmatic or cynical slumber. Thus, the principle of accommodation means more than just topicality; it means, as well, that the critic must attempt to comprehend in as systematic a fashion as possible the relationship between his profession and the needs of the community at large—a task that one could argue defines the theoretical enterprise Knapp and Michaels want to bring to an end.

The third principle is the "principle of judgment." However difficult it may seem today to draw any hard and fast distinctions between the authentically creative imagination and the merely conventional, degraded, or empty form, the critic must make the attempt—especially if he is going to ask others to devote their lives to a vocation dedicated to the appreciation and analysis of cultural productions. If the last principle is crucial to the theoretical enterprise, then this one is crucial to the practice of criticism. Even Emerson, for all his antinomianism, does not ask his audience to abandon Christianity in despair or to found a new religion; rather he enjoins them to infuse the old forms with the new spirit of his doctrine of the soul. Similarly, although Frye claims that it may become increasingly difficult to distinguish a maniac's anxiousness from creative energy, he does not propose to stop trying to do so, as the title of his piece indicates.

The fourth principle, that of "programmatic action," means that whether the critic points to the living examples of particular individuals or holds up models of a critical system, he ought to propose some program of intellectual activity, no matter how experimental, provisional, or revisionary. This principle is obviously the hardest to define to everyone's satisfaction. But given the examples of Emerson and Frye, let me attempt to speculate on some practical suggestions. Both Emerson and Frye in their talks provide occasions for what in "Spir-

itual Laws" Emerson calls our moments of "revisal" or "correction."
These are "epochs of our life" in which "a silent thought by the way-
side as we walk . . . revises our entire manner of life and says—'Thus
hast thou done, but it were better thus' " (206). In other words, Emerson and Frye act on our imagination in a way that calls us to judgment. They suggest why we must convert to a faith in the creative
power of the human imagination. Whether or not we can summon up
the will for such a faith is an open question.

The fifth principle, that of "formal self-effacement," means that no
matter how obviously or subtly one presents oneself as either a cultural Messiah or a plain honest man ("one of us"), the critic should subordinate the impulse to promote himself to the larger communicable
vision he is proposing for critical evaluation. On the face of it, this
principle would seem to be the one that needs little or no comment.
We all detest the critic who encourages a cult of personality to spring
up around him, no matter what kind of cult or personality may be
involved. Both the later Eliot's studied modesty and Bloom's chronic
afflatus often detract from the fine points they would make.[25] Neither
Emerson nor Frye, despite their self-projections, seems like either the
sly priest with an insidious doctrine to insinuate or the great man
with the big voice. However one sees their textual identities, Emerson and Frye put themselves forward as heralds of a positive vision of
spiritual laws and imaginative creation. They are trying to articulate a
vision for their particular communities. Their styles, which facilitate
rather than frustrate communication, testify to this motivation. But
their representative status does not depend solely on the authority of
their styles; rather, it depends as much—perhaps more—on the
quality and care that their styles reveal.

Finally, the sixth principle is that of "self-revision." However unpropitious the times, however similar he or she makes critical idealism and critical nihilism seem, the critic should try to ground the
education of students on a heuristic or regulative ideal of critical activity that can lead them out of their apprenticeship to any particular
system or methodology into their scholarly maturity so that they may
become the originators of their own stances and accommodating theories.[26] Recall Emerson and Frye once again. They do not turn against
the soul or the imagination, or even against the ministry or the profession of psychiatry, simply because the age seems to demand an ironic

image of its accelerated grimace. Instead they critique the present decadence in the name of an intentionally open-ended, admittedly prophetic vision of human potential—a vision clearly derived from the cultural past. That is, they too practice monumental history in Nietzsche's sense and take the risk that their "modest proposals" *for* something might also make them seem eligible, in some people's eyes, for the madhouse.

I offer these six principles in barest outline. I do so not simply for provocation's sake. The profession is in horrible shape, and we must begin addressing the situation seriously. If you were a graduate student now and had just finished reading "Against Theory," would you willingly choose to belong to a profession that appears to be openly and irremediably nihilistic? Whoever *did* enter the profession would help to turn it into a haven for the hopelessly neurotic, at best, or, at worst, an asylum for the purely pathological. And unless one has some perverse, self-destructive need to play (whether intentionally or not) Sancho Panza to one's own Don Quixote, or Emerson of "Experience" to Emerson of "Self-Reliance," or even Knapp and Michaels to their own Fish, the question of the function of criticism at the present time demands to be treated and not left to the sublime cynicism of Schopenhauer or any of his belated avatars: "The mind, tormented so greatly, destroys, as it were, the thread of its memory, fills up the gaps with fictions, and thus seeks refuge in madness from the mental suffering that exceeds its strength, just as a limb affected by mortification is cut off and replaced with a wooden one."[27] Could it be, I wonder, as Schopenhauer's remarks ironically suggest, that what, for the sake of argument, one can fairly characterize as revisionary madness could also be seen as an uncanny restoration to health? Could it be that our profession had to go through its deconstructive phase in order to begin over again, what was apparently lost in new critical method having been supplemented by even more powerful interpretive techniques grafted from continental sources? Would this mean that the critic best embodies Freud's image from *Civilization and Its Discontents* of man as a prosthetic god? Or does this mean only that the would-be revisionist who entertains such a vision is possessed by a "gaiety transfiguring all that dread," because he may soon become as plainly mad as the next university don?[28]

7 Critical Change and the Collective Archive

For a complex set of reasons, some of which I will explore in this chapter, critics today have little good to say about their work or, at times, even about themselves. Listen to what one of America's leading literary critics recently has said on the subject:[1]

All of the current critical schools in the United States and Britain and France and Germany, I guess, almost without exception . . . could be linked together. Whether you call it deconstruction, Marxism or neo-Marxism, feminism, black and hispanic, New Historicism, it is exactly what Nietzsche called Resentment with a capital R. They really should be called the School of Resentment. The last critics with whom I can fully empathize would be Ruskin and Pater and Oscar Wilde. I mean, it strikes me that criticism and literature are either primarily aesthetic or they're something other than criticism and literature. But I sometimes wonder if there can be five people beneath the age of 40 now teaching literature in the better universities and colleges in the United States who have ever in all their days loved a poem for being a poem or a story or a novel for being a story or a novel. They are looking for social utility; they are looking for something. . . . The primary question always has to be, "is this a good poem, or is it just verse?"

That it is Harold Bloom who is making this indictment of the School of Resentment is, of course, almost amusing. Bloom is the critic who, in attributing a fiercely competitive sense of anxious belatedness to the Great Dead, made the public attribution of a resentful will-to-power motive informing every text virtually respectable in contemporary criticism. If any one critic can be said to be responsible for a lowering of the tone of criticism, of making criticism more the embodiment of what Nietzsche, referring to *ressentiment,* calls "the spirit of revenge," rather than of magnanimity, it is certainly Harold Bloom.

Bloom's remarks against so-called political correctness are important, however, not simply because they expose the fundamental contradiction of his own prominent position. Nor does their importance lie in their rearguard, elitist, and humanistic recuperation of the purely aesthetic formulation of literature and literary study. The fact that Bloom sounds more like William Bennett, Reagan's former Secretary of Education, Bush's former Drug Czar, and Arnold's would-be heir, is telling, but not crucial to my argument. What is crucial is that these remarks expose the representative anxiety of the profession concerning the highly vulnerable sense of place that any critic, including (perhaps especially so) a major critic, now feels. Although Bloom characteristically casts this anxiety of place, of status, in generational and Oedipal terms, what his remarks really disclose is the revisionary conditions of work in the profession of literary study. These are perceived to be conditions of perpetual change that promote the ideology of perpetual novelty. Historical changes envisioned and executed for particular institutional and political ends of liberation are subsumed by and in the formal processes of revisionism as merely the latest examples of the profession at work, or as in Bloom's psychologizing indictment, the profession's venerable business of *ressentiment* as usual operating under the guise of "making it new."

To discover the most effective analysis of the forms of change within interpretive communities such as professions, however, we must turn to the latest work of Stanley Fish. But before doing so, I must admit that I am less interested here in all the details of his typically brilliant analyses than I am in the demoralizing vision of the profession that his neutrally stated conclusions unintentionally promote. For the purpose of my present argument, I am willing to stipulate that his analyses are generally persuasive, even as I plan to challenge the key unexamined belief in the continuing power of instrumental reason underlying his representation of the institutional mechanisms of change in the profession's ideological practices. Fish concludes a recent article entitled "Change" with characteristic insouciance:[2]

> Perhaps the most persistent charge against the notion of interpretive communities is that it seems to make disciplinary and professional activity its own end. But, since that end itself is continually changing, the charge can be cheerfully embraced because it says only that the members of a community will always believe in the ends for which they work, and that therefore their work will never be ended even though it will be ceaselessly transformed. (444)

Fish's conclusion captures in pure form the vision of the profession as profession, as an endlessly self-revising interpretive community with no definite final end in sight, other than the perpetuation of its own ceaselessly transformed and transforming, revisionary or modernizing, projects. Fish has already claimed that such a vision of the profession neither promotes nor inhibits any particular social agenda or course of political action or historical change. Whether partisans of the "right" or the "left" ultimately prevail in professional terms is made entirely the "determination of empirical fact," according to the victorious community's established procedures, that will take place after the successful takeover operation has occurred. In short, Fish's "theoretical" model of change would be entirely practical and pragmatic, and not predictive of specific changes, even as it does represent itself as the general intelligible form of all such changes of the professional guard imaginable. "In all of these cases, and in any others that can be imagined, a theory of change is inscribed in the self-description that at once directs and renders intelligible the characteristic labors of the workers in the community" (442).

I think Fish is basically correct here. History does emerge in criticism as the assumed theory of change implicit in any interpretive community's self-description of its labors. The key and worrisome point in this last quotation, however, is the innocuous-sounding phrase "renders intelligible." According to what standard is the process of rendering intelligible going to be carried out and judged, especially while the struggle for control of any aspect of the profession is still continuing? Or rather, according to whose standard of judgment is any of the mechanisms of professional change to be analyzed and evaluated? Clearly, it must be a community's—or at least some group's—standard, but which community or group? And is there a standard of judgment that all interpretive communities or critical groups in the profession share in common? And, finally, is this commonly shared standard of judgment, as the above quotation suggests, universally "true," that is, simply the state of affairs for any and all imaginable cases of critical change? From one set of representative remarks, Fish does appear to endorse a particular standard of judgment as the standard of judgment currently and continually operating in the profession:

> Does an interpretive community encourage or license change by relieving its members of any responsibility to the world or to the text, or does it inhibit change by refusing to take into account anything that is contrary to its assumptions and interests? The bulk of this essay has been concerned to demonstrate that this question, in either its left or right versions, is misconceived: since an interpretive community is an engine of change, there is no status quo to protect, for its operations are inseparable from the transformation of both its assumptions and interests; and since the change that is inevitable is also orderly— constrained by evidentiary procedures and tacit understandings that at once enable change and are changed by what they enable—license and willful irresponsibility are never possibilities. (440)

The standard of judgment that Fish takes as operative in the profession now and throughout all the changes to come is one that recognizes endless modernization, constant change, as definitive for any profession as a profession and yet clearly enforces an orderly form of all such changes upon the community by means of the enabling constraints of certain "evidentiary procedures and tacit understandings"—that is, by means of the post-Enlightenment mode of human rationality known as instrumental reason. Given this belief, Fish reassures his community, "license and willful irresponsibility are never possibilities."

For example, in his commentary on the essays collected in *The New Historicism* entitled "The Young and the Restless," Fish argues that the contributors who speak to theoretical matters all worry about the same problem or impasse—how to do new historical research with valid truth claims while accepting the now-established poststructuralist principle of the textuality of all facts. Fish's response to their dilemma is interesting and typical of his practice and position. He claims that the principle of the textuality of all facts is one that functions solely in the critical practice known as theory, whereas doing specific historical research, making specific historical claims and mounting specific arguments in their support are particular activities in the critical practice known as literary or cultural history writing. For him, there is no necessary connection between the practice of theory and the practice of history; that is, no necessary consequences for the practice of history follow from the principles of theory. New historicism or any other form of poststructuralism is merely a theoretical superstructure, as it were, that rests upon and is governed finally by the same pragmatic base of rational argument and empirical criteria of judgment, that is, upon the strategies of rhetorical persuasion, as has always been the case. Styles of persuasion may change somewhat; what counts as a good argument or proof may fit the moment, but the general forms of persuasion, the appearance of rationality (or, shall we say, rationalization), the appeal to what the community knows conventionally to be the case—all these things constituting the schemes of critical reason remain fundamentally the same.

> A conviction that all facts rest finally on shifting or provisional grounds will not produce shifting and provisional facts because the grounds on which facts rest are themselves particular, having to do with traditions of inquiry, divisions of labor among the disciplines, acknowledged and unacknowledged assumptions (about what's valuable, pertinent, weighty). Of course, these grounds are open to challenge and disestablishment but the challenge, in order to be effective, will have to be as particular as they are; the work of challenging the grounds will not be done by the demonstration (however persuasive) that they are generally challengeable. [3]

Theory, in short, has no practical consequences or effects at the level of everyday or "normal" criticism. Only the practical counts for

Fish, and it does so in terms of long-established criteria of rational or, rather, rationalizing argument and appeals to empirical facts that everyone in one's community conventionally admits. Although Fish does acknowledge the principle that each interpretive community may decide again what counts as reasonable or factual, he also claims that in practice the intelligible forms of critical work continue, however much or little their theoretical and material contents change. Fish's pragmatism, in sum, is really the latest mode of formalism. To displace any one historical claim by another thus requires, in Fish's view, that we play the current version of the long-established game of arguments and proofs, and so the conventional forms of debate go on, acting to inhibit if not to preclude from the conceptable space of critical debate new objects of analysis or newly recovered materials of the past. An analogy with the legal profession may be appropriate here. The basic structure and procedures of contestation in the profession remain generally the same despite new laws, new precedents outmoding older ones, new styles of law giving, and new theories of law. That is, the system of legal practice retains its basic shape and structure of authority. The law is Fish's model for how a profession works, and because it is, he can claim that "licence and willful irresponsibility are never possibilities" in literary study, because our formal "evidentiary procedures and tacit understandings" work to preclude the very emergence of all truly radical possibilities, which have always been dismissed "out of court," as it were, as merely "license and willfull irresponsibility."

Fish's version of instrumental reason, these "evidentiary procedures and tacit understandings," is greatly revised and qualified for the contemporary scene. No individual autonomous faculty of rationality, as in Kant, Fish's "reason" is simply a community's agreed-upon set of "evidentiary procedures and tacit understandings," a historically specific form of human rationality, clearly masquerading as a universal standard of reason, whose successful deployment is the prerogative of certain classes of people within highly selective social and professional circumstances. (As we shall see, Fish later identifies this "reason" as "rhetorical man.") Such selectivity, however, necessarily restricts considerably and often effectively proscribes the power of such reason to make a significant structural difference in the larger world or even within the confines of the profession or those of any of its interpretive communities. The often intricate and sophisticated arguments of Fish himself are examples of the kind of reason his practice assumes and would necessarily replicate through all the changes to come. As his essay "Change" concludes, any other form of reason, or of "unreasonable" (read: historically revolutionary) change cannot even be recognized:

> The question of change is therefore one that cannot be posed independently of some such self-description [of a community's work and implicit theory of change] which gives a shape to the very facts and events to which the question [of change] is put. Does this mean, then, that we can never say "what really happened" because we can only say what happened under some description or account? Not at all. Every description and account—including the descriptions and accounts that make up this paper—is an attempt to say what really happened. If the claim to be saying that is contested (as it often is), it will not be contested by some view of the event independent of description but by a compe ting description, and the competition will be adjudicated with reference to the norms, standards, and procedures understood by the community to be appropriate to the determination of empirical fact. (442)

The problem with Fish's position here concerns less his competitive model of critical change, although I will challenge it shortly, than it does his vision of deciding between competing descriptions. Surely Stanley Fish knows how members of an interpretive community obtain the common understanding of "norms, standards, and procedures"—by the authoritative imposition of power upon people's minds and sometimes their bodies? Surely he knows, too, that the best argument within any interpretive community does not necessarily win widespread acceptance in either critical or political arenas? Besides, even if the best argument did usually win out in literary study, there is no reason to assume that the "norms, standards, and procedures" of instrumental reason are necessarily appropriate in other than current professional contexts. Why does Fish need to make such naive-sounding assumptions? Perhaps the use of the legal term "adjudicate" in the passage is a clue—to what, I will show, is the essentially irrational, broadly aesthetic basis of his position.

Fish is a professor of English and of law, and when he speaks about the legal profession in this essay, he admits that one of its founding beliefs is necessarily a convenient fiction, which for all its fictionality is indispensable and constraining on all its members, regardless of their legal philosophy or "theory":

> The enterprise of law, for example, is by definition committed to the historicity of its basic principles, and workers in the field have a stake in seeing the history of their own efforts as the application of those principles to circumstances that are only apparently new (i.e. changed). That is why a judge will do almost anything to avoid over-turning a precedent, and why even those who hold to the doctrine of legal realism—the doctrine that the law is whatever the courts happen on that day to say it is—are uncomfortable with that doctrine and wish that they held to something else. In short, the very point of the legal enterprise requires that its practitioners see continuity where others, with less of a stake in the enterprise, might feel free to see change. (441)

And are we to draw the further conclusion that now a similarly ironic situation holds true for the profession of literary study—whereas we are committed to seeing change and to "making it new," others, outside the profession, "with less of a stake in the enterprise, might feel free to see" continuity? Whether or not Fish's conclusion does indeed entail this further conclusion of mine, his vision of the fictional foundations of the legal enterprise's necessary belief in an ideal continuity can provide a clue to why Fish assumes the standards, norms, evidentiary procedures, and tacit understandings of instrumental reason. In taking the law as his model of a profession (something Magali Larson's *The Rise of Professionalism* licenses him to do), Fish is both ignoring literary study's difference from the law, its unrationalized object of analysis, and tacitly admitting that his commitment to the current professional mode of instrumental reason is serving him and his interpretive community in the same way as the legal profession's rigid belief in the sanctity of precedent: as a useful fiction without which he could not imagine the familiar, self-revising, and aesthetically pleasing pattern of change he articulates in the essay. (The profession of literary study as a self-transforming, purely formal system is a seductive reincarnation of his idea of Renaissance texts as self-consuming artifacts.) The belief in rationalized, orderly, con-

tinuous change is necessary to the ever-modernizing professional es-
tablishment or ironic "status quo" of fashionable change to which he
belongs. This "interpretive community" subscribes to what could be
called—following Fish's own account given above—the doctrine of
critical realism. This would be the belief in the Humpty-Dumpty
principle of professional politics: that criticism is really whatever the
"community" of apparently like-minded leading critics and their disciples happen on that day to say it is.

Whether or not my last speculative barb hits the mark, I think we
have seen enough of Fish's vision of change to draw certain conclusions. First of all, although his practical "theory" of change deper-
sonalizes the modernizing procedures of the profession, making the
endless displacement and strategic resentment Bloom worries about
less a matter of individual or even obviously generational animus, it
retains as the form of all change imaginable this very mode of endless
displacement for its own sake. In fact, it conceives of a permanent
structure of displacement as the fictional origin of critical judgment.
Such revisionism is conceived in terms of interpretive communities
committed to the apparently impersonal practices of instrumental
reason. But this idea of human rationality is actually (in large part) no
more than an updated, professionalized, 1980s- and 1990s-styled
version of the conventional understanding of the "taste" and "common sense" that distinguishes a cultural elite from the untutored
masses. Second, Fish's model of change authorizes no clear direction
for change. Outcomes are no more than what the sum total of the individual professional projects of contestation happen at any one time
to add up to within an interpretive community or within the sum
total of interpretive communities in the profession. In this fashion,
the free-market, utilitarian, positivistic, and pragmatic view of classical liberal capitalism has been displaced from individuals and at-
tributed to interpretive communities, so that although Fish would
never maintain that individuals are finally "free agents," however
much different contexts might make them "feel free," his representation of the model of professional change does grant all the power for
basically beneficial choice to the operations of the invisible hand of
the interpretive community of the profession as a whole. Typically, a
politically demoralizing idea is "cheerfully embraced" by Fish, the
good professional, and put to rhetorical use for his own "representa-

tive" self-aggrandizement. One could propose a democratic rationale for the modesty Fish appears to display in refusing to authorize a specific agenda for change. One could claim that Fish does not want to play the prophet and coercively predetermine the shape of changes to come. However, one must also remind oneself that such a refusal to take the lead and play the speculative theorist or prophetic critic occurs in the context of promoting a vision of change dependent on the acceptance of professional elites continuing to operate their modernizing procedures according to a conception of instrumental reason appropriate for the standard of taste and value current in late-capitalist America. In short, such a refusal to play is playing at refusal and really accepting things as they are, as how things must and even should always be. And the final conclusion to be drawn from Fish's latest work is that despite its trappings of realism and worldly-wise, even cynical reason, the vision of change presented there is in its sublimity but not in its instrumentality truly a vision that should be familiar to us from the romantics and even more so from the deconstructive critique of the romantic practice of attempting to represent in sublime or "romantic" images of natural objects and processes, matters that are entirely cultural and textual—indeed, often purely rhetorical. Fish's representation of a continuously changing interpretive community that is a self-regulating, self-perpetuating, self-transforming ensemble of revisionary forms without specific content is, to my mind, as sublimely aesthetic as anything in Harold Bloom's theories. Fish's theoretical conception of critical change is really a figure of speech projecting a spectral fiction that would impersonate all the anonymous force of natural fact. Fish, like Homer, would be identified with nature in his performance.

With this topic of the displaced romantic sublime we are indeed back to Harold Bloom and an understanding of "community" based purely and simply upon naked self-interest. Let me cite Jonathan Arac, one of Bloom's recent critics, on the nature and sources of his critical vision:

> The classical source for literature as fragmentary and competitive is Longinus *On the Sublime*. Longinus helped extricate the romantics from the dilemmas of eighteenth-century poetry and was crucial to Bloom's new romantic criticism. Longinus is extravagant and difficult, and since Bloom rarely cited him, many readers have not appre-

ciated his place in Bloom's work. Longinus held that the sublime was
disjunctive, a power that "scatters everything before it like a thunder-
bolt," in a moment. This power derived from the grandeur of the human mind, "the echo of a great soul," and was freed from any natural
mimesis. It offered a theory of inspiration that depended on no divinity. Men became gods to one another, as the "effluences" of past
greatness filled the young writer. To achieve full power, however, one
must leave such passive receptivity and emulatively combat one's predecessor, as Plato did Homer, "entering the lists like a young cham-
pion matched against the man whom all admire." Thus Bloom's agonistic metaphors joined a tradition of discourse. Likewise, another of
Bloom's important, apparently idiosyncratic notions: the Scene of Instruction. To achieve the sublime, one may conjure up the great past
writers as judges and exemplars: the "ordeal" of this ghostly "tribunal" will yield us the power to immortalize ourselves, or else it will
quell us if our spirits are inadequate.[4]

Bloom's sublime vision of the fiercely competitive "ordeal" of facing the "ghostly tribunal," his "scene of instruction," is the religious
and explicitly personalized version of Fish's secularized, rationalized
(hence seemingly more "enlightened"), and depersonalized but no less
self-interested notion of the interpretive community of change. Fish's
model of "norms, standards, and procedures" that decides which of
the competing critical descriptions an interpretive community adopts
as its own takes on in Bloom's criticism the form of the Longinian
"ghostly tribunal" and the ordeal or scene of judgment, which Bloom
generally reads into the processes of poetic and critical canon formation. The models of change that Bloom and Fish propose are really
interchangeable, equivalent parts of the profession's self-justifying
ideology that attempts to ensure the replication of the profession's
basic structure of power relations into the future without substantial
change. Furthermore, the force of these competitive models of professional work and critical change, whether represented in explicitly "visionary" (Bloom) or more "instrumental" terms (Fish), functions in
the same fashion to constrain the production, distribution, and acceptance of all alternative views. The result is that the conditions of work
in the profession are felt to foster an ideology of self-interest for the
individual and his group to the point of being essentially destructive
of any conceivable possibility of human community of shared beliefs,

values, and general life experiences that transcend narrowly defined, often improvised professional strategies and goals. What Fish, as we will see in chapter 8, calls "rhetorical man" is really a rationalization of demonic alienation.

At this point, a question arises concerning how anyone can perceive the limits of this pervasive model of professional work. To what can one compare it? Whence comes the alternative cooperative vision of the social character of work? Fredric Jameson in a recent essay provides the best answer I know, when he introduces "some notions of Jean-Paul Sartre [in the *Critique of Dialectical Reason*] which seem to open up new avenues for exploration":

> For Sartre, social praxis—which always involves solving problems and confronting contradictions—also always tends to leave a kind of residue, what he calls the practico-inert. This residue, this dead mark or trace of a now extinct praxis, survives to form a part of the new situation, the new dilemma or contradiction, which people confront in their new historical present. Would it therefore not be plausible to suggest that what is called social character is to be seen as just such a residue, just such a form of the practico-inert, just such a scar left in the present by the outmoded and forgotten practices of the past?[5]

By "social character" Jameson means not simply the social dimensions of collective projects but also the kind of subject formation now all but totally outmoded in our late-capitalist epoch, a form of human subjectivity that still possesses a residual if now not entirely appropriate sense of that much-abused word "community." (One can catch glimpses of this fading phenomenon in the relations between representative members of formerly subaltern groups now making their way upon the world-historical stage, such as women, people of color, and postcolonial peoples.) Jameson continues his analysis with a critical surmise:

> We may conjecture, for example, that in a certain communal situation certain kinds of character traits prove necessary and effective in overcoming specific concrete social difficulties and dangers: forms of puritanism, for example, or authoritarian family structures organized around a patriarch. When the problems in question are surmounted, these specific collective stances—something like the muscular contraction of a body resisting a specific weight and pressure—do not go

away but persist without function, in the forgetfulness of the purpose they once served (and I may add that this forgetfulness of the crucial role of forgetfulness in social reproduction is not the least problem with contemporary appeals to social memory). Social "character" would then be this persistence of traits which have lost their function and which now exist as givens or data, as elements of a new situation and as themselves problems which must be overcome (as in various efforts to alter collective habits which have become counterproductive). (553)

What I want to suggest, following Jameson's lead here, is that literature is the place in our culture where one can still discover the persistence of collective stances, those symbolically overdetermined but otherwise apparently outmoded forms of communal vision. In fact, I want to define the aesthetic dimension of literariness, of powerful imaginary effects, as what after Foucault we could call "the collective archive"—that is, as the cultural site for the conscious preservation of the often repressed history of humanity's collective projects, all its supposedly "nonrational" models of community, tradition, and change, both canonical and subversive. (This is, of course, especially but not exclusively true of the novel.) By turning to the literary tradition, even with all the institutional problems of canonization still in mind, we can recuperate the idea of a collective project yet to be realized, which can give shape and direction to the future of the profession and, more important, of society, and so provide a more viable basis of comparative judgment on the present state of things. Our work of critical change can then take on a larger meaning than merely the narrow self-interest of the resentful individual or the self-justifying group. In this way, too, our work can be related, via the mythological resonance of literary language, to the universalizing projects of liberation, which often use the language of myth and religion to express their purposes, both here in this country and around the world. In short, our work of critical change would have a coherent imaginative vision of what we want change to make possible.

Does this mean that just any model of the collective project drawn from the literary tradition is itself necessarily viable and appropriate? Well, obviously not. Then how does one determine what is an unfinished vision of human community that can still be realized, rather than only another exhibit in a museum of muscular poses? The beginning of an answer is, I think, that critics must look to the immediate contexts in which they do their work—not only the local work of teaching, of course, but also the work in which they are engaged within the specific field or subdiscipline of the profession. We must take our lead, as it were, from what we perceive as the needs of our areas of study. Ideally, we critics will not stop there, but at least we must begin definitely somewhere in a concretely historical opposi- tional manner. In this way, we can better avoid the fate of resurrecting from the past what would only be, in Jameson's formulation, a com- plex of "counterproductive" albeit "collective habits" (553) that would also have to be radically altered for the needs of our time.

I want to explain further why we need this corrective vision of the collective archive by looking at the latest work of Gerald Graff and Richard Poirier, both of whom propose to renovate literary study without such a vision. In a recent critical history of the institution of American literary study, Gerald Graff has argued that the profession as a whole has been plagued for the last century or so by an ideological split between those who accept in one form or other the scientific and professional model of specialization and those who, opposing such re- ductive professionalization, desire in some way or other to have a more pervasive influence on modern culture. Whether staged as a contest for professional power between scholars and generalists, crit- ics and humanists, pragmatists (Fish) and theorists (Jameson), or de- constructionists and new historicists, this ideological split has con- tinually haunted literary studies, and it has been accompanied by a process of institutionalization that Graff calls "patterned isolation."[6] What Graff means is that as each new development in critical method or ideology appears, it is assimilated into its own separate compart- ment or "niche" in the profession, its own "interpretive community" in Fish's phrase. This enables everyone on the local level to evade fac- ing directly the challenge posed to the first principles other ap- proaches necessarily entail, especially in light of the many polemical theoretical and antitheoretical manifestos over the years. At the same time, this "liberal" or "pluralistic" mode of assimilation and institu- tionalization, while it makes for a minimum kind of "peaceful co- existence," also insures that the latest critical innovations will quickly become mere routine, even as the essential split between scientistic specialization and critical humanism continues to inspire a fiercely competitive situation made all the more fierce, since the institution, in the name of academic freedom, can never permit any "final solutions." In this viciously circular fashion, professional change occurs as the periodic displacement of routine by novelty and novelty by routine.

The study of American literature proves to be no exception to the general rule. Its distinctive feature, Graff claims, is its origin in the promise it held out that, as a viable, interdisciplinary mode of cultural studies, it could successfully oppose the hegemony of New Critical formalism. In fact, according to Graff, the major works of American literature studies, from *Maule's Curse* (1938) and *American Renaissance* (1941), through *Symbolism and American Literature* (1953), *The American Adam* (1955) and *The American Novel and Its Tradition* (1957), to *The Machine in the Garden* (1965) and *A World Elsewhere* (1966), all tend to deploy in their analyses cultural archetypes, based upon "a very limited number of works" (221). And these analyses continue to celebrate the very aesthetic and moral features of irony, paradox, ambiguity, symbolism, existential complexity, tragic vision, and so on that New Criticism assigned to all literary texts. The disillusioning result, Graff concludes, is that if during this period all "literature was New Critical," then "American literature was somehow a bit more so" (220). In the attempt to displace and assimilate its rival, therefore, American literature studies continues to preserve many of the major elements of the New Critical complex, even as it still adopts the radically opposing stance of cultural studies—an outcome that Jameson's comments on Sartre cited earlier would theoretically predict.

The Renewal of Literature: Emersonian Reflections (1987), Richard Poirier's latest contribution to American literature studies and indeed to contemporary criticism as a whole, clearly confirms Graff's general point about the cycle of novelty and routinization in the profession.[7] I think it also replicates some of the major features of the discipline to which it belongs, even though while explicitly endorsing the method of close reading, it nonetheless also condemns the aristocratic ideology of New Critical modernism. The major disciplinary feature of American literature studies that this study replicates is the formulation of a culturally specific archetype, that of the transcendental American genius of revisionism, based on a very limited number of works—in this instance, texts by Emerson, William James, Stevens,

and Frost that constitute a subtly pervasive Emersonian countertradi-
tion to Arnoldian humanism and Eliotic modernism. And this restrictive genius-archetype, it is nevertheless claimed, defines the essentially American nature of all American literature. Here we see, in
other words, one of the hoary "classics" of American literature—
Emerson, that transcendental pragmatist of imaginary compensation
for all ills—once again trotted out in a currently fashionable revival of
ideal cultural types à la Max Weber and Karl Mannheim. (I have nothing against ideal cultural typologies, only against their facile and
fashionable invocation.) Indeed, Poirier makes Emerson and his heirs
more radically "new" and "deconstructive" (because so casually, non-
chalantly so), than Foucault, Nietzsche, or any of their many followers can even pretend to be. (The temptation to do this with Emerson is hard to resist.)

It is around the subject of "genius" that Poirier most clearly discloses at work the endless displacement ideology of the profession and
the increasingly common desire to transcend the evident vicissitudes
that such critical practice produces. Poirier argues, based on Emerson, that literature "is supremely the place where . . . the reader and
writer become indistinguishable" (77). Yet such identification is neither a sympathetic imaginative one nor something that makes us
"better citizens or even wiser persons" (77). Instead, this identification of reader and writer enables us to "discover how to move, to act,
to work in ways that are still and forever mysteriously creative" (77).
"Genius," Poirier continues in this vein, "describes those moments
when language and the person using it reach a point of incandescence.
It marks the disappearance of individuality on the occasion of its triumph" (80). This self-destructive mode of individuality, in which
language and subjectivity fuse together, defines "genius" (as Poirier
presents it) as a compensatory dream, quite horrific and antisocial, in
which good professionals of the type Fish's vision of change would
promote, can find momentary release from the vicissitudes of meaningless change, despite their feeling ever-threatened with the prospect of being made obsolete "has-beens." And yet, this dream of
genius would go even further in the name of compensation by obliter-
ating material "things" themselves, a project expressing a nihilistic
attitude of mind: "Why, under the Emersonian dispensation, should
anything at all be preserved as an example to the future? Why not

erase every sentence just as soon as it is written and read? Wouldn't that be the purest form of action as Emerson imagines it?" (83). Poirier's argument thus concludes in this vision of a self-destructive mode of individuality that in seeking to evade the endless repetition of professional displacements, change for mere change's sake would consign to the future only its own disintegrating gestures of *ressentiment*, as it exits the world of human practices altogether: "Genius involves itself in processes which, when they arrive at practical expression, especially in any mode of writing, become immediately filled with the apprehension of dissipation and loss of energy. To overcome this apprehension we need to convince ourselves, as Emerson says in the essay 'Art,' that 'the real value of the Iliad, or the Transfiguration, is as signs of power' " (85).

In these passages, everything goes—and goes on: text, author, reader, things themselves. All is dissolved into the ceaseless process of rhetorical transition that defines the ideal type of the American Genius, whose only enemy is the lapse into the habitual, the merely practical, the material—that is, the socially reproducible. The resort to Emerson is evidently a last-ditch effort of a major representative of one entrenched interpretive community in the field of American literature studies once again to undergo in a distinctive fashion the modernization of himself and his corner of the discipline, in the face of the inevitable outmoding, the becoming a personal and collective "has been," that necessarily defines the profession and its various "areas of study" as being "professional" in the first place. Signs of power? I think not.

Where are we to discover a vision of human relationship not reducible to Bloom's, Fish's, and Poirier's world of resentful competition and strategic displacement? In the collective archive of literature to which Jameson's remarks led me there are many such visions. I choose Wallace Stevens's late poem of the 1940s, "Large Red Man Reading," because it is appropriate to the previous discussions of vision, change, the sublime, and imaginative compensation and because it offers an alternative prospect. In fact, the poem supports both a resentfully competitive and a magnanimous vision, depending on in which context—narrowly professional or broadly imaginative—we elect to read it.

There were ghosts that returned to earth to hear his phrases,
As he sat there reading, aloud, the great blue tabulae.
They were those from the wilderness of stars that had expected more.

There were those that returned to hear him read from the poem of
life,
Of the pans above the stove, the pots on the table, the tulips among
them.
They were those that would have wept to step barefoot into reality,

That would have wept and been happy, have shivered in the frost
And cried out to feel it again, have run their fingers over leaves
And against the most coiled thorn, have seized on what was ugly

And laughed, as he sat there reading, from out the purple tabulae,
The outline of being and its expressings, the syllables of its law:
POESIS, POESIS, the literal characters, the vatic lines,

Which in those ears and in those thin, those spended hearts,
Took on color, took on shape and the size of things as they are
And spoke the feeling for them, which was what they had lacked.[8]

Read in the specialized terms of contemporary criticism, the poem
justifies Bloom's anxiety of influence theory of literary history. "Large
Red Man Reading," in this light, expresses a latecomer's vision, in
which the usually repressed desire to see oneself as the primal source
for the greats to whom one feels anxiously indebted beautifully if self-
deceivingly articulates itself. Consider how the "he" of the poem provides, through his acts of reading the changing colors of the heavens,
all that the ghosts of his literary ancestors lacked. He creates "the
poem of life" and speaks "the feeling for them." In this fashion, Stevens would become more powerfully original than any of his precursors, especially Walt Whitman. The transcendental American genius
for forgetting the past and delighting in the changes that destroy one
here strikes again.

Or so it seems. But read in a less restrictive way, the poem sounds a
radically different note. If we take the speaker and his ghosts not in
their purely literary roles as the belated modern poet and his sublime
predecessors but rather in their human roles as survivor and his dead,
we get a very different poem. That Stevens composes the poem during

the time when he is losing family members to death reinforces such a reading. In this different light, "Large Red Man Reading" becomes a poignant expression of the pathos of desire that would triumph over death, a pathos made all the more piercing by the poem's repeated, self-conscious use of the subjunctive mood for its grand vision of the poem's "setting" solar protagonist reading the great blue and then purple tabulae of the twilight heavens for all his ghosts. The creative act, in this context, is not an anxious repression of precursors; it is instead the generous, even noble (if self-consciously doomed) vision of giving imaginative life back to the dead—for the collective archive, as Stevens performs it here, is the communal memory of exemplary acts read from the changing horizons of one's world and rearticulated, with feeling, thereby blooding the ghosts of the dead and making them real again. This poem is thus an allegory of the literary act as creative reading, a poetic outlining of a being, once lost, now reenvisioned, and worthy of becoming an instructive model of future existence. Literary texts at their best are thus inhabited not only by the distorted traces of the political unconscious but also by the spectral lineaments of noble magnanimity.

Consider, as another and final instance, the famous and much-disputed concluding vision of Joyce's "The Dead," a long coda to *Dubliners* intended to be a more sympathetic reappraisal of Ireland, otherwise viciously satirized in the rest of the collection.[9] Does Gabriel Conroy, the protagonist, as he contemplates the snow that is now general over Ireland, really suffer a surprising release from his paralyzing egotism in shedding "generous tears" (223) for his wife's sense of lost love? Or is this just Joyce's last savage twist of the ironic knife, as we recognize Gabriel's defeat in love expanding, self-absorbedly, into the snowy apocalypse of the very universe? This is the critical dispute. And the reason for it is the mistaken critical focus on Gabriel. At story's end, it should be on what Greta and Gabriel Conroy and Joyce are making of Michael Furey. This is the story's focus, for Furey is the figure of romantic Ireland dead and gone and now returning to haunt the dismal present with a vision of greater possibilities. Furey is now more actively alive in Greta's memory, her husband's imagination, and Joyce's own text than any of the other Dubliners. Joyce, through the Conroy's final bedroom drama, recovers and delivers for critical understanding a mode of passionate being that dissolves, by contrast, the diminished present of mean-spiritedness and hypocrisy into slushy fragments. An outmoded or superannuated style of existence—romantic self-sacrifice—reappears both to judge all the living and the dead in post-Parnell Ireland by its higher standard and to offer that standard of a nobler vision to another generation for possible heroic repetition. Such magnanimous visions drawn from the collective archive of literature can counter the mindless competitiveness and reductive displacements of the critical institution both by reminding us of the larger horizons of earlier epochs, when modernization was not yet all in all, and by guiding our work to make the future more (not less) human. [10]

8 Pragmatists of the Spirit
Late Bloom and Company

Harold Bloom has spent an entire career professing his highly individual sense of the romantic imagination in a time, to echo Pound from *Hugh Selwyn Mauberley,* generally unpropitious for its appreciation. Beginning to write in the age of Eliot and the new criticism means that Bloom in Shelley's *Mythmaking* (1959) has to demonstrate both his ability as a close reader, which he does and has continued to do brilliantly, and the continuing importance of understanding the romantic origins of our modernity. He does so in this book by adapting to Shelley in particular Northrop Frye's mythic approach to the vision of cultural archetypes first rediscovered by the romantics and then disseminated by Frye himself in *Fearful Symmetry: A Study of William Blake* (1947) and *Anatomy of Criticism* (1957). Thereafter, despite occasional appreciative readings, Bloom has confronted general cultural and specific literary intellectual climates either ignorant of or hostile to his prophetic style of romanticism. Consider, for example, as Bloom produces his famous tetralogy of theory in the mid-1970s, how the ersatz neoromanticism of the 1960s counterculture and the 1970s linguistic determinism of imported theory combine to reduce the reality of the imagination simultaneously to a degraded New Age commonplace and a logocentric fiction of Western narcissism. What a truly revolting development such a disillusioning spectacle must have been for Bloom. And despite his provocatively imaginative revision of Freud's Oedipal theory of the family romance in which each belated poet aggressively strives to rescue the muse from her imaginative degradation at the hands of his poetic ancestors by repeatedly, defensively, and variously revising them, Bloom has achieved general public recognition only with the essays collected in *Agon: Towards A Theory of Revisionism* (1982). [1] The reason for this belated achievement of widespread popularity lies in the essays' insistence on their Emersonian or American difference from continental theory and popular romanticism alike. Bloom defines this difference rhetorically as the essays' inherent self-regarding pragmatism, by which he means their revisionary insistence on always asking of a prior text, "What is it good for, what can I do with it, what can it do for me, what can I make it mean?" (19). This American difference opposes what Bloom sees as the evaporation of literary or critical personality into the spectral anonymity of textuality and discourse, thereby preserving the traditional American dream of the self-made individual in contemporary critical culture. It is for this reason that, since *Agon* and even before his work on the Bible or Shakespeare, Bloom increasingly gets cited in newspapers and magazines as an authority in attacks against theory and current academic culture.

In *Agon,* Bloom approvingly cites Richard Rorty on American pragmatism's always already postphilosophical stance (19). Bloom thus begins his general public association with the "neopragmatism" of Rorty himself, of course, but also—surprisingly, given their self-proclaimed "left" orientations—that of Fish, Barbara Hernstein Smith, and their critical disciples. Bloom thereby moves to center stage in the general public debate about American culture. This public association becomes so intimate and seminal in Rorty's case, however, that in the now-classic statement of what "neopragmatism" or "contingency theory" is, *Contingency, Irony, and Solidarity* (1989), Rorty starts from Bloom's notion of a "strong poet" as the revisionary foundations for his radically antifoundational position (20, 22, 28–

30, 34–35, 40–42).[2] Since *Agon,* where Rorty, who once reviewed Bloom approvingly, played authority figure for Bloom, the roles clearly have been reversed once again.

What Rorty and any revisionary company of "neopragmatists" mean by "strong poet" is really what Bloom has all along meant by the romantic imagination, which in his latest work defines the nature of the imagination per se, from the Hebrew Bible to Shakespeare, Freud, and beyond. Confronted by the purely contingent, that is, arbitrary, accidental, or gratuitously determined situation of being chosen by a tradition of thought, belief, and feeling made by others, into which one is born and raised, the "strong poet" is the one who is able at least to redescribe some aspect of the tradition in a new way, telling a more comprehensive, interesting, and original story about it in a persuasively provocative vocabulary uniquely one's own. (In this regard, Bloom, Derrida, and Heidegger are more inventive than Rorty.) For late Bloom and company, "strong poet" is what every one of us—imaginative writer, philosopher, critical reader—aspires to become. Our aspiration for an immortal name not to be scattered, they claim, may provisionally inspire different group projects of revisionism—really, the bureaucracy of the revisionary imagination—such as canon reconstruction, in literary or any other humane study. But this is preliminary to the emergence of the central or major figures in such collectivities once the appropriate context for seeing their originality has thus been institutionally established. I find the best shorthand statement of the revisionary American pragmatism of late Bloom and company, which takes one of Milton's devils, Belial, for its exemplar, to be the following passage in Stanley Fish's "Rhetoric." I believe he calls the Bloomian "strong poet" by the simpler, more useful, and very telling name of "rhetorical man." Notice how Fish projects any sense of belatedness onto the "fellows" of his "rhetorical man":

> As rhetorical man manipulates reality [i.e., current conventions], establishing through his words the imperatives and urgencies to which he and his fellows must respond, he manipulates or fabricates himself, simultaneously conceiving of and occupying the roles that become first possible and then mandatory given the social structure his rhetoric has put into place. By exploring the available means of persuasion in a particular situation, he tries them on, and as they begin to suit him, he becomes them.[3]

This vision is, of course, entirely imaginary but no less revealing for that. Bloom in his recent work since *Agon*—including *Ruin the Sacred Truths: Poetry and Belief from the Bible to the Present* (1987, 1989) and his extensive commentary in *The Book of J* (1990)—has now for the first time a general American audience increasingly receptive to his vision of what I would call, updating it for our moment, "the contingent imagination."[4]

The problem with "the contingent imagination" as practiced by late Bloom and company is implied in Fish's celebration of "rhetorical man." First of all, in its use of the synecdoche "rhetorical man," Fish abstracts from all the differences of gender, ethnicity, race, class, and family to create his imaginary ideal of the self-determining male individual whose rhetorical performance, however taking off from conventional codes, ends single-handedly by putting into place the larger structures of his culture and society. Even if we credit Fish with intending to mean by "rhetorical man" all those in the profession who espouse the contingent imagination in the way he does, we still must question the notion of a would-be protean agency scoping out the rules of the rhetorical game, transforming them in terms of an impossible desire for mastery, and thereby transforming the entire culture and projecting onto others (colleagues and disciples) one's own sense of contingent belatedness. This is the myth of genius in neopragmatist, purely rhetorical guise. Self-creation of this heroically self-deluded, openly "demonic" sort envisioned in Fish's representative statement is, as we shall see apropos Bloom, a regressive self-delusion in the strong sense, especially since it makes it virtually impossible for critics to work productively together to draw from the collective archive of canonical and noncanonical works those positive and negative exempla so necessary for orienting the serious discussion of moral values.

I want to look at Bloom's latest work in order to portray this contingent imagination in all its fullness, before analyzing it in light of critical positions in the later work of Foucault and Kristeva, who are, I can't help repeating, two of the strangest theoretical bedfellows ever imagined. Thanks to Foucault's later stress on the ethical stylization of the subject's sexuality and Kristeva's recent psychoanalytic theory of creative mourning, we will be able to see why late Bloom and company can only be "pragmatists of the spirit," and so ultimately professors of the purely imaginary desire for cultural mastery. As we shall see, late Bloom and company are chronically in mourning for the heroic ideal of individuality lost in practice to our postmodern mass culture. Because they are so attached to this ideal, their works can only function as (in Rorty's candid terms) "private fantasies" or, at best, as transient gambits of upward professional mobility. The contingent mask of neopragmatist revisionism defines the pure form of professionalism in literary studies today. But now, however, we must examine late Bloom as the representative member, the first among equals, of his company of spiritual pragmatists.

Three moments in *Ruins the Sacred Truth* define the limits of the contingent imagination as envisioned and practiced by late Bloom and company. The first moment occurs in the chapter on Shakespeare's originality, which Bloom claims consists in "the representation of change by showing people pondering their own speeches and being altered through that consideration."[5] In support of this formulation, Bloom, following A. C. Bradley's lead, cites Hegel from *The Philosophy of Fine Art*. Hegel, too, praises Shakespeare for the dramatic depiction of characters possessing "intelligence and imagination" that become "free artists of themselves" by virtue of "the [changing] image in which they . . . contemplate themselves objectively as a work of art" (54). For Bloom, what Hegel's praise endorses is his own notion that in Shakespeare an imperial or all-consuming form of human passion for subjective freedom emerges that conditions and contains all subsequent representations of character, personality, or the subject. This imperial form of the subject as the contingent imagination changes primarily in terms of the projected and objectified world of images it pragmatically soliloquizes, in which it can repeatedly read its own progressively emerging ideal status as a work of art. (If this sounds more like Bloom's practice than Hegel's theory, it's no accident.) This subjectivity can respond only to its own changing style of appropriating and revising commonly shared reality, which for Hegel is radically historical if not, of course, essentially material, but which for Bloom is what he characterizes as "a cosmological emptiness marked by the limits of truth [or literalism] and meaning [or apocalyptically imaginative revisionism]" (4). For Bloom, therefore, there cannot be an independent or extrasubjective reality beyond the limits of truth and meaning to be found in the containing forms of the human imagination as defined by a few great sublime figures such as the Yahwist, Homer, Dante, Chaucer, Shakespeare, Wordsworth, Tolstoy, and Freud. These imaginative masters, free artists of themselves all, have defined our world of images for us, in radically diverse ways, and so have projected their sense of belatedness onto us. Reality, in this context of the contingent imagination, can only be a hungry void waiting for the next sublime genius to try to fill it. Otherwise, the only reality that the rest of us can know is the one that befalls us "contingently," ready-made but open to further revision, from the hands of the original creators as we happen to encounter them and become their epigones. This contingency Bloom also calls our "facticity," (7) and it inspires our revisionary responses, our competing imaginative world of antithetical images in which we are to find our own grand reflections. While Rorty, Fish, and company would never buy such a grandiose pathos, they certainly do share Bloom's vision of the contingent imagination confronting arbitrary conventions of saying things after sublime models that we work to revise in accordance with what Rorty sees as our wish to become different, our desire to become a name in our own right.[6] Between the vast unimaginable void of reality without the work of the creators and the grand containing imaginative forms of our culture with them, there defensively stands the belated, would-be sublime revisionist of the moment: such is the phantasmagoric world of the contingent imagination, as Bloom representatively envisions it.

The second moment in *Ruin the Sacred Truths* defining the limits of the contingent imagination occurs in Bloom's later discussion of Wordsworth's revisionary response to a major containing mental form in our culture by the name of Milton.

> The two-part Prelude of 1799 completes the work of *Paradise Lost* in destroying the distinction between sacred and secular poetry. What it celebrates ultimately is neither nature nor God, and not even a presence transcending Wordsworth's own creative force. Rather, the poem praises Wordsworth's own transport, his own exalted sublimity, the pathos of the Miltonic bard emancipated from any representations that could inhibit the fully imagined self. (139)

Bloom here claims that Wordsworth so internalizes and repressively forgets the imaginative world of his precursor who contains him that what is left for him is a visionary vacancy, which he mistakenly calls nature, for his fully imagined self to occupy. As Keats first notes when he defines Wordsworth's characteristic mode as "the egotistical sublime," the God and nature of Milton's epic vanish into Wordsworth's visionary dreariness, his creative transport beyond all representations other than those of his poetic self. With Shakespeare begins the process Hegel saw (and Bloom after him in a now-classic 1968 essay "The Internalization of Quest Romance") as the revisionary withdrawal of reality into the objectified structure of human culture for purposes of aesthetic contemplation and of making room for the human subject's changing world of images. Here with Wordsworth, we get the intensification, adaptation, and application of this revisionary process to the original work of such revision produced by Shakespeare and Milton. Bloom thus sees in Wordsworth the commencement of our self-conscious modernity that would belatedly contain the containing forms of an always already revisionary reality forever void without us. Troping upon the void of reality as our precursors did, who first envisioned the void without their imaginations, we would and must so repressively trope upon them in turn endlessly.

The third defining moment in *Ruin the Sacred Truths* tells us why we are condemned to a perpetual troping, and provides us with the best transition to Bloom's extensive commentary in *The Book of J*. In speaking of "Freud and Beyond" in our modernity, Bloom claims he is returning to where his story begins in both this book and his life, with his outrageous reading of the Hebrew bible, in an incredible attempt to define how Freud returns the entirety of Western culture to an essentially Jewish sense of pragmatism:

> Abraham, arguing with Yahweh on the road to Sodom, haggled with God over the number of righteous men required to prevent the destruction of the city but knew he was nothing in himself when face to face with Yahweh. Yet in his humane desperation, Father Abraham pragmatically needed to act momentarily as if he were everything in himself. Already, Abraham was Freudian man, which is only to say that Freud's [defensive] conception of the human [mind] is surprisingly biblical. (162)

The "act"—both fiction and action—by which Abraham haggles with God is indeed sublimely memorable. Abraham at first claims that if he can find fifty innocent men in Sodom then Yahweh should spare the cities of the plain from his wrath for their contempt of him. Once Yahweh agrees to this first figure, Abraham boldly reduces the number, Bloom claims, getting down to ten innocent men before it is to no avail, as Yahweh's wrath will not be finally contained, even if this effort is still greatly to Abraham's credit. Abraham's haggling with God, Bloom says, exemplifies the all-and-nothing sense of what I'm calling the contingent imagination that ever must improvise its design of values so as to feel as a god, all in all, even while being, in fact, less than nothing before the god with which it must contest its claims—whether that god be called Yahweh, Shakespeare, or, in Freud, the death-driving superego. The three critical moments from *Ruin the Sacred Truth* thus characterize the contingent imagination as an increasingly internalized defensive troping upon perpetually receding, ever-earlier figurative origins in one's imaginative history, both personal and cultural. In short, the contingent imagination, as Bloom representatively practices it, is the latest form of aesthetic compensation for his (and our) pragmatic alienation as academic intellectuals.

We come now to the primary reason for Bloom's current influence and the popularity of contingency theory in American criticism. While recognizing and promoting the view that all of what we see has been made arbitrarily by other and prior human hands, a contingency theorist is "a pragmatist of the spirit," to adopt Bloom's own formula from *The Book of J* (44).[6] That is, such a theorist still desires the sublime vision of impossible contest for more than human status, what Thomas Weiskel in *The Romantic Sublime* identifies as "the essential claim of the sublime . . . that man can, in feeling and in speech, transcend [even momentarily] the human."[7] Despite the lip service in Rorty, Fish, and other "neopragmatists" given to the role of social and professional conventions and practices in our lives, they still believe that, as you recall Fish putting it apropos his example of Milton's Belial, "rhetorical man manipulates" the reality of these discourses and establishes "through his words the imperatives and urgencies to which he and his fellows must respond," thereby fabricating himself and "simultaneously conceiving of and occupying the roles that become first possible and then mandatory given the social structure his rhetoric has put in place" (483).

While the synecdochal nature of "rhetorical man" is clear, so, too,

is the claim of the sublime in Fish's stance here, as he would impersonate this demonic figure in his grandly synoptic vision of infinitely
pliable human culture. Only a would-be "demon" could think human
beings so manipulable. Similarly, one could say that what makes contingency theory contingent is finally this personal vision of imaginative possibility becoming literally necessity for others. What has once
befallen oneself, one has revised and has made befall others. That is,
the desire for apotheosis becomes, for the contingent imagination,
the desire for symbolic immortality as a sublimely successful instance
of "rhetorical man" persuasively at work mastering culture and acting
like a force of nature on others. All these pragmatists of the spirit
want the ironically self-conflicted agon with the authority of a transcendent reality, the contest with the divine, but a "divine" of the
cultural pantheon of genius that is nevertheless made entirely by human hands alone. The aim is in one's turn to be assimilated to this
Western pantheon of imaginative heroes. But what happens in their
revisions is, as Fish proposes, that they begin by "exploring the available means of persuasion in a particular situation" to try them on,
whether suitable or not, only to end up, I would contend, becoming
what they behold, for better or worse in their own and our eyes.

In his commentary to *The Book of J*, Bloom has given us a definitive
portrait of what he has become: the representative American celebrant
of the contingent imagination. Bloom claims that his fiction of the J
or Yahwist author of certain major strains in the Pentateuch is neither
logically probable nor scholarly creditable but is, for him, nonetheless imaginatively compelling. For Bloom, J is a woman writer of the
post-Solomonic court (tenth century B.C.E.), a contemporary of the
court historian who authored the second book of Samuel. She shares
with him the memory of lost Davidic splendor in a disillusioning epoch of increasing division, degradation, and, ultimately, cultural dispersion. The vision of the Patriarchs and of their radically incommensurate god, Yahweh, who is as much radically self-contradictory as he
is transcendent of humankind, exemplifies more the Patriarchs' own
divinely formed natures than religious anthropomorphism. For this
vision reflects back, according to Bloom, from J's aggressively nostalgic yet ironically repressed memory of the ever-blessed David and
his gloriously problematic reign. (The figure of David never directly
appears in *The Book of J* but is kept offstage, casting a luminous shad-

ow over all.) In articulating this intentionally preposterous claim, Bloom comes to celebrate Yahweh, the god who haggles with Abraham over human lives, who attempts to murder his prophet Moses, and who fears his own wrath at the people of Israel on Mt. Sinai before arbitrarily choosing to give the Blessing of ever more life (which Bloom says is a name not to be scattered) to one after another forerunner of David, ideal object of his most intense and sustained electionlove.

Bloom aims in *The Book of J* to recover from the normative and revisionary traditions of Judaism, Christianity, Islam, and their secular variants a radical sense of J's incommensurate originality that, like Shakespeare's and Freud's, still contains our imagination of reality, temporality, and personhood. The aim, in other words, is so to recover this originality as to see oneself, vis-à-vis other revisionists, in the figure of Yahweh enthroned and feasting on Sinai before the elite of all the children of god as if the entire cosmos were turned upside down now beneath one's feet: "Under his feet there was the likeness of a pavement of sapphire like the very sky for purity" (256). To become sublime is ever to appear thus, an incommensurate mortal god to the coming generations. (By this Bloom means something like a "nonrational" fact of nature, a pure contingency.) Bloom's audacity here goes beyond his taking on an impossible critical task of offering logical or scholarly justification for his extravagant claims, for he does manage to elaborate at considerable imaginative length his essential vision of J's Yahweh who still contains us, the following excerpt of which gives the gist: "J's attitude toward Yahweh resembles nothing so much as a mother's somewhat wary but still proudly amused stance toward a favorite son who has grown up to be benignly powerful but also eccentrically irascible. Such a stance feels ironic, but again, how are we to categorize such an irony?" (26). Ironic indeed is Bloom's comic vision here as he revises Yahweh into a divine child. In effect, as the imaginative progenitor of this Jewish mother-version of J, who in turn produces the patriarchal tradition from Abraham to Freud and beyond, Bloom would thus become the father of the god of his and all of our "feary" fathers. Bloom's rescue of the abjected mother is to make her the ideal source of the tradition abjecting her.

What can we make of this bizarrely self-indulgent yet still powerful vision? Is it merely the last representative gasp of a romantic bourgeois humanism shared alike in least common denominator fashion by conventional humanist and pragmatist critic? Is it, in short, simply the contingent imagination's corresponding god-image? I think Foucault, particularly the later Foucault of the second and third volumes of *The History of Sexuality,* can help us to understand this contingent practice of self in American criticism. In what follows, I am clearly using Foucault to "perfect" or socialize Bloom, and so put certain aspects of his work to use for my own ends.

According to Foucault, the agonistic structure of the self, whether in Hellenic, Roman, or Judeo-Christian modes, entails the ascetic stylization of human sexuality practiced by a self-described "noble" elite in essentially slave cultures. The ultimate aim of such stylized self-discipline is to provide for the possibility of individual variation in the forms of cultural life to be recalled as exemplary models by posterity. The practice of self as a sublime agon, more specifically, depends upon and generalizes the homoerotic bond informing the pedagogic situation, in which the wisdom of the older mentor and the passion of the youth have been internalized dialectically as a ceaseless self-overcoming plural subject for a historically specific elite. Master and student become figures in the mask play of such plural subjects now representing the differential relations between given and transformed qualities of self. Similarly, one can see how Bloom in enacting his revisionary practice of criticism has internalized in the relations between precursor and ephebe the basic dynamic of the pedagogic pair. In this fashion, late Bloom becomes for his company of pragmatists of the spirit a useful (because heroically self-revising) mask for their own liberal agonistic play in relation to some precursor or other, a play in which their own homoerotic bond to their imaginative or actual masters, or both, has been sublimated.[8] According to Gilles Deleuze in his *Foucault,* the general aim of such mask play is to define "a relation to oneself which resists codes and powers [of normalization], to mark the resistance of a style."[9] Bloom's chronic hostility to the prophet Jeremiah, especially memorable in *Ruin the Sacred Truths* (12–19), centers on and is explainable by the major trope for the prophet's torturous relation to Yahweh, that of divine ravishment, a too-literal figuration for the surprisingly squeamish Bloom, and a definition of the self-overcoming relation to oneself that, however resistant to codes and powers of normalization, shows a resistant mark of style not sublimely transformed enough for Bloom's representatively American macho tastes. Late Bloom and company are, in short, pragmatists of the spirit in order to mark the sublime resistance of their styles to the relentlessly reductive mechanisms of what Kenneth Burke has called "the bureaucratization of the imagination" that define the modern state and its polity. [10] They would all stand out individually as original figures, "free artists of themselves," against the background of the banal masses, our "slaves" of economic production and popular culture. As Foucault puts it in the introduction to *The Use of Pleasure,* volume 3 in *The History of Sexuality,* concerning the object of his own revisionary exercises: "[It is] to learn to what extent the effort to think one's own history can free thought from what it silently thinks, and so enable it to think differently." [11] The relations of revisionism and repression in contemporary criticism could not be more perfectly expressed even by Bloom himself. And what Foucault underscores, Bloom and company would downplay: the social determinations of the imagination.

I think, however, that Kristeva in such works as *Tales of Love* (1983, 1987) and *Black Sun* (1987, 1989) provides the most comprehensive psychoanalytic formulation of the motive for this elitist resistance of style. For my purposes here, her more succinct Lacanian definition of the processes of identification that Freud first theorized, which is given in the recently published essay "Identification and the Real" (1990), will do quite nicely. The first part of the quotation (down through "the imaginary and the real") should be read as proposing a normative model of psychic development via the processes of identification with the Other that moves from the purely imaginary through the culturally symbolic to the confrontation with human finitude in the reality of death:

> Let us therefore understand identification as meaning this movement by which the subject comes into being, through a process where he or she becomes one with another, identical to him- or herself. I am not saying that the subject model him- or herself on the Other, which would be a characteristic of the formal plastic uncertainty of mere comparison. On the contrary, transferred to the Other, in identification, I become One with the Other throughout the whole range of the symbolic, the imaginary and the real. Freud evokes the intensity of an Einfuhlung, an empathy appropriate to certain amorous, hypnotic or

even mystical states. He also indicates that the primary identification of the subject occurs with a primitive figure which he calls [an imaginary] "father in the personal prehistory" (*Vater der personlichen Vorzeit*), and which, he argues, possesses the sexual attributes of both parents.[12]

From the rest of this quotation, I want to conclude that the emerging style of "neopragmatism" as an increasingly dominant mode of thought and writing in American culture and as a hegemonic form of professional life in American theory necessarily entails this revisionary identification with what is the intellectual equivalent of the pre-Oedipal imaginary father, a figure inheriting all of the narcissistically invested characteristics of the abjected pre-oedipal mother-child fusion state that, mutatis mutandis, attends the original empathetic identification with one's intellectual masters. Bloom's imaginary mother for Yahweh is a good case in point. Instead of seeing such psychoanalytic formulations as an inappropriate generalization of the family romance and misapplication of its paradigmatic force to the interpretative moment in the critical act, it would be better to see any later act of identification—professional or otherwise—as necessarily involving all the phases of the empathetic imagination, however supposedly primary, radically ambivalent, or rationally critical. Given such a perspective, one can begin to see why in Bloom's commentary in *The Book of J* all distinctions—generic, discursive, cognitive— disintegrate into a heavily cadenced prose melange that repeatedly regresses to ever-earlier origins to end up in the following passage, which sounds so much like his mother/father Emerson in "History," where all of time becomes the epic theater for the sublime mask plays of oneself:

> Throughout this book, I have asked the reader to work back through three stages of varnish, plastered on by the rabbis, the Christian prelates, and the scholars, stages that converted J into Torah, Torah into Hebrew Bible, and Hebrew Bible into Old Testament. To read J, you need to clear away three sealings-off, three very formidable layerings of redaction. But if you will do the work, then as Kierkegaard says, you will give birth to your own father. Yahweh and Superego are after all versions of yourself, even if the authorities have taught you to believe otherwise. To say it another way, J's Yahweh and Freud's Superego are grand characters, as Lear is a grand character. Learning to read

J ultimately will teach you how much authority has taught you already, and how little authority knows. (306)

The best commentary on this climactic passage is in fact Emerson from "History," where he defines the "private man" as the belated inheritor of all the ages, an ironically self-divided and indeed plural subject like that of Emerson's postmodern pragmatist offspring, which must freely envision its self-conscious agon as an ever early (because never finally defined) mobile self, a self of pure never-to-be-realized possibility: "The philosophical perception of identity through endless mutations of form makes him know the Proteus. What else am I who laughed or wept yesterday, who slept last night like a corpse, and this morning stood and ran? And what see I on any side but the transmigrations of Proteus."[13] Late Bloom and company, those nostalgic pragmatists of the American spirit one and all, can be then nothing more than what their imaginary father, Emerson, here conceives as these perpetually disintegrating masks of Proteus. In sum, they have become what he beheld in a perfect fulfillment of their own prophecy of the contingent imagination.

The contingent imagination's compensatory dream of evading the psychosexual and social determinations of intellectual agency so as to become a self-determining protean imagination (or self-made "rhetorical man") may be heroic-sounding in our postmodern age of ever-diminishing personal possibilities. It is, however, a dangerously seductive vision leading critics to the dead end of endless individual self-transformation to no end. Unlike both Foucault's historical formulation of the plural subject and Kristeva's psychoanalytic conception of the necessarily social nature of identification and identity formation, both of which we have seen before and will see again, the practice of the contingent imagination by late Bloom and company can never lead them or anyone else to work together to draw ethical sustenance from the collective archive of noble examples of effective imaginative agency that literature and culture in fact provide because it ends up sounding more like a demonic postmodern parody of absolute idealism than like anything else in the modern history of thought:

Dear Reader: I wonder if you may not sometimes have felt inclined to doubt a little the correctness of the familiar philosophic maxim that the external is the internal, and the internal the external. Perhaps you have cherished in your heart a secret which you felt in all its joy or pain was too precious for you to share with another. Perhaps your life has brought you in contact with some person of whom you suspected something of the kind was true, although you were never able to wrest his secret from him either by force or cunning. Perhaps neither of these presuppositions applies to you and your life, and yet you are not a stranger to this doubt; it flits across your mind now and then like a passing shadow. Such a doubt come and goes, and no one knows whence it comes, nor whither it goes. For my part I have always been heretically-minded on this point in philosophy, and have therefore early accustomed myself, as far as possible, to institute observations and inquiries concerning it. I have sought guidance from those authors whose views I shared on this matter; in short, I have done everything in my power to remedy the deficiency in the philosophical works.[14]

Now here is a mask play for us with real bite.

9 A Postmodern Poetics of Critical Reading

Richard Rorty in *Contingency, Irony, and Solidarity* defines critical reading as a revisionary redescription. Rorty understands all texts in terms of the new vocabulary or, more weakly, the new configuration of established vocabularies they deploy (9). The purpose of such critical reading is primarily to place oneself, via the more or less transparent mask of the Other, in a story that grants the pleasures of ironic reflection. Any assumption of critical reading's larger professional, social, or historical effects Rorty simply dismisses as a fantastic and potentially dangerous pretention. Besides, for Rorty, large-scale historical change is pure happenstance, an unpredictable change in our habits of speaking, not a grand intentional act of a people. [1]

His contrast of Heidegger and Proust encapsulates his view perfectly. Heidegger responds to the apparent exhaustion of the Western tradition by redefining "the ultimate business of philosophy" as a major representative of his "nation of philosophers." [2] It is "to preserve the force of the most elementary words in which Dasein expresses itself, and to keep the common understanding from leveling them off to that unintelligibility which functions . . . as a source of pseudo-problems" (*BT,* 262). Heidegger's career, as Rorty sees it, is thus the repeated identification and reinterpretation of the latest "litany" of "the most elementary words" that have sublimely struck him. Heidegger's project is a single-handed and vain attempt to resuscitate traditional philosophy (metaphysics) and with it the entirety of Western culture.

For Rorty, the primary problem with this self-deluding heroic effort is that Heidegger thinks his individual acts of critical reading can have world-historical effects and implications. As Heidegger's idiosyncratic readings become even more so, and his claims for his philosophical project become ever more grandiose, he appears, as the rest of the world ignores him, silly. Or, as Rorty briefly considers the one serious attempt Heidegger made to give his work a larger political effectiveness—his rectorship of the University of Freiburg as a member of the Nazi party in 1934—Heidegger appears viciously stupid. By believing that his philosophy should have greater effectiveness, Heidegger not only misunderstands the alienated situation of the professional philosopher in the modern world by thinking it can and should be overcome at all costs, he also prepared the ground for this abysmally disastrous episode in his career. For Rorty, pursuing private fantasies in the public sphere is always destructive.

Proust, on the other hand, is Rorty's liberal hero of modern sanity because he redefines and redescribes the novel genre and his life in an avowed fiction with a purely personal interest. But Proust's "success" in influencing Rorty (or anyone else) is purely "accidental," or contingent upon the later writer's own "private" revisionary project and Proust's usefulness for that project:

> Proust succeeded [where Heidegger failed] because he had no reason to believe that the sound of the name "Guermantes" would mean anything to anybody but his narrator . . . But Heidegger thought he knew some words which had, or should have had, resonance for everybody in modern Europe, words which were relevant not just to the fate of people who happen to have read a lot of philosophy books but to the public fate of the West. He was unable to believe that the words which meant so much to him—words like "Aristotle," *physis,* "Parmenides," *noein,* "Descartes," and *substantia*—were just his own private equivalents of "Guermantes," "Cambray," and "Gilberte." (*CIS,* 118)

Typically, Rorty redescribes the interpretive project for critics and philosophers alike in a broadly psychological way that proscribes any general revolutionary import. The poetics of critical reading are thereby made pragmatically appropriate for a self-confessed, "postmodern," liberal bourgeois, American humanist of the later twentieth century. Critical reading is thus suitably domesticated by Rorty for Rorty—and his many followers.

I begin with this introductory discussion of Rorty on the poetics of critical reading because in discussing the books under consideration— Richard Shusterman's *T. S. Eliot and the Philosophy of Criticism,* Jonathan Arac's *Critical Genealogies: Historical Situations for Postmodern Literary Studies,* and Gilles Deleuze's *Foucault*—I plan to stress the interpretive tension in them between what can be called, after Rorty, the Heideggerian aspiration and the Proustian recognition. In essence, then, I don't quarrel with Rorty's initial characterization of critical reading. It can be an act of revisionary redescription that deploys new and established critical vocabularies. This revisionary project's repeated purpose is to stage a self as the ironic (because self-conscious) hero in a story of one's own invention. Each critical reading represents a new self-fashioning by using the texts and authors one is redescribing as elementary materials for the production of a novel critical vocabulary, an innovative discourse that functions as one's latest critical mask. Thanks to Bloom, Rorty, and others, work in the humanities has become what these influential critics have beheld. In essence, then, I recognize the force of Rorty's Proustian recognition scene. I also see how the essential narcissistic limits of critical reading in a modern or postmodern mass culture are extremely constraining for humanistic intellectuals. One does largely talk to oneself, or even in the best of circumstances, to a few others, about such esoteric matters as the poetics of critical reading.

However, certain humanistic intellectuals, in their own times or in ours, come to have a greater influence. Heidegger and Proust and Rorty himself are obvious cases in point. And such influence can have and has had more than merely psychological effects. Disciplines have been remade, as well as personalities. And in a few, admittedly rare instances, cultures have been transformed by the combined influence of such master figures as the ancient Greeks (for the Renaissance, to give one obvious example). The power of Freud's redescription is still so great that not even the most backward Americans can escape speaking through his words and thinking in terms of his ideas. As Wallace Stevens put it so well in "A Postcard from the Volcano," what we say of something can become for subsequent generations an integral "part of what it is."[3] And significant change ever entails the potential for violence.

My point in saying all this is not to claim such grand significance for these books. Rather, it is to point to an aspect of critical reading that Rorty slights and Heidegger, in *Being and Time* especially, makes much of. Criticism and theory, like the rest of the human sciences, are essentially historical. That is, they read the texts of the past in order to discover there the residual possibilities of meaning that can be developed now to meet the emerging needs of one's future and that of one's profession or culture. The highly contestory structure of the human sciences demonstrates how critical reading is more than merely a private affair. Critical self-fashioning is a historical, even exemplary act that would redefine the possibilities of human being for others as well as for oneself, since we are, to use Heidegger's telling language, "being in the world." The cultural implications of the most abstrusely philosophical speculations are inescapable, although they sometimes are minimal or not generally useful. But sometimes such speculations are greatly influential. In any event, shorn of this larger possible horizon, why should anyone ever bother to write? Surely, promoting "solidarity" among postmodern tale-tellers to minimize "pain" in the world, as Rorty recommends, is in itself not enough motivation.

More immediately important for the literary critic and theorist, however, is mastering the play of Heideggerian (or sublime) aspiration and Proustian (or ironic) recognition. Ideally, this play manifests itself in a dynamic balance of critique and appreciation. In fact, however, when there is no such balance operating, even in an approximate manner, then there are abrupt, unexplained oscillations from one interpretive mode to another. Sometimes, the overwhelming dominance of a single mode—monumental appreciation or savage critique—discloses the ugly face of the critic's *ressentiment,* whether in disguised or more open forms. In any event, the absence of balance betrays a failure in staging the poetics of critical reading. Unable to produce a new vocabulary or to reconfigure established ones, the critic delivers an incomplete intellectual framework that cannot rationally

justify all the stories—and their necessary "logics" and interconnections—that the critic desires to tell about his or her subject while
going about constructing a mask. In the following discussion of these
three books, we will see the vicissitudes of critical reading, as their
authors attempt to perform successfully their revisionary mask plays.

Richard Shusterman in *T. S. Eliot and the Philosophy of Criticism* argues that there is more systematic theoretical reflection in Eliot's apparently occasional criticism than one at first would suspect.[4] He reminds us in some detail of Eliot's early philosophical training, of his
doctoral dissertation on Bradley's idealist epistemology. He also
traces the continuing, previously little-appreciated impact of Rus-
sell's early philosophy and personality upon the increasingly pragmatist development of Eliot's self-consciously ironic mind. And finally,
Shusterman highlights the extraordinary range and satiric precision
of Eliot's later cultural criticism conducted under the banner of conservative Christianity. In fact, Shusterman sees in Eliot's later substitution of "culture" for "tradition" a complex self-revision that results in a more comprehensive and useful idea for cultural analysis and
critique, since "culture" refers to the entirety of the forms of a people's
life whereas "tradition" inevitably carries narrower, elitist implications.

Eliot's work for Shusterman thus stands in opposition to both facile
deconstructions of the history of literary theory (or its "tradition") and
equally facile Marxist critiques of modernism as simply protofascist
aesthetic ideology. Eliot in his most caustic cultural critiques, Shusterman finds, resembles Adorno more than he does Remy de Gour-
mont; and in his "practical" orientation toward poetry and morals,
with his great concern for a "useful wisdom," Eliot resembles more
the neopragmatist, postmodern storyteller, Rorty, than he does the
Catholic theologian of creativity, Maritain. Yet such resemblances,
especially to Rorty, have their necessary limits:

> A more epistemological objection to Rorty's proposal of using vo-
> cabularies to make texts do what we want is that this seems to under-
> mine the hermeneutic project of "edifying conversation" (Rorty's
> Gadamerian alternative to foundational epistemology) by turning all
> conversation into self-centered monologue. By making texts mean
> what one wants them to mean, one denies the alterity of the text and
> its ability to maintain a different point of view; but this is to deny

what makes literature so edifying and mind-expanding. In discussing Eliot's dialogical account of reading . . . we saw instead that to learn from and properly to enjoy literature we must to some extent submit ourselves to the work, even if ultimately we must critically assess it against our own experience and view of life. Paradoxical as it sounds, we do not always want poems (or people) to say and do just what we want them to. One reason we cherish and learn from literature and people is that they resist being manipulated as mere text-objects or sex-objects. (211)

Shusterman's Eliot is one possibility of the tradition that can be re-appropriated for our time by testing out his positions, testing them, as here, against those of Rorty and Gadamer, or, as elsewhere in the book, against those of other major representatives of the most influential contemporary schools.

In the seventh chapter, for example, Shusterman finds Eliot's transformation of the early idea of "tradition" into that of "culture" in the later criticism to be far more useful for doing culture criticism today than either Gadamer's idea of "prejudice" or Derrida's idea of tradition as merely "a genetic mode of explanation" (or "sedimentation") to be deconstructed:

> Tradition is most frequently taken, as Derrida takes it, as simply a genetic mode of explanation; and tradition's genetic aspect—its emergence and development from the past and its account of present features by relating them to the past—is obvious enough not to belabor here. What needs to be emphasized is that tradition also affords a structural standpoint, since many of tradition's past elements are still actively present alongside what they have helped generate and are thus available as terms of relations for structural accounts of the meaning of later elements. In other words, a tradition is not a mere sequence of clusters of random items, but [as Bourdieu puts it in *Outline of a Theory of Practice and Distinction*] a sequence of structures structured by the past and structuring the present and future. The main point in Eliot's early rehabilitation of tradition was this living presence of past tradition and the consequent conception of tradition as a structural and not merely a genetic order, and hence "as a principle of aesthetic, not merely historical, criticism." (187)

This passage, and indeed this entire chapter, is typical of the book as a whole. Shusterman deploys the language of contemporary theory,

Anglo-American and continental, to create a comprehensive framework or novel relational network in which Eliot's criticism can be re-
described, redefined, and revaluated—usually to the enhancement of
our appreciation of the critical potential it still possesses. He uses
Eliot as a structural vantage point from which to judge the adequacy
of current formulations in light of past formulations, even as he uses
the terms of the present to understand and, when necessary, elaborate
and critique the past, as in the case of Eliot's reactionary politics and
anti-Semitism.

In other words, Shusterman enacts perfectly the dialectical order
existing between past and present, authority and innovation, proposed in Eliot's most famous essay, "Tradition and the Individual Talent" (1919): "Whoever has approved this idea of order, of the form of
European, of English literature will not find it preposterous that the
past should be altered by the present as much as the present is directed
by the past."[5] Shusterman thus nicely balances, throughout this brilliant, readable book, sublime aspiration for himself (and his chosen
subject) and ironic recognition of his own (and his subject's) human
limitations. Eliot is his magnanimous mask, not a grandly strained or
cruelly demonic one.

T. S. Eliot and the Philosophy of Criticism is simply the best book on
Eliot's criticism yet to appear. It is carefully researched, eloquently
argued, comprehensively informed about the latest developments,
and lucidly and elegantly written. Shusterman re-creates Eliot as a
figure for its author's highest concerns in an exemplary way that demonstrates not only the necessity of self-interest in critical reading but,
as well, the continuing general viability of Eliot for our time.

Jonathan Arac's *Critical Genealogies* is certainly as fine a book as
Shusterman's, even if it is also more problematic.[6] It is at once both
more ambitious and more modest than a single-author study. It is obviously more ambitious, as illustrated by its three major interrelated
divisions, respectively entitled "The History of Romanticism in Contemporary Criticism," "The Discipline of Wholeness," and "History
in Contemporary Critical Practice." This sequence of titles suggests a
dialectical substitution of "history" for "romanticism" in contemporary criticism, after the necessary deconstruction of the organic ideology informing the founding Arnoldian assumptions of the discipline
of Anglo-American literary studies. The book is also more modest in
that it eschews definitiveness, and courts open-endedness by practic-

ing provisionality. The repeated gesture of suggestive introductoriness arises in part from the origins of the book's chapters in occasional pieces for various audiences, composed and revised over the last decade or so. But, finally, there is something self-consciously provisional about the book as a "whole," as is to be expected from a book whose central section deconstructs the idea of "wholeness" itself, or whose subtitle—"Historical Situations for Postmodern Literary Studies"— stresses the provisional and the plural. I admire this emphasis and have attempted to emulate it here.

Some reviewers do not read this provisionality as intentional.[7] Instead, they complain that this is really three books in one, with the result that none of these three projects is seen as comprehensively or definitively realized. Depending upon which major strand of the book one follows, it can be read, equally, as a thematic study of the fortunes of romanticism in contemporary criticism, as a institutional analysis of the Arnoldian translation of organicism into literary studies, or as a critical prognosis for the most viable uses of "history" in current criticism. Yet, even as I recount these three projects one cannot help but see their necessary interconnections. Romanticism, organicism, and history belong, however problematically, together; in fact, they emerge and are perhaps most memorably enshrined as a complex problematic in such literary and philosophical monuments of early nineteenth-century German culture as *Faust* and *The Phenomenology of Spirit.*

However, in its parts and as a "whole," the book itself only suggests such a full-scale critical historical framework. Mostly, it engages in finely detailed local analyses of one aspect or another of its three big concerns. Some of these critical analyses—of Harold Bloom, de Man, Jameson, Arnold, D. H. Lawrence's modernist revision of the sublime, F. O. Matthiesen's Arnoldian appropriation of the American Renaissance—are often richly suggestive preliminary sketches for the definitive major studies that would comprehensively confirm the many important claims made. Perhaps because of their even greater provisionality, some of the less finished analyses are often merely provocative. I am thinking of the new historicist critiques of Geoffrey Hartman and the New York intellectuals, and especially of the neo-Lacanian, feminist critique of Wordsworth.

The balance in Arac's text between his sublime aspiration and ironic self-recognition is itself extremely provisional. Wordsworth, for instance, appears at first worthy of severe critique—in Arac's reading of "Nutting"—for desiring symbolically to castrate Mother Nature as the poetic equivalent of actually displacing women here and throughout his poetry into a subordinate, ministering position, a displacement into a functionary of male culture that Arac claims, following recent feminist literary critics, was being enacted historically. (How intentional this finger-pointing style of criticism may be is not fully clear.) But thereafter, Arac finds Wordsworth of *The Prelude* to be an entirely positive figure: heroic prophet of both Baudelairean modernity and Benjaminian postmodernism. By not explicitly demonstrating at length but only loosely suggesting (47–49) the necessary connections between these different figures of Wordsworth, how one must also be or become the other, the poles of aspiration and recognition, appreciation and critique remain suggestively, provocatively, but also jarringly, extreme. Arac's Wordsworthian masks do not mesh well, suggesting again that he has not created a critical framework sufficiently comprehensive and definitive to tie up all the loose ends. His poetics of critical reading, in other words, still need to be perfected.

Chapter 8, "Walter Benjamin and Material Historiography," however, presents Arac's postmodern provisional style in its best light. There he tests out the possibilities of Benjamin's analysis of "metropolism"—the definitive formative power of the modern urban landscape upon the language and sensibilities of modern writers and their readers—by bringing into significant relation Wordsworth and Conrad, Baudelaire and Emily Dickinson. For both reasons of space and repetition in the inconclusive treatment of Wordsworth, I will focus on the latter conjunction.

What Arac finds at first is a remarkable aesthetic harmony between the two writers in terms of their disjunctive metonomyic perception of a transiently sublime, horrifyingly opaque, ordinary world. Modernity, as that patron saint of postmodern theorists, Benjamin, understands it, has clearly overtaken both poets. But, Arac rightly asks, how can this be the case with Dickinson, since hers is not a metropolitan environment by any apparent stretch of the imagination? Her room with a view of the cemetery in her father's house and her secluded garden in mid-nineteenth-century Amherst, Massachusetts surely don't impact the same as Paris upon the poetic sensibility. So how explain the similarities of poetic effects in their work that Arac deftly points out?

Arac, following Benjamin's general lead, argues persuasively, in detail, that the source of modernity's disjunctive metonymic style is not immediately the city in either Baudelaire or Dickinson. Rather, this experience of the cityscape is mediated for them both, becomes available to them for aesthetic perception and poetic purposes, via the sudden pervasiveness of the modern newspaper. The newspaper's sensational format, after all, is a paradigmatic case of metonymic, collagelike perspectivity and disjunctiveness, a kind of protocubist or mosaiclike effect that Eliot in *The Waste Land* and Joyce in *Ulysses* will fully exploit.

> It's not just that both [Dickinson and Baudelaire] lived in the era of high capitalism, but that some of the key mediations by which commodity exchange affected perception were also shared between Amherst and Paris. In both cases, the mosaic dispersion of advertisements over the page offered a new field for perception arising from the great expansion of the market for commodities. (211)

In this way the newspaper mediated the mosaic dispersion of high capitalism's primary locale, the urban metropolis.

Arac thus proves very resourceful in both saving the possibility of Benjamin's materialist historiography and revising it, making it more historically specific and critically sophisticated in its conception of cultural mediation and diffusion. Recognizing the confines of Benjamin's productive influence is the result of Arac's judiciousness here. This is a considerable achievement for him and postmodern critics more generally. As Paul de Man remarked, "in the profession you are no one unless you have said something" about Benjamin.[8] And Arac has said his "something" here to our great benefit.

Arac balances wonderfully the critic's aspiration to sublimity that would turn his critical mask of "Benjamin" opportunistically against itself and the recognition of the necessary limits to all such resentfully aspiring turnabouts.

> We reach back to rescue from the danger of oblivion a figure [of Benjamin] that inspires us but also threatens to embarrass us. We find ourselves in Benjamin as he found himself in Baudelaire. Unless we

can also establish critical distance from Benjamin, as Benjamin did from Baudelaire, we can only play the farce of his tragedy. (214)

Perhaps this problematic of influence, self-consciously and elegantly thematized here, is what haunts the rest of *Critical Genealogies*, making for its radical provisionality?

If Shusterman fully knows his power as a critical interpreter and so can show his appreciation of (as well as reservation for) Eliot's work, then Arac, it seems, doesn't generally know his own strength and so doesn't know how much he can afford to appreciate those he reconstructs and revaluates, however partially. This is true except in the case of Benjamin, whose focus on sublime fragments and whose own fragmentary style clearly strike in Arac a sympathetic yet (self-)critical chord.

Although I have perhaps been a bit hard on *Critical Genealogies*, it's not because of lack of respect. This book is the finest collection of theoretical essays seriously reflecting on the possibilities of writing a critical history of literary modernity from Wordsworth to deMan yet to appear. It promises a future definitive study, and, in many of its chapters, more than begins to make good on that promise. Deleuze in *Foucault* has no problem balancing critique and appreciation, sublime aspiration and ironic recognition, the Heidegger and the Proust in himself.[9] This is so because in his poetics of critical reading Deleuze gives up even the pretense of critical distance and completely transforms Foucault into his own revisionary mask, a prophetic mouthpiece of the Deleuzian theories of subject formation and schizocriticism. Foucault, for his friend, is a "new archivist" of the nonrational bases of rational knowledge and a "new cartographer" of the configurations of power that permeate knowledge to construct individual yet essentially interchangeable subject positions in the modern disciplinary society.

Deleuze also sees Foucault as the Theorist as Outsider. He is ever "thinking otherwise," of the Outside of Otherness. Foucault can explore the fissures in the archive and the lapses in discipline that inevitably accompany the power/knowledge of our scientific regime of truth. This is so because the representative spaces in a culture can never be entirely saturated by the appropriate images of the prescribed norms. And Foucault is the first to exploit this fact fully. Historical formations (or "strata" in archeological analysis) and strategies of power (on nonstratified, generally circulating disciplinary forces) combine in Foucault to produce the contours of an "inside" (or subjectivity). So in volumes 2 and 3 of *The History of Sexuality,* for example, Foucault emphasizes the styles of "the relation to oneself" that different cultures with their different moral codes permit to inform the process of individual subjectivation. To Deleuze (and to me), then, the late Foucault answers those critics who say he never seriously addresses the question of agency. In this way, too, Foucault discloses the all-important differences in ethical stylization that defines cultures— such as ancient Greece and modern Europe—as different.

Deleuze has Foucault envisioning how the cultural "Outside" (the external cultural world and the haunting specter of what is also external to its norms) gets folded over by power/knowledge as it operates the regime of truth of the disciplinary society. This "folding" is like a Möbius strip, a figure with an "inside" entirely on the surface. How this is precisely done, and to what degree people are empowered to give some ethical shape of their own to these "figures" of the subject, are the things that distinguish a coercive culture from a less coercive, or even comparatively noncoercive culture.

Despite his uncritical monumentalization of his friend, Deleuze's statements about the phenomenon of doubling in Foucault do make an important contribution to our understanding. His remarks come in the last chapter on subjectivation, entitled, intriguingly enough, "Foldings; or the Inside of Thought." I cite now a cento of passages that summarize Deleuze on his "Foucault" on the theory of the subject:

> The unthought is therefore not external to thought but lies at its very heart, as that impossibility of thinking which doubles or hollows out the outside. . . . The inside as an operation of the outside: in all his work Foucault seems haunted by this theme of an inside which is merely the fold of the outside. . . . The theme which has always haunted Foucault is that of the double. But the double is never a projection of the interior; on the contrary, it is an interiorization of the outside. It is not a doubling of the One, but a redoubling of the Other. It is not a reproduction of the Same, but a repetition of the Different. It is not the emanation of an "I," but something that places in immanence an always other or a Non-self. It is never the other who is a double in the doubling process, it is a self that lives me as the double

of the other: I do not encounter myself on the outside, I find the other in me. . . . It resembles exactly the invagination of a tissue in embryology, or the act of doubling in sewing: twist, fold, stop, and so on. (97–98)

Deleuze's major point is that the regions eluding the hegemony of the normal—such as that of the "mad"—constitute the Outside of power/knowledge and its current regime of scientific rationality. This is the Outside of the unthought haunting thought. It is this Outside, in its unthought relation to thinking, that folds over itself to form the figure of an Inside, what can be called a "oneself." The "oneself" is a complex doubling reflection made up of heterogeneous yet textually interwoven fragments from the discourses of established and transgressive subjectivities. Foucault posits "the relation to oneself" in the late work to discuss the different ethical stylizations of sexuality in different cultures. This "relation to oneself" is an overdetermined and overdetermining, provisional discourse of self, a textual phenomenon that I call the "Over-Self." It affords multiple subject positions for "individuals" to occupy and form themselves, according to the moral codes of a particular society and the professional codes of a particular discipline or field of knowledge. This "Over-Self," however, is not an "individual" production. It is the dominant, albeit composite, mask of a culture. It is always already inherently self-parodying, given its provisional, composite status. At best, it appears as a dynamic balance of facets, a coherent story of successful mask play—that is, as the magnanimous poetics of critical reading. Deleuze's transformation of Foucault into a prophetic mask of his "schizosubjectivity" discloses in radical form the poetics of critical reading. A culture authorizes a range of possible instances of its dominant, composite mask, from which people select and revise their latest incarnations, appropriating and being appropriated by their culture, as they make themselves be made into "individual" subjects. Critics, practicing the poetics of reading, redescribe the terms in which these masks can be understood. As a result, the unthought of a culture can begin to be thought as the unthought, thereby leading to the production of new masks, new discursive embodiments for the recurring blind spots of reason. These new cultural possibilities are in principle critically different from the established norms of a society.

The productive power of critical reading must be balanced by an appreciation for the achievement being read; otherwise, as we see elsewhere in this book, the monumental or satiric transformation of the Other into one's plaything just memorializes one's *ressentiment* of another's "genius." Sublime aspiration, balanced by the recognition of one's limits, permits the unthought to be thought in new masks generally available to others for their use. Shusterman's "Eliot" throughout, Arac's "Benjamin," and, at moments, Deleuze's "Foucault" can become, I think, just such innovative masks or "Over-Selves."

10 Selves in Flames
Derrida, Rorty, and the New Orthodoxy in Theory

Near the conclusion of his *Of Spirit: Heidegger and the Question,* Jacques Derrida imagines what an assembly of various theologians might say to Martin Heidegger, in light of his attempts to speak differently "of spirit," and especially in light of his attempt to do so in his famous interpretation of Georg Trakl's poetry (1953).[1] Heidegger wishes to speak in a way that avoids or evades all previous common uses of the term "spirit," particularly those revised, mediated, and disseminated by the ontotheological tradition. Derrida's imaginative invocation includes in the sublime tribunal theologians orthodox and heterodox, Moslem and Christian, and, of course, Jewish. In this scene, Derrida ventriloquizes his question, as if through the mask of himself as a believer: "When you speak of ["spirit"], of flame and fire-writing in the promise, in accord with the promise of return towards the land of pre-archi-originarity [echoing equally tropes of Eden and of the Promised Land], it is not certain that you would not receive a comparable reply and similar echo from my friend and coreligionary, the Messianic Jew" (111). In short, Derrida here— carefully, via the double negative, the grammatical form of the dialectical negation of the negation—turns the tables on Heidegger for a moment. (About what precedes and follows this "dramatic" moment, more later.) And this turnabout raises the specter that Heidegger is unthinkingly repeating the Jewish archetype (or mythologem) of "spirit" precisely when he thinks he is proposing an original return to a pre-Judeo-Christian, long lost, and indeed pagan (Greek) conception of "spirit" that only Old High German retains a ghostly vestige of, which somehow Trakl and now Heidegger after him have managed to stumble upon once again. Given Heidegger's involvement with the Nazis and his sincerely opportunistic use of "spirit" and related categories in their support during the 1930s, this scene of turnabout, this comic auto-da-fé of flame befuddled by flame, truly would be fair play, especially in light of Heidegger's postwar refusal, with one infamously insensitive exception, ever to address openly the question of the Final Solution, the Holocaust.[2] Derrida, a Jew and lifelong student of Heidegger's texts, is thus telling a story, staging a "mask play," in which his "teacher" is really speaking Hebrew just as he thinks he is "originally" speaking ancient Greek by way of the presumably privileged relation of Old High German to this "great" dead language.[3]

I begin with this penultimate scene from *Of Spirit* because it displays in its most interesting and complex form the problematic defining what I'm calling the "new orthodoxy in theory," which all three of these volumes in their different ways reflect. To put it simply and, unfortunately, a bit reductively, I see theory now as a "field" for the performance of a certain cultural ritual of postmodern intellectuals. The "theorist" assembles from the collective archive figures, texts, contexts, issues, problems, and questions and reconfigures them into a story told according to the constraints of professional conventions upon personal desire, as these constraints apply—unevenly, to be sure—to the theorist in question. (A Derrida or Rorty has more freedom in this respect than a lesser-known person.) A suitable mask play is thereby performed, in which pressing intellectual, political, and personal matters are played out but in a conventional form that privileges the contingent imagination of professional revisionism. In this diminished way, as Hegel first claimed in *The Phenomenology of Spirit,* intellectual "culture" truly becomes a "discipline" that the modern alienated critic is to produce and consume as a series of "selves," since the story told, the mask play performed, as a whole (and not solely in any of its figures or masks) constitutes the critic's self at each moment. "Plot" is truly the self, if not the soul, of this drama. The critic thus projects and reflects upon a continuously changing totality-in-the-making of textual agency with no final form in sight, since the Hegelian tropes of Absolute Knowledge and Absolute Spirit are conventionally unavailable in a relativistic epoch.[4]

In different ways, these three volumes perform this cultural ritual of critical intellectuals repeatedly-in-the-making. *Redrawing the Lines: Analytic Philosophy, Deconstruction, and Literary Theory,* edited by Reed Way Dasenbrock, presents eleven leading figures from analytic philosophy and literary theory reflecting on the current assimilation of deconstruction into an Anglo-American institutional context. The traditional resource of analytic philosophy—systematically logical critique of ordinary and poetic language, of judgment and justice, and of scientific rationality and truth—are now being supplemented by the problematic of reading and intertextuality, of grand narratives giving way to self-conscious story fragments or tales, of reason's sublime limits in the awe-ful metaphysics of presence, or power's cunning practices of repression and empowerment. In sum, this collection, as a whole, brilliantly and eloquently testifies to the incredible increase in the array of materials that the encounter between these two traditions—analytic and continental philosophy—has now placed largely at the disposal—appropriately enough, given their initial training in literary study—of literary theorists. Both Dasenbrock in his useful introduction and Anthony J. Cascardi in a fine afterword make this very clear by focusing their expositions and arguments so much on the contribution to the volume by Charles Altieri. In following their lead, I don't mean to slight any of the other contributors, who discuss in provocative and effective ways the coalescence of topics I cite above; constraints of space require that I, too, focus on Altieri's essay.[5] Besides, if an avowed humanist theorist now openly practices and theorizes criticism as mask play, then we can see how institutionalized revisionism has become.

In "Judgment and Justice under Postmodern Conditions; or, How Lyotard Helps Us Read Rawls as a Postmodern Thinker," Altieri wittily brings together John Rawls and Jean-François Lyotard less to explore their reciprocal inadequacies, although he does this with his

customary brilliance, than to demonstrate that Lyotard in his statements on judgment and justice typically adopts the postmodern move
of bringing to bear on the specifics of any argument or situation an
absolute irony dissolving all human conditionality and agency—and
hence all ethics—into a purely Nietzschean laughter. The soberer
Rawls, despite his limitations—his lack of Lyotard's self-critical
"spirit"—at least forces us to consider the specific circumstances of
any so-called rational claim to justice, and such restraint entails, Altieri shows by implicit recourse to Wittgenstein's linguistic analysis
of "forms of life," critical consideration of the site in which we make
and analyze all such claims. That is, Altieri demonstrates how all
modern critical intellectuals, existing in historically specific professional and disciplinary situations, derive the terms, figures, arguments, problems, issues, and styles from the Western "cultural
grammar" we have assimilated and been assimilated by—to varying
degrees, of course. Our revisionary desires, positing "potential identities" (86), play themselves out according to the speculative "logics" of this cultural grammar, so that our empirical and textual dimensions combine to compose an open-ended critical dialectic of
actual and hypothetical "selves," all within the general postmodern
context.

Altieri's point is not to argue against various efforts to transcend
our Western intellectual conditioning by enlarging the canon, cri-
tiquing Enlightenment rationality, or politicizing the traditional formal questions of aesthetics. Rather, it is to dramatize, contrastively,
the limits of these efforts, which are even more limited when such
conditioning is ignored, or easily—all too easily—dismissed by critics such as Lyotard and others whose claims to possessing a systematic
political position or ethical theory are just so much badly informed,
bad-faith, self-congratulatory rhetoric. If Lyotard, a postmodern philosopher, has not much of a political theory, how can postmodern literary critics hope to have any coherent position not reducible to "political correctness" clichés? I now quote, at some length, from Altieri's complex conclusion:

> But as we try to live in accord with certain hypothetical possibilities
> we may be able to give expression to modes of behavior that are poten-
> tial within our own psyches and within our own cultural traditions,
> although rarely realized in the marketplace. These potential identities

are as public as any tribal obligations. They get their claims upon us from the symbolic order sustained by cultural traditions, and they require our accepting certain determinate communal criteria. . . . We cannot be sure we do not delude ourselves in casting ourselves as free to make such identifications. . . . If one cannot escape the empirical self, one can try to bracket it and to find in such hypotheticals other aspects of our nature that can then effect practical judgment to the degree that they focus or intensify commitments to justice that are already part of the social fabric we inherit. Such experiments require replacing the consolations of metaphysical theater [Nietzschean laughter], however ironic or pataphysical, by the demands of a publicly constructed tribunal for which we take responsibility as its authors and its addresses, since the condition of going on stage is being able to become authors identified with their characters. The play we see will rarely warrant rave reviews because the parts are . . . difficult to play. . . . But in this theater [that the profession is becoming] there is no more valuable lesson than that difficulty, because the constant pressure of our incommensurable differences reminds us that this is the only show in town we cannot afford to let close down. Only within its confines can we correlate the fundamental public need of postmodernity—the need for shareable norms within an increasingly diverse society—with the central private need defined by modernism—the need to be able to establish expressive identities capable of resisting intellectual climates that try to reduce everything to race, epoch, and milieu. (86–87)

Altieri thus wishes to steer a middle course between the absolute positivity of an Enlightenment rationality and the absolute negativity of a post-Enlightenment irrationality. Self-making is for him, therefore, the public dramatization, according to professional norms open to critique and change, of significantly different personal desires, in a collective attempt, from various disciplinary perspectives, to constitute and to revise a postmodern social self based upon the analysis and appreciation of distinctive aesthetic forms of both the postmodern present and (especially) the modernist past.

The limits of Altieri's representative position are best seen, curiously enough, in what Richard Rorty in his latest volume has systematically made, somewhat belatedly, of Harold Bloom's theory of revisionism. *Contingency, Irony, and Solidarity* tells the story of what Rorty dubs "ironist culture," in which leading—and following—intellectuals, in discovering the radically contingent nature of society, language, and the self, become ironically revisionary, Bloomian "strong poets." They now seek to propose ever more interesting and novel "fictions," "original" redescriptions of modern culture, that would provide both new analytic vocabularies and new redeployments of established vocabularies. Their aim is to keep the story-telling game going on indefinitely, with the only "absolute" self-consciously embraced as such being that of "solidarity," by which Rorty means the collective effort to reduce the sources of physical and psychological pain. The only constraint on the revisionary game of "ironist culture" for Rorty is the recognition that "private fantasies" and projects of "self-creation" must not be played out as if true in the "public sphere," since if they are, others (and ultimately, perhaps, oneself) could get hurt. If taken as true, our "projects of self-creation" are liable to result in a Heidegger, when what we want, really, is a Proust. That is, we want the aesthetic satisfactions of modern life's epic redescription and not the shameful, embarrassing tableaux of intellectual complicity with politics. As ironist theory and culture become ever more sophisticated, therefore, liberal democratic political discourse should staunchly reaffirm, in the simplest of terms, its most fundamental principles, in order to avoid conflating the two realms of "private fantasies" (theory) and "public policy" (practice) that constitute together our postmodern, admittedly bourgeois, "ironist culture." In sum, then, what Altieri would tentatively join together under the aegis of professional disciplines and their conventions of liberal rationality, Rorty would keep, in theory at least, asunder. This is precisely because Rorty believes "the strong poet" in a critic uses the discipline, its norms and conventions, as materials for his or her new differentiated or contrastive invention.

As we can see from the following quotation, however, Rorty, in judging the difference between a Heidegger and a Proust, implicitly assumes the existence of the professional academic context that Altieri makes explicit:

> When Nietzsche and Heidegger stick to celebrating their personal canons, stick to the little things which meant most to them, they are as magnificent as Proust. They are figures whom the rest of us can use as examples and as material in our own attempts to create a new self by writing a bildungsroman about our old self. But as soon as either tries

to put forward a view about modern society, or the destiny of Europe, or contemporary politics, he becomes at best vapid, and at worst sadistic. When we read Heidegger as a philosophy professor who managed to transcend his own condition by using the names and the words of the great dead metaphysicians as elements of a personal litany, he is an immensely sympathetic figure. But as a philosopher of our public life, as a commentator on twentieth-century technology and politics, he is resentful, petty, squint-eyed, obsessive—and, at his occasional worst (as in his praise of Hitler after the Jews had been kicked out of the universities), cruel. (119–20)

Who are "the rest of us" who can profit by Heidegger's and Nietzsche's "good" examples, even as we lament, as cautionary tales, their "bad" actions? And where do we exist that we can afford to produce our own bildungsromans? Why is Heidegger's praise of Hitler so repellent not after any of the number of hideous things he did to the Jews but, specifically, after he expelled them from "the universities"? The answers are clear: Rorty assumes the position of the critical intellectual in the disciplinary, professional, academic context of judgment that Altieri makes explicit, even as a Proust or a Nietzsche must assume their positions in a literary or philosophical tradition.

What Altieri has explicitly proposed that our intellectual project ought to be—a disciplined self-making responsibly carried out according to the revisionary norms and rational conventions of our established, liberal professions (or "critical humanism," for short)—is precisely what Rorty, following Bloom, assumes modern "ironist culture" already is, has largely been, and should continue to be. But Altieri's prophetic superannuation points to something more important and serious than the participation of the new theoretical orthodoxy in the society of the spectacle, with its stress on novelty and celebrity for their own sakes. It points, rather, to the modern tradition of proposing as a solution (emergent or recently established) what precisely is the real problem: the nonrepresentative status of intellectual life (what Rorty calls "ironist culture"), especially as it exists in America. This is something that the recent "political correctness" debate with its multiple misrecognitions makes all too clear.

To put it even more bluntly, Altieri, Rorty, Bloom—and any number of other postmodern theorists and practitioners—want us to be content with the conception of intellectual life as a continual "self-creation." The problem with this notion is not that it makes intellectual life into a cultural amusement park, a Disney World for highbrows; that, after all, would entail a representative status for intellectual life as a whole, since so much of our society is geared toward producing the amusement park effect. The problem is that what we do within the profession, if it is continual textual "self-creation" without life-altering consequences, is clearly a luxury that no other group in our society can afford. In other words, the fact that people like Altieri, Rorty, or Bloom once again successfully remake themselves in and through their textual productions and performances is not something that really matters to very many other people nowadays, or ever. That I successfully follow their example or not—whatever that may mean—is even less interesting to me. The only way "projects of self-creation" (Rorty's phrase) can significantly matter is if they are placed in larger than personal or purely professional intellectual contexts. In short, it is a Heidegger or a Pound, and not a Proust, who should become a "central" figure and should absorb our critical attention. My point is not to demean literature or to celebrate political reactionaries; it is to call for our focus on all figures whose work would be "wordly." Insofar as the intellectual's career of "self-revision" reflects and has an impact upon the historically important issues of the culture as a whole, it is to that extent that "self-revision" becomes worthy of extended analysis and meditation. Representative status—demonstrated at considerable scholarly length and not simply asserted or assumed—is the only thing that confers legitimacy on the prospects of "self-making." And, quite frankly, most members of what I'm calling the "new orthodoxy in theory"—and I include myself among their number—are neither sufficiently complex and interesting nor broadly representative of an entire culture at a particular crisis moment. The new Church of Revisionism may have a number of prophets and priests, but it has few laypersons.

Lack of representative status is certainly not Heidegger's problem. The recent debates on his Nazi affiliations, inspired by Victor Farias's 1987 book, recently published in English as *Heidegger and Nazism,* have spilled over into the newspapers and electronic media both here and abroad. Proposals for banning the teaching of his works have been seriously discussed. I cannot go into all the complexities of these debates here. So what follows is only a general sketch meant to place

Derrida's profoundly serious (self-)revision of Heidegger in its appropriate context.

Heidegger's philosophy, early and late, deploys certain sets of terms, figures of speech, and "stories" about the fate of Western culture that position his work along a continuum with the writings of Ernst Junger, a leading fascist intellectual and friend of Heidegger; of those former Freikorps officers who later formed the nucleus of the Nazi leadership; and of the "young conservatives" who inherited the aristocratic posturings of the decadent German mandarins of Weimar. Heidegger, like these others, laments the triumph of Enlightenment ideals of liberalism, democracy, cosmopolitanism, bourgeois rationality, and scientific and technological progress. Heidegger, like these others, sees in all such modern developments the emasculation of the authentic spirit of unique individuals and great peoples. Heidegger, like these others, favors 1) a "spontaneous" order of rank among individuals and peoples insofar as they are capable of fundamental thinking; 2) the heroic leader principle; 3) a linguistic nationalism; 4) a spiritual conception of nobility; and 5) a romantic religiosity connected directly to a supposedly peasantlike respect for the earth. In these preferences, Heidegger is much closer to the romantic revival that rediscovered Friedrich Hölderlin in time to make him essential reading in the trenches than he is to Nietzsche, that self-described "last good European," who always, and equally, scorned Enlightenment pretensions and reactive romantic posturings. And in what Heidegger both said and did and didn't say or do before, during, and immediately after the Second World War, careers and lives, to one degree or other, at times hung in the balance.

To put this in the most representative fashion possible, what Heidegger, like these others, opposes is what we, following Kant, call "modernity." And what Heidegger, like these others, proposes is what we, following Lyotard, call "postmodernity." For what Heidegger and his peers hate is the specter of a triumphant, democratically leveling, rationalistic universalism, and what he and his peers love is an endangered or embattled, distinctively different, passionately embraced localism. "Liberal" cosmopolitanism versus "conservative" provinciality is the cultural form of the political opposition between "liberal" and "conservative" conceptions and practices of state power. That is why Heidegger can inspire a Foucault and other poststructuralist theorists of power and politics, and why a Habermas can find them to be, for all their avowed "radicalism," neoconservatives. That is also why the "radical" celebration of the specific intellectual operating in the local situation to liberate the other of modernity, however defined, versus the universal intellectual presuming to represent an entire cultural moment is actually a contemporary opposition that recalls this earlier one between Enlightenment modernity (including Weimar) and romantic reactions (including the Nazis). We naturally want to be neither Weimar mandarins nor fascist sympathizers. In sum, the Heidegger case implicates in extremely complex and contradictory ways modern and postmodern intellectuals alike. It raises, in fact, the question of the relation existing between intellectual life and government policy—not only possibly in theory but also actually

Derrida launches a multidimensional reading of "spirit" in Heidegger. "Spirit" appears intermittently in Heidegger's work in different contexts and as different, at times contradictorily defined, German forms (*Geist, geistig, geistlich*) over more than a quarter-century, or from *Being and Time* (1927) through the infamous 1933 Rectorship Address ("The Self-Assertion of the German University") to the 1953 discussion of Trakl, "Language in the Poem." Derrida's major point is that at first Heidegger announces the imperative warning to avoid "spirit" because of its inescapable affiliations with both religious formulations and their secular transformations in modern, essentially Cartesian subjectivity. This project of "subject avoidance" is carried out in *Being and Time* via the invention of new terms ("anticipatory resoluteness") or the revision of older ones (*Dasein*) and the ironization of the mentioning of "spirit" in order to evade being made use of by conventional perspectives. This last strategy is best exemplified by Heidegger's deployment of scare quotations marks around "spirit."

After announcing this "destructive" project of avoiding "spirit" by tactics so prophetic of Derrida's own deconstructive moves, however, Heidegger next uses the term entirely without irony in the Rectorship Address to express support, however colored by obvious bad faith and complicated by unwitting self-contradictions, for the Führer principle as a model of reconstructing the university system and indeed all of German existence. Thereafter, Derrida claims, "spirit" largely disappears in Heidegger's texts until it resurfaces in the Trakl discussion, where Heidegger defines "spirit"—that is, the original ironized "spirit" of *Being and Time* and not the ironically unironic "spirit" of the Rectorship Address—not as "breath," which is too Judeo–Christian, but "flame," which is pre-Judeo–Christian, Greek, pagan— and, miraculously, close to what the Old High German sense of "spirit" once intimated.

Of course, Derrida points out that "spirit" as "flame" is clearly not purely pre- or anti-Christian, since, for example, God's "holy spirit" appears in the Bible as fiery pillars, bushes, and tongues. What are we to make of Heidegger's reading here, and how is it related both to the question of his complicity with Nazism and to the question of fundamental questioning—that is, to the form of questioning that raises the question of the meaning of Being?

Derrida sees in Heidegger's failure to follow his own imperative of avoiding "spirit" and in his unwitting repetitions of its subjectivist and religious meanings a fateful predisposition to be led to a prior affirmation of the unquestioned and unquestionable value of fundamental questioning—to a prior affirmation that cannot be distinguished from critical blindness. Moreover, Derrida sees in Heidegger's case an allegory of the fate of any critic's "deconstruction" of the ontotheological tradition. Derrida, in effect, reads into his "Heidegger" the "law" of deconstruction: that one can never definitively "overcome" the constellations of what he terms the "mythologems" and "philosogems" defining Western culture, however much one may be able to "master" (or "stage"), for a time, to one degree or other, different aspects of their interplay and reformulation.

To his credit, however, Derrida magnanimously grants Heidegger his final word of rebuttal to this critique (111–13), before Derrida gives the really last word to his envisioned sublime tribunal of theologians:

"Yes, precisely," [Heidegger's] interlocutors would then reply [to such a rebuttal], "that's just what we're saying, at the same crossing of paths, and these paths would be equally but otherwise circular: we are appealing to this entirely other in the memory of a promise or the promise of a memory. That's the truth of what we have always said, heard, tried to make heard. The misunderstanding is that you hear us better than you think or pretend to think. In any case, no misunderstanding on our part, from now on, it's enough to keep talking, not to interrupt. . . . The spirit which keeps watch in returning [*en re-verant*, as a ghost] will always do the rest. Through flame or ash, but as the entirely other, inevitably." (113)

Who, finally, can this "spirit which keeps watch in returning" be but "the entirely other, inevitably" that appears right here, "through flame or ash," as Derrida's unwittingly Jewish "Heidegger"?

So, then, Derrida, too, performs the cultural ritual of postmodern intellectuals-in-the-making as a mask play he produces or story he tells about one of his elected, truly representative precursors, thereby confirming with the highest, most profound, and thoroughly sophisticated practice of my "new orthodoxy in theory." As I end, however, I'd like to propose a different, ironically doubling reading of Heidegger's "blind" repetition of the Judeo-Christian conception of "spirit" precisely at the moment when he is claiming to disclose, via Trakl's poetry, its Greco-Germanic "otherness," long repressed and now, in 1953, released and returning. Suppose we adduce the context of the Holocaust and Heidegger's inexplicable silence in response to it. What then? Could it not be that Heidegger, who surely did know that the Judeo-Christian trope of tropes for spirit is "fire," is himself staging, as a self-elected expiation, his own comically humiliating, metaphysical pratfall or purely "spiritual" auto-da-fé? Could it not be, furthermore, that this "spectral" spectacle shadowing Heidegger's ostensible intentions, which Derrida has just deconstructively elaborated, would not so much enfigure the cosmic conflagration of the "meditative," Heraclitean "fire" of the great Aletheia essay of ten years before, as prefigure the nuclear apocalypse scenario that the then-new "super-weapon," the H-bomb, rightly inspired? Such a "self-explosive" Heidegger, in other words, would simply blow Derrida, Rorty, and the "new orthodoxy in theory" completely away. Wouldn't it be pretty to think that this "total" Heidegger were the true one?[6]

III Reconstructing a Practice

11 Smiling Through Pain
The Practice of Self in *The Rise of Silas Lapham*

*The Puritan wanted to be a man of calling {*Berufsmensch*}—we must be.*   —*Max Weber*

Two brief scenes from the latter half of *The Rise of Silas Lapham* interest me.[1] In the first scene, Penelope Lapham faces Mr. Corey, the rich young man who loves her but who everyone else had assumed loved her sister, Irene. He has come to find out why, after his confession of love, Penelope refuses to have anything to do with him, since no one has bothered, especially not his beloved, to explain the confusion to him. "He came toward her, and then stood faltering. A faint smile quivered over her face at the spectacle of his subjection" (253). In the second scene, also involving Penelope (alone with her mother), the girl's faint smile at Corey's subjection returns, only this time in a context that suggests the gradual dissolution of her resolve. When she learns that Corey had offered "on her account" to invest money in her father's business in his time of financial troubles, Penelope twice censures such efforts as vain and silly attempts to change her. However, in "repeating the censure" the second time, we learn that her mother thinks "her look was not so severe as her tone; she even smiled a little" (302). It seems a change is going to come.

It also appears as if the repetition of the spectacle of another's subjection has the power of changing one's cruel smile into a look whose smile betrays the diminishing severity of such cruelty. What initially is a smiling that arises from the example of one's power to cause another to stage his own subjection transforms itself, when reiterated, into a smiling that appears more promising, despite the repetition of the most painful contrary avowals. "Smiling through" in the first sense of "arising from" thus becomes "smiling through" in the second sense of "in spite of appearances to the contrary." A structure of resentment—conditioned by social, cultural, or sexual differences in position and power—arises from the assumption of moral superiority that another's willing subjection confirms. This ironic structure then gives way to a process of sublimation that bit by bit enables one to appreciate the subjected other's generous if misguided sacrifices. And Corey's sacrifices are truly generous, because his father, like his model, Mr. Bennett from *Pride and Prejudice,* has spent most of the family fortune in cultivating a life of leisured irony and aesthetic refinement.

In any event, Penelope cannot permit herself to have her rich young man, without a protracted and painful trial of both her own and his motives. *Tears, Idle Tears,* an imaginary sentimental novel in a grieving Tennysonian mode, is the immediate source of her inspiration for this course of action. It tells the tale of an old-fashioned heroine and hero who make wildly satisfying but unnecessary sacrifices for each other. In fact, their trial is endless and climaxes in their exorbitant sacrifice of personal happiness for romantic principle. Despite her own better judgment of this novel as incredibly unrealistic, Penelope, the clever, witty sister, nevertheless allows the novel to shape the romantic crisis of *Silas Lapham.*

As Walter Benn Michaels recently notes, however, the novel's "realism" repudiates this romantic subplot.[2] It does so dramatically, by subversively undoing, via these scenes of Penelope's resentful cruelty and lessening resolve, the sentimental ideology of heroic self-sacrifice informing popular novels of the time. And it does so discursively, by incorporating critiques of what Reverend Sewell, Howells's apparent spokesman on the topic, refers to as the genre's excessive "economy of pain" (41). Sewell complains that popular novels cultivate among the youth a dangerous prevalence of the imagination of self-sacrifice, which can even encourage a sensitive reader like Penelope, in the name of morality, to give up her love, rather than betray her sister's romantic hopes. Penelope thereby makes many others, besides herself, suffer needlessly.

Michaels, following the lead of these critical discussions, reaches the conclusion that the "popular novel," with its "monstrously [Sewell's word] disproportionate emphasis on love and self-sacrifice, turns out, surprisingly enough, to be the literary equivalent of the greedy and heartless stock market, which produces wealth out of all proportion to labor or merit." Moreover, Michaels continues, "Realism [is] Howells's literary equivalent of the Lapham's domestic economy and of the Reverend Sewell's 'economy of pain.'" Why? Because "all three stand in precarious opposition to the excesses of capitalism and the sentimental novel or, rather, to the excessiveness that is here seen to lie at the heart of both the economy and the literature" (41). This opposition between realism, precapitalist domestic economy, and a restricted economy of pain; and naturalism, speculative capitalism, and an excessive, nonrestrictive economy of sacrifice is precarious for Michaels because the ideal of intentional self-limitation informing Howells's trinity of traditional values is itself unrealistic, hopelessly outmoded by the emerging culture of mass—and massive—(self-)consumption.

Howells, for Michaels, is thus the exemplar of American realism—a much-disputed term that, like naturalism, he rightly prefers not to define. Suffice it to say, for Michaels, that Howells's fiction, especially *Silas Lapham,* composes a restricted economy of expenditure—psychic, financial, cultural—that hearkens back to the precapitalist era of domestic economy, of primitive and prudent enterprise (versus the current gambling speculation), as the utopian moment of active spirit (versus the decadence of the Gilded Age). Realism, as a life-style as well as a literary program, thus would stand in critical opposition to the irresponsibly excessive speculation—psychic, financial, cultural—of the emerging imperialist world order. The latter promotes a speculative expenditure standardizing all areas of the culture according to the developing logic of naturalism, which entails both the reification of spirit and the commodity fetishism of animating material things with our alienated desires that Marx analyzes in *Das Kapital.* Turn-of-the-century American literature, for Michaels, bears witness to, then, and exemplifies this emerging imperialist world order of consumer capitalism.

In this context, the effect of Howells's "realism" can only be to reinforce the processes it condemns, less because it produces novels at odds with their own explicit intentionsthan because the novels must monumentalize nostalgically past modes of economic and literary production perversely (because self-defeatingly) valued by these very novels precisely for their supreme irrelevance and original obsolescence. Consequently, what Howells proposes as critical opposition can only result in quixotic evasion. And Michaels's primary point is that such evasive literary transcendence of one's historical moment is simply not a viable possibility because Howells's writing—like all writing, especially since his time—necessarily always already demonstrates the reifying logic of a self-alienating naturalism that fetishizes the desires of and for selfhood. "What kind of work is writing? It is the work of at once producing and consuming the self or, what comes to the same thing, work in the market" (28). And what, then, is the self, according to Michaels? "[A] commodity, a subject in the market" (28). It is this very development, of course, that Michaels sees Howells in *Silas Lapham* vainly opposing with his unrealistic realism of the domestic "economy of pain" that would curb all those "excesses of capitalism and the sentimental novel or, rather, the excessiveness that is here seen to lie at the heart of both the economy and the literature" (41). Thus, Howells's novel makes a perfectly consistent if essentially irrelevant whole, clearly aligning and separating its old-fashioned good values and modern evils, even as it ironically reinforces their actual confusion by its adoption of a purely imaginary, monumentalizing opposition. Like the fiscal conservatism favoring the Gold Standard of "hard money," "realistic" opposition to the reifying logic of a naturalizing commodity fetishism (the cultural equivalent of wholesale capitalist speculation) can only "assert the ontological impossibility of what was already an historical fact" (178). In this contingent fashion, Michaels pragmatically combines neo-Marxist analyses with deconstructive assumptions about writing and the production of the self to critique Howells's quixotic realism in *Silas Lapham*.

The main problem with this reading is that it ignores the major contradiction in the novel—for, even as the novel dramatically criticizes and releases Penelope from her thralldom to the romantic ideology of moral heroism pervaded by sentimental fiction, *The Rise of Silas*

Lapham, in its main-plot focusing on the fate of its protagonist's business fortunes, dramatizes as exemplary the excessive "economy of pain" of this very moral heroism by enmeshing the girl's father ever deeper in it. In fact, expectedly, as Lapham's material fortunes fall, he begins to effect the "rise" of the title, morally speaking, just as, unexpectedly, the resentful cruelty of Penelope's romantic principle of heroic sacrifice sublimates itself ironically into a provisional trial of motives that leads to no such heroic catastrophe as her father suffers. These formally parallel plot lines that contradict one another involve scenes of misrecognition ripe for radical parody.

Lapham's "gambling" in the stock market starts to go bad as his former partner's recent speculative ventures also turn sour. This forces Lapham to invest increasingly heavily in order to expiate his guilt for originally buying Rogers out as the paint firm was beginning to make big money. The result is that Lapham is now increasingly vulnerable to Rogers, who, to repay what he owes Lapham, sells him at cost a losing venture whose only access road has just been purchased by a railway that can always put the "squeeze" on our hero whenever it wants. The result is that Lapham starts losing more and more capital, and so cannot match the innovations of his new young competitors in the paint business, who can now begin to capture an ever larger share of the market.

Lapham's house of cards now begins to tumble, even as he "accidentally" sets fire to his still-incomplete mansion (his "dream-house"), which is totally consumed by the ensuing conflagration and, naturally, no longer covered by insurance. It is at this sentimentally vulnerable point that Rogers melodramatically comes to Lapham representing some English buyers who want to purchase that losing venture Rogers originally sold to Lapham. Lapham refuses to sell at first, then says he will sell only if he can tell whoever the interested buyers are the truth about the ownership of the access road. Lapham insists on doing so because he sees in Rogers's new deal "the very devil" (323) that would rob him of the last shreds of his moral integrity in resentful revenge for past financial wrongs. In essence, Lapham believes Rogers is tempting him to repeat intentionally, on a grander scale, now under dire circumstances, the original wrong he had "unintentionally" committed in better times against his former partner. When Lapham learns that the English buyers don't care about the truth he has to tell about the access road because they represent a group of wealthy English aristocrats who want the land under any circumstances to build a model socialist community, Lapham reverses himself and now refuses to sell anyway. He claims that he would still be responsible for the evil consequences of the utopian aristocrats' foolhardiness, even if he, unlike Rogers, would not be guilty of perpetrating a fraud. Such fineness of conscience, condemning him and his family to bankruptcy and social ruin, now marks Lapham as a person as extravagantly sacrificial in commercial affairs as his daughter aspires but ironically fails to become in romantic matters.

Naturally, as Lapham's empire collapses after this great renunciation, the novel celebrates both his final victory over "temptation" and the return of his original enterprising spirit as he moves his paint business, in greatly reduced form, back onto the family farm. The following passage, at this climactic moment, is typical of the psychological realism and moral sentiment endorsed wholeheartedly and elaborately by the novel:

> Perhaps because the process of his ruin had been so gradual, perhaps because the excitement of preceding events had exhausted their capacity for emotion, the actual consummation of his bankruptcy brought a relief, a repose to Lapham and his family, rather than a fresh sensation of calamity. In the shadow of his disaster they returned to something like their old, united life; they were at least all together again; and it will be intelligible to those whom life has blessed with vicissitude, that Lapham should come home the evening after he had given up everything to his creditors, and should sit down to his supper so cheerful that Penelope could joke in the old way, and tell him that she thought from his looks they had concluded to pay him a hundred cents on every dollar he owed them. (351)

To make the contradictory connection between Lapham's endorsed form of moral heroism and his daughter's disapproved form even clearer, Penelope somewhat earlier claims that it is absolutely wrong to "profit by a wrong" (256). The language of capitalism here and throughout the novel is thus used to support a morality that the novel entirely disapproves as unrealistic in principle, even as it clearly approves such extravagant moral sacrifice in practice by enacting it in the fate of the hero. Similarly, when Corey sophistically proposes that

Penelope's form of suffering in life may be to be happy "when everyone else is suffering" (355), everyone in the family approves this version of Reverend Sewell's "economy of pain"—as does the entire novel, since the romantic subplot does end happily in the marriage of this unlikely pair. Once again, the business of morality and the morality of business are intertwined in a way the novel both approves and disapproves, even as Lapham heroically refuses himself the escape-hatch of such sophistry. Similarly, even though both father and daughter do submit to a trial of spirit, the girl's is clearly presented as suspect, while Lapham's is clearly presented as exemplary. In sum, *The Rise of Silas Lapham* is a novel radically at odds with itself.

Why is it right for the father to practice a form of excessive moral heroism that it is wrong for his daughter to practice? Why does the novel endorse the father's grim smiles (309) and cruel determination to see another (Rogers) subject himself and so confirm one's superior ethical status, even though it exposes these very same qualities to our critique in his daughter's case as she handles her lover? Shouldn't both forms of extravagant, unrealistic moral heroism be equally disapproved? (The excruciatingly painful nature of the romantic subplot precludes the excuse of comic relief or cautionary edification.) The problem with Michaels's argument, as we can now see, is that he evades this question of the novel's self-contradiction by making equivalent the excessive romanticism of the popular literature of the time and the excessive speculation of the stock market, so that he can also make neatly equivalent as their logical and axiological contraries Howells's restrictive (and quixotic) realism and nostalgic precapitalist (i.e., pre–Gilded Age) ideal of domestic economy. Michaels in this way can rationalize *The Rise of Silas Lapham* for purposes of his critical argument, but only at the expense of its messier and more dramatic aesthetic interest. As we have just seen, however, Howells's realism, which exemplifies itself in the exemplary fate of the novel's protagonist, is actually akin (if not equivalent) to the very excessive romantic ideology of moral heroism it condemns. Similarly, the language of business, of profit and loss, as moralized by the protagonist, is enunciated by his daughter in the service of a romantic ideal of useless sacrifice that Howells's realism totally opposes. Why, in short, these formally contradictory relationships?

One answer would be that the gender difference, with all its accompanying differences in status, position, and power, defines the difference between the novel's approval and disapproval of the modes of heroic self-denial. It is, after all, morally and aesthetically canonical for a man to practice an excessive form of renunciation, and largely unprecedented for women to do so. In addition, affairs of the heart are not taken as seriously, traditionally speaking, as the worldly affairs of "men at work"—either in war or in business. This answer is too easy, however: for *The Rise of Silas Lapham* portrays all of its major characters as involved in an excessive economy of pain that requires for self-definition forms of self-sacrifice that span the spectrum from relatively petty to sublimely monumental. Consider, for one comic example, how Irene Lapham upbraids her sister for being "such a ninny as to send [Corey] away" on her "account" precisely at the moment when Penelope has decided finally to accept his marriage offer: "Penelope recoiled from this terrible courage; she did not answer directly, and Irene went on, 'Because if you did [send him away for her sake], I'll thank you to bring him back again. I'm not going to have him thinking that I'm dying for a man that never cared for me. It's insulting, and I'm not going to stand it. Now just you send for him!'" (358). Although we are meant to be amused at Irene's "haughty magnanimity" (358), we are also instructed by it. The self in this novel produces itself out of the experience of practicing a stylization of life that entails all forms of renunciation, from the least to the most self-destructive. The genealogy of this practice of the self that I call "smiling through pain" is identified by the narrator only once in the novel, by the by, as it were, in a sentence explaining why Persis Lapham must take upon herself the ultimate—and originary—blame for her husband's ruin. For it is she who first, foremost, and continually forces upon him a memory of guilt and the consequent need for expiation, so far as the Rogers affair is concerned. "She came back to this [explanation for Lapham's fate], with her helpless longing, inbred in all Puritan souls, to have some one specifically suffer for evil in the world, even if it must be herself" (277). Is the novel's formal self-contradiction, therefore, the aesthetic expression of its Puritan heritage, or even of what Geoffrey Galt Harpham has recently termed, after Nietzsche, "the ascetic imperative" that is not only common in Western culture but "common to all culture" (xi)?

The problem with this admittedly speculative formulation is that it is a questionable transhistorical explanation that exceeds the necessities of critical argument. Must we really "rise" to the universal level to understand Howells's self-contra-dicting novel? Clearly not. Must we then perform, on the other hand, as John W. Crowley in *The Black Heart's Truth* does for *A Modern Instance,* an exhaustive psychobiography, "a literary psychology," of the writing of *The Rise of Silas Lapham?*[3] Between minute particulars of the life and times and the critical history of all culture, I propose a middle ground of "typical" analysis, in the Weberian style, of the kind of modern soul the characters in the novel are supposed to aspire to realize through their self-imposed sufferings—a process the novel itself performs best via its formal contradiction of being in its own unique way the kind of novel this novel condemns. In short, I propose that *The Rise of Silas Lapham* embodies an ascetic aesthetic not only appropriate to the Puritan origins of the American self, but typical of the post-Enlightenment era.

Harvey Goldman, in *Max Weber and Thomas Mann: Calling and the Shaping of the Self,* presents the best brief description of this type of the ascetic spirit that I am proposing the novel itself most fully realizes, even as all its characters, especially the Laphams, and most especially Silas Lapham, aspire but fail, by comparison, as fully to realize.[4] (The faded gentility of the Corey family testifies to the superannuated status, the comic irrelevance, of their cultural class in the ethical world of the novel.) I cite now a long but I think useful passage from Goldman on the ascetic "type" of personality:

In fact, the "type" of the first great entrepreneur is essentially the same as the "type" of the figures who reappear as the politician, scientist, artist, and entrepreneur of Weber's later essays. Aloneness, an inclination to ascetic labor, devoted service to a god, self-denial and systematic self-control, a capacity to resist their own desires as well as the desires, pressures, or temptations of others—these are the qualities all of Weber's *Berufsmenschen* [men of calling] acquire through their submission in the discipline of the calling to an ultimate ideal or goal. The key to their character lies, first, in the subjugation of the "natural" self and second, in its transformation and fortification through the discipline of the calling as a unique relation of service to their ideal or god: the self is transformed into a personality in a process of formation that shapes it through a calling and equips it for a calling. For the Puritans the life in this calling, carrying out the actions that they believed served their god, became the source of certainty for religious men to the uncertainties of death and salvation. For secular men too, according to Weber in his later work, the life in a calling, fitted for the modern situation, holds out the only hope against the threat of purposelessness, directionlessness, and the meaningfulness of death in a civilization now unable to draw on more traditional solutions, dominated as it is by the advance of rationalization. (19)

My point in citing this passage is not simply to allegorize the novel's main character. The qualities, traits, and intentions of the ideal type of the ascetic spirit, of the Protestant ethic, as it relates to the rise of capitalism and its later nineteenth-century transformation, do correspond generally, however, to those one finds in Silas Lapham at both the beginning and the end of his career, after he suffers, like Milton's Samson in the mill, the various temptations of a refined and cruelly extravagant life-style that he had aspired to make his own. But I also want to propose a more complicated argument—that the novel itself, in the way I have suggested, embodies this ascetic spirit. Formal, aesthetic contradiction would thus be necessary for the realization of the process of ascetic embodiment. That is, contradiction would be formally intentional in the novel. Nietzsche's *On the Genealogy of Morals* analyzes the law of asceticism precisely in these terms as the endless clash of opposing forces (of will and the body's resistance and inertia). This is what makes possible and defines self-overcoming nature in any ascetic discipline of self making:

> This secret self-ravishment, this artists' cruelty, this delight in imposing a form upon oneself as a hard, recalcitrant, suffering material and in burning a will, a critique, a contradiction, a contempt, a No into it, this uncanny, dreadfully joyous labor of a soul voluntarily at odds with itself that makes itself suffer out of joy in making suffer—eventually this entire active "bad conscience"—you will have guessed it— as the womb of all ideal and imaginative phenomena, also brought to light an abundance of strange new beauty and affirmation, and perhaps beauty itself.—After all, what would be "beautiful" if the contradiction had not first become conscious of itself, if the ugly had not first said to itself: "I am ugly?"[5]

In this light, the smiles of Penelope and her father are as equally smiles at their own actively ravishing cruelty against themselves as they are their cruel reactions to the subjection of the Other. In fact, it would be primarily the sign of their own active subjection to a discipline of their own imposition if not of their own making. Such self-subjection, after all, is what Reverend Sewell, who is indeed Howells's spokesman, claims he is so "intensely interested" in at the novel's end: "the moral spectacle which Lapham presented under his changed conditions" (363). (Lapham's ever rougher appearance and manner of dress by novel's end allude to the type of the religious eremite.) What makes *The Rise of Silas Lapham* interesting is the moral spectacle of its own uniquely self-opposing aesthetic condition of having to preach formally against what it must find itself practicing as a novel, a situation that may define the nature of the genre itself.

What I am proposing here, however, is less the textualization of the ascetic spirit intimately involved in the rise of capitalism than what Nietzsche calls "the internalization of man" (84) first carried out by the movement of humankind into cities and recently renewed to an unprecedented degree by modern society. Nietzsche refers by this memorable phrase not only to the turning inward and against ourselves the practices of cruelty originally meant to be performed upon others; he is referring also to the subsequent sublimation into new forms of psychological discipline and defense. Finally, he is also referring to the combined effect of these two developments, to what a Foucauldian critic might call "the internment of human being" in a world where all the prospects of possibility, of infinite horizons, are increasingly withdrawn, blocked, and cut off by an ever-rationalizing world order of the imperial urban centers of a commercial civilization—precisely the world that Michaels argues, unlike Nietzsche or Marx (or Howells, for that matter), that we must accept as simply inescapable. Although Nietzsche is of course analyzing explicitly the situation of humankind first in prehistory and then during the originary moments of the Judeo-Christian tradition, his analysis is, I find, perhaps even more pertinent when read as a historically cast critique of his (and still largely our own) present moment.

We can see the specter of this process of internalization and internment, this loss of the possibility of infinitude, of what Wordsworth most memorably glosses as "something evermore about to be," not merely negatively in the reduced world of Howells's realism (or the even more diminished world of Michaels's naturalism); that is, not merely in what is officially repressed of an excessive, even irrational expenditure. We can also see it operating positively in the ways it principally conditions the major and minor outcomes of the plot. Penelope and Corey, on the one hand, are finally united as part of a package deal. Lapham agrees to let his young West Virginia rivals in the paint business buy him out on two conditions: that he keep control of the production of his deluxe line of paint, the Persis brand (named after his wife); and that Corey be taken into their newly expanded business as a partner (something he had always refused to do), so that Corey can finally put into practice his plans for the paint business in Mexico. Apparently, then, thanks to this threat of imminent departure, all the formerly embarrassing moral and social wrinkles are suddenly smoothed over. For Penelope now accepts his latest proposal. On the other hand, even the marginal utopian venture of the English aristocrats that causes Lapham so much moral anguish and enables his "rise" in moral stature is also intricately intertwined, as we have seen, with the torturous schemes of various entrepreneurs. In short, the ground of experience in the novel is wholly conditioned by the imperialistic economic order that is necessarily defined by the growing rationalization of the world and consequent diminishment of the sense of the infinite. (Such contingent historical determination, of course, does not mean an absolutely fixed fate, whether of a reductively materialist or discursive kind.)

By sense of the infinite I mean what Kant in *The Critique of Judgement* analyzes as the sublime.[6] For Kant, the sublime is that paradoxical experience in which the individual imagination reads its failure to represent in definite images some boundless totality like mountainous abysses or creative genius as the sign of the human mind's power to constitute via its abstract ideas the realm of experience itself: "for the imagination, although it finds nothing beyond the sensible to which it can attach itself, yet feels itself unbounded by this removal of its limitations; and thus that very abstraction [from such limitations] is a[n indeterminate] presentation of the Infinite, which can be nothing but a mere negative presentation, but which yet expands the soul" (115). The sublime's negative transcendence of experience Kant compares to the highest command of the Jewish law: "Perhaps there is no sublimer passage . . . than the command, 'Thou shalt not make to thyself any graven image, nor likeness of anything which is in heaven or in the earth or under the earth' " (115). The sublime experience thus realizes in the modern context the iconoclastic ascetic imperative of the Judeo-Christian tradition. A sublime aesthetic, therefore, necessarily depends upon texts of self-transcending images, upon an imagination that is radically and intentionally at odds with itself. And in a world where the experience of the sublime is increasingly rationalized out of existence, just as Michaels rationalized away the sublimely conflicted nature of Howells's novel, the only places where the ascetic spirit can practice and realize the sublime imagination are such self-opposing texts, which are the sites for our modern self-opposing culture to reveal itself.

Foucault in "What Is Enlightenment?" provides a useful gloss on what I am reaching for.[7] He focuses there on Kant and Baudelaire as defining figures of our "modernity," which he finds necessarily entails an "ironic heroization of the present" involving an "ascetic elaboration of the self" in the "different place" of art. Modernity, for Foucault, is thus primarily "an attitude, an ethos, a philosophical life in which the critique of what we are is at one and the same time the historical analysis of the limits that are imposed on us and an experiment with the possibility of going beyond them" (42, 50). In terms of my argument, then, *The Rise of Silas Lapham* would be the place where the emerging culture of speculative capitalism suffers an ascesis in the exemplary fate of its hero as sublimely embodied by this self-opposing text.[8] An immanent critique, a negative transcendence, a prototype of what I call "radical parody," enacts itself here in an ascetic transgression of the aesthetic limits of a novel that condemns itself as sublimely as its finally antiheroic hero does himself, as the narrator reports:

> All those who were concerned in his affairs said he behaved well, and even more than well, when it came to the worst. The prudence, the good sense, which he has shown in the first years of his success, and of which great prosperity seemed to have bereft him, came back; and these qualities used in his own behalf, commended him as much to his creditors as the anxiety he showed that no one should suffer by him; this even made some of them doubtful of his sincerity. . . . He saw that it was useless to try to go on in the old way, and he preferred to go back and begin the world anew, in the hills at Lapham. He put the house at Nankeen Square, with everything else he had, into the pay-

ment of his debts, and Mrs. Lapham found it easier to leave it for the old farmstead in Vermont [than she had thought she would]. . . . This thing and that is embittered to us, so that we may be willing to relinquish it; the world, life itself, is embittered to most of us, so that we are glad to have done with them at last; and this home was haunted with such memories to each of those who abandoned it that to go was less exile than escape. . . . He was returning to begin life anew. (352–53)

Lapham's final words to Reverend Sewell put in homelier fashion than the narrator's do what the nature of this "less exile than escape," this sublimely negative transcendence of our self-opposing culture, is really most like: " 'About what I done? Well, it don't always seem as if I done it,' replied Lapham. 'Seems sometimes as if it was hole opened for me, and I crept out of it. I don't know,' he added thoughtfully, biting his stiff mustache—'I don't know as I should always say it paid; but if I done it, and the thing was to do over again, right in the same way, I guess I should have to do it' " (365). If Kant is right that the most sublime passage of the Old Law is the prohibition of graven images, then the most sublime passage of the New Law must be the scriptural archetype of Lapham's striking, down-to-earth common-place: "He is risen."

12 John Cheever's "Folly"
The Contingent Imagination

John Cheever (1912–82), as we now know, was a deeply troubled man. For years, he felt compelled to lead a dual life. While his heavy drinking was well known, both his ruinous alcoholism and his self-destructive guilt over his gay preferences were long kept at the core of a secret world beyond the scope of the conventional upper middle-class confines of Westchester, New York. His wife and family, his big Revolutionary-era house, his selectively revised Wasp ancestry, even his several pedigree dogs—all were pieces of a thoroughly crafted normality, as he thought of it, which would compensate for his youthful and chronic sense of being an especially unwanted child. His mother delighted to recount how, at thirty-nine, she conceived him after one too many martinis, and how his father, ten years older than she, when learning of the mistaken pregnancy, vainly invited the abortionist to dinner. When his father suffered financial ruin in the depression—he was a shoe salesman, and not, as Cheever liked to claim, a shoe manufacturer—his mother had to support the family by opening a gift shop in their hometown of Quincy, Massachusetts. She salvaged for sale as curios the few items the family had inherited from the past. Maternal and wifely neglect and economic opportunism became one in Cheever's mind, as his mother usurped his alcoholic father's place as head of the household, and he took upon himself the burden of resentments of son and husband alike. After his childhood puppet theater and schoolboy story telling failed to meet his growing needs, Cheever turned readily then for affection, support, even tenderness to his brother Fred, who, seven years older, could afford to give all these things, plus money, since he had dropped out of Dartmouth College to get work. As the price for giving such love, Fred buggered his younger nineteen-year-old brother. During the many years Cheever took to establish a financially secure career as a *New Yorker* writer, making a life for himself according to the patterns he happened to find in his era, these familial "origins" remained covered over by the elaborate edifice he was constructing called "John Cheever," a process of fiction making as inventive as the creation of his many memorable characters and narrative personas. Recent selections from his journals continually return to and candidly reflect on the progress and price of this individual process of self-fashioning. [1]

I like to think of this reactive practice of compensatory identity formation in terms of an architectural analogy, that of the "folly," a good old-fashioned British term for the elaborate, intricate, and deliberately designed but wildly natural-seeming house just ripe for falling apart. In what follows, I will examine John Cheever's "folly" in this sense of an imaginary construction as he himself discusses it in the journals and dramatizes it in his radical self-parody, "The Lowboy." My aim is neither to condemn him for his compensatory identity formation nor to celebrate his self-critical reflections on it. Rather, it is to define the limits of a certain currently representative practice of the imagination that describes itself as being radically contingent, by which, as we have seen, is meant a professionally accredited revisionism that uses the historical or social determinations of an interpretive situation for imaginary self-aggrandizement. Cheever, of course, recognized the radically contingent nature of American culture in his own life and work. He put the matter most succinctly in "A Vision of the World," a story reflecting the rapidity of change in modern America, included in the collection *The Brigadier and the Golf Widow* (1964): "What I wanted to identify then was not a chain of facts but an [imaginary] essence—something like that indecipherable collision of contingencies that can produce exaltation or despair [and that can] grant my dreams, in so incoherent a world, their legitimacy."[2] Cheever in this story and really throughout his career seeks the sudden discovery of an aesthetic essence that transforms chains of facts into an epiphany of meaning for him and for his class of readers. This "discovery" and "transformation," Cheever sees by the 1960s, are as much projective constructions as his "folly" of a persona. By selectively examining Cheever's life and work, then, in which the American postwar literary imagination recognizes so starkly its own radical contingency, we can trace from this recent past the outlines of our probable future should we continue to espouse the philosophy of contingency.

I believe that a definition of the limits of contingency philosophy is timely now, for it could be fairly argued, I think, that the most prevalent discursive practice in American intellectual culture is at the present time what one of its recent critics calls "contingency theory." Contingency theory is a least common denominator, so-called pragmatist philosophy informing such superficially different critical practices as Bloom's and Rorty's revisionism or the various American forms of poststructuralism, especially the different "new historicisms" and "new Americanisms" of race, class, and gender study. It is the most avowedly literary and imaginative of intellectual practices pretty much defining the conventions of professional advancement in literary studies. Whether identifying itself as "cultural poetics" or "revisionism," it disbelieves, like Cheever's narrator from "A Vision of the World," in real essences. That is to say, critics today are universally nominalists. They believe not in abstact universals but only in the power of names to simulate general truths. The chance collision of contingencies—their hazardous play—creates the literary form of the "American dream." Contingency theory, more specifically, is the position claiming that since the advanced study of language and culture has finally disabused us of the notion of universals such as humanity or nature as having anything but an imaginary or rhetorical existence, we now know for sure that there are no real unchanging essences at the basis of the world we see and act in, or of the self that each of us feels he or she is, or of the community—professional or otherwise—to which we belong. What we take for universals are the various nominalist fictions of the world, the self, and the community that are merely contingent historical productions of figures (or "tropes") that have become institutionalized because they happen to serve the interests of currently dominant groups. While it might sound flippant to sum up contingency theory's antifoundationalism by repeating Yeats's epithet from "High Talk," "All metaphor," it would not be fundamentally wrong.[3]

Contingency theory necessarily ascribes to us the power of revising our images of ourselves and our world. In principle, there cannot be any necessary transcendent realities, except for death, that the human will to reconstruction has to accommodate, but this does not mean that just anything goes. For contingency theory does also recognize that there are social and professional conventions, collectively adopted and adapted rules—language games or established vocabularies—that, no matter how ingenious one's would-be revisions may be, can act with all the force of nature or fate on anything one may want to do or say if one does not know how to play the academic game well. In short, contingency theory is an ironic poststructuralist updating of romantic and liberal American beliefs in self-making genius to the parodic point at which it begins to sound like the gist of Emerson's "Self-Reliance" and "Fate" coming simultaneously out of both sides of the mouth.[4]

Since they do not believe in the real existence of such universals as the true, the good, and the beautiful, or in any transhistorical perspective, contingency theorists in contemporary America condemn themselves to the ever-changing spectacle of cultural conventions and their pragmatic revisions, whether ironically entertained in "private fantasies" or more publicly modified in professional acts. The advantage of this situation is that no one group or "world-historical" subject can persuasively claim, by successfully impersonating, representative or universal status. Each person or collectivity is in principle no more privileged than any other. What counts is the way arguments are conducted in the ongoing conversation of modern (and now postmodern) "ironist culture." And the standards or norms by which such arguments are adjudicated are the currently enforced and empowering professional criteria and conventions of instrumental reason. Everything else is ruled out of court beforehand. Such a world as contingency theory generally outlines is, however, as Rorty's cold-war liberalism in *Contingency, Irony, and Solidarity* suggests, wholly compatible with the experience of contingency to be found discussed in Cheever's journals and dramatized in his fiction during the 1950s. Even today, it is a world that, however postmodern and revisionary it may aspire to be, must operate within the generally pervasive discursive and cultural practices and forms of postwar America. The result is that contingency theory, as performed by Fish, Rorty, and their fellow travelers, may be greatly provocative, but it cannot be genuinely oppositional, however often a Stanley Fish may be mistaken as such by the popular media.

The reason it cannot be is that contingency theory does not provide a standard or measure sufficiently comprehensive and stable, recognizably moral, and historically appropriate for this standard to function as the old universals once could for emerging subjects and communities to appeal to convincingly, with evident credibility and validly. The professional processes of endless modernization, of displacement for displacement's sake, defines our culture of instrumental reason. This process of professional fashion cannot accommodate the prospects of epochal revolution of the kind we have seen, in which appeals to reason, justice, or nonalienated creativity are so crucial in the formation of large public movements for radical change. As we will see from Cheever, the only kind of radical change imaginable for the professional devotees of contingency appears to be innocently (and so impossibly) apocalyptic, truly American (or Emersonian) reflections of a frustrated desire for total transformation of the entire cosmos, a futilely utopian and finally self-destructive imagination. The lesson Cheever would thus teach contingency theorists is devastatingly cautionary, to say the least. My own perspective, despite appearances to the contrary, is not hostile to the vision of contingency, only to the form this vision has taken in the professional context of postmodern American theory. Foucault and Nietzsche, as well as Cheever, also possess this vision of contingency. The difference, I think, lies in the transhistorical (if still historical) nature of their focus. For Foucault and Nietzsche, as for Cheever in his chronicles and fictions of families and family histories, there are large-scale recurrent regularities—mores, codes, stylizations of behavior, social customs—which constitute a more slowly changing resource of value-laden (if often irrational) perspectives, practices, and styles of judgment, what, following Foucault and Jameson, I call the collective archive. It is this collective archive of canonical and noncanonical imaginative forms and practices that can act as a source of general (albeit not necessarily universal) standards of critique, something that reaches beyond the scope of professional conventions at least. It is some such notion of the collective archive of cultural memories and practices that informs, I believe, similar critical speculations of Charles Altieri on "cultural grammar" and of Jurgen Habermas on "the ideal speech act" situation. My own preference, however, is for this Foucauldian notion of the collective archive, especially as we have seen it developed in relation to the self in volumes 2 and 3 of *The History of Sexuality.* Foucault describes the self there as a mobile and plural subject that the pedagogic experience of mentor and student constitutes and exemplifies, as most famously celebrated in the relationship of Socrates and Plato. The unwitting formation of a plural subject or agency—not an "I" but what could be called the "oneself"—of such an internalized pedagogic pair, Cheever demonically parodies in "The Lowboy" for his own self-critical purposes.

I will continue now with a Cheever journal entry from the mid-1950s that bears crucially on this matter. By this time, Cheever has already moved from 59th Street in New York City to Westchester. He and his family are not yet living in the big house in Ossining, but are still living in Scarborough on the large Vanderlip estate in a reconverted gardener's house. In this entry, Cheever reflects on one possible explanation for his brother's unhappy life and alcoholic collapse that an intimate friend has just recently suggested to him. The sudden, even accidental nature of this possible discovery is typical of the journals as they seek repeatedly for one explanation after another of his own and his family's unhappinesses:

> I can readily imagine it all. He was happy, high-spirited, and adored, and when, at the age of seven, he was told that he would have to share his universe with a brother, his forebodings would, naturally, have been bitter and deep. They would have been deepened by the outrageous circumstances of my birth. I was conceived mistakenly, after a sales banquet. My mother carried me reluctantly and my father must have been heard to say that he had no love in his heart for another child. These violent scenes must have given great breadth and intensity to his own conflicts. His feeling for me was always violent and ambiguous—hatred and love—and beneath all of this must have

been the feeling that I challenged him in some field where he ex-
celled—in the affections of his parents. I have felt for a long time that,
with perfect unconsciousness, his urge was to destroy me. I have felt
that there was in his drunkenness some terrible cunning.[5]

Cheever has reconstructed here the primal scene of his family romance, and he has done so based on the chance insight of a friend.
Underlying his own and his brother's present-day personas is, perhaps, just such an imaginary scene. The amazing discovery Cheever
makes is his recognition that his brother's alcoholism may be the result of "some terrible cunning," as if his brother counted on Cheever's
competitive emulation to lure him, already a heavy drinker, down the
same path of self-destruction.

This is truly a demonic insight, and leads in the next paragraph of
the entry to a reflection that rises to visionary intensity. The echoes
range from chivalric romances and metaphysical poetry to the ghosts
of Poe's gothic shudders to Yeats's gnostic theories from *A Vision,* in
which the souls after death provide, by their dreaming back over their
last lives' unfulfilled possibilities, the future scripts of our own.[6] The
reader should recall that Cheever's father is already dead by this time,
his mother has just died, and installments of his long-awaited first
novel, *The Wapshot Chronicle,* are soon to appear in the *New Yorker:*

> Here then are three worlds—night, day, and the night within the
> night. Here are the passions and aspirations of the dead, moving free-
> ly among us with malevolence and power. Here is a world of open
> graves. Here is a world where our imagery breaks down. We have no
> names, no shapes, no lights, no colors to fill out these powers, and yet
> they are as persuasive as the living. Out of his window he can see the
> city shining in the light of day and he adores it but he will be moti-
> vated less by this vision than by his remembrance of a scream heard in
> a dark stairwell fifty years ago. They seem to destroy him and to
> counsel him to destroy me. We seem to be at one another's throats. We
> hear the lashing of a dragon's tail in the dead leaves, piteous screaming
> of a child whose eyes are plucked out by a witch, we smell the damps
> of the snake pit. This suggestion or disclosure seems very important
> to me and I pray it will be as helpful to Fred.[7]

The moment of his own birth (or does the imagery also suggest the
moment of conception?) is the moment from which the insatiable

dead continue to speak to his brother, making it impossible for him to see the shining City on the Hill of modern America. Instead, all he can perceive is not a vision but a remembered voice screaming, that of his mother probably in the throes of giving birth to his new brother. Although this screaming blends with the unnamed child's "whose eyes are plucked out by a witch," it could also be Fred's long screaming from the nightmare life of "the night within the night," which clearly now is beginning to engulf John Cheever as well. Ironically, as his final remark here implies, Cheever plans to share this insight with his brother. Perhaps, this is, in "perfect unconsciousness," a measure of his revenge for the supposed "terrible cunning" of Fred's seductively attractive urge to (self-)destruction.

The general intellectual framework of categories that can contain such a vision from Cheever's journals is obviously psychoanalytic. But, like most modern American writers, Cheever loathed psychoanalysis, always making fun of its psychobabble and playing with the various analysts he patronized in order to placate his wife. I think that what is more important than any possible containing intellectual framework of categories is how the entry originates and develops: "B. tells me Fred is suffering from something that happened to him before his adolescence and I think it may have been my birth. I have tried for years to uncover the turning point in his life but this had never occurred to me. This is a clinical or quasi-scientific disclosure, but it seems to me as rich as any other revelation. I can readily imagine it all."[8] The vision originates from an occasional remark, and develops its richness "as any other revelation" would. That is, Cheever's attitude in all this is pragmatic, his focus is as much literary as moral ("I have tried for years to uncover the turning point in his life"), and his spontaneous vision of imaginary origins, especially as it elaborates itself in the second of the two paragraphs, is wholly improvisatory. This radically pragmatic, simultaneously aesthetic and ethical, and thoroughly improvisatory stance is what I mean by the contingent imagination. In his many later interviews, Cheever liked to define literature, particularly the kind of fiction he wrote, as a contemporary mode of lyric, even visionary poetry: "writing is a force of memory that is not understood."[9] That is, writing befalls us, and compels our revisions, as Harold Bloom will later claim, too. In this understanding, as in his entire stance as a writer, Cheever is practicing what contingency theorists preach. Take, as one brief example, the following passage from Stanley Fish, which sums up perfectly what a variety of contingency theorists, from Harold Bloom to Richard Rorty and Barbara Herrnstein Smith, all claim to believe:

> As rhetorical man manipulates reality [i.e., current conventions), establishing through his words the imperatives and urgencies to which he and his fellows must respond, he manipulates or fabricates himself, simultaneously conceiving of and occupying the roles that become first possible and then mandatory given the social structure his rhetoric has put into place. By exploring the available means of persuasion in a particular situation, he tries them on, and as they begin to suit him, he becomes them. [10]

As William Blake put it repeatedly in his visionary prophecies concerning the children of this world, "they became what they beheld." Similarly, what Fish is saying is that contingency critics are manipulative, pragmatic, self-aggrandizing and self-transforming opportunists. As Rorty puts it apropos the difference between Heidegger and Proust, or as Bloom puts it apropos the difference between Freud and Shakespeare, or as Fish puts it apropos the difference between Milton's Milton and Fish's Milton, whether we officially espouse truth or not, we are all of the devil's party, that is, the party of the revisionary imagination, whether we know and admit it or not. Fish, for example, derives his "positive" generalization about "rhetorical man" from Milton's critical characterization of Belial, one of Satan's fellow devils.

There are, of course, many problems with this position, but I am only going to deal with one of them here via my analysis of Cheever. [11] The practice of the contingent imagination may mean one can persuade oneself of anything, but as Cheever's journal entries testify and his stories and novels dramatize, this apparent freedom of individual self-fashioning cannot lead to personal or professional security. In fact, what it most often leads to in Cheever are self-destructive gestures of apocalyptic disillusionment, from a throwing away of everything from one's last identity to a final carnival of possible identities all of which are discarded because they can be, to the catastrophic negation of the very possibility of having any other identity ever again, a horrifying mode of imaginative suicide that the contingent imagination ironically entertains. While one could read in these terms the shape of Cheever's life and career up to the 1977 publication of *Falconer,* I want to use just one story, "The Lowboy," to outline such a possible reading as part of my comparative analysis of the contingent imagination in Cheever and in the practice of contemporary theory.

First, however, I want to establish the connection between Cheever's private vision and the public circumstances that help to make it representative. In so doing, I am demonstrating how, as Fish puts it, this rhetorical man, "John Cheever," conceives and occupies the possible and then mandatory roles of the social structure that "his rhetoric" has helped to "put in place." Since "The Lowboy" concludes with an ironic apocalyptic vision of discarding all the mementos of the past, I will now cite a letter about "the end of the world" written around the time of the story's composition ("The Lowboy" was composed in the late 1950s and included in the 1961 collection of short stories entitled *Some People, Places, and Things That Will Not Appear in My Next Novel*). My aim is to define the historical situation for the practice of the contingent imagination in the story. Writing to Josephine Herbst in early October 1958, a lifelong friend and correspondent who suggests the "liberal" political world they once had in common, Cheever remarks at some length about the possible confluence of "the end of the world" and his own psychic "going to pieces again," one way of looking at the subject of "The Lowboy." Here is what he has to say:

> It seems to me now that the world may be disintegrating although this could be a reflection on my sanity. I think it has to do with the bomb. But how can anyone who has watched the sky deny that in the last six month this has changed; and I don't like it. Yesterday at around four in the afternoon it seemed to me that Dulles had plainly pushed the wrong button. An unearthly green light was beating out of the west. Overhead there was a mackerel sky, mares tails and dark brown cumulus. Either I am nutty or something has gone very wrong upstairs and I don't mean my personal upstairs. . . . This seems to me to be very nearly the end of the world. . . . It may be all that green light outside the window. [12]

Is this what has happened to that all-American "green light" of Fitzgerald's Gatsby? (Cheever was a lifelong devotee of Fitzgerald's work.) In any event, the cold-war political framework quite literally defines here the psychosocial mind-set in which Cheever is trying, not too successfully, to work ("I have lost my taste for it"). And, as we shall see, more subtly in "The Lowboy" than in the very broadly done "The Brigadier and the Golf Widow," which is about the wicked lengths people will go to get the key to a family's bomb shelter, Cheever will represent critically the social roles to which his characters are condemned. The practice of the contingent imagination, whether in literature or theory, can at best disclose, given its radical contingency, only such dead ends. No matter how ironically self-opposing or wildly elaborate or even baroquely natural-seeming it may become, the contingent imagination can never become a viable alternative to the large, nearly mythical, intellectual and political frameworks, what Blake calls "mental forms," that its revisionary practice often helps unwittingly to underwrite.[13]

"The Lowboy" of John Cheever is a story about the intimate associations of property, ancestry, familial rivalries, and personal identity. It is, in other words, a story about the structures of *ressentiment* long operative in our culture. The narrator tells how his brother, Richard Norton, a small and spoiled child of a man, has built up a nearly perfect "picture-puzzle" (406) of a life. Only sole possession of the lowboy that stood in their parents' house, acquired from the once rapacious Aunt Mathilda, can possibly provide the missing piece to complete the picture, thereby satisfying Richard's strange passion for a definitive self-fashioning. And yet, once the object of Richard's selfish quest has been finally possessed, the narrator surmises that his brother must now face all of the most painful memories the lowboy can conjure. A climactic visionary scene detailing the breakdown in family relations over several generations is so destructive for his brother that it results, the narrator imagines, in a terrible conflagration, which in its ironic turn causes the narrator to imitate his own vision by discarding all of his possessions, including, as the final biblical-sounding sentences stressing purity and renewed innocence suggest, his entire way of life with all of his property: "Cleanliness and valor will be our watchwords. Nothing less will get us past the armed sentry and over the mountainous border" (412). We will selectively return to this apocalyptic scene in which the narrator becomes what he beheld to discuss its echoes of Auden in his most Yeatsian manner imitating Milton on the covering cherub and the way back to paradise. (Yeats and Auden were Cheever's two favorite modern poets.) But first, I must discuss structure and point of view in "The Lowboy."

Cheever divides with an ellipsis of asterisks the two major sections of the story. Each of these major sections he further divides into inverted mirror images of one another, thereby creating a chiasmus. Up to the ellipsis, there are two parts consisting first, in the opening set piece excoriating the narrator's spoiled brother for his smallness of stature and temperament; and then, in three subsequent movements progressively unfolding the nature, purpose, and completion of the quest. After the ellipsis, there are also two parts consisting, first, in three movements progressively unfolding the initial, developing, and final consequences of the brother's successful quest; and then, in the narrator's supplementary act of dispossession, a set piece in which he discards all remembrances of the past. Given this severely symmetrical yet ironically inverted specular structure, those final sentences, especially considering their visionary difference in diction and symbolic resonance from the surrounding low mimetic mode of modern social comedy, leap out at the reader.

The chiasmus mirror-effect of the story's reflexive structure strongly suggests the possibility of a similar ironic inversion in point of view. Indeed, as one would expect in a 1950s story, the narrator appears potentially unreliable from the very start, with his mock extravagant opening set piece that begins: "Oh I hate small men and I will write about them no more but in passing I would like to say that's what my brother Richard is: small" (404). This gesture too much reminds one of the overly intimate stranger at the cocktail party from whom, at the first opportunity, one practically bolts away. In addition to this comic clue, as the narrator's catalog of his brother's "small" characteristics continues—so prophetic of Randy Newman's song "Short People"—these physical details become one predominant moral feature. The narrator's spoiled whining suggests a demonic narcissism that recognizes others only insofar as they can play a role in the poorly cast, shabby genteel drama Richard Norton performs, "perhaps, for eternity" (404). Smallness, in the moral sense of pettiness, is, of course, what the self-regarding narrator also manifests in his brilliantly mocking catalog made up wholly at his brother's expense. When one then considers that Cheever was a small man, that his brother was the larger one, and, as the journals and the story of the same period, "The Scarlet Moving Van," attest, given to authoritative-sounding yet purely vain directives, and that Cheever was often accused by his wife of using people for his own private psychomachia, the story's ironic elaboration of point of view begins to take on, perhaps, monumental complexity. Plot, structure, and point of view—all suggest that this realistic social comedy, like Cheever's later novels, *Bullet Park* and *Falconer,* is also a representative visionary portrait of a single but sharply divided mind, as is typical of the genre.

"The Lowboy" is thus a greatly overdetermined work, beginning with this title. It refers, of course, to the suggestive object of the Norton brothers' rivalry. As goal of their quest, it symbolically takes on many conflicting associations. The title also refers to the smallness in stature and in motivation, to the physical and moral "lowness" of both Norton "boys" dramatized here. Richard Norton's smallness and spoiled nature mirror and are mirrored by the narrator's disarmingly candid brotherly resentment and pettiness. When the lowboy is accidentally "injured," for example, as it is being transported in the narrator's station wagon to his brother's house, the childishly spiteful narrator remarks that while he cannot be blamed for the accident "in fact," he could be blamed "in spirit" (407), as if wish were father to such chance events. The narrator is thus the other, more spontaneous brother's ironic self-consciousness who makes conscious the various emotions shared spectrally by both brothers as if they were two halves of one deeply troubled psyche.

In such a suggestive context, the lowboy itself acquires many possible meanings. First of all, it represents the way of life of the Norton brothers' parents, particularly of their mother. When he makes his claim to it after Aunt Mathilda offers it to the narrator, Richard confesses, "I feel that it was the center of our house, the center of our life before Mother died. If I had one solid piece of furniture, one object I could point to, that would remind me of how happy we all were, of how we used to live . . ." (405). The lowboy thus stands for a now-vanished form of life, an order long gone but now viewed with an intense nostalgia that the experienced reader knows covers an often considerable pain or grief.

Second, as the narrator says when introducing the subject, the disposition of the lowboy is just the kind of thing that inspires his family's only seriously emotional "displays" (404). That is, the lowboy also stands for all the jealous rivalries and resentful acquisitiveness associated with the brothers' struggle for the finest property so typical of their class. (As it turns out, the lowboy is a lost Barstow piece from 1780, and a museum's curator's priceless dream.) Third, as both brothers recognize, the lowboy, with its "polish of great depth" (406), represents for Richard the "final piece in the puzzle of respectability" that he has been composing for years since they both shared a suggestively "checkered, troubled, and sometimes sorrowful past," an all-too-common, even seedy "chaos" out of which Richard at least has engineered his "dazzling rise" (406). Finally, in the descriptions of the lowboy's great "carved claw feet" (reminiscent of the dragon-witch's from the journal entry?), of its being "carried tenderly" when "injured" in the accident (407), of its "dark ring" stain where its pitcher of seasonal flowers rested—an image shining through the ruddy varnish "like something seen under water" (406)—and of its power to summon forth, especially from Richard, the passions of love (adoration, devotion, jealousy, and grief at loss or possible betrayal), the lowboy becomes a gathering symbol, taking on all the characteristics—economic, social, moral, psychological, aesthetic, and even natural—of the grand fetish.

I think, however, that the most fruitful way to understand this gathering symbol as a whole comes from Julia Kristeva's already classic study of depression, melancholy, and creativity, *Black Sun*. The depressive or melancholic is, as Freud first surmised, in mourning for what, following Lacan's semiotic revision of Heidegger's ontological analysis, Kristeva calls the loss of "the Thing." By "the Thing," Kristeva means the infant's original fantasy of return, after separation from the mother has begun, to the pre-Oedipal and preobjective imaginary bond or fusion state of mother and child. Out of this desire all subsequent distinctions of "the real"—sexual, moral, and rational—arise. The impact of the child's initiation into civilization's symbolic chain of laws and conventions occurs by means of primary identification with what Freud in *The Ego and the Id* first describes as the imaginary father of individual prehistory. The "lost Thing" is also like this later primary identification with the imaginary father of individual prehistory in that it incorporates as fantasy all of the sexual features of both parents despite its otherwise quite specific gender characteristics. In addition, the "lost Thing" is the matrix out of which the critical and self-critical faculty begins to develop once the supervention of the primary identification with the father imago occurs. For the writer, Kristeva proposes, the literary use of language, its multidimensionality at the acoustical, cognitive, and mythical levels—its playful semiotic interruption of rational semantic discourse—would recover and embody the "lost Thing." In this literary capacity, Kristeva posits the "lost Thing" as "the real that does not lend itself to [univocal] signification, the center of attraction and repulsion, seat of sexuality [beyond or before the phallic signifier], from which the object of desire will become separated."[14] For "the depressed narcissist" mourning its loss, "the Thing" thus stands primarily for the self in its repeated temporal dispersion. The concept of "the Thing" is as voraciously overdetermined as what the concept signifies. For Cheever in "The Lowboy, this would mean that Richard plays depressed narcissist to the narrator's artist, as much as the latter plays a role in the former's performances, "perhaps, for eternity" (404). In this ironic fashion, Cheever could be seen as dramatically staging what Kristeva critically theorizes by dividing himself into these dialectically related Norton brothers.

The climax of "The Lowboy" is much like the summoning of the dead in Yeats's visionary poems. As such, it ironically testifies to the self's temporal dispersion, its literal genealogical dissemination:

> It would have been raining on the night I imagined; no other sound transports Richard with such velocity backward in time. At last everything was perfect—the pitcher, the polish on the heavy brasses, the carpet. The chest of drawers would seem not to have been lifted into the present but to have moved the past with it into the room. Wasn't that what he wanted? He would admire the dark ring in the varnish and the fragrance of the empty drawers, and under the influence of two liquids—rain and whiskey—the hands of those who had touched the lowboy, polished it, left their drinks on it, arranged the flowers in the pitcher and stuffed odds and ends of string into the drawers would seem to reach out of the dark. As he watched, their dull fingerprints clustered on the polish, as if this were their means of clinging to life. By recalling them, by going a step further, he evoked

them. and they came down impetuously into the room—they flew—
as if they had been waiting in pain and impatience all those years for
his invitation. (409)

The spirits who come are liberated Grandmother DeLancey; her
daughter, artist Aunt Louisa; Louisa's son, Timothy, a musical prodi-
gy and a suicide at fifteen; Uncle Tom, his broken father; Aunt
Louisa's aimless and promiscuous sister, Aunt Mildred; and Mildred's
resentful alcoholic husband, Uncle Sidney. All are fabulous examples
of failure in personal relations that together compose "the fascination
of pain" the past exercises over Richard. He is now condemned to pure
observation, paralyzed by their representative "folly" of constructing
"false selves" to the point at which he cannot act to prevent the ghost
of "stinking drunk" Uncle Sidney from scattering the fire that consumes all—Richard, his lowboy, his house and family, in an ultimate
conflagration. Or so the Cheever narrator, as is typical in his brother
fables, envisions it.

This powerful visionary scene leads to the narrator's own supplementary apocalypse:

> I took the green glass epergne that belonged to Aunt Mildred off the
> sideboard and smashed it with a hammer. Then I dumped Grand-
> mother's sewing box into the ash can, burned a big hole in her lace
> tablecloth, and buried her pewter in the garden. Out they go—the
> Roman coins, the sea horse from Venice, and the Chinese fan. We can
> cherish nothing less than our random understanding of death and the
> earth-shaking love that draws us to one another. Down with the
> stuffed owl in the upstairs hall and the statue of Hermes on the newel
> post! Hock the ruby necklace, throw away the invitation to Buck-
> ingham Palace, jump up and down on the perfume atomizer from
> Murrano and the Canton fish plates. Dismiss whatever molests us and
> challenges our purpose, sleeping or waking. Cleanliness and valor
> will be our watchwords. Nothing less will get us past the armed sen-
> try and over the mountainous border. (411–12)

After staging this psychosocial drama of apocalyptic change and
manic mourning, a virtual comic Freudian-sounding hymn to the
contingent imagination ("We can cherish nothing less than our random understanding of death and the earth-shaking love that draws us
to one another"), Cheever in the final Audenesque and Miltonic lines

would apparently wash his hands of the whole thing—family romance, class struggle, historical crisis—in this representative visionary gesture of religious-sounding conversion to renewed innocence and the romantic transcendence of time. The coming together of all these things in the gathering symbol of the lowboy's fiery consummation is a perfect instance of what Cheever's narrator in "A Vision of the World" means by an imaginary "essence": "that indecipherable collision of contingencies that can produce exaltation or despair" (515). A reader's provocatively interesting problem at the end of "The Lowboy" is that he or she cannot tell which of these emotions Cheever primarily means to evoke. The stylistic disjunction in diction and symbolic resonance of the last three sentences in the story is made more acute by both the formal if ambiguous closure of the inverted specular structure and the dense complexity of point of view. This ironic gap signals a passionately wished-for apocalyptic transcendence of human temporality—which must end up taking, like all things in nature, "the form of an arc" (411)—that the story's opening set piece already mockingly suggests is impossible. Its similar "once and for all" gesture, you will recall, quickly gives way to the "in passing" of the essentially ironic human story: "Oh I hate small men and I will write about them no more but in passing I would like to say that is what my brother Richard is: small" (404).

In "The Lowboy," then, Cheever has rehearsed, as if fully before the fact, the public fate of the contingent imagination in America. Without belief in the real existence of universals or a viable transhistorical if still historical alternative, it can only accommodate itself to the rules of the current game, the established vocabularies, the psychosocial conventions of the time. This accommodation is necessarily a self-opposing, ironic, and temporary accommodation, a playing for time until one can seize one's opportunity, since one always wants to revise the rules in terms of one's interests, however they happen to be momentarily conceived. Such fundamental compromise results inevitably, when one faces the prospect of death, in no Nietzschean "amor fati" but in a belated self-mourning protest for the unrealized and now unrealizeable possibilities one has had to sacrifice in order to play the game well. Such monumental mourning culminates, as here, in the familiar apocalyptic desire for the total transcendence of the past so typical of modern American culture.[15] The agonistic structure of plu-

ral agency in late Foucault and the conflicted mourning for the lost
fusion state of mother-child in recent Kristeva mirror each other as if
they were primitive origin and sophisticated end. However that may
be, in Cheever's "The Lowboy," we see the radically contingent, historically conditioned bitter comedy of the two-in-one, all-American
Norton brothers, with the fiercely disputed lowboy as their thoroughly overdetermined self-image. Wholly "rhetorical *man*" (italics
mine), as Fish indiscriminately calls us all, thus becomes, as here in
Cheever's radically prophetic self-parody of the small Norton boys,
the petty mask of the narcissistic revisionism critics like Fish so resentfully must behold and become. In the theater of self that the profession, like the rest of America, is now, Fish and others of his kind
have had the purely aesthetic essences of their lives already written out
for them—and critiqued—by Cheever, that ghost of their selves to
come:

> Some people make less of an adventure than a performance of their
> passions. They do not seem to fall in love and make friends but to cast,
> with men, women, children, and dogs, some stirring drama that they
> were committed to producing at the moment of their birth. This is
> especially so on the part of those whose casting is limited by a slender
> emotional budget. The clumsy performances draw our attention to
> the play. The ingenue is much too old. So is the leading lady. The dog
> is the wrong breed, the furniture is ill-matched, the costumes are
> thread-bare, and when the coffee is poured there seems to be nothing
> in the pot. But the drama goes on with as much terror and pity as it
> does in more magnificent productions. (404)

Oh, indeed it does! "—*mon semblable,—mon frere.*"

13 Imaginary Politics
Emerson, Stevens, and the Resistance of Style

"Your condition, your employment, is the fable of you."
—*Emerson, "Poetry and Imagination"*

I would walk alone,
Under the quiet stars, and at that time
Have felt whate'er there is of power in sound
To breathe an elevated wood, by form
Or image unprofaned; and I would stand,
If the night blackened with a coming storm,
Beneath some rock, listening to notes that are
The ghostly language of the ancient earth,
Or make their dim abode in distant worlds.
Thence did I drink the visionary power;
—*Wordsworth,* The Prelude *(1850), Book Second, ll.303–11*

For Amy Zaffarano Rowland

"Ecstasy," according to Emerson in "The Method of Nature" (1849), is "the law and cause" of being (92). [1] He means that the in-coming of energy ever becomes the out-going of expression in act or word projected beyond the material limits of individual entities. Poems and beehives are but two examples. Individuals are "vents for the current of inward life which increases as it is spent" (90). Each person, for Emerson, expresses genius uniquely if unconsciously, like someone "always spoken to [and through] from behind, and unable to turn . . . and see the speaker" (90). A ravishing, heavenly music arises out of such transcendental ventriloquism so long as the individual does not allow the contingent aspects of life to obstruct the essential flow. When one does so, either the energy accumulates to the point of mountainous explosion, or the "voice" of genius "grows faint, and at last is but a humming in the ear" (90): All would-be Ariels can become mere Calibans in the end. The poet's voice, therefore, is either like an underground river coming out into the light, or else it is like a volcanic devastation reduced to an irritable noise.

Emerson intends "the work of ecstasy," like the title "The Method of Nature," to be a bit oxymoronic. Ecstasy and nature, work and method are pairs of synonymous antinomies when set in opposition on the basis of a critical standard of ideal or universal spontaneity. Nature methodized, of course, is a Popean turn of phrase defining the sup-posed essence of art. But spontaneity and method conjoin to recall Wordsworth's definition of romantic poetry from the preface to *Lyri-cal Ballads* as a spontaneous overflow of powerful feelings recollected in tranquility. Meanwhile, the project of stepping out of oneself, the prospect of going beyond one's limits, both recalls Kant's critical phi-losophy of epistemological and moral transcendence and anticipates Heidegger's existential ontology of human being as repeatedly thrown into the there of being beside oneself. This rapid meta-morphosis of conflicting allusions back and forth between early and later periods and between Anglo-American and European sources rep-resents Emerson's ecstatic method of composition and, I think, Ste-vens's typical poetic working. And, as we have seen, radical parody depends upon such pervasive intertextuality and its scenes of multiple misrecognitions.

For Emerson, in "Spiritual Laws," such subjective agency is inter-woven with the idea of vocation.[2] You are what you are called by your talent to do. And you do what you are in the specific work only you can do.

> Each man has his own vocation. The talent is the call. There is one direction in which all space is open to him. He has faculties silently inviting him thither to endless exertion. He is like a ship in a river; he runs against obstructions on every side but one; on that side all ob-struction is taken away, and he sweeps serenely over a deepening chan-nel into an infinite sea. This talent and this call depend on his organi-zation, or the mode in which the general soul incarnates itself in him. He inclines to do something which is easy to him, and good when it is

done, but which no other man can do. He has no rival. For the more truly he consults his own powers, the more difference will his work exhibit from the work of any other. His ambition is exactly proportioned to his powers. The height of the pinnacle is determined by the breadth of the base. Every man has this call of the power to do somewhat unique, and no man has any other call. The pretence that he has another call, a summons by name and personal election and outward "signs that mark him extraordinary, and not in the roll of common men," is fanaticism, and betrays obtuseness to perceive that there is one mind in all individuals, and no respect of persons therein. (310)

The passage resonates with religious overtones (and male chauvinism). As Emerson's own final remarks underscore, however, it also points, via the ship analogy, to a secular, communal, and nontranscendental theory of vocation. Although he does not use the term here, the idea informing this analogy is what throughout his "Human Culture" lectures (1837–38) he calls "abandonment." Bereft of any conventional, familial, or religious authorization, each of us is totally given over to abandonment. We fluently abandon ourselves in turn to action, to the only action one's talent proposes as the calling to do one's unique work. There is in this overdetermined sense of abandonment a hedonic more than an ascetic imperative, virtually with the sensual appeal of sexual surrender. And as the ship analogy also implies, such unique work is necessarily artisanlike, a specialized skill, and part of a collective effort of equally unique works done by equally different others. Such a vision incorporates, of course, the art of steering well. In thus collectively yet uniquely "going with the flow," each one acts out his talent as an intentional role in the grand enterprise of humanity that is forever in passage "over a deepening channel into an infinite sea." I mean to invoke such a dialectical theory of individual yet collective agency (or democratic "genius") whenever I use the term "the plural subject" here. And, after late Foucault and Kristeva, I see it as a basically literary subject, because only the class of literary intellectuals has the most opportunity to maximize such "abandonment" to their vocation, although this does not imply that other groups of workers have no such opportunities at all. But literary intellectuals, in their works, constitute the primary radical and utopian measure by which we can judge the often parodic difference between the communal ideal of free human agency and the actual degraded forms of our alienation. Only in Emerson's vision of people working skillfully to-gether and moving toward their equally individual yet collective fates, can we get a sense of the world for which his vocational theory of abandonment urges us to work.[3]

My point in proposing this Emersonian version of agency is to sug-gest that there is a variety of literary forms of agency, with Emerson's being but one predominant form.[4] There are, apparently, several the-ories of agency in Emerson, one other of which, because it is so influ-ential, I will examine now for its possible relationship to what I am calling the vocation of abandonment.[5]

At first blush, "The Over-Soul," with its transcendental Plotinian religiosity, could not be further from the practical analogy of the ship in the river, with its material urgency of finding the ways to our own work, for the union of soul and Over-Soul announces the apocalypse of the mind:

> The things we now esteem fixed shall, one by one, detach themselves, like ripe fruit, from our experience, and fall. The wind shall blow them none knows whither. The landscape, the figures, Boston, Lon-don, are facts as fugitive as any institution past, or any whiff of mist or smoke, and so is society, and so is the world. The soul looketh steadily forwards, creating a world before her, leaving worlds behind her. She has no dates, nor rites, nor persons, nor specialties, nor men. The soul knows only the soul; the web of events is the flowing robe in which she is clothed. (388)

The moments when the individual soul opens to receive the divine influx of the Over-Soul are when this apocalyptic productivity arises. Emerson's heady spouts of literary vision are here prefiguring, I think, the climactic scene of creative making in Stevens's "The Idea of Order at Key West" (about which more shortly), even as it is echoing the meditative provocation in Wordsworth's "The Solitary Reaper."

However, the image of the best-established things in our world de-taching themselves, one by one, and falling, "like ripe fruit," sug-gests a more historical material sense of the revolutionary transforma-tion attendant upon apocalyptic agency. It suggests the abandonment of these things to the internal logic of their own developmental, often self-parodic unfolding; that is, it suggests the prospect of their unwit-ting abandonment to the vocation of perishing. While Aristotle is hardly the usual source for citations when interpreting Emerson, his sense of beings striving to perfect themselves unto the death would be the most traditionally appropriate philosophical prefiguration of this vision, even as Freud's discovery of the death drive as the individual organism's unique way to and work of death would be the most appropriate modern variation. Nietzsche's *Zarathustra,* you may recall, uses Emerson's imagery in the opening sections of his book that evokes the coming of the Overman. These figures of romantic organicism, whether finally traceable to Aristotle or not, transume mere biologism, I believe, due to their imaginative recognition of the repetitive mortal structure of human temporality remarkably akin to Heidegger's existential analysis in *Being and Time:* "These things we now esteem fixed shall, one by one, detach themselves, like ripe fruit, from experience, and fall. The wind shall blow them none knows whither." Emerson's tropes theorize agency, much as does his "Poetry and Imagination" when it defines the poet as an embodied trope, in terms of the vocation of abandonment, a calling working through a revisionary turning.[6]

Emerson makes the fact that this theory is essentially literary and not religious abundantly clear in the most famous passage in the essay, a passage that resounds backward through the authors he cites to the classical sources so fascinating to the late Foucault—the very same classical sources (such as Plutarch) that Nietzsche uses for his model of self-overcoming selves, his aristocracy of souls.

> Humanity shines in Homer, in Chaucer, in Spenser, in Shakespeare, in Milton. They are content with truth. They use the positive degree. They seem frigid and phlegmatic to those who have been spiced with the frantic passion and violent coloring of inferior, but popular writers. For they are poets by the free course which they allow to the informing soul, which through their eyes beholds again, and blesses the things which it hath made. The soul is superior to its knowledge; wiser than any of its works. The great poet makes us feel our own wealth, and then we think less of his compositions. His best communication to our mind is to teach us to despise all he has done. Shakespeare carries us to such a lofty strain of intelligent activity, as to suggest a wealth which beggars his own; and we then feel that the splendid works which he has created, and which in other hours we extol as a sort of self-existent poetry, take no stronger hold of real na-

ture than the shadow of a passing traveller on the rock. The inspiration which uttered itself in Hamlet and Lear could utter things as good from day to day, for ever. Why, then, should I make account of Hamlet and Lear, as if we had not the soul from which they fell as syllables from the tongue? (396)

What Emerson is calling "The Over-Soul" is really a treasure hoard of masks. Shakespeare, Milton, Spenser, and so on constitute a collective archive of literary agents abandoning themselves to their self-overcoming vocation of being passed on to future generations and used—not, like disposable capitalist commodities, consumed once and for all, but, like Foucault's vision of the open strategic games of love and friendship, repeatedly consumed and renewed in their serious playing as select practices of self: "a society of souls."[7]

Unfortunately, however, Emerson concludes "The Over-Soul" with a vision that sounds more like alienation than plural agency:

The soul gives itself, alone, original, and pure, to the Lonely, Original, and Pure, who, on that condition, gladly inhabits, leads, and speaks through it. Then it is glad, young, and nimble. It is not wise, but sees through all things. It is not called religious, but it is innocent. It calls the light its own, and feels that the grass grows and the stone falls by a law inferior to, and dependent on, its nature. Behold, it saith, I am born into the great, the universal mind. I, the imperfect, adore my own Perfect. I am somehow receptive of the great soul, and thereby I do overlook the sun and the stars, and feel them to be the fair accidents and effects which change and pass. More and more the surges of everlasting nature enter into me, and I become public and human in my regards and actions. (400)

Here only the lonely can love one another, but, in "Experience" and elsewhere, each can only repel the other, infinitely. This would be the vocation of abandonment, with a vengeance, in the most literal and brutal of senses, which corresponds to Emerson's chronic refusal to do the entire work of mourning, preferring, as in the case of his brother, Charles, to say he has abandoned the other first, even before death has supervened. This climactic passage of "The Over-Soul" also anticipates what Kristeva and other psychoanalytic critics see as the narcissistic rage for celebrity in our postmodern media culture: "I, the imperfect, adore my own Perfect." As I argue elsewhere in this book in detail, each first-person singular is poor and vacant until the dream of the fabulous universal third person appears reflected back from the latest media mirror. Is it Jay Gatsby or "Bob," the American psycho of *Twin Peaks,* who inhabits us all? What a prospect, ripe for parody, such possible misrecognitions make!

Even this popular degradation of Emerson's active soul involves in alienated form the vocation of abandonment as we drift along and imaginatively merge, on occasion, with our media extensions. It is the price we pay in America for giving democratic access to the greater vision of the active soul that higher education affords. Because the literary production of texts, with its semantic overdetermination and ironic stylistic complexities, tends to resist the purely throwaway commodification of dreams our consumer culture would uniformly enforce, it is primarily literary art that should be the vocation to which, each in his or her own unique way, we would yet collectively abandon ourselves.

A poetic of intertextuality based on such an Emersonian conception of natural vocation internalizes the perpetual abandonment of each prior position in the chain of allusions, transforming the accompanying moment of loss into a renewed impetus for further imaginative mobility. Abandonment in every sense becomes a vocation for the poet, since the standard of perfection is a nature that is ever on the way to its predetermined but unknown fulfillment or realization in some ultimate but apparently unreachable expression. If Hegel temporalizes Aristotle's sense of nature's final form, Emerson's transcendental skepticism refuses any certain knowledge of the goal, however inevitable it may be. By means of such intertextual liberality and openness, then, a writer achieves a more universal albeit unconscious frame of reference, the ironic form and play of which traces the lineaments of a writer's sources of authority. And one can read this meditative genealogy, with its variable resistance of style, for the imaginary politics, or the political dimensions of the imaginary and its captivating powers, that such play allegorically enacts.

I begin with this Emersonian poetics because it establishes succinctly the American romantic conception of genius that Stevens inherits. It is well known that Stevens read Emerson at Harvard and after, having received from his mother the 1903–04 twelve-volume *Collected Works.* And it has been generally well demonstrated by

Harold Bloom and others that Stevens, whatever his degree of indebtedness to the French Symbolists, also owed much to Emerson. One brief but salient example of this compelling connection previously mentioned crystallizes when one reads the central vision of "The Idea of Order at Key West," with its young woman on the shore singing beyond the genius of the sea and making her own exemplary world, and the central vision of "The Over-Soul," with its perpetually youthful soul (personified as the muse), "creating a world before her, leaving worlds behind her," for whom, as she progressively advances, "the web of events is the flowing robe in which she is clothed" (155). This closing image of the Emerson "Over-Soul" accounts for (among other things) the ghostly "empty sleeves" (128) at the opening of the Stevens poem. Such an Emersonian vision of genius haunts Stevens as he ever inquires of its mysterious making and unmaking of worlds, "whose spirit is this?"

The experience of genius that Emerson proposes and Stevens meditates is what psychoanalytic theory calls "projective identification." A natural object or process, a person, a collectivity, a work of art, or even an abstract ideal can elicit a regressive act of psychic incorporation on the original model of the most intense aspects of the mother-child fusion bond. Such later or secondary identification of self and world, if strong enough, can thus reactivate the repressed feelings associated with this primary fusion state. These feelings include not only what we call "love," of course, but also a rage to possess and consume or to be possessed and be consumed that knows no bounds. The loss of this state of primary fusion and its subsequent, always inadequate (because derivative and temporary) avatars of identification fuel the quest for perfect fusion with further rage—a rage at both the original wound of loss and its later reopenings. The psyche, in this light, becomes a composite belated assemblage of abandoned projective identifications, like a landscape of volcanoes that have all blown their tops.

Julia Kristeva in her recent essay "Identification and the Real" develops this psychoanalytic theory of psychic composition beyond Freud's and Lacan's work on mourning and melancholia, death and the imaginary.[8] She argues that in the case of "symbolic sublimation" the child unlearns the fusion with the mother, who in our culture must suffer abjection so that the child may move beyond image-thing perception to linguistic symbolization and cognition. Instead, the child now primarily identifies with the next figure in the chain of the family romance, the imaginary father of individual prehistory. This is an alternative figure standing between the abjected mother and the oedipal patriarch. It is like the figure in Emerson's vision in his essay on Swedenborg or like that in many of Stevens's poems. It incorporates the gender characteristics of both sexes. The child's fantasy of the phallic mother becomes this vision of the maternal patriarch, a development complicating Western misogyny. Such catechresis preserves and advances at the same time the desires of the psyche via a chiasmic or crisscross troping. As Kristeva puts it, the process of primary identification does not complete itself in the pre-Oedipal period until, "transferred to the Other, in identification, I become One with the Other throughout the whole range of the symbolic, the imaginary, and the real" (168). This powerfully generalized *Einfuhlung* or "empathy" is "appropriate to certain amorous, hypnotic, or even mystical states" (168). For Kristeva, then, "the primary identification of the subject," when completed, "occurs" with a primitive figure of the imaginary father possessing "the sexual attributes of both parents" (168).

Thanks both to Stevens's meditative, often ironic incorporation of Emerson and to this reading of Kristeva's revisionary theory of identification, we can see more clearly the full outlines of the drama of genius Stevens performs in his poetry. The poetry is always a reflection upon and of a transcendental or first idea. This is the idea of an intense experience of identification virtually to the point of fusion. The poetry is thus a later imaginative reasoning about this first idea of original and ecstatic empathy, the pure form of an apocalyptic (and hence clearly ambivalent) love that creates and re-creates selves and worlds the way the poet does personas and words. It is as if Stevens is ontologically, not just historically or literally, belated. His existence, that is, is ironically ecstatic, always beyond itself in reflection, with experience always to be imaginatively (re-) discovered. It is a web of afterwords reflecting poignantly, wryly, comically, or self-parodically upon the "memory" of an experience he must first (re-)construct, and then repeatedly interpret. It is as though he is reading the shape and size of the maternal/paternal mountain as well as the intensity of the explosion, from the ruins of the original eruption that has given him birth.

With such a poetic project, it is no wonder that the defining quali-

ty of Stevens's style is a dense and complex allusiveness sometimes to
the point of absolute obscurity. His use of allusion, as Harold Bloom
first develops, differs totally from T.S. Eliot's more familiar conspicuous kind. And in the work of two recent critics, Eleanor Cook
and Barbara Fisher, we can begin to see the full range of his far-
fetching figures.[9] Classical references (to Virgil), medieval allusions
(to Dante and the Provençal poets) are also made, resonating darkly
amid the already slightly askew tropings upon Emerson, Shelley,
Wordsworth, or Milton. These allusions almost but don't quite echo
their apparent sources. As Cook nicely glosses this phenomenon, Stevens's evasive echoing is a form of "transitory allusion"—what Emerson calls rhetorical power, "the shooting of the gulf." Such "glancing"
reference tends to just skip by its source so that, as Cook puts it, "we
do not take over the full context of the original" (88). Fisher is excellent on the way the poetry thus consists in a variable psychic space of
such allusive evasions or evasive allusions, a grandly abstract yet
changing pattern of pleasurable if hauntingly ambiguous or undulat-
ing resonances making up the "temenos" or "templum" feel of a sacred
enclosure that Stevens's most hieratic poetry inspires (152). It is within this maternal-like mental space that the poetry stages its often
comic drama of identification with the genius of the imaginary father
taking on much of the context's mothering aspects.

As we shall see, this resistance of Stevens's style to conspicuous allusion, and so to complete (sometimes even partial) lucidity, composes his imaginary politics, in which familial, personal, and social
relations become different qualities of his inclusive psychic landscape.
The result is that his poetry stands firmly in opposition to the reductive modern commodification of aesthetic objects for ideological or
commercial purposes of any stripe. Stevens, in short, produces his
dense networks of repressed and often virtually unnameable intertextuality in order to project a palpable if still "fluent mundo," as his
version of what Kristeva in *Black Sun* terms "the lost Thing"—that is,
the sadly inscribed fanciful "memory" of the mother-child disintegrating fusión bond.[10] Interior paramour, "fat girl," muse figure,
or created paradisal site—all are his tropes for this "lost Thing" that
the poetry would recover by allusively embodying. The imaginary
politics that Stevens thus practices in and through the resistance of his
style is a belated modernist preservation of the apocalyptic romantic

desire for the return to Eden, a desire that seeks definitive personal and political expressions that remain impossible and so are provocations to disastrous frustrations.

The conclusion of "A Postcard from the Volcano" contains a paradigmatic expression of Stevensian allusiveness. Since most critics agree that, in Frank Lentricchia's memorable phrase, the poem's opening mood is one of "authoritative wistfulness," even if they disagree over its significance, I will accept that characterization, too, for most of the poem. [11] But its conclusion is anything but wistful, however authoritative sounding it continues to be. (If anything, the last three stanzas sound even more authoritative.) The poem ends to my ear on a note not of wistfulness but of ever-increasing defiance, as the final lines accumulate and mass into a climactic scene of opulent if impersonal self-display: [12]

> Children,
> Still weaving budded aureoles,
> Will speak our speech and never know,
>
> Will say of the mansion that it seems
> As if he that lived there left behind
> A spirit storming in blank walls,
>
> A dirty house in a gutted world,
> A tatter of shadows peaked to white,
> Smeared with the gold of the opulent sun. (159)

It may be that the dying social and cultural order of 1935 will be replaced by a more innocent, know-nothing order to come, but the children of that future (and our present) epoch will have to speak of the past, however unwittingly, in the terms that past fashioned for itself and handed on to the future in the only styles of perception, feeling, and language still available for use. And the poem's final four lines, I believe, compose a single monumental apocalyptic image whose ghostly lineaments ironically suggest the superbly artificial and literate volcano that a Stevens would put together and elaborate, van Gogh–like, in order to drive his point home with a vengeance. And this is a point that goes far beyond his play on the banal "wish you were here" of postcard convention. "So you think I am an outmoded elitist chauvinist aesthete," one can almost hear Stevens chuckling demonically (and somewhat anachronistically) to himself as he composes these lines; "well, then, here's your 'real me' for you, in the grandly decadent style."

By attending to the formal features of tone, imagery, and rhythm, one can hear what critics who focus on the purely social dimensions often miss: comically heroic defiance of all merely social pressures. Moreover, if one pays close attention to the play of allusion in the poem, then the defiance becomes, if possible, even more pronounced. The title and setting of the poem, for example, allude directly to Nietzsche's widely cited, extravagantly aesthetic injunction from *The Gay Science* to "live dangerously" by building our cites on "the slopes of Vesuvius." The last four lines amass similar apocalyptic images that transform to Stevens's own purpose of comic defiance four sets of literary allusions. Shakespeare's King Lear and Hamlet, I think, animate "A spirit storming in blank walls," and Milton's scenes of cosmic devastation from *Paradise Lost* construct "A dirty house in a gutted world," I am almost certain. Meanwhile, both Shelley's abstract Power from "Mount Blanc" and his Demogorgon from *Prometheus Unbound* weave the deep, spectral truth of "A tatter of shadows peaked to white." Finally, Stevens's own early solar impersonations, especially the golden utopian vision of male power in the famous seventh stanza of "Sunday Morning," appear to shine playfully through in the grandly self-deprecating, self-asserting last line of the poem. Stevens ironically composes all such revisionary imagery of dangerous literary strength without any sentimental evasions: "Smeared with the gold of the opulent sun." This perversely glorious aestheticism ("smeared") is the inescapable hallmark of his modernism.

In this putting-together of a pattern of allusive evasions (hence my resistance to identifying his sources definitively), Stevens constructs the psychic space or matrix in and out of which his major version of the imaginary father, that figure symbolizing the mother-child bond even as it would transcend it, may mountainously arise and be equally celebrated and degraded (hence, Stevens's "smear" job). In this powerfully ironic fashion, Stevens both extends the abjection of the mother to incorporate partially the imaginary father and transfers back to her some of the reflected glory of her volcanically active poetic offspring, the prophetic persona pronouncing this final outrageous pun.

In "How to Live. What to Do" Stevens sketches the plot of his dream songs. The first two lines allude, glancingly to be sure, to

Yeats's contemporaneous poem, "Byzantium" (1933), and its opening
line "The unpurged images of day recede" (248).

Last evening the moon rose above this rock
Impure upon a world unpurged.
The man and his companion stopped
To rest before the heroic height. (125)

For Stevens, there is no possible escape in vision or into the afterlife
that would satisfy the poetic imagination's desire for ideal purity, a
perfection of (self-)expression impossible to attain even as it is ever
possible to envision. Instead, Stevens's ironic reduction of Yeats's visionary poet and his ghostly companion, of Byzantium's moonlit (or
starlit) landscape and of San Sophia, attests to the persistence of the
desire not for purity per se, as for the "fuller fire" (125) of a sun not
"flame-freaked." That is, more life and capacity, not the spectral overview of life and power, is what one really wants.

The bare scene of poet and muse (the original pedagogic pair), confronting the moonlit tufted rock of literary tradition, dramatizes perfectly the title as a romantic listening to the rising wind:

There was
Only the great height of the rock
And the two of them standing still to rest.

There was the cold wind and the sound
It made, away from the muck of the land
That they had left, heroic sound
Joyous and jubilant and sure. (126)

If this "heroic sound" in its redoubled and so reassuring jubilation
means to allude to Emerson's vision of the creative voice of the soul,
then the resonance of the couple's archetypal situation, moving "away
from the muck of the land," refers not only to the contemporary
American world of "mickey mockers" (see "The American Sublime");
it may also refer to the exit scene of *Paradise Lost,* when Adam and Eve
leave paradise, with all the world before them, going about their solitary way. The major difference between this literary archetype and
Stevens's poem lies in the attitude of listening that would complete
the return to Paradise now stalled. It is as if in leaving "the muck of
the land" Stevens's couple is listening back to a prophetic recitation

of their world to come in Paradise. Or, it may be that the heroic sound of the wind they are listening to may only tell them of the laughter of Satan. Such opposing intertextual possibilities make "How to Live. What to Do" a little resonating world.

Rather than settle on one or two sets of possible identification here, however, it would be more productive to see Dante and Petrarch, along with Emerson and Milton, hovering in the air and inhabiting their many "majesties of sound" (125). (Allusions to *The Tempest* and Wordsworth's *The Prelude,* Book Second, ll.303–11, and even *The Waste Land* can also be heard, despite the differences in landscape or other details.) The tufted rock and the clouds its ridges embrace "like arms" (125) could then be taken for this poet's latest expression of the literary tradition's imaginary father (or poetic word) and abjected mother (or nature), with the former's mountainous tuft chiasmically suggesting something of the latter's visionary curl. The poem thus is a powerfully resonant allegory of the modern poet's dilemma when facing tradition in a land of muck (or America). Remember too well, and become a luminous sputtering, a "flame-freaked sun" (125). Forget too well, and become speechless, imageless, songless, without mediator or savior: "There was neither voice, nor crested image, / No chorister, nor priest" (126). Allude evasively, however, and then listen all night to the bracing "cold wind" as it sublimely responds by articulating "the great height of the rock" in "heroic sound / Joyous and jubilant and sure" (126). That is, sublimate the desire for a purified mother tongue to express eloquently the patriarchy, and the poem can then embody differentially, in ceaseless interplay of interpretive possibilities, the Other of tradition in one's own unique and spontaneous voicing.

"A Dish of Peaches in Russia," however, makes the repeated experience of this unique unconscious voicing sound close to psychosis. Twice the poem asks, "Who speaks?" And the poem gives more than two answers to this question. A Frenchman, a Spaniard, a lover, or, perhaps, a Russian exile: all are possible speakers for portions of the poem, which as a whole has yet another, formal narrative voice in which the other voices are barely contained. The poem takes off from a contemporary magazine article about a Cezanne held captive by the Kremlin in the Hermitage. What results from this point of departure is the poet's meditation in his room. He pictures a dish of peaches and becomes in turn different personas as he would imaginatively experience in this round the full sensuous delight of the meditative fruit. Each persona permits another perspective to emerge in this experimental attempt to comprehend the sensuous quality of the peaches in the aesthetic form of the poem:

> With my whole body I taste these peaches,
> I touch them and smell them. Who speaks?
>
> I absorb them as the Angevine
> Absorbs Anjou. I see them as a lover sees,
>
> As a young lover sees the first buds of spring
> And as the black Spaniards plays his guitar.
>
> Who speaks? But it must be that I,
> That animal, that Russian, that exile, for whom
>
> The bells of the chapel pullulate sounds at
> Heart. The peaches are large and round,
>
> Ah! and red; and they have peach fuzz, ah!
> They are full of juice and the skin is soft.
>
> They are full of the color of my village
> And of fair weather, summer, dew, peace. (224)

Here sound is less heroic than sensual, breeding more sounds in the heart, with the "pullulating" echo of chickens suggesting Williams's proletarian portrait of the red wheelbarrow, even as the prospect that it may be the Cezanne itself speaking must be entertained, until the poem's conclusion. For the poem concludes with a return to the previously unidentified site of origin, the poet's room. The Hermitage and Kremlin, Anjou and the Angevine, Spain, France, and all their masks are left behind, abandoned, absorbed into the final reflection on the poet's psychic splitting or plural subjectivity, whose ferocious nature is provoked by these peaches, the only objects, after the curtains drift off, that remain in the end:

> The room is quiet where they are.
> The windows are open. The sunlight fills
>
> The curtains. Even the drifting of the curtains,
> Slight as it is, disturbs me. I did not know
>
> That such ferocities could tear
> One self from another, as the peaches do. (224)

Such tearing of one self from another resounds complexly, to say the least. It is as if the poet has become and is turning from himself as his own precursor.

The psyche in Stevens is largely a contingent assemblage of abandoned object identifications. It is an accumulated deposit of spectral images or specular memories. Only the earliest, simplest, and most capacious model of organization, that of the mother-child dyad, can accommodate all these later precipitations of identity. In this context, the ferocious tearing of self from self that the peaches inspire resembles a continual process of giving birth. It is a repeated standing outside of or beside oneself. This is a poetic life whose law is a cultivated ecstasy, and whose cause is knowledge of the self as Other. The imaginary politics entailed by this psychic economy requires the Other as the different in order to express itself as such ferocious tearing. The peaches must be both artificial—painted—and elsewhere—in the Hermitage—so that they can provoke the splitting of the subject into a series of romantic, at times sentimental personas within the self-reflexive ironic frame of a poetic act of knowledge. "Who speaks?" is, then, an urgent and not a rhetorical question, since within the endless frame of imaginative intertextual reference in a Stevens poem any one of several selves may claim to be speaker with as much right as the purely formal narrating voice, for that formal poetic persona is so less aesthetically interesting than any of the voices sounding through its mask.

The proliferation of selves as personas and poetic masks reaches its limit, however, when in "Chaos in Motion and Not in Motion" the self that does speak amid whatever ferocious dramatic effects still occur can no longer credit any object with sensuous or passionate investment sufficient to carry off the latest performance with conviction. A dissemination of selves results in a dispersal of objects. "Pro forma–ism" or "a going through the motions" may become the norm. So desire rehearses itself as a mobile or motionless, purely operatic chaos. All is very affective in a stagey way. A depressingly cold comic scenario unfolds:

> Oh, that this lashing wind was something more
> Than the spirit of Ludwig Richter . . .
>
> The rain is pouring down. It is July.
> There is lightning and the thickest thunder.

It is a spectacle. Scene 10 becomes 11,
In Series X, Act IV, et cetera.

People fall out of windows, trees tumble down,
Summer is changed to winter, the young grow old,

The air is full of children, statues, roofs
And snow. The theatre is spinning round,

Colliding with deaf-mute churches and optical trains.
The most massive sopranos are singing songs of scales. (357)

The entire theater of the world, facing its apocalypse, has become a
poor man's version of Wagner produced by a grandiloquent fool. The
ironic consequence of a hyperdeveloped poetic self-consciousness is
not only the absence of any object adequate to one's desire; it is also
the reduction of desire to a mindless childish violence for which
papier-mâché is the only appropriate medium. This powerfully empty act of the mind removes the poet's comic surrogate, Ludwig Richter, turbulent Schlemihl, from the only whole he knows—the previous round of identifications and abandonments:

And Ludwig Richter, turbulent Schlemihl,
Has lost the whole in which he was contained,

Knows desire without an object of desire,
All mind and violence and nothing felt.

He knows he has nothing more to think about,
Like the wind that lashes everything at once. (358)

The fatal condition of knowing desire without an object of desire
means that the speaker identifies with the primary processes as if before the appearance of object relations. In other words, object relations, already no longer real, have been abandoned for the apocalypse
of the mind in the narcissistic immersion in a purely preconscious
knowing: no thought or feeling is possible, only an affectless screen-
ing of desire. This fixation upon the imaginary per se is like the picture of a kiss offered to a splintering mirror, a freeze-frame for the
finale of the reel, a chaos in motion and not in motion indeed. Here
radical (self-)parody, with all its possible scenes of multiple misrecognition, reaches its limit. The resistance of style in Stevens may begin
as a resistance to ideological and commercial commodification, but it
must end as a kind of self-resistance, as a resistance to the poet's psy-

chic demise in his own reflexive medium: a postmodern Urizen awash in the waters of his own production. The recapitulation of the mother-child fusion bond becomes a total dissemination in such poems as "Chaos in Motion and Not in Motion." This defines Stevens's plight. "Large Red Man Reading," in this claustrophobic light, performs his deliverance. By distancing his plight via the ironic surrogate of Ludwig Richter, Stevens merely delineates it in a finer tone. In "Large Red Man Reading," however, Stevens repeats the movement from the earliest position of desire, to which he has now regressed, forward to the figure of the imaginary father, thereby creating a space in which objects of desire, however transparently "fictional" they may be, can once again appear, even as he simultaneously takes an imaginative stand as if in the aboriginal world of the first word's utterance. This final fiction of his new first word is justified by the psychological justice of the poet repeating the normative model of imaginative development here, from abjected mother to imaginary father and his poetic law.

> There were those that returned to earth to hear his phrases,
> As he sat there reading aloud, the great blue tabulae.
> They were those from the wilderness of stars that had expected
> more.
>
> There were those that returned to hear him read from the poem of
> life,
> Of the pans above the stove, the pots on the table, the tulips among
> them.
> They were those that would have wept to step barefoot into reality,
>
> That would have wept and been happy, have shivered in the frost
> And cried out to feel it again, have run fingers over leaves
> And against the most coiled thorn, have seized on what was ugly
>
> And laughed, as he sat there reading, from out of the purple
> tabulae,
> The outlines of being and its expressings, the syllables of its law:
> Poesis, poesis, the literal characters, the vactic lines,
>
> Which in those ears and in those thin, those spended hearts,
> Took on color, took on shape and the size of things as they are
> And spoke the feeling for them, which was what they had lacked.
> (423–24)

The title persona may be the sun, an Indian chieftain, Whitman in either or both guises, or a self-parodically phantasmagoric, breathless Stevens on the lecture circuit, an Emerson manqué. This allusive ambiguity or variable reference to possible avatars of the imaginary father frees the poet's desire from its too-perfect identification with the engulfing medium of its abject self-reflection, releasing desire to the ecstatic and progressive performances of the symbolic chain of signifiers and so symbolically transuming death in this protean social (because discursive) reality of being's poetic law of endless metamorphosis.

The ghosts resuscitated by the poem of life may be as much the abandoned revisionary identifications of the poet as his actual or imaginary ancestors. His once-novel psychic personas or spectral masks from the earlier poetry such as "Hoon" or "The Sleight-of-Hand Man" may be reappearing here. They are supplied with what they had lacked on their quest for the stars by Stevens's imaginary father, this solar creator, or "fuller fire," who as day changes to evening pleases himself in outlining with his breath the prophetically literal divinations of being and its law: "Poesis, poesis." The volcanic personality who needed to know "how to live" and "what to do" and who chased his own disseminated selves to the wilderness of stars until all became a fixation upon and in a chaotic void, here recovers his resistance to the death of the imagination by publicly avowing his imaginary father. This is a variably composite figure curiously enshrined in the domestic realm of pots and pans, as if this father has through his feeling taken on or preserved the primary quality of the abjected maternal imago. Such is Stevens's normative model of imaginative development in its final mode. The ideal of psychic wholeness necessarily incorporates all the culturally marked features of human being in poetic form.

Not only do we now see how the sexual politics of the family romance tend to work out in Stevens via this creative repetition of the normative model of psyche development, we also can read from its dynamics a cautionary lesson useful for educating our own desire for political criticism. The promotion of race, class, and gender studies under the aegis of poststructuralism, postmodernism, or the new historicism challenges the traditional patriarchal canon in the name of all those who have suffered abjection in our culture. As such, the abjected mother can readily be taken as the representative type toward which this ideological criticism moves as it would perfect its celebration of difference in a politics of identity appropriate to each of its constituencies. The danger in such a purely oppositional position, as we can see imaginatively outlined in these (self-)opposing lyrics from the course of Stevens's career, is that the perfection of such politics may lead to the collapse of the self into the purely reflexive world of its own rhetoric without reference to the reality of objects with which its desire once identified in its difference from the allegedly false ideals of the culture it had critiqued. In the Emersonian terms with which we began, such criticism, like Stevens's poetry at times, may be in jeopardy of refusing "the work of ecstacy" (86), the project of standing outside or beside oneself, and so is unable to become self-critical by identifying with and avowing its imaginary fathers, remaining instead completely captivated by the perpetual embrace of abjection that Nietzsche defines as the fate of *ressentiment*. Playing the victim seeking justice and justification for too long can end up victimizing all concerned, for good. In short, a little aesthetic (and analytic) distance could prove salutary.

CONCLUSION
On Becoming Oneself
in Frank Lentricchia

"il miglior fabbro"

In many ways, Frank Lentricchia is a leading oppositional figure among those who do American criticism. Initi-
ated into the profession during the latter days of the New Criticism,
schooled in close reading, disciplined by the sublime example of
modernist masters, Lentricchia in his first book on the "radical poetics" of Yeats and Stevens, *The Gaiety of Language* (1968), nevertheless
supplements his insightful formalist analyses with a history of
nineteenth-century literary appropriations of Kant and post-Kantian
philosophical developments. He does so in order to contextualize his
chosen poets' collective imaginative and theoretical achievement,
which he identifies, hesitantly, as "a poetics of will" that he is uncertain may not really be "a poetics of anti-will."[1] Not only is Lentricchia
moving to theory prior to its heyday in the early and mid-1970s, he is
also going beyond formalism prior to the 1970 publication of Geoffrey Hartman's influential essay collection of that name. Moreover, in
raising the question of the individual will and its role in culture, however uncertainly, Lentricchia foregrounds the problems of imaginative and critical agency that preoccupy him, and now us, so urgently.

Similarly, in the mid-1970s, at the height of European theory's major impact, when things American, modern, and subject-centered are generally out, and things continental, (post-)romantic and anonymously textual (or discursive) are generally in, Lentricchia publishes in 1975 his second book, *Robert Frost: Modern Poetics and the Landscapes of Self,* which relies on a pragmatist understanding of conscious intention.[2] He thereby begins the renovation of modernist studies even as he anticipates the return to the subject of modern American culture and its distinctive historical origins, which seriously begins to occur on a large scale only later in the decade. In his next book, *After the New Criticism* (1980), Lentricchia does double work: he participates significantly in theory's academic institutionalization by writing the first general overview of theory's post–World War II developments; but he also provides, presciently, the first sustained and fully informed critique of theory. Theory has become, as we recall, a new formalism for this historically engaged American critic sympathetic to (albeit sometimes critical of) Western Marxism and Foucault's brand of poststructuralism.[3]

Lentricchia comes entirely into his own with *Criticism and Social Change* (1983). He positions himself concretely and personally here by provocatively choosing Kenneth Burke as his American theoretical exemplar, over against the professional choice of many other critics at the time, Paul de Man. Lentricchia also announces and thematizes the conflict of historical origins and intellectual aspirations—the problematic of American cultural assimilation—that has become so central to the problematics of the new historicism, postcolonial (or "subaltern" studies), and new Americanist projects. In publicly choosing Burke over de Man, a maverick American literary intellectual simultaneously of the old left and one of its most formidable critics, Lentricchia chooses the politically committed yet highly self-conscious philosopher of the literary symbolic over the ironically self-opposing and highly sophisticated (and once so very influential) mandarin of theoretical reflection. Lentricchia justifies this critical choice of Burke, surprisingly, as expressing loyalty to his origins—a choice made in the name of his own and his family's material experiences of class, ethnic, and gender differences. For it is Burke's dramatistic criticism of the socially symbolic action to be discovered in aesthetic encodings of such differences, and not deMan's hieratic deconstruction, that can expose the cultural work that literature in fact performs. Such differences, along with those of race, are automatically overlooked by theory as de Man practices it. Sooner than Lentricchia then thinks, however, such differences come to provide the primary topics of contemporary critical investigation.[4]

Lentricchia thus encapsulates, prefiguratively, the experience of his generation of oppositional literary critics. He goes beyond formalism, turns to theory, historicizes its development, criticizes its emerging professional excesses, and thematizes the minute historical particulars of both imaginative agency and the institutional realities of the proposed American difference in late-capitalist culture. From formalism to theory, from theory as a new formalism in disguise to theory as openly postmodern cultural politics—such could be the self-description of Lentricchia's career and that of his generation. In these ways, we can see that the subject of his criticism, however familiar it finally seems, has always been the fate of the imagination in modern culture. Lentricchia has been concerned about how the imagination has been conceived, practiced, and policed. As one can see, he has discovered and taught, virtually from the beginning of his career, beyond the specifics of such conceptions, practices, and policings, that there is not one imagination, narrowly aesthetic or symbolist derived from Coleridge, Kant, Poe, and his French champions, but there are in fact several imaginations, all of them postromantic in the strong sense, yet each significantly different from the other. This is especially true for Lentricchia in the case of the twentieth-century American imagination. Yet, as we shall see, there remains a basic family resemblance among these imaginations.

As I sort out and categorize these imaginations in action (a process based loosely on Hayden White's typology of the historical imagination in *Metahistory*), I discern essentially four types. They can best be characterized by the intellectual movements they have respectively most informed: aestheticism, totalitarianism, pragmatism, and criticism. Aestheticism, of course, finds its great ancestor in Kant, while totalitarianism follows Hegel, pragmatism revises Emerson, and criticism enshrines Arnold. Lentricchia accepts each of these ancestors as historical points of reference, except Arnold, preferring instead to substitute the actual experiences of difference—economic, social, sexual, cultural—for some grand literary or critical paragon. As we shall see, in writing recently on Pound, Lentricchia does disclose via his appreciative and critical comments the profile of his perfect cultural critic.

Another way of characterizing these types of imagination is rhetorically or figuratively, in terms of what Kenneth Burke calls the master or ancestral trope, the performative god-term, especially prized by each of them. Aestheticism is the mode of metaphor, of the desire to be different and to be in a stylish world elsewhere: "I am the king in the palace now." Totalitarianism is the mode of synecdoche, of the desire to subsume all the different parts of a vertiginously multiple life within a totalizing and invariable whole or system: "I am the state." Pragmatism is the mode of metonymy, of the desire for ever-emerging wondrous associations of ever-new personal possibilities without end and without definitive consequences: "The crown and scepter, the head and good right arm of the state—c'est moi? Wouldn't it be pretty to think so, or would it?" Criticism, finally, is the mode of irony, of the desire to become and remain flexible and open to the necessities of self-revision within the broadest possible public context: "I am content always to criticize things as they are."

I do not want to multiply complexities in a Shandyean manner, yet I do find in Lentricchia that each of these imaginations may also be self-divided. Aestheticism, as in Pound, may be active and insurrectionary, literally and socially, or it may be, as in early Yeats, far from provocatively innovative, becoming passive and pessimistically escapist. Totalitarianism can take the aristocratic or vanguard party form of fascist authoritarianism or communist oligarchy; or, antithetically, it can inspire dystopic and paranoid visions, an Orwellian Big Brotherism or a Foucauldian panoptical discipline of power. Pragmatism appears either as the anti-imperialist, barbarically anarchic and wildly antinomian, loose-cannon individualism of the later William James, or as the wishy-washy, Charlie Brownish postmodern bourgeois liberalism of Rorty's contingency theory of "private self-creation." Finally, criticism can be, as it usually is in Burke, a consciously complex style of critical engagement, at once imaginatively sympathetic and ironically self-reflective. Or, it can regress to its romantic and aesthetic roots in Kant's earlier aestheticism, which anchors his critical philosophy, by adopting the sophisticatedly belated and disillusioned posture, as in de Man, of cloistral retreat. In this complex light, we can see that Lentricchia's project throughout his career, really a historicizing of Frye, aims at giving a critical anatomy of these imaginations in action as they play crucial roles in the modern world.

Both the popular media, such as the *New York Times Magazine,* and the intellectual media, such as *Critical Inquiry,* now recognize Lentricchia's representative status as an academic oppositional figure. Both kinds of forum generally do so, however, in the most superficial terms possible: that of celebrity gossip, thanks (in part) to the notorious photograph on the back of *Criticism and Social Change,* which Lentricchia has recently revealed is a radically (self-parodic) spoof of the media's scenes of multiple misrecognition. Just imagine: "The Dirty Harry of critical theory," as the *Village Voice* identifies him, the central figure in the current prominence of Duke University's English department, as the *Chronicle of Higher Education* characterizes him, the editor-in-chief of the critical collective that has revamped *South Atlantic Quarterly* almost overnight into a major journal—these "Frank Lentricchias" have a collective sense of humor, and can be ironical at their own expense![5]

More seriously, in "Don DeLillo," Lentricchia focuses on the former's emergence into popular consciousness due to the controversy sparked among influential neoconservative critics like George Will by *Libra,* an intentionally "unpatriotic" novel about the Kennedy assassination. In his sustained meditation on the media creation of "Lee Harvey Oswald," Lentricchia comments critically on the system of celebrity production and assassination of which he has recently been a partial and purely symbolic victim. The brilliance of this performance lies in the ironically allegorical fashion in which Lentricchia theorizes the general situation of the postmodern subject per se, via his intensely particular reflection on DeLillo's novel.

> In the radical sense of the word, Lee Harvey Oswald is a contemporary production, a figure who is doubled everywhere in *Libra,* even, most harrowingly, in strategic places, in the narrative voice that DeLillo invented for this book. . . . The disturbing strength of *Libra*— DeLillo gives no quarter on this—is its refusal to offer its readers a comfortable place outside of Oswald. DeLillo does not do what the media right convicts him of doing—imply that all Americans are would-be murderous sociopaths. He has presented a politically far

more unsettling vision of normalcy, of everyday life so utterly enthralled by the fantasy selves projected in the media as our possible
third person, and, more insidiously, an everyday life so enthralled by
the charisma of the media, that it makes little useful sense to speak of
sociopathology or of a lone gunman. Oswald is ourselves painted
large, in scary tones, but ourselves.[6]

In what Lentricchia calls the "theater of self" (14) that the sociopathology of postmodern America especially encourages, our lives
are like DeLillo's "imagined biography of Oswald, a plotless tale of
aimless life propelled by the agonies of inconsistent and contradictory
motivations, a life without coherent form except for the form implied
by the book's [astrological] title" (14). We are, like Oswald, negative
Librans, barely balancing a myriad of possibilities. For, as Lentricchia
cites the DeLillo narrative voice as saying, we are "somewhat unsteady
and impulsive. Easily, easily, easily influenced. Poised to make the
dangerous leap" (14). Into what? Blindly into some role or other, like
Stanley Fish himself or his "rhetorical man," in one or another of the
coercive yet captivating narratives of our self-alienation already
scripted and being revised in and as American cultural history. However much we may deny or critique such narratives, they are still there
to ensnare us, most likely when we think we are hatching our most
authentic little plots. Following DeLillo's lead (here and in *White
Noise*), Lentricchia traces this all-too-probable contemporary fate, a
horrific yet historically specified marriage of Foucault's discursive
nightmares and Lyotard's visions of our postmodern condition, all the
way back from DeLillo and Fitzgerald, through Dreiser and Emerson,
to the pilgrim fathers and mothers on the Mayflower. Each generation
of American dreamers, it seems, is convinced that its given identities,
its first persons (or "I's"), are barren, poverty-stricken, empty vessels
set loose from the ruins of some literal or figurative Europe (or other
original homeland), to await once in America the sublimely apocalyptic appearance of the fabulous universal third person, the new self-
made American identity ex nihilo, standing there and staring back at
us from the radiant surface of the latest mirror of our culture: book,
newspaper and magazine, film, TV newsreel, video cassette, and so
on. In this eerie light, the distinction between reality and imagination begins to blur. All the imaginations in action that Lentricchia

anatomizes over the course of his career thus lead up to and make possible this historical vision of the saturnalia of contingent masks in postmodern American culture.

Both in *Ariel and the Police* and in his latest book, *American Modernism,* his contribution to the new *Cambridge History of American Literature,* Lentricchia not only explores the historical formation of this postmodern condition but also provides us with the example of a self-critical theoretical practice. His mask play stages an alternative conception of the critic and of criticism's function at the present time. This alternative oppositional criticism can best be elucidated by reading Lentricchia's latest work in terms of the late Foucault's idea of the plural subject and Kristeva's revisionary understanding of imaginary identification.

My own position is close to Lentricchia's as I have so far outlined it. (Clearly, he is my Kenneth Burke.) Where it varies is in my reliance on late Foucault and recent Kristeva, neither of whom Lentricchia discusses. I rely on them for, respectively, a historical meditation and a revisionary psychoanalytic treatment of intellectual identity formation. As I read them, and following Lentricchia's lead, critical identity (especially in postmodern America) involves the sublimation of the vulnerable sympathetic reader's initial response (our negative libran reaction) to an imposing imagination in action. The critic internalizes this sublime wound of aesthetic possibilities as a specular doubling, a spectral scene of instructive mourning for a momentarily usurped and so somewhat resentful and sharply self-divided subjectivity. This interpretive process sets up the psychic agency I call "oneself," a radically ambivalent dialectic of self-overcoming identification and critical differentiation, loving transference and defensive distantiation. The source for this internalized agon is the ancient classical model of self-development derived from the complex ever-changing relationship of the pedagogic pair of mentor and student with their (at least) latently erotic bond. Critical identity becomes an internalized economy of such imaginative pairings, a psychic school of formative influence, a continuing mask play of "oneself" in this inescapably plural sense. As such, critical identity is necessarily and radically socialized, indeed inescapably if internally political, fundamentally dynamic, self-consciously erotic, and so, almost by definition, constitutionally ironic. For me, the ethical aim of such identity formation, when wittingly practiced, comes about in that magnanimous avowal of one's imaginary father(s) that defeats the social pathology of (self-)destructive *ressentiment*. If the material sites of the collective archive of canonical and noncanonical works in our culture are the various institutions and media for the preservation, circulation, and dissemination of knowledge, then what I have just characterized as critical identity formation constitutes both the collective archive's psychosocial site and its changing human face.

I think this agonistic bonding of the pedagogic pair is what informs the historical context of first and third person sociopathology that Lentricchia adduces in "Don DeLillo." Male bonding, even across generational, ethnic, and racial lines, is the only thing, in the arena of personal relations, that traditionally America liked to think it did even partly well. *Libra* represents in the Oswald-Kennedy bond its demonic postmodern parody: the former plays Mordred and not Percival to the latter's King Arthur. Lacking a definite identity, being all too easily influenced because cut off from historic roots, this representative fate of Oswald's constitutes what it means to be an American as much as does the dream of impersonating a fabulous figure of one's own creation. In America, perhaps, only the educational institution can provide an important albeit minimum basis for collective intergenerational judgment. And we need this basis for judging such wildly self- and other destructive dreams of fabulous identity as Thomas Sutpen's doomed dynastic "design" in Faulkner's *Absalom! Absalom!* or Oswald's pathetic postmodern parody and pastiche of all such imperial designs in DeLillo's *Libra*. The problem with most American appropriations of poststructuralism—new historicism, new Americanist criticism, neopragmatism—is precisely that whatever they may preach, they nevertheless practice, because of this postmodern American condition, their own belated versions of the sublime dream of the heroically self-made individual: DeLillo's everaspiring celebrity Oswald from *Libra,* however uncomfortably, may indeed be one of us.

In *Ariel and the Police: Michel Foucault, William James, Wallace Stevens,* Lentricchia takes to task three contemporary critical formations: new historicism, neopragmatism, and essentialist feminism. He does so because, unlike Michel Foucault, William James, and Wallace Stevens, these critical movements subsume the problematic struggles of such particular (and plural) imaginations in action within the conventional hierarchies of professional discipline. These movements, Lentricchia claims, thereby supervise and homogenize, policing by making uniform, such heterogeneous Ariels most often for self-serving careerist purposes. That is, the unique differences of Foucault, James, and Stevens just become grist for the mills of professionalism. Filial ingratitude could be the motto of these critical movements, even as saving Ariel (or the particular imagination) certainly is Lentricchia's. Each of these critical positions, after claiming a radically contingent basis, reinscribes the aesthetic dream of the self-made, freestanding, singular subject beyond the reach of history, thereby belying their initial socializing claims. As "Don DeLillo" may already suggest, these critics do so because they are unaware that the postmodern American condition of Oswalds-in-the-making, narrative shards adrift in or bumping wildly about a culture of inherited masterplots, also applies to themselves. Twentieth-century fiction repeatedly traces the evolution of fatal design out of mere chance. As DeLillo dramatizes in *Libra,* once Oswald the aimless shard enters the plot of the CIA-Mafia-Cuban-Exile conspirators, his own end, like that of his ideal double, Kennedy, is fatally sealed. Similarly, as Lentricchia shows, some theorists of the postmodern end up getting hooked by one or another version of the greatest American grand narrative of them all, that fabulous dream of the self-originating, purely aesthetic subject, the transcendental self that springs full-blown from its own Platonic conception of itself.

Lentricchia in *Ariel and the Police* traces Stephen Greenblatt's trail of self-contradiction. He starts from Greenblatt's full embrace of the new historicist nightmare vision from Foucault's *Discipline and Punish,* in which history is a totalitarian system of metadiscourses of power supervising and disciplining every molecule of life, with no exit for subjective agency to escape. Lentricchia concludes his hunt with Greenblatt's expressed desire for and fundamental conviction of a "will to play" in the epilogue to his 1980 classic of contemporary criticism, *Renaissance Self-Fashioning.*[7] As Lentricchia cites him, Greenblatt ends by contradicting his espousal of new historicism (really, of any historicism), when he claims that "the will to play flouts society's cherished orthodoxies, embraces what the culture finds loathsome or frightening, transforms the serious into the joke and

then unsettles the category of the joke by taking it seriously, courts
self-destruction in the interest of the anarchic discharge of its energy.
This is play on the brink of an abyss, absolute play" (100). Greenblatt, given his new historicist discursive determinism, has no logical
justification for such a vision of the will to play, which is already an
absurdity on its face, a subject ripe for radical parody. For where could
such a will, particularly in the world of *Discipline and Punish,* whose
prototype Greenblatt claims to find emerging in the Renaissance,
come from? In any event, this passage echoes, I think, Schiller from
Letters on Aesthetic Education and Nietzsche from *The Gay Science.* [8] Naturally, the passage also has a then-contemporary resonance in early
Derrida and Foucault, particularly their surprisingly similar remarks
on the visions of totally excessive psychic economy and of transgression in Bataille. But while such resonances make Greenblatt's illogi-
cal position historically understandable it cannot make it any more
logical. Lentricchia's analysis of this passage primarily in terms of
Greenblatt's own postmodern American situation of disillusioned liberalism, with its considerable debt to Emersonian transcendentalism,
is remarkably perspicacious:

> The personal story that {Greenblatt} tells in the epilogue of {*Renais-
> sance Self-Fashioning*] functions as a cautionary tale of the archetypal
> political awakening of liberal man to the realities of power. His advice
> is to imaginatively interiorize the dream of self-fashioning because
> only by so doing will we keep ourselves from being swept away in
> history's narrative of repression, in the inevitable movement to the
> carceral nightmare as the daylight world of everyday life. [Yet] Green-
> blatt tells us at the end that the human subject which he (and we)
> wanted to be autonomous and believed to be so "begins to seem re-
> markably unfree, the ideological project of the relations of power in a
> particular society" [97]. . . . So the Foucauldian new historicist ac-
> count in its entirety—both what it believes to be the truth and what
> speaks through and undoes that belief {the will to play" in Green-
> blatt]--is the best if unwitting account of new historicism and its
> political quandary that I know. Hating a world that we never made,
> wanting to transform it, we settle for a holiday from reality, a safely
> sealed space reserved for the expression of aesthetic anarchy, a long
> weekend that defuses the radical implications of our unhappiness.
> (101)

Lentricchia here exposes how the totalitarian nightmare imagination of Foucault's *Discipline and Punish* effectively inspires the resurrection of the aesthetic imagination's compensatory dream of escape from reality into a sublime vision of the freely self-fashioning dilettante of absolute play. How far the self-made critic of American culture to be found in Emerson has fallen here! Lentricchia thereby reads the critical mask play of these interrelated imaginations from the dramatic intersection of Greenblatt's new historicist text and his postmodern American context.

Similarly, in his analysis of Steven Knapp and Walter Benn Michaels's controversial 1982 essay "Against Theory," Lentricchia reads the mask play of imaginations in action within their influential brand of neopragmatism, which generally celebrates William James and not C.S. Peirce. Given their ostentatious claims to pragmatist critical pedigree, one might expect that, like the later William James, the antinomian father of pragmatism, Knapp and Michaels would practice an open-ended metonymic criticism, variously political, aesthetic, historical, and theoretical. Instead, they do what all their neopragmatist brethren now also do: They set themselves up, as Lentricchia shows, as synecdochal or representative masters of the entire critical field. For they presume to know, a priori, what counts as theory (viz., strong, foundational, and thus self-doomed attempts to survey and master, systematically from outside and above, the field of critical practice), and what does not count as theory (viz., provisional, improvisatory conceptualizations of practice for getting some critical job of work done). Lentricchia here betrays the self-contradiction at the heart of their "Against Theory" project.

However much they may claim there is nothing more to theory than practice, professional convention, and social belief, and that therefore theory, with its presumption to a priori knowledge, can and should simply be dismissed, their own rhetoric nevertheless performs in practice as if they were imperial subjects laying down the law of their neopragmatist vision for everyone and for all time. Lentricchia succinctly puts it this way: "Pragmatism (the vigilante within) is always on the verge of vanquishment, of giving belief over to [such absolutist practice of] theory (the totalitarian within)" (125). In other words, the mask play of the pragmatist and totalitarian imaginations in action, like that of the aesthetic and totalitarian imaginations in

Greenblatt's case, are here dialectically interrelated on the pedagogic model of magisterial presence and prodigal student (Stanley Fish, you recall, became the professional mentor of Michaels), until the supervention of the critical imagination, which, as Lentricchia performs it, can read so well the auguries of such far-from-innocent critical mask plays.

As we will shortly see in his provocative critique of Sandra Gilbert and Susan Gubar's "essentialist feminism," Lentricchia can read such mask plays of imaginations in action performing themselves as the dramatic intersection of text and context not simply because he draws intellectual sustenance from rough and ready Kenneth Burke and his socially symbolic criticism of motives rather than from well-modulated and refined Northrop Frye and his idealist vision of mythic archetypes. It is also because the other-than-professional circumstances primarily account for Lentricchia's distinctive critical ability. His situation as a second generation Italian-American male—unlike Italian-American women, it has been unusual hitherto for this demographic category, as they say, to make it in significant numbers into the ranks of professional intellectuals—necessarily foregrounds historically specific aspects of class, ethnic, and gender differences. This foregrounding or underscoring helps to explain Lentricchia's nearly preternatural sensitivity to differences and nuances of style in the largest sense of the word. I do not mean to imply by making this claim that for a critic to be a self-aware insightful analyst of style he or she must play the game of moral one-upmanship on the world historical stage of cultural victimage. Far from it. What I am instead claiming is that the power of subjective agency in Lentricchia's representative case, as he himself repeatedly says, is fully historical in nature (and fully historicized in his later criticism). It is never merely a matter of sublime individual genius, whether implicitly his own or ostensibly Burke's (or any other writer's). It is also that this (like any) imaginative agency is necessarily plural, made up of scenes of instruction in which literary and personal ancestors compete for attention, since imaginative agency, as I have suggested here and argued earlier in the book at greater length, is grounded in the collective archive and its fostering of critical change by means of its accumulated resources of canonical and noncanonical, positive and negative exempla. The mask plays of imaginations in action in Lentricchia's work are clearly informed by this collective process of critical identity formation.

Basically, with Gilbert and Gubar, Lentricchia accuses them of what Toril Moi in *Sexual/Textual Politics* defines as "essentialist feminism." Lentricchia is referring to the kind of feminist criticism in which a fundamental biological difference in identity along gender lines, which marks women's writing as fundamentally different, is asserted or presumed. The upshot of such criticism is that the patriarchal hierarchy is simply reversed, with women becoming the morally privileged victims in the material history of repression. In such criticism, they are thus always being represented, with distinction, as the moral superiors of imperially empowered males, regardless of all socially specific, historically constructed differences, especially those of class, between people within the same culture and between different cultures. Feminists of the Gilbert and Gubar sort are therefore in danger of erecting into dogma a "Manichean allegory," a "formalism of gender," that is the mirror image of the patriarchy's naturalistic ahistoricism and that would grant to the essentialist feminists in question the rhetorical right to lord it over the entire field of critical and cultural studies as if they were, from Lentricchia's perspective, the self-appointed queens in theory:

> If history, as Gilbert and Gubar argue, is a repetitive sexist drama (not easy to argue otherwise) with men in the pilot-controlling role of the oppressor, and women in the role of selfless victim, then history may be in danger of being translated into Manichean allegory and the very category that Moi and others invoke in order to explain the transformation of biology into history—she calls it interchangeably, the "social" or the "cultural,—this category will be banished behind the scenes almost as quickly as it is invoked. With the social banished behind the scenes, history begins to look very much again like biology, biology like metaphysics, and the writing of feminist literary criticism like a ritual of scapegoating propelled by paranoia. (179)

And, from Lentricchia's perspective, it is also propelled by the American dream of sublime self-aggrandizement in one of its more virulent postmodern critical forms. Just as Greenblatt embraces Foucault's totalitarian dystopia of history as all-powerful suffocating discourses only to retreat into a weak-kneed liberal posture of aesthetic self-fashioning; just as Knapp and Michaels espouse the radical contingency of pragmatism only to reproduce the panoptical desire for total supervision and disciplining of the entire theoretical field at their hands; so, too, Gilbert and Gubar, in the name of the radical ideology of difference, apocalyptically separate all men and women into the very same homogenizing antithetical archetypes of biological determination that the patriarchy loves, only in doing so simply reversing their evaluations. Ironically enough, the current institutional consequences of such deeply self-conflicted rhetorical strategies is the simultaneous resentful dismissal or confinement of all imaginary fathers and the virtual professional apotheosis of their critical "authors."

As his statements in several recent interviews attest, Lentricchia knows from his own and his family's material experiences that class differences, which are not natural but historical, can make as much difference for males from excluded groups as can gender differences for women. Similarly, he knows that not all women until recently were in the position of homebodies just tending the children and the simulated hearth. Both his own mother and his grandmother had to work to help support the extended family. Such class differences are radically contingent, as Lentricchia reiterates, and, as we will see shortly in more detail, they account for the particular situations of modern American poets and their distinctive achievements more thoroughly than simply the application of one abstract theoretical category of analysis, whether gender-based or not. In Gilbert's and Gubar's case, their conception of poetic vocation derives from the aristocratic model of inherited estates, so historically inappropriate for a country in which Wordsworth's democratic dream of the vast majority of poets being middle class, would indeed become a reality. America's poets rarely experience such inheritance in fact or fancy, are mostly fearful of falling to the lower depths, and are ever conscious, in each generation, of starting over again from next to nothing to make their own new ways in the business of poetry. (By "middle class," Lentricchia means neither idly poor nor idly rich, but working for a "more-than-subsistence" livelihood.)

In each of these cases—Greenblatt's new historicism, Knapp and Michaels's neopragmatism, and Gilbert's and Gubar's essentialist feminism—Lentricchia reads the mask play of imaginations in action as shaping the criticism in question often to the point of distortion, the self-contradiction of working at cross-purposes with itself. Despite their explicit claims to the contrary, despite the irony that two of these three cases involve pairs of critics, and despite the fact that all three cases represent now-widespread critical developments, the formative self-contradiction generally playing itself out is the one Lentricchia discusses so memorably in "Don DeLillo." This is, as you recall, that whatever we may believe and say in theory, our critical practice at any moment may betray us as being Oswald-like narrative fragments awhirl in our postmodern world, chronically in danger of making the dangerous leap and becoming ensnared by some master narrative or other. In our time, of course, this usually means the grand narrative of the American dream's fabulous third person, the heroically self-made universal individual, the Jay Gatsby, Sister Carrie, or Ralph Waldo Emerson—any and all those figures that we witness perpetually changing in response to their own words, who haunt what Lentricchia dreads may really be our Lee Harvey Oswald–like everyday lives.

> DeLillo writes that Oswald "wanted to carry himself with a clear sense of role." But who is this "he" who wanted a "role," just who is it that stands in the wings waiting for a part in the theater of self? It doesn't much help to say that he is someone named "Oswald" who can get up from a chair where he's been reading a book, calmly walk over to his wife, pummel her with both fists, then return to the chair and resume his reading, quietly. The identity of the negative libran is an undecidable intention waiting to be decided. And astrology is the metaphor in *Libra* for being trapped in a system whose determinative power is grippingly registered by DeLillo's double narrative of an amorphous existence haphazardly stumbling into the future where a plot awaits to confer upon it the identity of a role fraught with form and purpose. (14)

The feature of Foucault, James, and Stevens that, whatever their limitations, sharply distinguishes them, for Lentricchia, from the American critical formations of new historicism, neopragmatism, and essentialist feminism that would appropriate and discipline these figures, is precisely what DeLillo and Lentricchia also possess: a strongly particular imaginative grasp of their actual historical situations. The problem with contingency theory, therefore, is that it is not really historical enough.

The constructively critical moment in *Ariel and the Police* comes mainly in its second half on Wallace Stevens. It is here that Lentricchia first develops, via his particular readings of his chosen poet, the theoretical-historical perspective of cultural-political analysis that informs his magisterial *Cambridge History* volume on modern American poetry entitled *American Modernism*. Lentricchia lays out the situation at the turn of the century facing the young man who wants to become a poet. All too briefly here I will summarize his deliberately provocative view of this situation from both books.[9]

Such a young man lives at a time when American imperialism, modern capitalist discipline and commodification, the savvy marketing of sentimentality for insatiable consumption by passive readers, and the feminization of intellectual life—its chronically self-hating and too often self-defined "genteel" status—combine to enshrine as aesthetic paradigm the belated Fireside poetic of Edmund Clarence Stedman (scholar and anthologist), Ellery Sedgewich (editor of the *Atlantic*), and Jessie Belle Rittenhouse (poet and anthologist). In his chapter on Robert Frost in *American Modernism*, Lentricchia succinctly characterizes the modern poet's antipathy to Belle Rittenhouse and her influence with special panache:

> In her various writings and anthologies she could say who was in and who (usually by omission) was out, and though recent historians have not ratified any of her choices and do not know her name, she was a force who represented both in her female person and her taste the aesthetic grain that the emerging modernist male poets worked against: the principle of "the Feminine in literature," as Eliot put it, which he was none too anxious to give space to in *The Egoist;* the "Aunt Hepsy" that Pound saw as typifying poetry's contemporary audience in the United States; one of those—again Pound—who had turned poetry (for serious people) into "balderdash—a sort of embroidery for dilettantes and women." (3)

This poetic, which Palgrave recommends in his statement of principles in *The Golden Treasury*, repeatedly reproduces a watered-down Keatsian or Tennysonian lyric, abstracted from what it sees as the hard grit of life, vaguely pointing some noble moral, in the Hallmark-card style of traditional verse forms, and so suitable for immediate framing in *Harpers* or the *Atlantic* by pages of advertisements. This is the world in which Palgrave's *Golden Treasury* is indeed king. Lentricchia with fierce verve also depicts in his Frost chapter what Palgrave's genteel followers made of this anthology poetic of splendid isolation. *The Golden Treasury* is clearly more various and representative of poetic tradition than this: "No narrative, no description of local, regional cast; no humor (the antithesis of the lyric mode according to Palgrave); no intellect at meditation; nothing occasional; nothing dramatic—no textures of blank verse because lyric in its purity excludes the dramatic voice in its speaking cadences; certainly no vernacular. . . . no ironists allowed" (3–4). Lentricchia's point is not that Palgrave consistently put his principles into practice, only that others did. Confronting such a scene of misrecognition, is it any wonder, Lentricchia asks, why Stevens and Pound, Eliot and Frost, feel less the anxiety of influence vis-à-vis their great romantic ancestors (although they surely do), than the anxiety of their imminent emasculations at the dainty hands of cultivated America, or that they, in strategic reaction, celebrate the heroic vitality of business and power, however much they may also come to lament the consequences of these counterideals.

American Modernism, Lentricchia's contribution to the new *Cambridge History of American Literature,* has three major parts. Part 1, in three chapters ("From Gentility to Joyce," "Lyric in the Culture of Capitalism," and "Philosophers of Modernism at Harvard, ca. 1900"), substantiates in greatly effective detail the picture that I have just been able to sketch of the poetic situation at the turn of the century.[10] Two things that I must leave out of my present discussion for reasons of space and appropriateness are the climactic role of Joyce's *Ulysses* in establishing modernist aesthetics in opposition to the washed-out neurasthenic gentility of conventional culture and the prophetic role such Harvard philosophers as George Santyana, William James, and Josiah Royce played in shaping modernist poetics, particularly the poetic of the image. (This last point is Lentricchia's deliberate effort simultaneously to downplay the traditional role of Bergson and Hulme in the history of modern poetry and to foreground the formative role of mostly American sources.) The sec-

ond part of *American Modernism* interprets the representative careers of
Frost, Stevens, Pound, and Eliot as the defining gestures in modern
American poetry. Like his elevation of the Harvard philosophers here
or, in *Ariel and the Police,* his attacks on three prominent critical formations, this move, too, is intentionally agonistic, indeed provocatively so, especially in light of Gilbert's and Gubar's recent multi-
volume feminist treatment of much of this same material in *No Man's
Land: The Place of the Woman Writer in Modern Literature.* Finally, Part 3
of *American Modernism* discusses briefly the complex relations of culture and identity along lines already suggested in *Ariel and the Police.*

Although I have elsewhere commented at length on Lentricchia's
views of Stevens and so will concentrate on his exemplary reading of
Pound in *American Modernism* (it best embodies the spirit of the book),
I should say something about the brilliant counterpointing effect of
these chapters, which typifies the organization of the whole volume. [11] Both Stevens and Pound, as Lentricchia rightly sees them, derive primarily from different (if subtly interrelated) aspects of Emerson. Stevens, on the one hand, rehearses Emerson's transcendental
desire (from *Nature*) for an original, vividly transparent relation to nature. He does so by translating it into his late-capitalist desire for an
original, vividly transparent relation of the connoisseur-gourmand to
the rich and strange commodity fetched imperially from around the
globe by the new economic world order: the original avant garde
painting from Paris, exotic teas from Ceylon, fresh foot-long bananas
from the Philippines. (The greatest danger to this upper middle-class
desire, of course, is the "democratic" proliferation of mass market
simulacra and scaled-down or ersatz approximations of such original
goods.) Such would-be aristocratic commodity desire perfectly
characterizes the poetic moment in Stevens as a moment of always-
anticipated and ever-deferred consumption of the ever-new and
always-fresh object of desire: a consumer's paradise of purely acquisi-
tive foreplay. In this ironic fashion of ever-postponed climax, Stevens
impersonates and updates for the times the very internalized "mask"
(4) of the pallid lady-poet, who consumes emotion for all occasions in
her opportunistic verse, that he begins his career by abjecting. (We
recall that he opts instead for the Whitmanesque or Lawrentian uto-
pia in the famous seventh stanza of "Sunday Morning," with its ring
of naked well-built men singing their paeans to their masterful lord,

the sun.) The result of this ironic turnabout in such late lyrics as "The World as Meditation," however, is that, through the ever-patient Penelope and related figures, Stevens finally abjures the imperial system of "far-fetchings," that is the late-capitalist world order endlessly feeding with commodities his narcissistic form of desire. As he does so he painfully recognizes the perpetual postponement of any final reunion of imagination and reality, desire and its material object (Penelope and Ulysses), as the sole desire he can ever finally know. As such, the abjected lady-poet returns with a vengeance. Pound, on the other hand, as we shall see in some detail, starts from what he plausibly sees as Emerson's vigorous sense of the American psyche (from "History" and "The American Scholar"). Emerson, as Pound understands him, sees the American scholar as the virgin site where all "the transmigrations of Proteus," all the self-interpretations of the Sphinx constituting human history, can finally fulfill themselves: what before was merely possible at last becomes embodied as the American psyche. History for Emerson (as for Pound and Lentricchia) is the collective archive of imaginative possibilities, at best only half realized, or perverted by accident or mistaken intentions or human stupidity. These possibilities are to materialize in and as the mask plays of the consummate American virtuoso, the poet, who is therefore "a liberating god" ("The Poet"). "We as we read must become," Emerson counsels (and Pound obviously took him to heart), "Greeks, Romans, Turks, priest and king, martyr and executioner, must fasten these images to some reality in our secret experience, or we shall learn nothing rightly" ("History"). For such a figure, Stevens's sexual poetics of late-capitalist desire can be but one part to improvise. (Pound's conspicuous connection to Browning is his defensive mask for this deeply formative Emersonian influence.)

Lentricchia, in this compelling manner, counterpoints the mask play of Stevens and Pound, significantly opting in his ironic performance for the latter figure over the former as the more inclusive and worldly imagination—for, despite Pound's embrace of fascism, which cannot be redeemed by saying he also writes good poetry, Pound, unlike the schizoid poet–insurance executive, at least knows cultural, social, and economic practices are mutually enmeshed, equally overlapping and reciprocally enveloping one another in diverse ways, not neatly separable (without severe psychic and political consequences) into the routine workweek and the aesthetic holiday weekend. However uncertainly useful such knowledge was to Pound, it is fully useful to Lentricchia.

Pound the youthful dreamy aesthete, the energetic entrepreneur of modernism, the imaginative philologist of the troubadours, the fly-by-the-seat-of-his-pants Chinese scholar, the creative Old English and Latin "translator," the crank economic theorist, the rabid fascist sympathizer, the fierce anti-Semite, the mad bad poet of the Pisan cage, and the bizarrely silent figure in the St. Elizabeth's cell—all these "Pounds" and more besides—begin for Lentricchia as any good American does: with no definitive identity that he can recognize as his own, but with a host of inherited personas or masks to take on and with only the principle of modernization itself (endless change as radical innovation as poetic metamorphosis) to guide him.

> In the period spanning the many stylistic changes from his earliest poems to his early Cantos, Pound changed not at all on the value of metamorphosis for the sort of writer (himself) who explained the process of writing to himself in his earliest poems as an experience of walking into nonsense—becoming Christ, Villon, or Dante, God or a tree—a writer who would project the psychic value of his own aesthetic experience as the real value of reading his poems. Pound's reader would also be freed from the self of the moment, liberated into some strange and bracing identity, joining the writer in mythic experience in order to take on with Pound what he, like Pound, does not possess. (35–36)

As Lentricchia goes on to say, both Pound and his reader are not versions of everyman, but typically American men, in need of "virtù"—that is, in need of the virtuoso's liberation from the "fixed and crystallised" shell of convention one's latest mask is always liable to become. This is a liberation into the perpetual avant-gardism, "the ruling philosophy of everyday life in the land of opportunity and infinite self-development" (36). For Pound, as Lentricchia reads him, this liberating experience of the poet and his reader both parallels the processes of everyday life in America and gives the best "antidefinition of literature as writing without historically prior and persistent identity, writing without a prior 'self' to rely on—a nonidentity of sheerest possibility, an absence of essence" (36). While individual exiles in this or other countries may have experienced a similar "absence of essence," Pound's uniqueness derives from his being born into a country of such essential absence of identity. Such an "absence of essence" defines the contingency theory informing many philosophical movements in the twentieth century, from existentialism through neopragmatism. For Lentricchia, however, this fact of historical contingency and "absence of essence" never licenses the belief that we can simply kick ourselves free of our material origins into purely aesthetic "projects of self-creation" (Rorty's phrase), with no historical or psychic consequences. For example, this "antidefinition of literature" is what Pound describes as "constant transformation" and what Lentricchia portrays as "constant rebirth into a newness of (these are equivalents) an American and a modern literary selfhood" (36). A country of people all out to make it new is the rationale for such equivalency. As Lentricchia sarcastically enjoins us, lest we get too giddy with such pretty prospects, "Never mind that 'constant transformation' also describes the dream of consumer capitalism, avant-garde of capitalist economics" (36). Here, as throughout this chapter and indeed the entire volume, Lentricchia typically reminds us of the imaginative limitations as well as the imaginative achievements of his chosen figures, by remarking the material conditions of their lives.

Lentricchia next distinguishes between Pound's American (or Emersonian) sense of metamorphosis and any classical precedent in a fashion that returns us to a main theme of culture and critical identity in America:

> Metamorphosis is the unprecedented master category in Pound's literary theory. In spite of the explicit Ovidian allusion [which earlier poets also invoked], the theory is not Ovidian. Nor does Pound draw upon a notion of biological metamorphosis: the man who comes "before" the glass can not be traced, not even obscurely, as a surviving form in the new self (hence Pound's [repeatedly] shocked "I"?). But if there is to be metamorphosis in any recognizable sense of the word, there must be a prior something which undergoes transformation. If the prior "something" is, as in Pound, a determinate nothing, a hole needing filling and fulfilling, valuable ("golden") precisely because of its amorphic condition, then Pound, like Emerson, has pressed metamorphosis to the edge of its limiting boundary: [what has become] the classic American dream, self-origination ex nihilo. Pound theor-

izes metamorphosis, a process of self-emergence, as Emerson had theorized it: on a condition of potential-for-self only, not on the transformation of one self into another; a condition without a memory out of
which a self might emerge which is nothing but memory, and so—
the irony and paradox of Pound's career—no self at all. (36–37)

This portrait of Pound and his reader is as powerful as it is, I submit, precisely because it is likewise a portrait of Lentricchia and his
reader, or, potentially, of any American writer and any American
reader, or of any Jay Gatsby and any Nick Carraway. All the masks of
imaginations in action begin to resonate through this figure of Pound—
aesthetic, totalitarian, pragmatist, critical—in a process of surprised
mutual recognition and as a persuasive scene of instruction that creates this critical portrait of the American: a man without qualities but
with a legion of names to come.

Such critical vision does not mean, however, that, like Emerson
before him and DeLillo's Oswald after him, Pound, as Lentricchia
reads him, (and as we read Lentricchia) is simply condemned, in
Yeats's haunting refrain, to be only "mad as the mist and snow." What
saves Pound—and by implication his critic and reader—in the early
Cantos at least, is "the artistic arrangement of the documents" (68).
What finally matters is not the fanciful production of the fabulous
third-person dream of self-originating American identity ex nihilo
but the careful, patient, actively meditative placement of all the
words—historical, philosophical, poetic—that we can collect from
the archive about a subject. (Here we see the continuing constructive
influence of Foucault's practice of critical genealogy.) The oppositional result of such an imaginatively particular "arrangement of the
documents"—of such artistry—can be, as here, the dramatic performance of intellectual identity formation in an interpretive moment of
some temporal complexity, considerable ethical resonance, and formative cultural influence. Or, the inspiring payoff can be, as it is in
the following example from the Stevens chapter, the exemplary imaginative care with which the critic in his style subtly performs his
many-faceted judgments: "As a student at Harvard, Stevens learned
to distrust (in a thickening fin-de-siècle atmosphere) overtly moralizing art" (37). This sentence does many things. The ironic enactment
of the soon-to-be definitively overcome American belatedness vis-

à-vis the "mother" country England (Stevens leaves that Anglophiliac bastion, Cambridge, for the Big Apple shortly after the turn of the century), the reflexive envelopment of the parenthetical remark, and the pointed positioning of *le mot juste*—"overtly"—for maximizing the dramatic effect of the negative aesthetic take on "moralizing art": all of these things collectively make the creative performance of this beautiful (because fully animated) sentence's rhetoric a minor example of Lentricchia's major critical art.

Consider, as final example of this "active soul," Lentricchia on Pound's portrayal of his Renaissance hero, Sigismundo Malatesta, whose "unswerving devotion to the building of the Tempio Malatestiana in Rimini" here becomes legendary:

> The arrangement of the documents is dramatic: Pound's purpose is to conjure his obscure hero (Canto 8 opens with incantatory rhetoric), show him in the act of emerging from corruption, his voice freeing itself, sailing above, somehow uncontaminated; a voice elegant, dignified, gracious, lyrical, and promising violence, a man whose passion rescues him even from the evil that he does. The strength of Pound's showing lies not in the narrative of Sigismundo—its confusions overwhelm even Pound—but in the rhetorical effects he manages in honor of his hero. Pound loves the man, and his love creates a verbal habitation that insulates him from the garbage of his circumstances. (68)

As Lentricchia concludes his study of Pound on Malatesta, he focuses on the sublimely ironic juxtaposition of the "swamp of political confusion" (70) his beloved hero has faced and the signature statement, as Pound relates it, on Malatesta's temple of art: "He, Sigismundo, templum aedificavit" (70). Art—Sigismundo's, Pound's, Lentricchia's—intimately confronts politics, for it, like critical identity, is an imaginative form of politics:

> From this swamp of political confusion, this comic litany of the months and seasons of byzantine betrayal, spoken, no doubt, in some smoke-filled backroom, comes a line from another level, elevated in syntax and tone, with a Latin phrase at the end (like an anchor of final authority) telling us what Malatesta did—the Latin working for Pound (as languages other than English often did) as some talismanic discourse, the facilitor of magical transcendence from politics to the

plane of art [and back again]: "He, Sigismundo, templum aedificavit." "He, Sigismundo"—a phrasing repeated often in the Malatesta group—not only clarifies just who it is among these obscure
political actors that Pound is talking about, but adds the sound of
awe, like an epitaph which registers the shock of the memorialist,
that in the midst of all this, he, Sigismundo, did what he did: "In the
gloom the gold gathers the light against it." (70)

The complex pedagogic imperative of this sublimely attractive, indeed "talismanic discourse" is that of critical analogy—as Pound may
be to Malatesta and Lentricchia may be to Pound, so, too, the reader
may be to both the critic and his doubled subject. Unlike the American dream of the singularly self-made yet impossibly universal third
person, which is something just too fabulously ideal and individualist
to be believed, the "oneself" here is a historically grounded, socially
made (architecture is a public art), and impersonally plural dialectical
subject. This vision is then a sublimely particular, politically posi-
tioned, and nobly magnanimous imagination in critical action.[12]
Here the contingent imagination is truly both historical and imaginative.

Pound, whose imagination of the modern has been imprisoned in
the obscurity produced by a strange combination of antiquarian commentary and reductive ideological critique, is here seen on analogy
with his chosen hero, a Renaissance man of powerful virtue and savage
devotion to art, whom Pound rescues from his captivity in near-
historical oblivion. Similarly, Lentricchia practices his critical art on
Pound's behalf, with the implication that the reader is to go and do
likewise for his or her chosen figure. Amid all the purely professional
processes for grinding the particular achievements of writers into
grist for the latest mills of careerism, celebrity, and professionalism to
no end, I find this truly artistic performance of imaginative gener-
osity that still sees all the historical and political limitations, to be
courageous and bracing, an aesthetic use of the collective archive of
creative exempla for constructively socializing and humanizing purposes—that is, the anchoring of our culture of critical identity in the
plural authority of "oneself." Pound-Malatesta, as I see Lentricchia
envisioning this relation, perfectly balances his earlier reading of the
DeLillo-Oswald relation, as the major parts of his theoretical portrait

of the ever-elusive American subject: "In the gloom, the gold gathers the light against it."

This performance thus dramatizes what Kristeva (after Lacan and Freud) analyzes as the imaginary father of individual prehistory. This is a supremely social and androgynous figure of primary identification with the symbolic order of culture immediately beyond the mother-child fusion state. It stands in relation to the Oedipal patriarch and the abjected mother much as Jesus Christ stands in relation to Yahweh and nature: as an alternative to both repression and abjection, as sublimation—that is, as sacrifice *and* resurrection. Kristeva reminds us, however, that the imaginary father never makes an appearance as any single figure alone. It is always implied by an entire constellation of figures in a text or over the course of a career. The imaginary father, as Foucault (after Nietzsche and Hegel) also recognizes, embodies the agonistic constitution of the self, that plural subject (or "oneself") that is the historically specific and ironically self-overcoming mentor-student bond in its various formal permutations, such as here: Malatesta-Pound, Pound-Lentricchia, critic-reader, and so on. This passage thus represents a sublimely particular interpretive gathering of dialectically interrelated temporal moments making up the American mask play (modern, renaissance, postmodern), whose continued imaginative resonance is generously offered for our edification. Such is the genuinely oppositional culture of self-overcoming critical identity. Rather than new historicism's weakly liberal poetics, neopragmatism's chilling professionalism unbound, or essentialist feminism's apocalyptic separatism—three of the most influential modes of criticism today—here is American critical theory performed as cultural politics radically in and effectively for our time that moves perpetually into "another intensity."[13]

Notes

Preface

1. All citations from Joel Porte, ed., *Emerson: Essays and Lectures* (New York: Library of America, 1982) are given in the text. For a discussion of this essay, see Robert D. Richardson, Jr., "Emerson on History," in Joel Porte, ed., *Emerson: Prospect and Retrospect,* Harvard English Studies (Cambridge: Harvard University Press, 1982), 49–84.

2. See, especially, the final section in *The Poetics of Mourning: Emerson, Stevens, Cheever* (Chapel Hill: University of North Carolina Press, forthcoming).

3. See Charles Altieri, *Canons and Consequences: Reflections on the Ethical Force of Imaginative Ideals* (Evanston, Ill.: Northwestern University Press, 1991). In his recent two volumes of philosophical papers, *Objectivity, Relativism, and Truth* and *Essays on Heidegger and Others,* Richard Rorty applies his self-described edifying conception of philosophy as an imaginative project of self-creation to major modern representatives of both the Anglo-American analytic and continental deconstructionist traditions. "Moral Identity and Private Autonomy" (193–95) reflects briefly on Foucault's entire career in light of his late work, only to rediscover Charles Taylor's critique (see my discussion in the introduction) that Foucault's theory of the regime of truth as a product of power relations invalidates his own truth claims, even as his desire for a *rapport à soi* conflicts with his criticism of bourgeois liberalism. As my introduction details, Rorty, like Taylor, fails to credit Foucault's radical sense of experience, which, as Gilles Deleuze in Foucault notes, is indeed compatible with pragmatism when the latter is properly conceived.

4. For further discussion of the relationship between criticism and autobiography, see

my *Tragic Knowledge: Yeats's Autobiography and Hermeneutics* (New York: Columbia University Press, 1981). See also my two essays on Said: "The Romance of Interpretation: A 'Postmodern' Critical Style," *boundary 2*, 8, 3 (Spring 1980), 259–283; and "Criticism Worldly and Otherworldly: Edward W. Said and the Cult of Theory," in *boundary 2* 12, no. 3 and 13, no. 1 (Spring/Fall 1984): 379–408. And for a discussion of Foucault's relation to edification and pedagogy, see James W. Bernauer, *Michel Foucault's Force of Flight: Toward an Ethics for Thought* (London: Humanities Press International, 1990) and Stephen J. Ball, ed., *Foucault and Education* (New York: Routledge, 1990). Finally, as my conclusion makes fully explicit, Emerson is a figure whose work both bears striking resemblances to certain contemporary developments in the theory of the subject, such as those I find in late Foucault and Kristeva, and informs, often implicitly, the desire of different critics—neopragmatist, new historicist, essentialist feminist—for a self-originating discourse of ideal or perfected individualism radically at odds with their social claims.

Introduction

1. Stanley Fish, "Reply," in "Forum," in *PMLA* 194, no. 2 (March 1989): 219–21.

2. See my *The Romance of Interpretation: Visionary Criticism from Pater to deMan* (New York: Columbia University Press, 1985); and *Lionel Trilling: The Work of Liberation* (Madison: University of Wisconsin Press, 1988).

3. See their interviews with Imre Salusinszky in his *Criticism in Society* (New York: Methuen, 1987), 122–48 and 176–206, respectively. The contingent imagination, as I have characterized it, is now professionally hegemonic as witness John Bayley's review of John Ashbery's *Flow Chart* in the *New York Review of Books* 38, no. 14 (August 15, 1991), 3–4, entitled "Richly Flows Contingency." Bayley, the archtraditionalist, openly and suavely revises Ashbery, the slick postmodernist, into the mask of deconstructive "Victoriana" (4). He thereby clearly reveals that such revisionism is the influential way the critical game must now be played by all. Just imagine it: John Ashbery as the "postmodern" Victorianist mask of an aging Oxford don. It is enough, one hopes, to make both Ashbery and Pater a bit uncomfortable at least.

1. *Mask Plays*

1. See Edward Said, "Reflections on American 'Left' Literary Criticism," in *The World, the Text, and the Critic* (Cambridge: Harvard University Press, 1983), 158–77; and Frank Lentricchia, *Criticism and Social Change* (Chicago: University of Chicago Press, 1983), especially 145–63.

2. See Allan Bloom, *Closing of the American Mind* (New York: Simon and Schuster, 1987); Gerald Graff, *Literature Against Itself* (Chicago: University of Chicago Press, 1979); and M.H. Abrams, "The Deconstructive Angel," in Robert Con Davis and Ronald Schleifer, eds., *Contemporary Literary Criticism,* 2d ed. (New York: Longman, 1989), 554–64.

3. The materials discussing these things are proliferating rapidly. Here are some highlights: Jacques Derrida, "Like the Sound of the Sea Deep Within a Shell: Paul de-Man's War," in *Critical Inquiry* 14 (Spring 1988): 590–652; "On Jacques Derrida's 'Paul deMan's War,'" in *Critical Inquiry* 15 (Summer 1989): 765–811; and, in the same issue,

Derrida's response to these responses, "Biodegradables: Seven Diary Fragments," 812–73. The best guide to the Heidegger debate is Joseph Kronick, "Dr. Heidegger's Experiment," in *boundary 2* 17, no. 3 (Fall 1990): 116–53. See also the "Symposium on Heidegger and Nazism," edited and introduced by Arnold I. Davidson in *Critical Inquiry* 15 (Winter 1989): 407–88. The best information on Heidegger in this regard so far is Hugo Ott, *Martin Heidegger: Unterwegs zu seiner Biographie* (Freiburg: Campus, 1988). See also J.P. Stern's review, "Heil Heidegger," in *London Review of Books* (April 20, 1989): 7–9.

4. See Richard Rorty, *Contingency, Irony and Solidarity* (Cambridge: Cambridge University Press, 1989); and Stanley Fish, *Doing What Comes Naturally* (Durham, N.C.: Duke University Press, 1989).

5. See, on this question of cultural studies as the latest form of philosophical anthropology, Paul A. Bové, *Intellectuals in Power: A Genealogy of Critical Humanism* (New York: Columbia University Press, 1986), especially 239–310.

6. For one recent example of critical reflection on the subsequent use of similar materials, see Charles S. Maier, *The Unmasterable Past: History, Holocaust, and German National Identity* (Cambridge: Harvard University Press, 1988), 9–33.

7. See Diana Trilling, ed., *The Portable D.H. Lawrence* (New York: Penguin Books, 1977), 36–63.

8. Klaus Theweleit, *Male Fantasies*, vol. 1: *Women, Floods, Bodies, History*, trans. Stephen Conway (Minneapolis: University of Minnesota Press, 1987), 197; hereafter cited in my text as *T1*.

9. On modern forms of asceticism in relation to ancient practices, see Geoffrey Galt Harpham, *The Ascetic Imperative in Culture and Criticism* (Chicago: University of Chicago Press, 1987).

10. Klaus Theweleit, *Male Fantasies*, vol. 2: *Male Bodies: Psychoanalyzing the White Terror*, trans. Erica Carter and Chris Turner in collaboration with Stephen Conway (Minneapolis: University of Minnesota Press, 1989), 184–85; hereafter cited in my text as *T2*.

11. See especially "The Struggle for Power as a Struggle Between the Homosexual and the Anti-Homosexual," Theweleit, Male Fantasies, *vol.* 2, 330–46.

12. For Theweleit's comments on Benjamin's formulation, see especially *Male Fantasies*, vol. 1, 79, 218, 226, 393, 430–31, 432, 434; and vol. 2, 127n, 128, 382, 355–57.

13. See Margaret Mahler, *On Human Symbiosis and the Vicissitudes of Individuation*, vol. 1: *Infantile Psychosis* (New York: International Universities Press, 1970). Mahler anticipates here, in a more sophisticated analytic form, the recently popular "codependency" tracts, such as Melody Beattie, *Codependent No More* (New York: Harper and Row, 1989) and Ann Wilson Schaf, *Co-Dependence: Misunderstood and Mistreated* (New York: Harper and Row, 1986).

14. See Jacques Derrida, *Spurs: Nietzsche's Styles*, trans. Barbara Harlow (Chicago: University of Chicago Press, 1979), 51–55.

15. Theweleit derives this antioverview critique from Foucault's *Discipline and Punish: The Birth of the Prison*, trans. Alan Sheridan (New York: Pantheon Books, 1977), even as he derives his idea of the subject of desire as a productive desiring machine from Deleuze's and Guattari's *Anti-Oedipus: Capitalism and Schizophrenia*, trans. Robert Hurley et al. (Minneapolis: University of Minnesota Press, 1983). Martin Heidegger, *What Is*

Called Thinking?, trans. Fred D. Wieck and J. Glenn Gray (New York: Harper and Row, 1968), 62.

16. For a radically oppositional perspective on this debate see William V. Spanos, "Heidegger, Nazism, and the Repressive Hypothesis: The American Appropriation of the Question," in *boundary 2* 17, no. 2 (Summer 1990): 199–280.

17. In an unpublished paper, "Paul deMan: An American Tale?" I suggest that both his later career of systematically forgetting his collaborationist past (and the ideology informing that collaboration) and his response to it after World War II were anticipated by already existing stereotypes in American culture, some of which go back to Emerson.

18. See my *Tragic Knowledge: Yeats's Autobiography and Hermeneutics* (New York: Columbia University Press, 1981) and *The Romance of Interpretation: Visionary Criticism from Pater to deMan* (New York: Columbia University Press, 1985).

19. See my *Lionel Trilling: The Work of Liberation* (Madison: University of Wisconsin Press, 1988).

20. For the most comprehensive understanding of modern irony so far, see Alan Wilde, *Horizons of Assent: Modernism, Postmodernism, and the Ironic Imagination* (Baltimore: Johns Hopkins University Press, 1981).

21. Martin Heidegger, *An Introduction to Metaphysics*, trans. Ralph Mannheim (Garden City, N.Y.: Doubleday Anchor, 1961), 23; hereafter cited in my text as *IM*. Mannheim consistently translates as "essent" Heidegger's word for "being," by which he usually means "entity" and sometimes means "being" thought of in distinction to "Being." Heidegger means by such a distinction to try to think the ontological difference between the entire realm of "beings," including human "being" (*Dasein*), and the anti-foundational ground of this realm, "Being." I have attempted to make the difference in the uses of what Mannheim translates as "essent" as clear as I can in my commentary. Also, Heidegger explains in his preface (xiii) how he has marked the revisions in this lecture series: "Matter in parenthesis was written while I was reworking the text. The square brackets contain remarks added in the ensuing years." Mannheim also includes explanatory words after key terms in his translation, rendering *Dasein*, for example, sometimes as "existence," sometimes as "being-there," with *Dasein* following in parentheses. This necessitates his changing Heidegger's carefully presented markings of revision. In the passages that I quote here, I have restored Heidegger's practice as described above.

22. George Steiner, *Martin Heidegger* (New York: Viking Press, 1978), 73–126, anticipates this point. See also Heidegger's *Question of Being*, trans. Jean Wilde and William Klubock (New Haven: College and University Press, 1958). This text, originally an open letter to Ernst Jünger, discusses the latter's work quite knowledgeably.

23. The best study of the soldierly aesthetic is Harvey Goldman, *Max Weber and Thomas Mann: Calling and the Shaping of the Self* (Berkeley and Los Angeles: University of California Press, 1988), 187–208.

24. See Derrida's reading of this text, "Of Spirit," in *Critical Inquiry* 15 (Winter 1989): 457–74.

25. This does mean, of course, that the text may bear some resemblance to the unpublished materials.

26. Martin Heidegger, *Being and Time*, trans. John Macquarrie and Edward Robinson (New York: Harper and Row, 1962), 42–44.

27. See my *Lionel Trilling*, 67–135, for a discussion of this issue.

28. Derrida in "Of Spirit," 459–60, makes much of this belief. See also *Of Spirit: Heidegger and the Question*, trans. Geoffrey Bennington and Rachel Bowlby (Chicago: University of Chicago Press, 1989), 58–72.

29. I have been led to this interpretation by Thomas Mann's *Reflections of a Non-Political Man*, trans. Walter D. Morris (New York: Fredrick Unger, 1983).

30. Derrida does not notice this implication as he interrogates Heidegger's still-"metaphysical" assumptions about the German and Greek languages' power to give an apparently unmediated vision of being. See again Derrida's "Of Spirit," 459–60.

31. Ibid., 457–60.

32. See *An Introduction to Metaphysics*, 157, for one such fugitive reference to Hegel; and 166–67 for both a reference to Heidegger's infamous Rectorship address in praise of the Führer and an emphatic identification of his philosophy with the "true spirit" of national socialism.

33. For an entirely different and brilliantly realized analysis of Heidegger, especially of his later career, see Gerald Bruns, *Heidegger's Estrangements: Language, Truth, and Poetry in the Later Writings* (New Haven: Yale University Press, 1989).

34. For this view, and much more, I am indebted to many conversations with Paul Bové.

35. On this topic, see William V. Spanos, *Repetitions: The Postmodern Occasion in Literature and Culture* (Baton Rouge: Louisiana State University Press, 1987), 277–313, and his previously cited "Heidegger, Nazism, and the Repressive Hypothesis."

36. See Bruns, *Heidegger's Estrangements*, especially 150–73, for a different view of this highly debatable question.

37. I distinguish Derridean from deManian deconstruction, because in its appropriated American form the latter reduces temporality to the rigor of its own textual problematic, thereby spatializing it by transforming it into a question of differential textual spacing. See Jonathan Arac, *Critical Genealogies: Historical Situations for Postmodern Literary Studies* (New York: Columbia University Press, 1987), 97–113, 239–59.

38. See my "What Was Foucault?" in Jonathan Arac, ed., *After Foucault: Humanistic Knowledges, Postmodern Challenges* (New Brunswick, N.J.: Rutgers University Press, 1988), 71–96.

39. For one version of this story, See Rorty, *Contingency, Irony, and Solidarity*, especially 162–98.

40. For an effective explanation and appropriation of this idea, see James Bernauer, "Oedipus, Freud, Foucault: Fragments of an Archaeology," in David Michael Levin, ed., *Pathologies of the Modern Self* (New York: New York University Press, 1987), 349–62.

41. See Rorty, *Contingency, Irony, and Solidarity*, especially 122–37.

42. On this topic, see Peggy Kamuf, *Signature Pieces: On the Institution of Authorship* (Ithaca: Cornell University Press, 1988).

43. For a self-consciously comic play on this gesture, see Frank Lentricchia, "Andiamo!" in *Critical Inquiry* 14 (Winter 1988): 407–13.

44. This argument is also deployed throughout Gerald Graff, *Profession Literature: An Institutional History* (Chicago: University of Chicago Press, 1987), 247–62.

45. Rorty, *Contingency, Irony, and Solidarity*, 59.

46. See A. David Napier, *Masks, Transformation, Paradox* (Berkeley and Los Angeles:

University of California Press, 1986), especially 1–29. On p. 23, there is a picture of a similar tripartite Kwakiutl mask.

2. What Was Foucault?

1. All citations of this essay are taken from the version of the text to be found in Donald F. Bouchard, ed., *Language, Counter-Memory, Practice: Selected Essays and Interviews by Michel Foucault*, trans. Donald F. Bouchard and Sherry Simon (Ithaca: Cornell University Press, 1977), 113–38. Hereafter all page references to this work will be given in my text.

2. See Tracy B. Strong, *Fredrich Nietzsche and the Politics of Transfiguration* (Berkeley and Los Angeles: University of California Press, 1975).

3. My three examples are Lydia Blanchard, "Lawrence, Foucault, and the Language of Sexuality," in *D. H. Lawrence's "Lady": A New Look at Lady Chatterley's Lover*, ed. Michael Squires and Dennis Jackson (Athens: University of Georgia Press, 1985), 17–35; Allan Megill, *Prophets of Extremity: Nietzsche, Heidegger, Foucault, Derrida* (Berkeley and Los Angeles: University of California Press, 1985), 181–256; and Paul A. Bové, *Intellectuals in Power: A Genealogy of Critical Humanism* (New York: Columbia University Press, 1986), 209–37. All page citations from these works will be given in my text.

4. My decision to focus on "What Is an Author?" was based, in part, on the inclusion of this essay in the highly influential anthology edited by Josué Harari, *Textual Strategies* (Ithaca: Cornell University Press, 1979).

5. Significantly, Blanchard does not refer to any other major work by Foucault.

6. As quoted in Michel Foucault, *The History of Sexuality*, trans. Robert Hurley (New York: Pantheon Books, 1978), vol. 1, 157.

7. See my "The Power of Nothing in *Women in Love*," in *Rhetoric, Interpretation, Literature*, ed. S. Mailloux (Lewisburg: Associated University Press, 1983).

8. See the entry for "Inspiration" in *Princeton Encyclopedia of Poetry and Poetics*, ed. Alex Preminger, enlarged ed. (Princeton: Princeton University Press, 1974), 396–98. See, also, Linda Hutchen, *A Theory of Parody* (New York: Methuen, 1985).

9. For the best reading of the theoretical modernization of romantic studies, see Jonathan Arac, *Critical Genealogies: Historical Situations for Postmodern Literary Studies* (New York: Columbia University Press, 1987).

10. Bouchard, *Language*, 99.

11. As quoted in ibid., 163.

12. See the entry for "Parody" in Preminger, *Princeton Encyclopedia*, 600–602. See, also, Fredric Jameson, "Postmodernism, or, The Cultural Logic of Late Capitalism," in *New Left Review* 146 (1984): 64–65.

13. Bouchard's remarks in the footnotes to "What Is an Author?" and Megill's history of the critical relations between Foucault and Jean Wahl, who presided at the session where "What Is an Author?" was first delivered, both provide a biographical motivation for Foucault's parodic self-critical display in this initial statement.

14. Foucault's claims that certain recent critical developments grant writing "a primordial status" ("What Is an Author?" 120) are taken by Bouchard to refer to phenomenology. I think they refer as well to that philosophy of language associated with Barthes and Derrida that has come generally to be known by the term *deconstruction*.

15. The terms in which Foucault discusses this problem may have inspired, along with his critical remarks on those who grant "a primordial status" to writing, Derrida's

self-parodic play in *Spurs: Nietzsche's Styles* on the fragment in Nietzsche's own handwriting, "I have forgotten my umbrella."

16. See Thomas S. Kuhn, *The Structure of Scientific Revolutions,* 2d ed., enlarged (Chicago: University of Chicago Press, 1970).

17. All references to this work will be to the following edition: Fredrich Nietzsche, *Ecce Homo: How One Becomes What One Is,* trans. R.J. Hollingdale (New York: Penguin Books, 1979). Hereafter all citations will be given in my text.

18. For different discussions of Nietzsche's aestheticism, see my *The Romance of Interpretation: Visionary Criticism from Pater to de Man* (New York: Columbia University Press, 1985); and Alexander Nehamas, *Nietzsche: Life as Literature* (Cambridge: Harvard University Press, 1985).

19. For the most comprehensive and insightful overview of the modern-postmodern debate, see Jonathan Arac, ed., *Postmodernism and Politics* (Minneapolis: University of Minnesota Press, 1986).

20. On this subject, see my *Lionel Trilling: The Work of Liberation* (Madison: University of Wisconsin Press, 1988).

21. See Hayden White, *The Content of The Form: Narrative Discourse and Historical Representative* (Baltimore: Johns Hopkins University Press, 1987).

22. James Joyce, *Ulysses* (New York: Random House, 1961), 36.

23. Michel Foucault, *Death and the Labyrinth: The World of Raymond Roussel* (Garden City, N.Y.: Doubleday, 1968), 10.

3. Performing Theory as Cultural Politics

1. See Edward W. Said, "Traveling Theory," in *The World, the Text, and the Critic* (Cambridge: Harvard University Press, 1983), 226–47. See, also, Frank Lentricchia, "Michel Foucault's Fantasy for Humanists," in *Ariel and the Police: Michel Foucault, William James, Wallace Stevens* (Madison: University of Wisconsin Press, 1988), 29–102.

2. See Charles Taylor, "Foucault on Freedom and Truth," in David Hoy, ed., *Foucault: A Critical Reader* (New York: Basil Blackwell, 1986), 69–102.

3. See "Postscript: An Interview with Michel Foucault by Charles Ruas," in *Michel Foucault: Death and the Labyrinth: The World of Raymond Roussel,* trans. Charles Ruas (Garden City, N.Y.: Doubleday, 1986), 184.

4. See Jürgen Habermas, "Lecture IX: The Critique of Reason in Foucault as an Unmasking of the Human Sciences," in *The Philosophical Discourse of Modernity: Twelve Lectures,* trans. Frederick Lawrence (Cambridge: MIT Press, 1987), 238–65.

5. For a critical summary of these charges, see Paul A. Bové, "Foreward: The Foucault Phenomenon: The Problematics of Style," in *Gilles Deleuze, Foucault,* ed. and trans. Sean Hand (Minneapolis: University of Minnesota Press. 1986), vii–xl.

6. All citations from Michel Foucault, *The Use of Pleasure: The History of Sexuality,* vol. 2, trans. Robert Hurley (New York: Pantheon Books, 1985) and *The Care of the Self,* vol. 3, trans. Robert Hurley (New York: Random House, 1986) are given in the text.

7. See "Nietzsche, Genealogy, History," in Donald F. Bouchard, ed., Donald F. Bouchard and Sherry Simon, trans., *Michel Foucault, Language, Counter-Memory, Practice: Selected Essays and Interviews* (Ithaca: Cornell University Press, 1977), 139–64.

8. On this topic, see Paul A. Bové, *Intellectuals in Power: A Genealogy of Critical Humanism* (New York: Columbia University Press, 1986).

9. For a discussion of the continuing critical fascination with the sublime, see my *The*

Romance of Interpretation: Visionary Criticism from Pater to de Man (New York: Columbia University Press, 1985).

   10. See Arnold I. Davidson, ed., "A Symposium on Foucault," in *Critical Inquiry* (forthcoming). See also Didier Eribon, *Michel Foucault,* trans. Betsy Wing (Cambridge: Harvard University Press, 1991).

   11. On the topic of Foucault being "the masked philosopher," see Lawrence D. Kritzman, ed., *Michel Foucault, Politics, Philosophy, Culture: Interviews and Other Writings, 1977–1984,* 323–30.

   12. All citations from *On the Genealogy of Morals,* first essay, sec. 13, in *Basic Writings of Nietzsche,* trans. Walter Kaufmann (New York: Random House, 1968) will be given in the text.

   13. All citations from Julia Kristeva, *Black Sun: Depression and Melancholy,* trans. Leon S. Roudiez (New York: Columbia University Press, 1988) will be given in the text. For recent critical appropriations of Kristeva, see John Fletcher and Andrew Benjamin, eds., *Abjection, Melancholia, and Love: The Work of Julia Kristeva* (New York: Routledge, 1990); John Lecht, *Julia Kristeva* (New York: Routledge, 1990); and Shuli Barzilai, "Borders of Language: Kristeva's Critique of Lacan," in *PMLA* 106, no. 2 (March 1991): 294–305. Kristeva contributes an essay, "The Adolescent Novel," to the Fletcher and Benjamin collection. She suggests there that "the adolescent" as a psychoanalytic category does not solely refer to a developmental phase that is then superseded by maturity. Instead, she claims that it refers as much to an open or chronically unfinished type of subjectivity in which one lives "only by maintaining a renewable identity through interaction with another" (8), a subjectivity that for her defines novel agency. In this suggestion, which I develop here, Kristeva reveals some possible affinities both with Foucault's discussions of the "open strategic games" of love that inform the agonistic structure of the relation to oneself in the Greeks and with the revisionary literary understanding of the postmodern American subject. Clearly, Rousseau's novel *Emile, or On Education* and the so-called romantic invention of adolescence informs Kristeva's formulation. Also, needless to say, the isolation of a psychosocial type of personality, definitive for modern intellectuals and increasingly predominating in our postmodern American culture, does not entail simplistic judgments on the superiority of some ideal adult maturity vis-à-vis this adolescent identity formation. In fact, Kristeva's formulation puts seriously into question the existence of such "classical" psychoanalytic maturity beyond the imaginary specular structure of the adolescent or open-structure psyche.

   14. In our culture, as Lacan repeatedly demonstrates, the figure of the father opens the way to the symbolic order of conventional codes and laws.

   15. For further discussion of this topic, see my "The Prophet of Our Laughter: or, Nietzsche as—Educator?" in Daniel T. O'Hara, ed., *Why Nietzsche Now?* (Bloomington: Indiana University Press, 1981; reprint, 1985), 1–19.

   16. For further discussion of this topic, see my "The Reality of Theory: Freud in His Critics," in Joseph A. Buttigieg, ed., *Criticism Without Boundaries: Directions and Crosscurrents in Postmodern Critical Theory* (Notre Dame: University of Notre Dame Press, 1987), 177–201.

   17. For further discussion of this topic, see my *Lionel Trilling: The Work of Liberation* (Madison: University of Wisconsin Press, 1988).

   18. All citations from *The Collected Poems of Wallace Stevens* (New York: Knopf, 1954) will be given in the text.

19. For further discussion of this topic, see Fredric Jameson, *Postmodernism, or, The Cultural Logic of Late Capitalism* (Durham, N.C.: Duke University Press, 1991).

20. For further discussion of this topic, see my "The Resistance of Style," in *American Literary History* 2, no. 4 (Winter 1990): 781–83.

4. Aesthetic Relations

1. In John Frow, "Foucault and Derrida," in *Raritan* 5 (Summer 1985): 35, hereafter cited in my text as *F*.

2. Harold Bloom, *Ruin the Sacred Truths* (Cambridge: Harvard University Press, 1989), 55.

3. "Foucault and Derrida," 350. Although Frow finally gives the victory in this exchange between Foucault and Derrida to the latter, he does so only by ignoring the implications of the evidence from Foucault that he himself highlights.

4. Michel Foucault, "Nietzsche, Genealogy, History," in *The Foucault Reader*, ed. P. Rabinow (New York: Pantheon Books, 1984), 83.

5. Michel Foucault, *The Archaeology of Knowledge and the Discourse on Language*, trans. A.M. Sheridan (New York: Harper and Row, 1976), 95–96.

6. Gilles Deleuze, *Foucault*, ed. and trans. Sean Hand, with a forward by Paul A. Bové (Minneapolis: University of Minnesota Press, 1988), 97–98.

7. See my "What Was Foucault?" in *After Foucault: Humanistic Knowledge, Postmodern Challenges*, ed. Jonathan Arac (New Brunswick, N.J.: Rutgers University Press, 1989), 71–97.

8. "The Ethic of Care for the Self as a Practice of Freedom," in *The Final Foucault*, ed. James Bernauer and David Ramussen (Cambridge: MIT Press, 1988), 180.

9. Michel Foucault, *The History of Sexuality*, trans. Robert Hurley: vol. 2, *The Use of Pleasure* (New York: Pantheon Books, 1985), 67–68. Hereafter cited in my text as *UP*.

10. Michel Foucault, ibid.: vol. 3, *The Care of the Self* (New York: Pantheon Books, 1986), 211. Hereafter cited in my text as *CS*.

5. On the Friend Self and Lawrence Kritzman's The Rhetoric of Sexuality and the Literature of the French Renaissance

1. See the discussion in my *Lionel Trilling: The Work of Liberation* (Madison: University of Wisconsin Press, 1988), 29–66. For a discussion of Freud's "Mourning and Melancholia" and the dynamics of self-development, see chapter 1, 2–28. For more on this subject of friendship, see Marshall Carl Bradley and Philip Blosen, eds., *Of Friendship: Philosophical Selections on a Perennial Concern* (Wolfeboro, N.H.: Longwood Academic, 1989); Jacques Derrida, "From: 'Psyche: Inventions of the Other,'" in Peggy Kamuf, ed., *A Derrida Reader: Between the Blinds* (New York: Columbia University Press, 1991) 200–220 and also by Derrida, "The Politics of Friendship," trans. Gabriel Motyhin, in *Journal of Philosophy* 85, no. 11 (1988): 632–45; D.J. Enright and David Rawlinson, eds., *The Oxford Book of Friendship* (New York: Oxford University Press, 1971); Gilbert Meilsender, *Friendship: A Study in Theological Ethics* (Notre Dame: University of Notre Dame Press, 1981); Ronald A. Sharpe, *Friendship and Literature: Spirit and Form* (Durham, N.C.: Duke University Press, 1986); Paul J. Wadell, *Friendship and the Moral Life* (Notre Dame: University of Notre Dame, 1989).

2. See my chapter 3 for further discussion.

3. See my introduction for further discussion.

4. See Christopher Lasch, *The Culture of Narcissism* (New York: Norton, 1979), and my chapter 4 for further discussion. See, also, Heinz Kohut, *The Analysis of the Self* (Madison, Conn.: International Publishers, 1971) and *The Restoration of the Self* (Madison. Conn.: International Publishers, 1977).

5. See my introduction and chapters 6 and 11 for further discussion.

6. Joel Porte, ed., *Emerson in His Journals* (Cambridge: Harvard University Press, 1982). All citations from this volume will be given in the text.

7. All citations from Joel Porte, ed., *Emerson: Essays and Lectures* (New York: Library of America, 1982) will be given in the text. Emerson splits the subject into ontological and empirical selves, which he dubs, respectively, the Over-soul and the individual soul. For more on this topic, and how it relates to what I am calling "oneself," see chapters 5 and 13.

8. Freud, "Mourning and Melancholia," in Joan Riviere, trans., *Collective Papers*, vol. 4 (New York: Basic Books, 1959), 159.

9. Lawrence Kritzman, *The Rhetoric of Sexuality and the Literature of the French Renaissance* (New York: Cambridge University Press, 1991). All citations from this volume will be given in the text.

10. See Lawrence Kritzman, ed., *Michel Foucault: Politics, Philosophy, Culture: Interviews and Other Writings, 1977–1984* (New York: Routledge, 1988).

11. For further discussion, see the essays in part 2 and the conclusion here.

12. For further discussion, see my *The Romance of Interpretation* (New York: Columbia University Press, 1988), 93–146.

6. Revisionary Madness

1. See, e.g., Harold Bloom, *Agon: Towards a Theory of Revisionism* (New York: Oxford University Press, 1982), 16–51; Stanley Fish, *Is There a Text in This Class? The Authority of Interpretive Communities* (Cambridge: Harvard University Press, 1980); Edward W. Said, "Travelling Theory," in *Raritan* 1 (Winter 1982): 41–67; M.H. Abrams, "The Deconstructive Angel," in *Critical Inquiry* 3 (Spring 1977): esp. 426–29; and Gerald Graff, *Literature Against Itself* (Chicago: University of Chicago Press, 1979).

2. The situation is so bad as to provoke Paul deMan to write a book on the topic in his *The Resistance to Theory* (Minneapolis: University of Minnesota Press, 1983); the important title piece from his book has been published in *The Pedagogical Imperative: Teaching as a Literary Genre*, Yale French Studies, no. 63 (1982): 3–20.

3. I am not concerned with all the particulars of their argument; rather, it is the overall rhetorical strategy and effect that concern me. To borrow Bloom's notion, their essay in its entirely negative stance embodies the latecomer's resentful psychology too clearly.

4. The sources for their notion of "true belief" are various. Hans Gadamer's idea of "prejudice," for example, comes to mind. The point is that if one did a genealogy of their ideas one would discover that their position against theory depends entirely on assumptions that are theoretical.

5. Or "t-h-e-o-r-y."

6. Whether or not Knapp and Michaels's argument against Fish is at all plausible is not my concern. I suspect that he will take care of his own defense.

7. For one of the best discussions of this recent development, see Paul A. Bové, "Intellectuals at War: Michel Foucault and the Analytics of Power," in a forthcoming issue of *Sub-stance*. Bové analyzes Said's recent criticism of Michel Foucault (see n. 1) as a representative case.

8. Arthur Schopenhauer, *The World as Will and Representation,* 2 vols., trans. E.F.J. Payne (New York: Dover, 1966), vol. 1, 193.

9. Bloom's revisionary theory of the anxiety of influence is the closest contemporary notion, as Bloom himself knows; see esp. his *Poetry and Repression: Revisionism from Blake to Stevens* (New Haven: Yale University Press, 1976).

10. For a discussion of this dialectic of revisionism as it works itself out in deconstructive and Marxist critical texts, see my review of *The Political Unconscious* by Frederic Jameson and *Saving the Text* by Geoffrey Hartman, "The Ideology of Romance," in *Comparative Literature* 23 (Summer 1982): 381–89.

11. Friedrich Nietzsche, *Thus Spoke Zarathustra* (in *The Portable Nietzsche*), ed. and trans. Walter Kaufmann (New York: Penguin Books, 1954), 189.

12. For a further analysis of this self-destructive psychology, see my "The Prophet of Our Laughter: or, Nietzsche as—Educator?" in *boundary 2* 9 (Spring/Fall 1981): 1–19.

13. Their continued interest in questions of theoretical implication suggests as much. This seems especially true of Michaels; see, e.g., his "Is There a Politics of Interpretation?" in *Critical Inquiry* 9 (September 1982): 248–58.

14. For the most succinct history of recent criticism, see A. Walton Litz, "Literary Criticism," in *Harvard Guide to Contemporary American Writing,* ed. Daniel Hoffman (Cambridge: Harvard University Press, 1979), 51–83.

15. For the most virulent form of this return to the American pragmatist tradition of thought, see Bloom, *Agon,* 38–41.

16. I freely confess that this notion betrays a lingering realist theory of truth.

17. Ralph Waldo Emerson, *The Selected Writings,* ed. Brooks Atkinson (New York: Random House, 1968), 81; all further references to this work will be included in the text.

18. Northrop Frye, "The Imaginative and the Imaginary," in *Fables of Identity* (New York: Harcourt, Brace, 1963), 165; all further references to this work will be included in the text.

19. Frye, of course, not only "lowers" vision to the position of madness here, he also "raises" the torments of the madman to the heights of vision—or at the least leaves the question in suspense.

20. The materialistic and imperialistic overtones of this entire passage are quite striking. Space, however, prohibits further discussion.

21. That Walt Whitman came along to interrupt this romance of interpretation is one of those accidents of literary history that one must be grateful for.

22. Totalizer that Frye is, it is not surprising that he should work within the reserved, neoclassical prose idiom of Samuel Johnson, Matthew Arnold, and T. S. Eliot in order to revive the romantic tradition.

23. That Bloom's revisionary ratios also total six is, I believe, no accident.

24. I prefer to use the weak term "updating" instead of "revising" because what is involved is not a willful misreading and distortion of the text but the use of the inherent semantic indeterminacy (usually, quite limited) of any text for topical purposes.

25. Clearly I recognize the powerful self-projections in both Emerson and Frye. However, such self-displays do not appear to be the primary motivating factor.

26. With this latter qualification, I believe that I avoid the risk of simply repeating the revisionary pattern previously discussed, at least as it works itself out in such essays as "Against Theory." Without offering a vision of their own to replace theory, Knapp and Michaels can more easily be assimilated by the old guard, who do have a certain vision of what the future of literary criticism and theory should be.

27. Schopenhauer, *The World as Will and Representation,* vol. 1, 193.

28. Richard H. Finneran, ed., *The Collected Works of W.B. Yeats,* vol. 1: *The Poems,* revised ed. (New York: Macmillan, 1989), 294.

7. Critical Change and the Collective Archive

1. Stephan Salisbury, "Harold Bloom: A Massive Literary Undertaking," in the *Philadelphia Inquirer,* no. 317 (December 23, 1987): 4F.

2. Stanley Fish, "Change," in *South Atlantic Quarterly* 86, no. 1 (Fall 1986): 423–44. Hereafter all references to this essay will be given in the text. See also his *Doing What Comes Naturally: Change, Rhetoric, and the Practice of Theory in Literary and Legal Studies* (Durham, N.C.: Duke University Press, 1984).

3. Stanley Fish, "Commentary: The Young and the Restless," in H. Aram Veeser, ed., *The New Historicism* (New York: Routledge, 1989), 308.

4. Jonathan Arac, *Critical Genealogies: Historical Situations for Postmodern Literary Studies* (New York: Columbia University Press, 1987), 17–18.

5. Fredric Jameson, "On *Habits of the Heart,*" in *South Atlantic Quarterly* 86, no. 1 (Fall 1987): 553. Hereafter all references to this essay will be given in the text.

6. Gerald Graff, *Professing Literature: An Institutional History* (Chicago: University of Chicago Press, 1987), 5. Hereafter all references to this book will be given in the text.

7. Richard Poirier, *The Renewal of Literature: Emersonian Reflections* (New York: Random House, 1987). All references to this book will be given in the text.

8. "Large Red Man Reading," in *The Collected Poems of Wallace Stevens* (New York: Knopf, 1954), 423–24.

9. Robert Scholes and A. Walton Litz, eds., *James Joyce, Dubliners: Text, Criticism, and Notes* (New York: Penguin Books, 1969). All references to this book will be given in the text.

10. For a more traditional and avowedly humanistic treatment of this matter, see Charles Altari, *Canons and Consequences: Reflections on the Ethical Force of Imaginative Ideals* (Evanston, Ill.: Northwestern University Press, 1991).

8. Pragmatists of the Spirit

1. Harold Bloom, *Agon: Towards a Theory of Revisionism* (New York: Oxford University Press, 1982). All quotations from this work will be cited in the text. Here, with the exception of his many prefaces in several Chelsea House series, is the relevant Bloom bibliography between the Shelley book and *Agon: Blake's Apocalypse* (1961), *The Visionary Company* (1963), *Yeats* (1970), *The Ringers in the Tower* (1971), *The Anxiety of Influence* (1973), *A Map of Misreading* (1975), *Kabbalah and Criticism* (1975), *Figures of Capable Imagination* (1975), *Poetry and Repression* (1976), and *Wallace Stevens: The Poems of Our Climate* (1977).

2. Richard Rorty, *Contingency, Irony, and Solidarity* (New York: Cambridge University Press, 1989).

3. Stanley Fish, "Rhetoric," in *Doing What Comes Naturally: Change, Rhetoric, and The Practice of Theory in Literary and Legal Studies* (Durham, N.C.: Duke University Press, 1989), 488. Hereafter all quotations from this work will be cited in the text.

4. Although the "contingent imagination" is my own term, I am indebted for my critical understanding of contingency theory to an unpublished essay by Steven Cole, "Evading the Subject: A Critique of Contingency Theory."

5. Harold Bloom, *Ruin the Sacred Truths: Poetry and Belief from the Hebrew Bible to the Present* (Cambridge: Harvard University Press, 1987, 1989). Hereafter all quotations from this work will be cited in the text.

6. *The Book of J*, trans. David Rosenberg and interpreted by Harold Bloom (New York: Grove Weidenfeld, 1990), 44. Hereafter all quotations from this work will be cited in the text.

7. As cited in Bloom, *Ruin the Sacred Truths*, 117.

8. For more detailed discussion, see my chapter 2.

9. Gilles Deleuze, *Foucault*, trans. Sean Hand, with a foreward by Paul Bové (Minneapolis: University of Minnesota Press, 1988), 108. Deleuze is excellent on what he terms Foucault's pragmatism throughout this study. For contesting views of Foucault, including Richard Rorty's "Foucault and Epistemology," see David Couzens Hoy, ed., *Foucault: A Critical Reader* (New York: Routledge, 1986).

10. On this topic, see Frank Lentricchia, *Criticism and Social Change* (Chicago: University of Chicago Press, 1983).

11. Michel Foucault, *The History of Sexuality*, trans. Robert Hurley: vol. 2, *The Use of Pleasure* (New York: Pantheon Books, 1985), 9.

12. Julia Kristeva, "Identification and the Real," in Peter Collier and Helga Geyer-Ryand, eds., *Literary Theory Today* (Ithaca: Cornell University Press, 1990), 168.

13. Emerson, "History," in *Emerson: Essays and Lectures*, ed. Joel Porte (New York: Library of America, 1983), 251–52. This piece leads off *Essays: First and Second Series*, the definitive and most influential statement of Emerson's position.

14. Roger Poole and Henrik Stangerup, eds., *The Laughter Is on My Side: An Imaginative Introduction to Soren Kierkegaard* (Princeton: Princeton University Press, 1989), 33–34. This is an excerpt entitled "The Writing Cabinet," which, in a parable of genius, Victor Eremita, the pseudonymous "editor" of *Either/Or*, explains how he discovered the manuscript of the book he is now publishing.

9. A Postmodern Poetics of Critical Reading

1. Richard Rorty, *Contingency, Irony, and Solidarity* (New York: Cambridge University Press, 1989). Hereafter all citations from this volume will be given in the text.

2. Martin Heidegger, *Being and Time*, trans. John Macquarrie and Edward Robinson (New York: Harper and Row, 1962). Hereafter all citations from this volume will be given in the text.

3. Holly Stevens, ed., *The Palm at the End of the Mind: Selected Poems of Wallace Stevens* (New York: Vintage, 1972), 127.

4. Richard Shusterman, *T. S. Eliot and the Philosophy of Criticism* (New York: Columbia University Press, 1988). Hereafter all citations from this volume will be given in the text.

5. Frank Kermode, ed., *Selected Prose of T. S. Eliot* (New York: Harcourt Brace Jovanovich, 1975), 39.

6. Jonathan Arac, *Critical Genealogies: Historical Situations for Postmodern Literary Studies* (New York: Columbia University Press, 1987). Hereafter all citations from this volume will be given in the text.

7. See, for the most recent example, Paul B. Armstrong's review in *Journal of Aesthetics and Art Criticism* 47, no. 1 (Winter 1989): 83–85.

8. Paul de Man, *The Resistance to Theory* (Minneapolis: University of Minnesota Press, 1986), 73.

9. Gilles Deleuze, *Foucault,* ed. and trans. Sean Hand, with a foreword by Paul A. Bové (Minneapolis: University of Minnesota Press, 1988). Hereafter all citations from this volume will be given in the text.

10. Selves in Flames

1. Reed Way Dasenbrock, ed., *Redrawing the Lines: Analytic Philosophy, Deconstruction, and Literary Theory* (Minneapolis: University of Minnesota Press, 1989); Jacques Derrida, *Of Spirit: Heidegger and the Question,* trans. Geoffrey Bennington and Rachel Bowlby (Chicago: University of Chicago Press, 1989); and Richard Rorty, *Contingency, Irony, and Solidarity* (Cambridge: Cambridge University Press, 1989).

2. In a still unpublished 1949 lecture, Heidegger equates modern agriculture as a mechanized food industry with the manufacture of corpses in the death camps, the blockades that reduced countries to famine, and the making of hydrogen bombs. See Arnold I. Davidson, "Questions Concerning Heidegger: Opening the Debate," in "Symposium on Heidegger and Nazism," in *Critical Inquiry* 15 (1989): 423.

3. *Of Spirit* makes much of Heidegger's belief in the privileged relation of the German language to all things truly "spiritual" (that is, all things authentically "Greek"), in opposition to French and indeed all Latin-based or romance languages, which distort and trivialize, in the name of "humanism," the "spiritual" into mere cleverness and wit at best. See especially chapter 7 (58–72).

4. For more on this subject, see my "Mask-Plays: Theory, Cultural Studies, and the Fascist Imagination," in *boundary 2* 17, no. 2 (Summer 1990): 129–54.

5. Some of the other important contributions include those by Richard Shusterman, Christopher Norris, and, in reply to Norris, Richard Rorty.

6. I want to thank Mary Korman Tiryak for helping me to think through many of the issues raised here. In "The Nature of Language," originally three lectures delivered between December 1957 and February 1958 and published along with "Language in the Poem" (1953) in *On the Way to Language* (1959), Heidegger explicitly refers to the trope "tongues as of fire" (96) as a Judeo-Christian enfiguring of "spirit." This reference and its placement in the volume before "Language in the Poem"—the essay Derrida makes so much of for his argument—thus tends to support my speculative reading.

11. Smiling Through Pain

1. W. D. Howells, *The Rise of Silas Lapham,* ed. W. J. Meserve and David J. Nordloh (Bloomington: Indiana University Press, 1971). Hereafter all citations from this volume will be given in the text.

2. Walter Benn Michaels, *The Gold Standard and the Logic of Naturalism: American*

Literature at the Turn of the Century (Berkeley and Los Angeles: University of California Press, 1987). Hereafter all citations from this volume will be given in the text.

3. John W. Crowley, *The Black Heart's Truth: The Early Career of W. D. Howells* (Chapel Hill: University of North Carolina Press, 1985), x.

4. Harvey Goldman, *Max Weber and Thomas Mann: Calling and the Shaping of the Self* (Berkeley and Los Angeles: University of California Press, 1988). Hereafter all citations from this volume will be given in the text.

5. Friedrich Nietzsche, *On the Genealogy of Morals,* trans. Walter Kaufmann and R. J. Hollingdale (New York: Vintage, 1969), 87–88.

6. Immanuel Kant, *The Critique of Judgement,* trans. J. H. Bernhard (London: Hafner Press, 1951). All citations from this volume will be given in the text.

7. Michel Foucault, "What Is Enlightenment?" in *The Foucault Reader,* ed. Paul Rabinow (New York: Pantheon Books, 1984). All citations from this volume will be given in the text.

8. For more on this topic, see Geoffrey Galt Harpham, *The Ascetic Imperative in Culture and Criticism* (Chicago: University of Chicago Press, 1987).

12. John Cheever's "Folly"

1. For the details of Cheever's life and career here and throughout this essay, see the following: Benjamin Cheever, ed., *The Letters of John Cheever* (New York: Simon and Schuster, 1986); Susan Cheever, *Home Before Dark: A Biographical Memoir of John Cheever by His Daughter* (New York: Harcourt Brace Jovanovich, 1984); Scott Donaldson, *John Cheever: A Biography* (New York: Random House, 1988); and Scott Donaldson, ed., *Conversations with John Cheever* (Jackson: University Press of Mississippi, 1987). For indispensable bibliographical information on available primary and secondary sources, see Denis Coates, "John Cheever: A Checklist, 1930–1978," in *Bulletin of Bibliography* 36 (January–March 1979): 1–13, 49; and his "A Cheever Bibliography Supplement, 1978–1981," in R. G. Collins, ed., *Critical Essays on John Cheever* (Boston: G.K. Hall, 1982). Cheever's journals from the late 1940s through the late 1960s have been selectively appearing in four issues of the *New Yorker:* August 8, 1990 (38–64); August 13, 1990 (29–61); January 21, 1991 (28–63); and January 28, 1991 (28–59). Selections from the remaining journals have appeared in later issues of the *New Yorker* and are now available in a book: *The Journals of John Cheever* (New York: Knopf, 1991).

2. "A Vision of the World," in *The Stories of John Cheever* (New York: Knopf, 1978), 515. Henceforth all references to Cheever's stories from this volume will be given in the text.

3. On contingency theory, see Steven Cole, "Evading the Subject: A Critique of Contingency Theory," an unpublished essay. See, also, three of my essays: "Selves in Flames: Derrida, Rorty, and the New Orthodoxy in Theory," in *Contemporary Literature* 32, no. 1 (Spring 1991): 116–26; "The Poetics of Critical Reading," in *Poetics Today* 11, no. 3 (Fall 1990): 661–72; and, on Stanley Fish, "Critical Change and the Cultural Archive," in Michael Hays, ed., *Critical Symptoms: New Essays on Contemporary Theory* (Minneapolis: University of Minnesota Press, forthcoming). For the Yeats citation, see Richard J. Finneran, ed., *The Collected Works of W. B. Yeats,* rev. ed., vol. 1: *The Poems* (New York: Macmillan, 1989), 343.

4. While Harold Bloom in *Agon* (New York: Oxford University Press, 1982) may

have been the first to claim Emerson as the grandfather of "neopragmatism's" project of contingently out-talking all opposition, Stanley Cavell in several recent books, including *Conditions Handsome and Unhandsome: The Constitution of Emersonian Perfectionism* (Chicago: University of Chicago Press, 1990), and Richard Rorty in *Contingency, Irony, Solidarity* (New York: Cambridge University Press, 1989) have vigorously endorsed Emerson's centrality for any philosophically informed American criticism.

5. The *New Yorker* (August 13, 1990): 50–51.

6. Throughout his life, in most of his interviews, Cheever remarks on his great devotion to the work of two poets, Donne and Yeats. See Scott Donaldson, ed., *Conversations with John Cheever*.

7. The *New Yorker* (August 13, 1990): 61.

8. Ibid., 50.

9. Scott Donaldson, ed., *Conversations with John Cheever*, 108.

10. Stanley Fish, "Rhetoric," in *Doing What Comes Naturally: Change, Rhetoric, and the Practice of Theory in Literary and Legal Studies* (Durham, N.C.: Duke University Press, 1989), 483. Significantly, this essay also appears in Frank Lentricchia and Thomas McLaughlin, eds., *Critical Terms for Literary Study* (Chicago: University of Chicago Press, 1989), 208–22. This volume is quickly replacing M. H. Abrams, *A Glossary of Literary Terms* as the introductory text for new English majors and graduate students in the profession.

11. For a detailed analysis of most of these other problems, see the previously cited essay by Steven Cole, "Evading the Subject: A Critique of Contingency Theory."

12. Benjamin Cheever, ed., *The Letters of John Cheever*, 213–14.

13. For being able to see such connections I am greatly indebted to Donald E. Pease, *Deterrence Pacts: Formation of the Canon in the Cold War* (Madison: University of Wisconsin Press, 1992).

14. Julia Kristeva, *Black Sun: Depression and Melancholia*, trans. Leon Roudiez (New York: Columbia University Press, 1989), 8–14. For an effective and succinct introduction to Kristeva, see Jean Graybeal, "Kristeva on Language and 'the Feminine,'" in her *Language and 'the Feminine' in Nietzsche and Heidegger* (Bloomington: Indiana University Press, 1990), 5–26.

15. On this topic, see my *Lionel Trilling: The Work of Liberation* (Madison: University of Wisconsin Press, 1988), 3–28; 244–91.

13. Imaginary Politics

1. All citations from this essay come from Richard Poirier, ed., *Ralph Waldo Emerson* (New York: Oxford University Press, 1990), 82–96 and will be given in the text.

2. All citations from Emerson, unless otherwise noted, come from Joel Porte, ed., *Emerson: Essays and Lectures* (New York: Library of America, 1982), and will be given in the text.

3. Although it is clear that Emerson derived much inspiration from the German romantic writers and thinkers, including Hegel, he seems to have derived even more from their English mediators, Coleridge and Carlyle. In "Transcendental Failure: 'The Palace of Spiritual Power,'" in Joel Porte. ed., *Emerson: Prospect and Retrospect*, Harvard English Studies (Cambridge: Harvard University Press, 1982), 121–54, Michael Lopez makes some instructive comparisons especially between Emerson and Carlyle on the question of vocation and doing one's own work. Emerson, unlike Carlyle, never identifies the power

along with which one is to move as anything other than this unique (yet plural) and publicly active self. Carlyle, however, will practically identify it, for example, with the age's increasingly secular form of Puritanism that "can steer ships, fell forests, remove mountains;—it is one of the strongest things under the sun at present" (133). Emerson's interest, as Stanley Cavell says in *Conditions Handsome and Unhandsome: An Essay on the Constitution of Emersonian Perfectionism* (Chicago: University of Chicago Press, 1990), is in the ultimate perfection of spontaneity and creative power in each entity of the whole. Carlyle's more immediately opportune interest is in the currently steering worldly power. In "Aversive Thinking: Emersonian Representations in Heidegger and Nietzsche" (33–63), Stanley Cavell characterizes the reading relation in Emerson as the uncanny transference relation of an attained to an unattained possibility of oneself on the traditional philosophic model of the pedagogic pair of friends. I would argue that this secularization and internalization of the ontological and empirical dimensions of the subject, when radically democratized by modern higher education and mass media culture, takes the postmodern form of the narcissistic personality structure of grandiose ego ideal and wounded ego. For further discussion of this subject, see chapter 5. Where I differ with Cavell is on the question of "moral perfectionism" in Emerson. To speak exclusively in this fashion of Emerson is to harken back to the ascetic tradition of working on the self, which, through the hedonic overtones of "the vocation of abandonment," I believe Emerson is beginning to leave behind. For a related sense of "abandonment" in Emerson, see Cavell's "Thinking of Emerson," in *The Senses of Walden* (San Francisco: North Point Press, 1980). For a different critical sense of Emerson, see DonaldE. Pease, *Visionary Compacts: American Renaissance Writings in Cultural Context* (Madison: University of Wisconsin Press, 1987), 203–34.

4. See, for example, the still excellent discussion of Emerson in his time in O. W. Firkins, *Ralph Waldo Emerson* (Boston: Houghton Mifflin, 1915).

5. I have chosen "The Over-Soul," rather than "Self-Reliance," precisely because I think it partakes more immediately of its time with its transcendental religiosity. But even "Self-Reliance," one antithetical complement to "The Over-Soul" in *Essays: First Series,* ironically undoes the elaborate structure of self-trust it has erected in the climactic passage on the "Aboriginal Power" that makes all mere talk of "self-reliance" nothing but prattle. This self-subverting irony thus prepares the ground for the later move to the major message of "The Over-Soul" that the self is plural, even if we would want to question many of the terms in which its plurality is discussed.

6. "Poetry and Imagination," in Richard Poirier, ed., *Ralph Waldo Emerson: Oxford Authors* (New York: Oxford University Press, 1990), 448.

7. "Quotation and Originality," in Richard Poirier, ed., *Ralph Waldo Emerson,* 436.

8. All citations from this essay came from "Identification and the Real," in *Literary Theory Today,* ed. Peter Colher and Helga Geyer-Ryan (Ithaca: Cornell University Press, 1990), 167–76 and will be given in the text.

9. All citations from their work come from, respectively, Eleanor Cook, *Poetry, Word-Play, and Word-War in Wallace Stevens* (Princeton: Princeton University Press, 1988); and Barbara M. Fisher, *Wallace Stevens: The Intensest Rendezvous* (Charlottesville: University of Virginia Press, 1990) and will be given in the text.

10. Julia Kristeva, *Black Sun: Depression and Melancholia,* trans. Leon S. Rondrey (New York: Columbia University Press, 1989), 14.

11. As cited and discussed in my "Lava-Writing: A Status Report on Stevens and

Feminism, 1988," in "Stevens and Women," in *The Wallace Stevens Journal* 12, no. 2, ed. Melita Schaum (Fall 1988): 173–80.

12. All citations of Stevens come from *The Collected Poems* (New York: Knopf, 1954) and will be given in the text.

Conclusion

1. Frank Lentricchia, *The Gaiety of Language: An Essay on the Radical Poetics of W. B. Yeats and Wallace Stevens* (Berkeley and Los Angeles: University of California Press, 1968), 6.

2. Frank Lentricchia, *Robert Frost: Modern Poetics and the Landscapes of Self* (Durham, N.C.: Duke University Press, 1975); see, especially, 145–60.

3. Frank Lentricchia, *After the New Criticism* (Chicago: University of Chicago Press, 1980); see, especially, 349–51.

4. Frank Lentricchia, *Criticism and Social Change* (Chicago: University of Chicago Press, 1983); see, especially, 1–20.

5. For a sampling of Lentricchia's "media" exposure, see the following: the interview with Imre Salusinszky in *Criticism in Society* (New York: Metheun, 1987), 176–206; the response to Gilbert's and Gubar's counterattack in *Critical Inquiry* 14, no. 2 (Winter 1988): 407–14 (it is here that Lentricchia reveals the self-spoofing nature of the infamous photograph); the interview with David Latane in *Critical Texts* 5, no. 2 (1988): 6–17; the article by Robert Bliwise entitled "Lentricchia Between the Lines: Putting Life into Literature," in *Duke: Magazine for Alumni and Friends* 74, no. 4 (May–June 1988): 2–7; and the now-famous article by James Atlas, "The Battle of the Books," in the *New York Times Magazine* (June 5, 1988): 24–27; 72–75; 85; 94. The infamous photo in question shows a muscular Lentricchia, looking streetwise and "pumped," wearing a pullover with bold horizontal stripes, and standing up against a graffiti-strewn wall: an image designed both to debunk the stereotype of the shabby-genteel professor and to spoof Lentricchia's own "macho" reputation among his critics. While clearly succeeding in doing the former, this photo—until recently, anyway—has not been taken in the self-ironical spirit of the latter intention.

6. Frank Lentricchia, "Don DeLillo," in *Raritan* 10, no. 3 (Spring 1989): 16; 17–18. See, also, Frank Lentricchia, "The American Writer as Bad Citizen—Introducing Don DeLillo," and "Libra as Postmodern Critique," in Frank Lentricchia, ed., "The Fiction of Don DeLillo," in *South Atlantic Quarterly* 89, no. 2 (Spring 1990): 239–44 and 431–53, respectively. For more of Lentricchia on the subject of postmodern media and their relation to the American dream, see his "Tales of the Electronic Tribe," in Frank Lentricchia, ed., *New Essays on White Noise* (New York: Cambridge University Press, 1991).

7. Frank Lentricchia, *Ariel and the Police: Michel Foucault, William James, Wallace Stevens* (Madison: University of Wisconsin Press, 1988), 91–92. Hereafter all citations from this work will be given in the text.

8. For a discussion of Schiller's influence on Emerson, Nietzsche, and later cultural criticism, see my "Over Emerson's Body," in *The CEA Critic* 49, nos. 2–3 (Winter–Summer 1987): 79–88. Emerson's famous phrase "I am glad to the brink of fear" from the notorious "transparent eyeball" vision in Nature clearly haunts Greenblatt's idea of "absolute play" on "the brink of the abyss." That is, American transcendentalism still hovers over the corpus of Renaissance new historicism, giving it a distinctive American style of radical individualism, despite its collectivist pronouncements to the contrary.

9. Unless otherwise noted, all citations of chapters from Frank Lentricchia's *American Modernism* come from manuscript copy and will be given in the text.

10. Two of these chapters have appeared in earlier versions: "Lyric in the Culture of Capitalism," in *American Literary History* 1, no. 1 (Spring 1989): 63–88; and "Philosophers of Modernism at Harvard, ca. 1900," in *South Atlantic Quarterly* 89, no. 4 (Fall 1990): 787–834.

11. For my discussion of Lentricchia on Stevens, see "Saving Ariel: Wallace Stevens and the Sexual Poetics of Late Capitalism," in *Contemporary Literature* 29, no. 4 (Fall 1988): 624–31.

12. For further discussion on this topic of the work of critical magnanimity, see both my introduction here and my *Lionel Trilling: The Work of Liberation* (Madison: University of Wisconsin Press, 1988).

13. Lentricchia has recently written three experiments in the personal essay—"Making It to Mepking Abbey," "Lefthanded," and "My Kinsman, T.S. Eliot"–which show him moving into what Eliot calls "another intensity" of spiritual life (*Four Quartets*). As of now, the first of these essays is to be published by *Harper's Magazine*.

Index

Abandonment: Emerson's idea, 227–28; vocation of, 231

Abjected mother, 68, 97–98, 108; Bloom and, 159; ideological criticism and, 243–44; Stevens and, 236, 238, 242–43

Abnormal, production of, 83

Abraham, as Freudian man, 156–57

Abrams, M. H., 13, 113; *Natural Supernaturalism,* 48

Absence of essence, Lentricchia's idea, 264–65

Academic freedom, 144; political correctness and, 1–2

Academic institutionalization of theory, 246

Academic intellectuals, and contingent imagination, 157

Academic left, 36; change viewed by, 3; and cultural studies, 34; Fish and, 2–3, 6–7

Accommodation, 126–27; of contingent imagination, 223

Action, causes of, 65

Adolescent personality, Kristeva's concept, 69–70, 278n13

Adorno, Theodor, *The Authoritarian Personality,* 19–20

Aesthetic criticism, tradition and, 170

Aestheticism, 247; criticism and, 248

Aestheticization of politics, fascism as, 22

Aesthetic objects, 8

Aesthetics of existence, 64, 82–84, 94; ancient Greek, 87, 89–90; classical, and family romance, 69; demonstrative meditation and, 86; free agents and, 65; as mask play, 95; modern, 85

Aesthetic subject, 76

Agency: Foucault's idea, 66, 176; literary forms, 228; subjective, deconstruction of, 64–65

Agonistic structure of self, 96–97; Foucault's view, 86, 160

Agriculture, Heidegger's views, 284n2

Allusion in Stevens's poetry, 234–38, 243
Alterity, as scapegoat muse, 23
Alternatives, intellectuals and, 44–45, 46
Altieri, Charles, 212, "Judgment and Justice Under Postmodern Conditions; or How Lyotard Helps Us Read Rawls as a Postmodern Thinker," 181
America: contingent imagination in, Cheever and, 223; cultural assimilation, 246; male bonding, 252; non-representative status of intellectual life, 185–86; universal literacy, 97
American critical theory, 269
American critics, x–xi, 68–69, 130; and contingency theory, 157, 160
American culture, 23, 36; Cheever and, 208–9; parody in, 4
American difference, Bloom and, 151
American dream, 253, 268; contingency theory and, 209; Lentricchia's view, 257, 259
American genius of revisionism, 144–48
American identity, 250; Emerson and, ix–x; Pound and, 264
American imaginations, 247
American individuality, 66
American intellectuals, 36; and contingency theory, 209; Foucault and, 60–61; *see also* Intellectuals
Americanist projects, 61, 246
American literary theorists, 114
American literature: studies of, 143–46; turn-of-the-century, Michaels's view, 195–96
American philosophy, 5–6
American poets, 258; dilemma of, 238; Lentriccia's view of, 260
American pragmatism, 151–53
American realism, Michaels's view, 195
Americans, self-conception, 108
American tradition, neopragmatism and, 6
Analytic philosophy, 181
Analytic transference, 69
Ancestors: imaginary, avowal of, 9; of intellectual movements, 247

Ancestral trope, Burke's idea, 248
Ancient societies, subject formation, 84
Anglo-Catholicism, Frye and, 125
Annihilation of future, fascist imagination and, 32
Anticipatory resoluteness, Heidegger's idea, 188
Antidefinition of literature, Lentricchia's idea, 265
Antifoundationalism: of contingency theory, 210; of Rorty, 151–52
Antiknowledge, Foucault and, 46
Antisexuality of fascist imagination, 18
Antithetical readings, 25
Anti-will, poetics of, Lentricchia's idea, 245
Anxiety, of critics, 131
Aphrodisia, 86; ethics of, 88
Apocalypse of the mind: Emerson and, 228; in Stevens's poetry, 241
Apocalyptic scenes, Cheever and, 216–17, 222
Appreciation, xiii
Arac, Jonathan, 139–40; *Critical Genealogies,* 171–75
Archetypes, cultural, American, 145
Argument, subject of, 76
Aristippus, 90, 91
Aristocratic commodity desire, Stevens and, 262–63
Aristotle, 74, 228–29; Foucault and, 90
Arnold, Matthew, 247
Art: nature and, 226; and politics, Lentricchia's view, 267–68
Ascetic imperative, 200–201; sublime experience and, 205
Asceticism: Nietzsche and, 202; radical, fascist imagination as, 20
Ascetic self-denial, 87
Ascetic type, 201–2
Ashbery, John, 272n3
Assimilation, cultural, 246
Attribution of authorship, 54
Auden, W. H., Cheever and, 218
Auerbach, Erich, Bové and, 43
Augustine, Saint, 52
Auschwitz death camp, 17
Author-function, Foucault and, 56–57

Authoritative ideal, loss of, 105
Authoritative wistfulness of Stevens's poetry, 235
Authority, Bloom's view, 162–63
Authority figures: identification with, 99; narcissists and, 98
Authors: critical intellectuals as, 47–48; readers and, 86, 98
Authorship: Foucault and, 48–55; Nietzschean ideas, 58
Avowal: of imaginary ancestors, 8–9; of imaginary father, 98–99; of inspiration, 101

Batman, 33
Baudelaire, Charles Pierre: Arac's view, 174; Foucault and, 205
Beckett, Samuel, *Stories and Texts for Nothing,* 49–50
Being: Foucault's idea, 78; Heidegger's concept, 25–28, 31–33, 274n21, 275n30
Being-there, Heidegger's idea, 26–28
Belief, theory and, 114–16
Benjamin, Walter: Arac's view, 173–75; and fascism, 22
Berufsmenschen (men of calling), Weber's idea, 201–2
Bible, Bloom and, 156–59, 162–63
Biological determination, feminism and, 257–58
Bion the Borysthemite, 89–90
Bio-power, 34; production of, 39
Blake, William, 67, 215
Blanchard, Lydia, and Foucault, 38–40, 42, 45–47
Blank parody, 49
Blood flows, soldier-males and, 20–21
Bloom, Allan, 13
Bloom, Harold, 5, 6, 7, 70, 113, 130–31, 139–40, 214; and contingency theory, 215; *Agon: Towards a Theory of Revisionism,* 151–52; *The Book of J,* 153, 156, 157–59, 162–63; "Freud and Beyond," 156; "The Internalization of Quest Romance," 156, 165; Rorty and, 183–84; *Ruin the Sacred*

Truths, 76, 153, 154–57, 160; and Stevens, 147, 232, 234
Bolshevism, soldier-males and, 18, 20
Booth, Wayne, *The Rhetoric of Fiction,* 51
Bourgeoisie: and authorship, 54; liberal, pragmatism of, 248
Bourgeois self, 66
Bové, Paul: and Foucault, 44–47; *Intellectuals in Power,* 43–46
Boys, love of, 85, 86, 92–94
Bradley, A. C., 154
Bureaucratization of the imagination, 161
Burke, Kenneth, 161, 248, 256; and Lentricchia, 246, 248

Calamity, natural history of, 108
Calling, men of, Weber's idea, 201–2
Cambridge History of American Literature, 251, 260–61
Canetti, Elias, *Crowds and Power,* 17
Canon, literary: formation of, Bloom's idea, 140; reconstruction of, 152; traditional, challenges to, 243–44
Capitalism, and morality, Howells's views, 198–99
Capitalist desire, Stevens and, 262–63
Career, critical theory as, 119–20, 129
Cascardi, Anthony J., 181
Celebrity, 230–31; Lentricchia's views, 249–50
Centralizing imperial normalization, 65
Cervantes, Miguel, *Don Quixote,* Frye and, 123–27
Change, 3; Bloom and, 140; critical, 131–49; historical, Rorty's view, 165; revisionism and, 131
Cheever, Fred, 208; alcoholism of, 212–14
Cheever, John, 207–24; *The Brigadier and the Golf Widow,* 208–9, 217; *Bullet Park,* 219; *Falconer,* 219; "The Lowboy," 208–24; "The Scarlet Moving Van," 219; *Some People, Places, and Things That Will Not Appear in My Next Novel,* 216; "A Vision of the World," 208–9, 223; *The Wapshot Chronicle,* 213

Children, psychotic, soldier-males as, 22
Chomsky, Noam, and Foucault, 43–44
Christianity, and self-division of soul, 88
Class differences, 258
Classical culture: Foucault and, 68–69, 73; Heidegger's view, 30–31; and self, 64–67, 96
Classical pedagogy, 69
Classical sources, 229–30
Cloistral retreat, criticism and, 248
Closed games, 84; of truth regimes, 66
Coercive games, 84
Cold war, Cheever and, 216–17
Cole, Steven, 285n3
Collective agency, 227; classical culture and, 66–67
Collective archive, 4, 8, 65, 69, 73; contingent imagination and, 163; and critical change, 142–49; criticism and, 211–12, 252; Emerson's Over-Soul as, 230; experience and, 70; friend self and, 102; history as, 263; and imaginative agency, 256; Lentricchia and, 268; mask plays, 68, 71; new orthodoxy and, 180; and oneself, 98; repressive cultures as, 67; self-creation and, 153
Collective habits, counterproductive, Jameson's idea, 142, 143
Collective imaginative power, friendship and, 101
Collective subject, Heidegger and, 26
Comic defiance, Stevens and, 236
Commodity fetishism, 195; opposition to, 196
Common understandings, imposition of, 136
Communist oligarchy, 248
Community: Bloom's idea, 139; Jameson's idea, 141
Community needs, literary criticism and, 127
Compensatory identity formation, by Cheever, 208–24
Conscious intention, pragmatist understanding, 246

Consciousness as surface, Nietzsche's idea, 57
Constant transformation, Pound's idea, 265
Construction, of author, 54
Consumer capitalism, 231: American literature and, 195; postmodern criticism and, 72
Contingency theory, 6, 151, 157–58, 209–11, 215, 248; Cheever and, 214–15; Cole and, 285n3; Lentricchia and, 260
Contingent imagination, 7–9, 153–54, 163, 208, 215, 216–24, 272n3; Bloom and, 155, 157, 158; Cheever and, 214; Foucault and, 160; Lentricchia and, 268; subjectivity of, 154
Continuity, change and, 137
Convention: contingency theory and, 210; tradition and, Heidegger's view, 30–32
Conversation, as monologue, 169
Cook, Eleanor, 234
Cosmpolitanism, liberal, 187
Creation, destructive, fascist imagination and, 23
Creative imagination, criticism and, 127
Creative reading, 148
Creative repression, genius and, 57–58
Creative usurpation, narcissistic sense, 100
Creativity: Emerson's ideas, 122; and madness, Frye's ideas, 124
Critical agency: Lentricchia and, 245; plural, 72–73
Critical essays: Montaigne and, 106; narcissism of, 105–6
Critical fictions, Foucault's idea, 62, 69
Critical genealogy, Foucault's idea, 266
Critical humanism, 44–46, 47; Altieri and, 185; Foucault and, 43, 46, 91
Critical identity, 68, 70–71, 251–52, 269; collective formation, 257
Critical Inquiry, 249
Critical intellectuals, 15–16, 67–68; Altieri's view, 182; as authors, 47–48; and imaginary father, 68; *see also* Intellectuals
Critical meditation, Foucault and, 80

Critical method, cultural studies and, 34
Critical narcissism, 98–99
Critical negation, genius and, 58
Critical parody, 48–49; *see also* Radical parody
Critical practice, 14–15; judgment and, 127; Knapp and Michaels and, 118–19; madness and, 117–29
Critical reading: Heidegger and, 166; postmodern poetics of, 167–78; as revisionary redescription, 165
Critical realism, Fish's idea, 138–39
Critical reason, 134
Critical theory, 15, 47; and deconstructive irony, 31–32; and fascist imagination, 25, 33; Fish and, 115–16; Foucault and, 80; function of, 119–20; as profession, 119
Criticism, xiii, 161, 247, 248; feminist, Lentricchia and, 257; of Foucault, 61–62; function of, 129; historical nature, 168; as mask play, x–xi; narcissism and, 109; nineteenth century philosophy, 54–55; postmodern, 72–73; principles, 126–29; as radical parody, 101; satiric aims, xi; theory and, 119–20
——as profession, 129; Fish and, 132–33; ideological split, 143–44
Critics, x, 130, 209; role of, 120–26
Crowley, John W., *The Black Heart's Truth*, 201
Cultural archetypes, American literature studies and, 144
Cultural assimilation, American, 246
Cultural change, critical intellectuals and, 15
Cultural criticism, by Eliot, 169–71
Cultural elite, Fish and, 138
Cultural grammar, Altieri's idea, 182, 212
Cultural life, American, parody in, 4
Cultural politics, 15; American critical theory as, 269; postmodern, Lentricchia and, 247
Cultural studies, 15, 33–36; American literature studies and, 144; oppositional, 14

Cultural styles, Deleuze's idea, 176
Cultural work of literature, 247
Culture, 68; American, 4, 23, 36, 208–9; critical theory and, 25; and identity formation, 69; and individualism, Foucault and, 67; intellectual, Hegel and, 180; modern, influences on, 143; and Over-Self, 177–78; and poetics of critical reading, 177–78; postmodern view, 34; preservation of, 123–24; reality and, 156; regimes of truth, 78–79; repressive, Foucault and, 67; and self, 64; tradition and, Heidegger's view, 30; transformation of, 167–68
Curricular multiculturalism, 2

Darwin, Charles, 52
Dasein (being-there), Heidegger's idea, 26–28, 165, 188
Dasenbrock, Reed Way, *Redrawing the Lines: Analytic Philosophy, Deconstruction, and Literary Theory*, 181
Death: prospect of, 223; of the subject, Foucault and, 65; writing and, 50–51
Deconstruction, xii, 181; cultural studies as, 35; de Manian, 275n37; and fascism, 31–32, 33; Foucault and, 276n14; of subjective agency, 64–65
Deconstructionism: Derrida and, 189; of Emerson, 145
Deleuze, Gilles, 81–82; *Anti-Oedipus*, 17, 18; *Foucault*, 160, 175–78
DeLillo, Don: Lentricchia and, 249–50, 252, 253, 259; *Libra*, 249–50, 252, 253, 259
de Man, Paul, 13, 36, 114, 174, 246–47, 248, 275n37
Democratic political discourse, 184
Democratic society, critical intellectual role, 15
Demonic figure, Fish's rhetorical man, 141, 158
Demonic parody, media as, 4
Demonstrative meditation, Foucault's idea, 76–79, 80, 83, 86, 95
Depression, narcissistic, 98

Derrida, Jacques, 152; and cultural studies, 35; Foucault and, 74; Greenblatt and, 254; and Heidegger, 31, 187–90; *Of Spirit: Heidegger and the Question,* 179–81; *The Postcard,* 35; *Spurs: Nietzsche's Styles,* 23; and tradition, 170
Derridean deconstruction, 33
Descartes, René: *Discourse on Method,* 42; *Meditations,* 77
Desiring man, culture and, 64
Destruction of tradition, Heidegger and, 29, 30–33
Destructive creation, fascist imagination and, 23
Determinism, critical opposition to, 126
Dickinson, Emily, Arac's view, 173–74
Differences: American, 151; cultural, Lentricchia and, 246–47, 256, 258; radical ideology of, 258
Disciplinary practice, Foucault and, 83
Disciplinary society: fascist imagination and, 23; Foucault's idea, 36
Discipline: fascist imagination and, 21–22; philosophical, 27
Discourse: conditions of, authorship and, 54–55; Foucault's theory, 42–43, 66; of meditaton, 75; of pure demonstration, 74–75
——innovative, 55; of critical reading, 167
——practices of, 65; fascist imagination as, 18; initiators of, 52–53, 57, 58; power of, 79
Discursive construction, subject as, 82
Displacement, critical: judgment and, 138; Poirier's views, 145–46
Dissemination of author, 54
Domestic economy: Howells's ideal, 199; precapitalist, realism and, 195
Dominant males, in ancient societies, 84
Dominating powers, cultural, 79
Domination, play of, Foucault's idea, 63, 78–79
Double reading: demonstrative meditation and, 77; of Foucault, 79–80
Doubles: defective, and destructive creation, 23; Foucault's idea, 81–82, 176–77

Duality of Foucault, 43–44
Duke University, English department, 2

Economy of authorship, 51
Economy of pain, Howells's idea, 194–206
Ecstasy: Emerson's view, 225–26; fascist imagination and, 20; oppositional criticism and, 244
Eden, desire for return to, 235
Edifying conversation, Rorty's idea, 169
Education: democratic, and culture, 231; and narcissistic personality, 97–98; and self-development, 102
Educational resource, critical intellectual as, 15
Ego: fascist imagination and, 17–18, 24; formation of, revisionist theories, 17; narcissistic, 97–98; and reality, Kristeva's idea, 98; wounded, 108
Ego ideal, grandiose, 97–98, 108
Egotistical sublime, Wordsworth as, 156
Eliot, T. S., 234; Lentricchia and, 260, 262; Shusterman's views, 169–71; "Tradition and the Individual Talent," 15, 171; *The Waste Land,* 174
Elitist resistance of style, Kristeva and, 161
Emerson, Ralph Waldo, ix–x, 6, 68, 99–101, 121–29, 247, 272n4, 286n4, 286–87n3; "Art," 146; "Compensation," 108; "Divinity School Address," 121–29; and ecstasy, 225–26; "Experience," x, 230; "Friendship," 100–101; "History," 162–63; "Human Culture" lectures, 227; influences of, in Lentricchia's view, 262; *Journals,* 98; and metamorphosis, 265–66; "The Method of Nature," 225–26; "The Over-Soul," 70, 96, 287n5, and Stevens, 232; "The Poet," 263; "Poetry and Imagination," 225, 229–30; Poirier and, 145–46; Pound and, 263; *Quotation and Originality,* xviii; radical parody, 101–2; "Self-Reliance," 98, 287n5; "Spenser," 100, 101–2; "Spiritual Laws," 127–28, 226–27; and subject, 280n7; transcendentalism of,

231; Trilling's view, 96; and vocation, 226–30

Empathy, Kristeva's idea, 233

End of the world, Cheever and, 216

Enlightenment: Foucault and, 45; and romanticism, 188; satyr play, 47

Entrepreneurial type, 201

Error, in regimes of truth, 66

Essay genre, narcissism of, 106

Essays, Montaigne and, 106

Essence, imaginary, Cheever's idea, 223

Essent, Heidegger's concept, 25–28

Essentialist feminism, 269; Lentricchia and, 252–53, 256–58

Essential values, loss of, 7–8

Ethical literary study, 14–15

Ethical stylization, 83, 176; Greek, Foucault's analysis, 96

Ethical subject: formation of, 84; Greek, heautocratic structure, 90–91

Ethical telos, in Greek culture, 86, 87

European theory, 246

Evasions, allusive, in Stevens's poetry, 236

Event, Foucault's idea, 63

Experience: Foucault's view, 62–64; of imaginative agency, 70

Exteriority, self-referential writing as, 51

Facticity, Bloom's idea, 155

Family romance, 69; Bloom and, 151; Cheever and, 213; of Montaigne, 105–6; narcissists and, 97; Stevens and, 243

Farias, Victor, *Heidegger and Nazism*, 186–87

Fascism: in every man, 17; Heideggerian "turn" and 28–29; of Pound, 263

Fascist authoritarianism, 248

Fascist imagination, 16–24, 28; critical theory and, 25, 31–32, 33; cultural representations, 34; Freudian view, 34–35; Heidegger and, 26

Faulkner, William, *Absalom! Absalom!*, 252

Female sexuality, Kritzman and, 103–4

Femininity, soldier-males and, 18, 20

Feminism, 269; Lentricchia and, 252–

53, 256–58; and psychoanalytic theory, 17

Feminist American studies, xii

Feminist criticism, of Wordsworth, 173

Fiction writing, 79

Fiery spirit, Heidegger's idea, 31

Final solutions, 144

Fish, Stanley, 6, 7, 13–14, 113, 114, 151, 211, 224, 250, 256; and Bloom, 140; "Change," 132, 136; and contingency theory, 215; and critical change, 131–39; and critical theory, 115–16; and political correctness, 1–4; and revisionism, 5; "Rhetoric," 152; "The Young and Restless," 134

Fisher, Barbara, 234

Fitzgerald, F. Scott, 70; Cheever and, 216

Flame, spirit as, Heidegger's idea, 189–90

Flaubert, Gustave, *The Temptations of Saint Anthony*, Foucault and, 44

Folding of external world, Deleuze's idea, 176–77

Formalism: of Fish, 135; of gender, feminist, 257; Lentricchia and, 245, 246–47

Formal self-effacement, 128

Foucault, Michel, x–xi, xiii, 8, 34, 37–59, 60, 72–73, 100, 153, 224, 251; career of, 80; *The Archaeology of Knowledge*, 80, Megill and, 42–44; *The Care of the Self*, 66, 69, 82–83, 85–86, 91–95; and collective archive, 212; and contingency theory, 211; and disciplinary society, 36; *Discipline and Punish*, 18, 23, 60, 253–54, Lentricchia and, 255; "Fantasia of the Library," 44; *Fearful Symmetry: A Study of William Blake*, 150; and genres of writing, 74–79; and Greek culture, 86; Greenblatt and, 254; *The History of Sexuality*, 8, 35, 38, 42, 60, 61, 63–65, 80, 83–96, 160–61, 176, 212; and imaginary father, 68–69, 269; Kritzman and, 104; Lentricchia and, 252–53, 259–60; *Madness and Civilization*, 74; and Nietzsche, 64–65; "Nietzsche,

Foucalt Michel (*Continued*)
Genealogy, History," 79; *The Order of
Things,* 50, 81–82; pedagogic pair
concept, 69–70; problems with, 61–
64; and relation to self, 96; Rorty and,
271n3; and subjectivity, 76–83; *The
Use of Pleasure,* 60, 62, 66, 82–83,
85–86, 95, 161; "What Is an Author?" 37,48, 54–55; "What Is Enlightenment?" 205; *The Will to
Knowledge,* 60, 61, 83–84
Free agents: Fish and, 138–39; Foucault's
idea, 65
Free speech, political correctness and, 1–
2
Freikorps, 16–17
French intellectualism, Foucault and, 48
French Renaissance literature, Kritzman
and, 103–9
Freud, Sigmund, 9, 52; analytic transference, 69; Bloom and, 151; *Civilization
and Its Discontents,* 129; death drive,
229; *The Ego and the Id,* 220, Kristeva
and, 67–68; Foucault's view, 38; *Group
Psychology and the Analysis of the Ego,*
Kristeva and, 67–68; identification
theory, 161–62; influence of, 168;
"Mourning and Melancholia," Kritz-
man and, 105; and Western culture,
156
Friend self, xii, 97–101, 103, 105–6; as
split subject, 102
Friendship, 100–101; fate of, 95;
Foucault's ideas, 83, 84, 85–86; spec-
ular role, 96–97
Frost, Robert, Lentricchia and, 260, 262
Frye, Northrop, 121–29; *Anatomy of Crit-
icism,* 123, 150; Bloom and, 150; "The
Imaginative and the Imaginary," 121–
29; Lentricchia and, 256
Füher principle, Heidegger and, 188
Future: fascist imagination and, 32;
Heidegger and, 33; self and, 23

Games, strategic, Foucault's idea, 66
Gender: confusion of, Montaigne and,
104–5; differences, Howells and, 200;
roles, Emerson and, 100–101

Generational change: oppositional criticism and, 6–7; and political correctness, 1–3
Genetic aspect of tradition, 170
Genius, 40; American romantic conception, 231; democratic, 227; drama of,
Stevens and, 233–34; Emerson's
views, 225–26; Foucault's ideas, 53,
55; neopragmatist myth, 153; Nietzsche and, 57–58; Poirier's ideas, 144–
46; professionalization of, 42–43;
projective identification, 232; resent-
ment of, 178; sublime, and reality,
155
Genres of philosophical writing,
Foucault's ideas, 74–79
German intellectuals, and fascism, 35
German language, Hiedegger and,
284n3
Germanness, soldier-males and, 18
German tradition, Heidegger and, 30–
31
Ghostly tribunal, Bloom's idea, 140
Gilbert, Sandra: Lentricchia and, 256–
58; *No Man's Land: The Place of the
Woman Writer in Modern Literature,* 262
Giving birth to oneself, 106
*The Golden Treasury of the Best Songs and
Lyrical Poems in the English Language*
(Palgrave, ed.), 260–61
Goldman, Harvey, *Max Weber and Thomas
Mann: Calling and the Shaping of the
Self,* 201
Graff, Gerald, 13, 113, 143–44
Grandiose ego ideal, 97–98, 108
Greek culture: Foucault's analysis, 85,
86–91; Heidegger's view, 30–31
Greenblatt, Stephen, 255, 257–58; *Re-
naissance Self-Fashioning,* 253–54
Guattari, Felix, *Anti-Oedipus,* 17, 18
Gubar, Susan: Lentricchia and, 256–58;
*No Man's Land: The Place of the Woman
Writer in Modern Literature,* 262

Habermas, Jurgen, 212
Harpham, Geoffrey Galt, 109, 172, 200
Heautocratic structure: of Greek ethical
subject, 90–91; of self, 86

Hebrew Bible, Bloom and, 156–59, 162–63
Hegel, Georg Wilhelm Friedrich, x, 68, 156, 231, 247; and Heidegger, 31; *The Phenomenology of Spirit,* 180–81; *The Philosophy of Fine Art,* 154
Heidegger, Martin, 6, 13, 152, 167, 226, 284nn2, 3; *Being and Time,* 29–30, 168, 188, 229; Derrida and, 179–80, 187–90; and fascist imagination, 36; *An Introduction to Metaphysics,* 15, 24–33; "The Origin of a Work of Art," 30; Mannheim and, 274n21; Nazism of, 186–89; philosophy of, 187; psychic profile, 29–33; Rorty and, 165–66, 184–85; *What Is Called Thinking?,* 23
Heideggerian aspiration, 168
Herbst, Josephine, Cheever and, 216
Heritage, tradition and, 30
Hermeneutic circle, Heidegger and, 28
Hermeneutics of self-suspicion, 83
Heroes, imaginative, Western, 158
Heroic self-sacrifice, Howells and, 194–95, 197, 199–200
Heroic sound, Stevens's idea, 237–38
Hirsch, E. D., 114
Historical change: revisionism and, 131; Rorty's view, 165
Historical determination, 204
Historical mask plays, 68
Historical materialization, 68–69
Historical reality, creation of, 34
Historical research, poststructuralism and, 134
History: Arac and, 172; criticism and, 132; Emerson's view, 263; feminist view, 257; fictional, Foucault and, 41–42, 46; Foucault's view, 253–54; practice of, Fish's idea, 134; of present, 51; tradition and, Heidegger's idea, 29–30
Hölderlin, Friedrich, Heidegger and, 187
Holocaust, Heidegger and, 180
Homer, 54
Homicidal artist, 33
Homicidal rage, 32

Homoerotic bond, Foucault and, 160
Homosexual male, scapegoating of, 85–86
Horkheimer, Max, *The Authoritarian Personality,* 19–20
Höss, Rudolf, 17
Howells, William Dean, *The Rise of Silas Lapham,* 193–206
Human being, Heidegger's idea, 26–28
Human community, literary criticism and, 142–43
Humanistic intellectuals, 167–68
Humanities: institutionalizations of Foucault, 48; and revisionism, 5
Humanization of Foucault, 40–41
Human rationality, revisionist view, 138
Human relationship, views of, 146–48
Human sciences, critical reading and, 168
Human sexuality, ascetic stylization, 160
Human subjectivity, Jameson's idea, 141
Human temporality, fascist imagination and, 19, 23

Idea, organizing, Nietzsche's concept, 57
Ideal love object, quest of, 85
Ideals, revisionary, 118
Ideal speech act, Habermas's idea, 212
Identification, 98; critical intellectuals and, 67–68; Kristeva and, 161–62; projective, 232; reader-writer, Poirier's view, 145; in Stevens's poetry, 238
Identity: adolescent, Kristeva's idea, 69–70; American, ix–x, 250; critical, 70–71, 251–52, 269; Emerson's idea, 163; friend self and, 99; idealized, Emerson and, 70; intellectual, Kristeva and, 67; of Pound, 264
Identity formation: by Cheever, 208–24; intellectual, 255
Ideology, theory as, in Bloom's view, 13
Image, poetic of, 261
Imaginary, cultural studies and, 34
Imaginary ancestors, avowal of, 9
Imaginary essence, Cheever's idea, 223
Imaginary father, 108, 220–21, 269; American critics and, 68–69; avowal of, 98–99; critical identity and, 252;

Imaginary father (*Continued*)
   identification with, 162, 233;
   Kristeva's idea, 67–68; narcissist and,
   97–98; Stevens and, 234, 236, 238,
   242–43
Imaginary politics, 231, 243–44; of Ste-
   vens, 234–35, 240
Imaginary self-aggrandizement, 208
Imagination: bureaucratization of, 161;
   Lentricchia's views, 247–48; nature of,
   Bloom's idea, 152; radically con-
   tingent, 208; reality and, in American
   culture, 250; social determinations of,
   161; sublime, 205; types of, 247–49
Imaginative achievement, 8–9
Imaginative agency, 68, 256; experience
   of, 70; Lentricchia and, 245
Imaginative authority, critical intellec-
   tual as, 15
Imaginative heroes, Western, 158
Imaginative masters, 155
Imaginative Other, power of, 70
Imaginative suicide, contingent imagina-
   tion and, 215
Imitation, Emerson's views, 122
Immortality: aspiration for, 152; sym-
   bolic, 158
Imperialist world order, American litera-
   ture and, 195
Imperial nation-state, fascist imagination
   and, 23
Impersonal plural agency, 80
Indetermination, spaces of, Foucault's
   idea, 78–79
Individualism: comtemporary critics and,
   272n4; pragmatism and, 248
Individuality: Foucault and, 66–67; and
   mass culture, 154; self-destructive
   mode, 145–46; sexuality and, 83
Individual prehistory, 269
Individuals: accountability of, 65; self-
   made, 151
Individual self, friend self and, 102
Individual subjectivation, Foucault's
   ideas, 176–77
Individual will, Lentricchia and, 245
Initiating-replicating authors, 55

Innovations: critical, 143–44; textual,
   52–53
Innovative work, 40
Inspiration: avowal of, 101; Longinus's
   idea, 140
Institutional codes, and authorship, 53–
   54, 56
Institutionalization: of literary criticism,
   143; scientific rationality and, 78
Instruction, experience and, 64
Instrumental reason, 136; contingency
   theory and, 211; Fish and, 133, 135–
   37; interpretive communities and, 138
Intellectual consumerism, critic and, 72
Intellectual culture, Hegel and, 180
Intellectual identity, 266; Kristeva and,
   67
Intellectualism, French, Foucault and, 48
Intellectual life, postmodern ideas, 185–86
Intellectuals, 15–16, 44–45, 67–68; Altieri's view, 182; as authors, 47–48;
   and experience, 64; humanistic, 167–
   68; identity formation, 69; and imaginary father, 68; memory, 97; as narcissistic personalities, 97–98;
   postmodern, and experience, 64; and
   revisionism, 5–6
——American, 36; and contingency the-
   ory, 209; Foucault and, 60–61
Intellectual self-parody, 49
Intelligible forms of critical work, Fish's
   view, 135
Interiorization, doubling and, 81–82
Internalization of man, Nietzsche's idea,
   203–4
Internment of human being, 203–4
Interpretive communities: Bloom and,
   140; Fish's idea, 132–33, 135–36,
   138–39, 143
Interpretive modes, oscillations, 168
Interpretive self, 8–9
Invariable subject of pure demonstration,
   75–76
Ironic criticism, 248
Ironic hero, self as, 167
Ironic recognition, 167, 168; Deleuze
   and, 175; Shusterman and, 171

Ironic reflection, 165
Ironist culture: contingency theory and, 211; Rorty's idea, 183–85
Irony: conventional, 51; criticism and, 59, 248; fascist imagination and, 31–32; Heideggerian "turn" as, 25–26, 28; Pseudo-Lucian and, 92–94
Irresponsibility, Fish and, 133, 135
Italian-American males, 256

James, William, 6, 248, 261; Lentricchia and, 252–53, 259–60; neopragmatism and, 255
Jameson, Fredric, 15, 49, 82, 141–43, 144
Jeremiah, prophet, Bloom and, 160–61
Jerome, Saint, 52
Jesus Christ, 269
Jewish archetype of spirit, Heidegger and, 180
Jewishness, soldier-males and, 18, 20
Jewish pragmatism, Western culture and, 156–57
Journal writing, and subject, 100
Joyce, James: "The Dead," 148–49; *Finnegan's Wake,* 42; *Ulysses,* 59, 174, 261
Judgment, critical, 127; Rorty and, 185
Juhl, P. D., 114
Jünger, Ernst, 16, 187

Kant, Immanuel, 54–55, 226, 247; *The Critique of Judgement,* 204–5, 206
Kapp putsch, 17
Keats, John, 156
Kierkegaard, Soren Aabye, x
Killers, psychotic, 32
Knapp, Steven: "Against Theory," 114–16, 118–19, 129; Lentricchia and, 255–56, 258
Knowledge: theory and, 115; subject of, 75, 76–80, 83
Kohut, Heinz, 97
Kristeva, Julia, xiii, 8, 64, 68, 72, 100, 153, 161, 224, 230, 251; "The Adolescent Novel," 69–70; *Black Sun,* 67–68, 98–99, 161, 220–21; and friend

self, 97; "Identification and the Real," 232–33; Stevens and, 234; *Tales of Love,* 161
Kritzman, Lawrence D., *The Rhetoric of Sexuality and the Literature of the French Renaissance,* 103–9
Kuhn, Thomas, 52

Lacan, Jacques, 68
Language: Heidegger's views, 31, 284n3; sexuality and, 39, 40; of soldier-males, 18; structure of, and action, 65
Larson, Magali, *The Rise of Professionalism,* 137
Latin language, Heidegger and, 31
Law: literary criticism and, 137–38; as profession, Fish and, 135, 137
Lawrence, D. H., 47; Blanchard and, 39–40; Foucault and, 42, 46; and friendship, 100; *Lady Chatterley's Lover,* Foucault and, 38–40; *The Plumed Serpent,* Foucault and, 38; "The Prussian Officer," 19; *Women in Love,* 39
Lawrence studies, 40–41
Leftist academics, political correctness, 1–2
Leftist critics, and theory, 13
Legal profession: Fish and, 135, 137; literary criticism and, 137
Legal realism, doctrine of, 137
Lentricchia, Frank, xiii, 7, 13, 235, 245–69, 288n5, 289n13; *After the New Criticism,* 246; *American Modernism,* 251, 260–62; *Ariel and the Police: Michel Foucault, William James, Wallace Stevens,* 251–56, 260, 262; *Criticism and Social Change,* 246, 249; "Don DeLillo," 249–50, 252, 253, 259; *The Gaiety of Language,* 245; "Lee Harvey Oswald," 249–50; *Robert Frost,* 246
Liberal civilization, cultural studies and, 34
Liberal imagination, 30
Liberalism, American, 254; Foucault and, 60–61; pragmatism and, 248
Liberation: critical change and, 142; intellectuals and, 44–45

License, Fish and, 133, 135
Linguistic analysis, 65; Altieri and, 182
Linguistic determinism, 151
Literacy, universal, and relation to oneself, 97
Literariness, aesthetic dimension, 142
Literary art, as vocation, 231
Literary canon, multicultural, 2
Literary criticism: Bloom's view, 130–31; Fish's view, 137–38; ideological split, 143–44; *see also* Criticism
Literary intellectuals, and vocation, 227
Literary selfhood, American, 265
Literary studies, 14–15; contingency theory and, 209; ideological split, 143–44
Literary subject, 82; Bloom and, 76
Literary texts, 148
Literary theorists, 115
Literary theory, analytic philosophy and, 181
Literary tradition, and collective project, 142–43
Literary unreason, 84
Literature: cultural work of, 247; study of, 120
Localism, Heidegger and, 187
Longinus, *On the Sublime,* 139–40
Lost Thing, Kristeva's idea, 67, 98, 220–21; Stevens and, 234
Love: self-critical, 98; strategic games of, 66; unitary theory, 85
——of boys, 85, 86; ancient Greeks and, 92–94
Love object, loss of, 105
Lyotard, Jean-François, Altieri and, 181–82

MacNeil-Lehrer News Hour, 1–3
Madness: revisionism and, 116–29
Magnanimity of collective archive, 148–49
Mahler, Margaret, *On Human Symbiosis and the Vicissitudes of Individuation,* 17
Malatesta, Sigismundo, Pound and, 267–68
Male bonding, 252; fascist, 18

Male chauvinism of Emerson, 227
Male domination, 17
Male friendship: ethics of, 84; Foucault and, 83
Males: dominant, in ancient societies, 84; homosexual, scapegoating of, 85–86; self-determining, Fish's rhetorical man as, 153; writers, sense of creative power, 104
Male self, fascist, 18
Manichean allegory, history as, 257
Mann, Thomas, *Doktor Faustus,* 46, 49
Marginalized Others, narcissist and, 98
Married couple, erotics of, 69
Marx, Karl, 52; *Das Kapital,* 195
Mask play, 67–68; ancient aesthetics of existance as, 95; collective archive, 70, 71; critical identity as, 251; criticism as, x–xi, 14–36; of Derrida, 180; fascist imagination, 16–24; of Foucault, 73; Lentricchia and, 251, 255–57, 259; of narcissism, 98; of new orthodoxy, 180–81; Over-Self as, 177–78; pragmatists of the spirit, 160; revisionary, 168–69
Masks, 33; lost love and, 104; of modern reason, 80; Over-Soul as, 230; subject as, 82; triple, Native American, 36
Mass consumption, culture of, 195
Mass culture: critical intellectuals and, 15; individuality and, 154
Mass media society, identity formation in, 69
Master-slave analysis of subjective agency, 66
Materialist historiography, Arac and, 174
Maternal patriarch, 233
Media, and stereotypes, 4
Meditation, critical, Foucault's idea, 74–76, 79, 80
Megill, Allan: *The Archaeology of Knowledge,* 42–44; and Foucault, 41–44, 46–47; "Michel Foucault and the Activism of Discourse," 41; *Prophets of Extremity,* 41
Melancholy: narcissistic, 98; self-development and, 102

Memory: communal, 148; of intellectuals, 97; madness and, in Schopenhauer's view, 116–17
Men, frienship between, Emerson's views, 100–101
Men of calling, Weber's idea, 201–2
Mentor-pupil relation, 66, 69–70, 96–97, 160; friend self and, 102; in journal writing, 100; *see also* Pedagogic pair
Metamorphosis, Pound's idea, 265–66
Metaphor, aestheticism and, 248
Metaphysics of power, Foucault and, 44
Method, unreliable, 62
Metonymy, pragmatism and, 248
Metropolism, Benjamin's idea, Arac and, 173–74
Michaels, Walter Benn: "Against Theory," 114–16, 118–19, 129; Lentricchia and, 255–56, 258; and *The Rise of Silas Lapham*, 194–96, 199, 205
Middle class, Lentricchia and, 258
Milton, John: Fish and, 215; *Paradise Lost*, 237; Wordsworth and, 155
Minorities, and political correctness, 1–2
Misrecognitions, multiple scenes of, 4–5; in *The Rise of Silas Lapham*, 197
Mobile subject of meditation, 75–76
Models, theoretical, 120; of change, Fish's idea, 132, 138–39
Moderation, 87
Modern critical theory, Heidegger and, 15
Modern culture, influences on, 143
Modernism: Marxist critiques, 169; Poirier and, 144
Modernist poetics, 261
Modernist studies, Lentricchia and, 246
Modernity: aesthetic reshaping, 80; Arac and, 174, 175; Bloom's views, 156; Foucault's idea, 91, 205; Heidegger and, 187
Modern literary subject, 75
Modern reason, masks of, 80
Modern regimes of truth, 76, 78
Modern society: and internalization of man, 203–4; and scientific rationality, 77–78; and sexuality, 83; subject formation, 84

Modern subjectivity, Bloom's view, 76
Moi, Toril, *Sexual/Textual Politics*, 257
Montaigne, Michel Eyquem de: "De l'affection des Peres aux enfans," 105–6; "On Friendship," 96, 100–101; "De l'institution des enfans," 104–5; Kritzman and, 104–7
Monumental history, 121, 129
Moral codes, 83; questioning of, 84
Moral heroism, Howells and, 198–200
Morality: capitalism and, Howells's views, 198–99; of humanism, 45
Moral superiority, and subjection of others, 194
Mother-child bond, 67
Mourning: for abjected mother, depression as, 98; of self, 223; self-development and, 102
Mourning self, Kristeva's concept, 67
Multiculturalism, 2
Multiple misrecognitions, scenes of, 4–5, 197
Myth of sexual liberation, 38

Narcissism: and authorship, 100; fascist imagination and, 19, 24; and friendship, 101–2; Kritzman and, 106; Montaigne and, 105
Narcissistic personality, 97–98, 108–9
Narcissistic revisionism, 224
Nationalism, fascist, 18, 23
Native American mask, 36
Natural history: of authorship, Nietzsche's idea, 56–57; of calamity, 108
Naturalism, 195; self-alienating, 196
Nature: critical theory and, 25; Emerson and, 262; methodized, art as, 226; soldier-males and, 18
Nazi movement, *Freikorps* and, 17
Nazism of Heidegger, 24, 166, 180, 185, 186–89
Negation, critical, genius and, 58
Neoconservatism, 188; and political correctness, 1–2
Neopragmatism, x, xii, 6, 61, 269; Bloom and, 151–52; and identification with imaginary father, 162; Lentricchia and, 252–53, 255

Neopragmatist revisionism, 154
Neoromanticism, countercultural, 150–51
New criticism: American literature studies and, 144; Poirier and, 144
New historicism, xii, 33, 61, 246, 269; Fish and, 134; Greenblatt and, 253–54; Lentricchia and, 252–53
New order, fascist imagination and, 19
New orthodoxy in theory, 180, 186; Derrida and, 190
Newspapers, influence of, 174
Newton, Sir Isaac, 52
New vocabulary, Rorty and, 165
New Yorker, Cheever works in, 213
New York Times Magazine, 249
Nietzsche, Friedrich Wilhelm, 6, 68, 244; *Beyond Good and Evil,* xviii; and contingency theory, 211; *Ecce Homo,* 48, 55–58; Foucault and, 45, 48, 52, 56–57, 64–65; and friendship, 101; *The Gay Science,* 236, 254; Heidegger and, 31, 187; and internalization of man, 203–4; *On the Genealogy of Morals,* 20–21, 64–65, 202; Rorty's view, 184–85; "Why I Am So Clever," 48, 55–57; *Zarathustra,* 101, 118, 229
Nihilism: of antitheorists, 119; and fascism, 24; individuality and, 145–46
Nineteenth century: critical philosophy, 54–55; transcendentalism, and authorship, 54
Nineteenth century writers, Foucault's view, 52
Nixon, Richard M., 3–4; farewell address to staff, 97–98
"Noble" morality, Foucault and, 65
Nominalists, critics as, 209–10
Non-being, Heidegger's idea, 25–28
Noncanonical works, 8
Nonrelation, in culture, 79
Nonrepresentative status of intellectual life, 185–86
Normality, production of, 83
Normalizing codes, postmodern criticism and, 67
Novel genre, 203; American, Michaels's

view, 195–96; culture and, 69–70; Proust and, 166
Novelty, perpetual, ideology of, 131

Object: aesthetic, 8; sexual, Greek view, 85
Object formation, abjected mother and, 98
Oedipal theory, Bloom and, 151
O'Hara, Daniel T., *Lionel Trilling: The Work of Liberation,* 8–9
Omnipotent Being, Heidegger's idea, 28
Oneself, xii, 98–99, 105–6, 251; agonistic relation to, 96–97; critical agency as, 72–73; Deleuze's idea, 177; drama of becoming, 98; Foucault's concept, 80, 82, 83, 91, 94–95, 212; giving birth to, 106, 108; internalization of pedagogic ideal, 102; Lentricchia and, 268; mask play of, 90–91, 162–63; pedagogic relation to, 104–5; radical parody and, 102; relationship styles, 176
Open strategic games, 86; in ancient society, 84; classical self as, 66; reading as, 89–90, 95
Oppositional criticism, x, 6–7, 126; Lentricchia and, 247, 251
Oppositional intellectuals, 63
Organicism, Arac and, 172
Organic tradition, 30
Original experiences, tradition and, 30
Originality: and inspiration, 53; of Shakespeare, Bloom and, 154
Orthodoxies, current, xii
Oswald, Lee Harvey, 252, 259; Lentricchia and, 249–50
Other: cultural studies and, 34; destruction of, by soldier-males, 17–18; fascist imagination and, 20, 23, 24, 32; friendship with, 84; identification with, critical intellectuals and, 67–68; imaginative, power of, 70; as interiorized double, 81–82; narcissist and, 98
Outcomes: of critical change, Fish's model, 138–39; of revisionism, questions of, 6

Outside: interiorization of, 81–82; of
Otherness, Deleuze's idea, 175–77
Over-self, 95, 177–78
Over-soul, Emerson's concept, 228–30,
280n7

Palgrave, Francis T., ed., *The Golden
Treasury of Best Songs and Lyric Poems in
the English Language*, 260–61
Paranoia, totalitarianism and, 248
Parody, 48–49, 71; in American cultural
life, 4; Foucault and, 43, 45–47, 49–
53; in Lawrence's writings, 39–40;
modern, 79; postmodern, 59, 82
Passive object, sexual, 86–87
Passive subject, sexual, 85
Past defenses, fascist imagination and, 32
Pastiche, xi, 49, 71, 107; Foucault and,
73; Kritzman and, 103; in Stevens's
poetry, 72
Patriarchal canon, challenges to 243–44
Patriarchal hierarchy, female sexuality
and, in Kritzman's view, 103–4
Patterned isolation, Graff's idea, 143
Pease, Donald E.: *Deterrence Pacts,*
286n13; *Visionary Compacts,* 287n3
Pedagogic ideal, internalization of, 102
Pedagogic pair, 64, 251; Bloom and,
160; Foucault's idea, 66, 69–70, 83,
96–97, 212; intellectual psyche as,
67; interpretive self as, 9; in journal
writing, 100; and sociopathology, 252;
Stevens and, 237
Pedagogic relation to oneself, 97
Peirce, C. S., 6, 255
Pentateuch, Bloom's view, 158–59
Perpetual novelty, ideology of, 131
Personal identity, friend self and, 99
Personality type, ascetic, 201–2
Perspective, transhistorical, 8
Persuasion, forms of, 134
Phallic mother, fantasy of, 233
Philia, 87
Philosophical anthropology, 15
Philosophical subject, 75
Philosophical writing, Foucault and, 74–
77
Philosophy: of contingency, 209–11;
Heidegger's view, 165–66

Photograph of Lentricchia, 249, 288n5
Placement, cultural, of authors, 54
Plato, 85; *The Laws* and *The Republic,*
Foucault and, 88–89
Playing the friend, Emerson and, 100–101
Pleasure, fascist imagination and, 21
Plural subject, 227; critical identity as,
71; Foucault's idea, 212; friend self as,
102; in Stevens's poetry, 239–40
Plutarch, 85
Poetics: genteel, 260–61; modernist,
261; of will, Lentricchia's idea, 245
——of critical reading, 32; postmodern,
167–78
Poetic vocation, feminist concept, 258
Poetry, of Stevens, 233–44
Poets: Emerson's views, 229; vocation of
abandonment, 231
——American, 258; Lentriccia's idea,
260; Stevens's idea, 238
Poirier, Richard, 6, 143; *The Renewal of
Literature: Emersonian Reflections,* 144–
46
Political correctness, 1–3, 185; Bloom
and, 131
Political criticism, 243
Political unconscious, 15
Politics: art and, Lentricchia's views,
267–68; cultural, 15; Foucault and,
41–42; theory and, 13–14
Postcolonial studies, 246
Postconstructuralism, 6
Post-Enlightenment intellectual life, tra-
dition and, 30
Postmodern America: celebrity in, 230–
31; critical identity, 251–52; Lentric-
chia and, 250, 251
Postmodern criticism, xii, 67, 72–73
Postmodern critics, 71; American, 253
Postmodern cultural studies, 33–36
Postmodern intellectuals: and experience,
64; narcissistic, 97–98
Postmodernism, x, 49; Altieri's views,
182–83; contingency theory and, 211;
and fascist imagination, 31; Heidegger
and, 187; ironist culture, 184; of
Lyotard, 182

Postmodern subject, Lentricchia and, 249–50
Postromantic imaginations, 247
Poststructuralism, 134, 252
Potential identities, Altieri's idea, 182–83
Pound, Ezra: and aestheticism, 248; Lentricchia and, 248, 260, 262–69
Power: constructive, of imaginative Other, 70; discipline of, 248; dominating, and culture, 79; Foucault's ideas, 41–44, 46, 61–62; natural history of, 56; relationships, 65; and standards, 136; subject of, Foucault and, 75–80, 83
Powerlessness, sense of, 98
Practico-inert, Sartre's concept, 141
Pragmatism, 6, 247, 248; American, 151–53; of Fish, 135; Foucault and, 271n3; Jewish, Western culture and, 156–57
Precapitalist domestic economy, realism and, 195
Precedents, legal, 137–38
Preoedipal state, fascism as, 24, 32
Presentation of self, critics and, 128
Primal scene, fascist, 16–24
Primary fusion state, 232
Primary identification, Kristeva's idea, 233
Primordial spirit, tradition as, 30
Principles of criticism, 126–29
Prior texts, critical theory and, 25
Private fantasies, Rorty's idea, 184
Private man, Emerson's idea, 163
Problems with Foucault's theories, 61–64
Profession, critcism as, 129; Fish and, 132–33
Professional assimilation of innovative work, 40
Professional elite, Fish and, 138–39
Professionalism, neopragmatism and, 6
Professionalization: of genius, 40, 42–43; opposition to, 143, 165; self-serving, of critics, 253
Professional work, 140–41; and critical change, 143
Professors, and political correctness, 1–2

Programmatic action, critical principle of, 127–28
Projective identification, 232
Projects of self-creation, Rorty's idea 184, 186
Prosthetic god, man as, Freud's view, 129
Protestant ethic, and capitalism, 202
Protestant Romanticism, Emerson and, 125
Proust, Marcel, 167; Rorty and, 165–67
Proustian recognition, 167, 168
Provinciality, conservative, 187
Provisionality of Arac's *Critical Genealogies,* 172–75
Provisional nature of self, 15
Pseudo-Lucian, *Affairs of the Heart,* 91–94
Psyche: and projective identification, 232; in Stevens's poetry, 240
Psychic development, normative model, 161–62
Psychic profile of Heidegger, 29–33
Psychic splitting, Stevens and, 239–40
Psychic wholeness, ideal of, 243
Psychoanalysis, 39; Cheever and, 214
Psychoanalytic theory: Frye and, 123–24; revisionary, 14
Psychosexual discourse, 39
Public policy, Rorty's idea, 184
Pure demonstration, Foucault's idea, 74–76, 79
Puritanism, 20, 201–2, 287n3; Howells and, 200–201
Purity, ideal, Stevens and, 237

Questioning of being, Heidegger's idea, 26–27

Rabelais, François, Kritzman and, 107; *Quart Livre,* 107
Radical asceticism, fascist imagination as, 20
Radical change, contingency theory and, 211
Radical parody, xi, 4, 33, 49, 71, 101–2, 226; criticism as, 101; Foucault and, 73, 82; Kritzman and, 103, 107; *The Rise of Silas Lapham* and, 197, 205;

in Stevens's poetry, 72, 241–42; will
to play as, 254
Radical self-parody of Cheever, 208–24
Rational agency, 80
Rationalistic universalism, Heidegger
and, 187
Rawls, John, Altieri and, 181–82
Readers, 268; and authors, 54; of Pound,
264–66
Reading: creative, 148; of Foucault, 47;
open strategic game of, 89–90, 95
Real, productions of, 34
Realism of Howells, Michaels's view,
194–96, 199
Reality: Bloom's view, 154–56; culture
and, 156; fascist production, 18; and
imagination, in American culture, 250
Reason: critical, 134; Fish's idea, 135–
36; modern, masks of, 80; modern so-
ciety and, 77–78
Rectorship Address, Heidegger, 188–89
Reflective pastiche, 71
Regimes of truth, 76, 78–79, 84
Relation to oneself, Foucault's idea, 177
Religion, Emerson and, 121–22, 127,
227, 229
Representative status, lack of, 186
Repressed object, intellectual parody and,
49
Repression: contemporary criticism and,
161; genius and, 57–58; of sexuality,
106–7
Repressive sublimation of Foucault, 43
Resentment, structure of, 194; *see also*
Ressentiment
Resolve, Heidegger's idea, 27
Ressentiment, 9, 79, 168; Bloom and,
130–31; Cheever and, 217; critical
identity and, 252; of genius, 178;
Nietzsche's idea, 244; Poirier and, 146
Revisionary imagination: bureaucracy of,
152; madness as analogy for, 116–18;
postmodern, 116
Revisionary madness, 129
Revisionary psychoanalytic theory, 14,
17
Revisionary redescription, critical reading
as, 165, 167

Revisionism, 5–6, 121, 131, 186; American, 144–46; contemporary criticism
and, 161; contingency theory and,
211; contingent imagination as, 208;
institutionalization of, 181–82; and
madness, 116–29; narcissistic, 224;
neopragmatist, 6, 165
Rhetoric: of fascism, 19; of Kritzman,
108; revisionism as, 5; transcendental,
108
Rhetorical man: Cheever as, 216, 224;
contingent imagination and, 163;
Fish's idea, 135, 141, 152–53, 157–
58, 215, 250
Rhetorical persuasion, poststructuralism
and, 134
Rhetorical power, Emerson's idea, 234
Rightist critics, and theory, 13
Rittenhouse, Jessie Belle, 260
Romance languages, Heidegger and, 31
Romantic genius, American, 231
Romantic ideology of genius, 58
Romantic imagination, Bloom and, 150,
152
Romanticism: Arac and, 172; Enlighten-
ment and, 188; Fish's ideas and, 139
Romantic poetry, Wordsworth and, 226
Romantic self-sacrifice, Joyce and, 149
Rorty, Richard, 5, 6, 7, 13–14, 36, 119,
167, 271n3; Bloom and, 151–52;
Contingency, Irony, and Solidarity, 151,
165–67, 183–86, 210; and con-
tingency theory, 215, 248; and con-
tingent imagination, 155; and critical
reading, 167; and Derrida, 359; Eliot
and, 169
Roussel, Raymond, Foucault and, 59
Royce, Josiah, 261

Sadomasochism, fascist imagination and,
21–22
Said, Edward W., 7, 13, 113; and
Foucault, 43–44
Santayana, George, 261
Sartre, Jean-Paul, *Critique of Dialectical
Reason,* Jameson and, 141
Satiric aim of criticism, xi
Satyr play, Enlightenment, 47

Scapegoat, Other as, in fascist imagination, 23

Scapegoating of male homosexual, 85–86

Schiller, F. C. S., *Letters on Aesthetic Education*, 254

Scholarship, critical humanism and, 47

School of Resentment, Bloom's idea, 130–31

Schopenhauer, Arthur, 129; *The World as Will and Representation*, 116–17

Science, modern, and sexuality, 83

Scientific rationality, 77–78, 84

Scientific revolution, Kuhn's idea, 52

Sedgewich, Ellery, 260

Selective social determinations, misreading of, 7–8

Self, 15–16, 91, 96–97; agonistic structure, 87, 94, 160; American, 66; calling and, 201–2; classical culture and, 66–67; critical intellectuals and, 15–16; cultural studies and, 33, 35; Emerson and, x, 70; Foucault's ideas, 64–65, 91, 212; friend self and, 102; heautocratic structure, 86; interpretive, 8–9; as ironic hero, 167; literature and, 14–15; male, fascist, 18; Michaels's view, 196; Montaigne's idea, 105–6; mourning, Kristeva's idea, 67; oppositional politics and, 244; postmodern, Altieri's views, 183; pre-Oedipal, of soldier-males, 17–18; temporal dispersion of, 221–22

Self-creation, 5, 7; Altieri's view, 183; American, 253, 259; ascetic, 202; of Cheever, 208; contingent imagination and, 215–16; culture and, 64–67; Fish's idea, 152–53, 157; postmodernism and, 185–86; and renunciations, 200; Rorty's idea, 184, 248

Self-definition, as mask, 15

Self-denial, ascetic, 87

Self-depreciation, of Montaigne, 104

Self-determination, contingent imagination and, 163

Self-development: classical model, 251; Freud and, 102

Self-discipline, fascist, 20

Self-division: Heideggerian "turn" as, 27–28; of soul, 87–89

Self-effacement, of critics, 128

Self-fashioning: in Cheever's fiction, 217; critical, 168; textual practice, 80; *see also* Self-creation

Self-governance, male ethics, 84

Selfhood: literary, American, 265; naturalism and, 196

Self-interest: community and, 139; critical change and, 140–41; in critical reading, 171

Selfishness, causistry of, Nietzsche's idea, 56, 57

Self-judgment, radical parody as, 107–8

Self-made individual, American dream, 151

Self-mastery, Foucault's views, 87, 90–91

Self-parody, 48–49, 59; by Cheever, 208–24; Foucault and, 41, 49–53; by Lawrence, 39–40; of Over-Self, 177; unwitting, 4

Self-production, as plural agency, 82

Self-reference, in writing, 50–51

Self-reflective criticism, 248

Self-regulation, intellectuals and, 44–45

Self-revision: criticism and, 128–29, 248; Foucault and, 63

Self-sacrifice, heroic, 194–95, 197, 200

Self-suspicion, 83; modernity and, 91

Semi-Quixote, Wordsworth's idea, Frye and, 123

Sexual ethics, ancient Greek, 85

Sexuality, 38–40; ethical stylizations, 177; history of, Foucault and, 93; and individuality, 83; repressions of, 106–7; rhetoric of, 108, 109; and self, 64

Sexual liberation, 83; myth of, 38

Sexual metamorphosis, Montaigne and, 105–6

Sexual object, Greek view, 85

Sexual stylization, ethics of, 84

Shakespeare, William: Bloom's view, 76, 154; Emerson's views, 101, 229–30; revisionism of, 156

Shelley, Percy Bysshe: Bloom and, 150;

"Mont Blanc," 236; *Prometheus Unbound*, 236; Stevens and, 236
Shusterman, Richard, 175; *T. S. Eliot and the Philosophy of Criticism*, 169–71
Simulacrum, postmodern culture of, 98
Slave societies: ancient, 84; sexuality in, 160
Smallness, symbolic, in Cheever's "The Lowboy," 218–19
Smith, Barbara Hernstein, 151
Social character: Jameson's idea, 141–43; of work, 141
Social critique, narcissism and, 98
Social determinations: of imagination, 161; selective, misreading of, 7–8
Socialism, Heidegger and, 31
Socially symbolic action, 246–47
Social praxis, Sartre and, 141
Societies, differences in, 83–84
Sociopathology, Lentricchia and, 250, 252
Socrates, Foucault and, 88–90
Soldier-males, fascist imagination, 16–24
Sophocles, *Antigone*, Heidegger and, 28
Soul: Bloom's view, 70; Emerson's doctrine, 121–23, 127, 229–30, 280n7; self-division of, 87–89
South Atlantic Quarterly, 249
Spaces in culture, Foucault and, 175–76
Special interests, and revisionism, 5
Specialization, professional, 143
Specific intellectuals, Foucault's idea, 60–61
Spectral image, fascist imagination, 24
Specular structure of Cheever's "The Lowboy," 218–19, 223
Speculation, and naturalism, 195
Speech, politically correct, 1–2
Spirit, Heidegger and, 31, 179–80, 188–90
Standards: of critical judgment, Fish and, 133; production of, 83
Statement, Foucault's theory, 80–81
Stedman, Edmund Clarence, 260
Stereotypes, media and, 4
Stevens, Wallace, 226; "Chaos in Motion

and Not in Motion," 240–42; "A Dish of Peaches in Russia," 71–72, 238–40; and Emerson, 231–32; "Hoon," 243; "How to Live. What to Do," 236–38; "The Idea of Order at Key West," 228, 232; "Large Red Man Reading," 146–48, 242–43; Lentricchia and, 252–53, 259–60, 262–63, 266–67; poetry of, 233–44; "A Postcard from the Volcano," 168, 235, 236; "The Sleight-of-Hand Man," 243; "Sunday Morning," 236, 262–63; "The World as Meditation," 263
Strategic games, Foucault's idea, 66
Strong poet, Bloom's concept, 151–52; Rorty and, 184
Structure: of Cheever's "The Lowboy," 218–19, 223; tradition as, 170
Style, 58–59; elitist resistance of, Kristeva and, 161; subject of, 76, 79–80
Stylization of existence, ancient Greek, 89–90
Subaltern studies, 246
Subject avoidance, Heidegger and, 188
Subject formation, Foucault and, 82–84
Subjection, 194; in Greek culture, 86, 87; of self, 203
Subjectivation, individual, Foucault's ideas, 176–77
Subjective agency: deconstruction of, 64–65; master-slave analysis, 66
Subjective freedom, Shakespeare and, 154
Subjectivity: adolescent, Kristeva's concept, 278n13; cricital meditation and, 80; Foucault and, 78, 176–77; modern, Bloom's view, 76; of scientific rationality, 77–78
Subjects: aesthetic, 76; American, Lentricchia and, 269; as contingent imagination, 154; of demonstrative meditation, 77; Emerson and, 280n7; Foucault's views, 65–66, 91; as impersonal plural agency, 80; journal writing and, 100; of meditation, 75–76; play of, Foucault and, 86; plural, friend self as, 105; of pure demonstra-

Subjects (*Continued*)
tion, 74–76; sexual, Greek view, 85;
of statement, 80–81
——postmodern, xii; Lentricchia and,
249–50; of parody, 82
——split: friend self as, 102; of narcissistic personality, 97–98
Sublimation: imaginary father as, 269;
Kristeva and, 68, 232; repressive, of
Foucault, 43; resentment and, 194
Sublime: experience as, 63; Fish and,
158; Kant's idea, 204–5; Longinus's
concept, 140
Sublime aesthetic, 205
Sublime aspiration, 168, 178; Deleuze
and, 175; Shusterman and, 171
Sublime effect, textual production, 55
Sublime genius, and reality, 155
Superego: Bloom's view, 162–63; imag-
inary father and, 68
Symbolic immortality, contingent imag-
ination and, 158
Symbolic order, imaginary father as pro-
totype, 68
Symbolic sublimation, Kristeva's idea,
232
Symbolism in Cheever's "The Lowboy,"
218–20
Synecdoche: neopragmatism and, 255;
totalitarianism and, 248
System, idea of, 113–14

Teacher, prophetic, Emerson's concept,
122, 124–26
Teaching of criticism, 120, 128–29
Television, Fish and, 3
Temporality: Cheever and, 223; fascist
imagination and, 19, 23; Heidegger
and, 32–33; new historicism and, 33;
soldier-males and, 18
Texts: author's relationship to, 50; as crit-
ical fictions, Foucault, 62; soldier-
male, 27
Textuality of all facts, Fish and, 134
Textual practice, friend self as, 98–99
Theater of self, Lentricchia's idea, 250
Theoretical model of change, Fish's idea,
132

Theoretical practice, self-critical, 251
Theorists, 115, 120; constraints on, 180;
as Outsider, Deleuze's idea, 175
Theory: and change, 2–3; contemporary,
scapegoat muses, 25; Fish's view, 134–
35; Foucault and, 60–61, 80–82; historical nature, 168; incoherent, 62;
Lentricchia and, 246, 247; neopragmatists and, 255; new orthodoxy, 180;
opposition to, 113–16; and politics,
13–14; and practice of history, Fish's
view, 134; of statement, Foucault's
idea, 80–81
Theweleit, Klaus, 27; and cultural studies, 33; *Male Fantasies*, 15–24, 34–35
Thing, loss of, Kristeva's idea, 98, 220–
21
Thought, Deleuze's ideas, 176–77
Totalitarianism, 24, 247, 248
Totality machine, fascist, 18, 32; state as,
24; threats to, 20
Tradition: as collective archive, 4; convention and, 32; culture and, Eliot's
idea, 169, 170; Derrida's idea, 170;
Heidegger's concept, 29–32; Knapp
and Michaels and, 118–19
Traditional canon, challenges to, 243–44
Trakl, Georg, Heidegger and, 179–80,
188–89
Transcendence, American, 223
Transcendental anonymity of writing,
Foucault's idea, 51–53
Transcendentalism: American genius of,
145–48; critical philosophy of, 54–
55; of Emerson, 226–28, 231; and ge-
nius, 225–26; liberalism and, 254;
neopragmatists and, x; and pedagogic
pair, 70
Transcendental rhetoric, 108
Transcendental self, 253
Transdiscursive authors, 52–53, 55
Transference, 98
Transformation: fascist imagination and,
23; in Greek culture, 86
Transhistorical perspective, 8
Transitory allusion, in Stevens's poetry,
234
Trilling, Lionel, 30; and Emerson, 96, 102

Tropes: ancestral, Burke's idea, 248; contingency theory and, 210; embodied, poet as, 229
Truth: Foucault's idea, 62; regimes of, 66, 76, 78–79, 84
"Turn," Heideggerian, 24–33
Twentieth-century fiction, 253
Type, ascetic, 201–2

Unconscious creativity, 58
Understanding, tradition and, Heidegger's view, 30
Unhappy consciousness, 79
Universalism, Heidegger and, 187
Universalizing moral codes, 84
Universal norms, loss of, 7–8
Universals: contingency theory and; 209–10; contingent imagination and, 223
Universal third person, 70, 259, 268; American, 250
University system, Heidegger and, 188
Unreason, modern, Foucault and, 78–79
Unreasonable change, Fish and, 136
Unthought, of culture, 177–78
Urban society, 203; newspapers and, 174

Values, revisionism and, 7–8
Verbal power, Montaigne and, 104
Victimization, politics of, 244
Victorian repression, 39; liberation from, 83
Village Voice, and Lentricciа, 249
Violence, change and, 168
Virgil, Montaigne's essays, 106
Vocabularies, critical, 167, 168–69
Vocation, Emerson's idea, 226–28; of abandonment, 228–30; Emerson and, 230; media culture and, 231

War: fascism and, 18, 21–23; Nietzsche and, 21
"War in the Gulf," television show, 66
Weber, Max, 193; *Berufsmenschen* (men of calling), 201–2
Weiskel, Thomas, *The Romantic Sublime,* 157

Western culture, 47; author in, 54; end of, 38; fascism and, 18, 23; Foucault and, 66–69, 73; Freud and, 156; Heidegger and, 187; postromantic, 17; psychosexual discourse and, 39
Western heroes, imaginative, 158
Western tradition: Heidegger and, 165–66; multiculturalism and, 2
White, Hayden, 59; *Metahistory,* 247
Whitman, Walt, Stevens and, 147
Wicker, Tom, *One of Us,* 98
Will, George, 249
Will: Heidegger's idea, 27; poetics of, Lentricchia's idea, 245
Will to play, Greenblatt's idea, 253–54
Women: displacement of, by Wordsworth, 173; fascist imagination and, 23; and friendship with men, 101
Words, elementary, Heidegger and, 165–66
Wordsworth, William, 203; Bloom and, 155–56; *Lyrical Ballads,* 226; "Nutting," Arac and, 173; romantic poetry defined by, 226; "The Solitary Reaper," 228
——*The Prelude*: 225; Arac's view, 173; Bloom and, 155–56; Frye and, 123–24
Work, ideas of, 140–41
Wounded ego, 108; narcissistic, 97–98
Writer, frame of reference, 231
Writing: Cheever and, 214–15; fascist imagination and, 23; Foucault's ideas, 51–54, 276n14; Kristeva's views, 221; and self, 50–51, 196

Yahweh, Bloom's views, 158–59, 162
Yeats, William Butler, 15, 42; and aestheticism, 248; "Byzantium," 237; Cheever and, 218; Stevens and, 237; "The Tower," 113; *A Vision,* 213

Zarathustra, 74; Nietzsche's *Zarathustra,* 101, 118, 229